The Road to Independence

THE ROAD TO INDEPENDENCE

The Revolutionary Movement in New York, 1773-1777

By BERNARD MASON

University of Kentucky Press-Lexington
1966

For permission to quote material from the books noted below, the author is grateful to these publishers:

Charles Scribner's Sons, for *Father Knickerbocker Rebels* by Thomas J. Wertenbaker. Copyright 1948 by Charles Scribner's Sons.

The Bobbs-Merrill Company, Inc., for *John Jay* by Frank Monaghan. Copyright 1935 by the Bobbs-Merrill Company, Inc., renewed 1962 by Frank Monoghan.

The Regents of the University of Wisconsin, for *The History of Political Parties in the Province of New York, 1760-1776,* by Carl L. Becker, published by the University of Wisconsin Press. Copyright 1909 by the Regents of the University of Wisconsin.

Manufactured in the United States of America. Library of Congress Catalog Card No. 66-26691.

For my mother Sophie Mason
and in memory of my father Louis Mason

PREFACE

THE HISTORIAN of the Revolution in New York has no simple task in writing about his subject because New York has occupied an ambivalent position in revolutionary history. A rebel party did commit the colony to independence, but the presence of thousands of loyalists lent credence to the idea in a later age that the revolutionaries represented a minority. Furthermore, a later generation emphasized the Whigs' vacillation in 1775-1776 and attributed it in part to a major loyalist reaction. The effect of this interpretation was to obscure the general spread of hostility to Great Britain. Subsequent historical writing proceeded along these lines and tended to perpetuate an illusory description of the province. The evidence presented in these pages indicates the inadequacy of this view of New York and suggests a different interpretation. A tenable hypothesis which emerges from the data is that the Whigs were a decisive majority. Associated with this proposition are other relationships which yield illuminating insights for the exploration of the Revolution.

This book does not offer a strictly chronological treatment of its topic, even though it describes the trend of events from 1773 to 1777. Its point of departure is an analysis that stresses the strengths and weaknesses of the organization of the revolutionary movement. Although the Declaration of Independence was a decisive stage in the growth of the Revolution, in New York independence was only one-half of the great question. The other half, which was not resolved until the spring of 1777, was the nature of the new government. However, there was no orderly sequence in these two matters because Yorkers, leaders and general public alike, were discussing them simultaneously as interrelated problems in the spring of 1776. Therefore, the culmination of the Revolution for these people seemed to occur when the Convention of Representatives of the State of New York adopted the New York Constitution of 1777.

One of the problems peculiar to this era is that of classifying individuals according to their political behavior. The problem is "peculiar" because one of the consequences of the friction with Britain was the shattering and regrouping of the existing factions into Whigs (often also denominated Friends of Liberty, Liberty Boys and Sons of Liberty) and Tories (Friends of Government). Historians have usually characterized the factions' leaders as radical, moderate, or conservative but have not explicitly stipulated the criteria by which they arrived at these judgments. A major difficulty with the usage of these terms as indicators of political beliefs is, for example, that a person who might have been a radical in his opposition to the Lord North ministry might have been a moderate on the question of the right of suffrage.

One solution is to employ these three words in relation to specific circumstances. Thus, in one context the words indicate attitudes toward resistance to British policies; in another context they designate positions in relation to constitutional problems in the Convention. The radicals in the first context were the men who advocated uncompromising resistance to Britain and demanded that nation's complete retreat on the disputed affairs. During the winter of 1775-1776 men of this stripe were publicly contending for separation from the mother country. The moderates condemned the North ministry but kept a sharp vigil for means of compromise. Nonetheless, the moderates sponsored policies that steadily widened the gap between New York and Britain. On the question of independence they publicly favored delay but privately conceded in June, 1776, the necessity of the separation. Although the conservatives opposed ministerial measures, they also rejected vigorous opposition to those measures. The conservatives might have acquiesced in Lord North's conciliation proposals of 1775 or the Howe Olive Branch of 1776. When the formal break occurred in July, the conservatives discountenanced independence. Many men moved from one category to another under the pressure of events. Alexander McDougall by the spring of 1776 had broken with his radical associates and was firmly in the moderate camp. On the other hand, John Jay gradually abandoned his conservative position in 1775 for that of the moderates.

In the second context the lines of differentiation are much less clearly drawn than in the first. The radicals in the Convention sought to obtain a constitution that would allow maximum participation of the male citizenry on all levels of government. Although the moderates were not ready to go this far, their proposals would have given the middle and small landholders much greater weight in the government than those of the conservatives. An initial objective of the conservatives was to minimize political change and to preserve the power and influence of the wealthy in the governmental structure. However, the exigencies of politics compelled both moderates and conservatives to shift ground, so that there were occasions when many moderates were indistinguishable from conservatives.

My debts to others are numerous and it is a pleasure to acknowledge them. Professor Richard B. Morris, Professor Chilton Williamson, and Dean Harold C. Syrett contributed indispensable criticism from which I have benefited greatly. If the results are not commensurate with their efforts, the fault is mine and not theirs. My colleagues, Professors Amy Gilbert, Albert V. House and Bernard F. Huppe, took the time and trouble to read critically the manuscript. I owe a special debt to Professor Alfred B. Rollins, Jr., for his perspicacious comments and encouragement. Naturally all errors of omission and commission are mine alone. I am grateful to the Research Foundation of the State University of New York and the Harpur College Foundation for financial assistance. The invaluable help of the library staffs of the institutions hereinafter cited is acknowledged with gratitude. These acknowledgments would be incomplete without mention of the unflagging aid, never-failing good humor and encouragement of my wife Marjorie.

State University of New York
   at Binghamton
April, 1966   Bernard Mason

CONTENTS

LIST OF ABBREVIATIONS USED IN NOTES

Cal. Hist. Mss.	New York, *Calendar of Historical Manuscripts Relating to the War of the Revolution, in the Office of the Secretary of State* (2 vols.; Albany, 1868)
Cal. H. O. Papers	Great Britain, *Calendar of Home Office Papers of the Reign of George III, 1773-1775* (London, 1899)
Const. Gaz.	*Constitutional Gazette* (New York)
CUL	Columbia University Library
FDRL	Franklin Delano Roosevelt Library
Hist. Mss. Com.	Great Britain, Historical Manuscripts Commission, *Fourteenth Report, Appendix Part X* (Manuscripts of the Earl of Dartmouth) (London, 1895)
Jour. Prov. Cong.	New York State, *Journals of the Provincial Congress, Provincial Convention, Committee of Safety and Council of Safety of the State of New York, 1775-1777* (2 vols.; Albany, 1842)
Min. of Conv.	Minutes of the Convention which formed the Constitution of the State of New York, n.d., Abraham Yates, Jr., Papers, New York Public Library.
N.Y.G.	*New-York Gazette and Weekly Mercury*
NYHS	New-York Historical Society
N.Y.J.	*New York Journal*
N.Y.P.	*New York Packet*
NYPL	New York Public Library
NYSL	New York State Library
Pa. Jour.	*Pennsylvania Journal* (Philadelphia)
Riv. Gaz.	*Rivington's New-York Gazetteer*
Smith, Memoirs	Historical Memoirs of the Province of New York, William Smith Papers, New York Public Library
Stopford Mss.	Great Britain, Historical Manuscripts Commission, *Report on the Manuscripts of Mrs. Stopford-Sackville of Drayton House, Northamptonshire* (2 vols.; London, 1904-1910)

ONE

Introduction

HISTORY has bequeathed to posterity a strikingly incongruous image of New York in the era of the American Revolution at which later generations have gazed in some perplexity. Here was a people who proposed the Continental Congress because they opposed an individual colony's commercial boycott of Great Britain but who in that Continental Congress argued against an intercolonial stoppage of trade. Here was a people who patronized a zealous Whig press but whose largest newspaper was the most important Tory journal in the colonies. Here was a people who cheered tumultuously, and on the same day, both George Washington on his journey to assume command of the Continental Army and royal Governor William Tryon newly returned from England. These were the revolutionaries who sent troops to invade Canada but who provisioned British warships in New York Harbor. These were the rebels whose conservative leaders opposed independence but who were publicly discussing independence before the publication of Paine's *Common Sense,* who declared their independence of the crown of Great Britain but who enlisted in thousands in His Majesty's army, whose laboring and "middling" classes argued for democratic reform but who accepted a conservative state constitution almost without a murmur of criticism.

Historians, identifying, scrutinizing, analyzing, and interpreting the events of the Revolution in New York, have tended to substantiate this image. A reader who ranged over the literature saw a province whose political organization was for the most part bifurcated into radicals and conservatives. The radicals were characterized as the spokesmen for the masses, the conservatives as spokesmen for the wealthy merchants and landlords. The conflict between these two political parties was one of the two dynamic forces in the Revolution. The other, the drive to cut Britain's leading strings, functioned on a minimal level partly because Whigs and Tories were nearly equal in strength. One index of this political division was the manner in which the colony found its way to independence–almost in spite of itself. The reader accepted the idea that the Patriots managed the war with great difficulty because so many Yorkers were loyalists. This image of New York contains major inaccuracies and distortions and requires modification and clarification.[1]

---

[1] The principal sources of the preceding interpretation are Carl L. Becker, *The History of Political Parties in the Province of New York, 1760-1776* (Madison, 1909), *passim;* Alexander C. Flick, *Loyalism in New York During the American Revolution* (New York, 1901), *passim;* Alexander C. Flick, ed., *A History of the State of New York* (10 vols.; New York, 1933-1937), III, *passim;* Claude H. Van Tyne, *The Loyalists in the American Revolution* (New York, 1902), chap. v; Arthur M. Schlesinger, Sr., *The Colonial Merchants and the American Revolution, 1763-1776* (New York, 1939), *passim,* and the same author's *New Viewpoints in American History* (New York, 1922), chap. vii; Wilbur C. Abbott, *New York in the American Revolution* (New York, 1929), *passim;* Thomas J. Wertenbaker, *Father Knickerbocker Rebels: New York City During the Revolution* (New York, 1948), *passim;* Dorothy R. Dillon, *The New York Triumvirate: A Study of the Legal and Political Careers of William Livingston, John Morin Scott, William Smith, Jr.* (New York, 1949), chap. vii; Virginia D. Harrington, *The New York Merchant on the Eve of the Revolution* (New York, 1935), chap. ix; George Dangerfield, *Chancellor Robert R. Livingston of New York, 1746-1813* (New York, 1960), Part Two; Edward P. Alexander, *A Revolutionary Conservative: James Duane of New York* (New York, 1938), chap. vi; Merrill Jensen, *The Articles of Confederation* (Madison, 1940), pp. 30-35; Elisha P. Douglass, *Rebels and Democrats: The Struggle for Equal Political Rights and Majority Rule During the American Revolution* (Chapel Hill, 1955), chap. v; Evarts B. Greene, *The Revolutionary Generation, 1763-1790* (New York, 1943), pp. 190-97, 233-34· William H. Nelson, *The American Tory* (Oxford, 1961), pp. 42-45, 80-83, 92, 98-104, 125; John R. Alden, *The American Revolution, 1775-1783* (New York, 1954), p. 88.

Any new look at the history of the Revolution in New York should start with the problems created by the Tea Act of 1773. Its passage by Parliament in 1773 punctured the bubble of colonial economic recovery and political quiescence. The preceding three years, 1770-1773, were a period of flourishing trade for New York, a period in which the continuing boycott of British tea hardly affected the entering volume of goods. Although the nonimportation of tea was effective, New Yorkers did not cease to consume the beverage. They bought and drank large quantities of the smuggled commodity.[2] Amidst the increasing affluence, antagonism to Britain declined and the provincial political kettle simmered mainly in response to local stimuli. However, the kettle emitted sounds which indicated the approach of the boiling point when the colonials learned of the plans of the East India Company.[3]

The reasons for the colonial excitement were not difficult to discern. By shipping its tea to New York consignees, the John Company (East India Company) would eliminate intervening wholesalers and be able to undersell competitors in America. The critics charged that the company, having ruined its rivals, would raise its prices above existing levels to the detriment of the consumers. Even the smugglers had cause for concern because the East India Company was to have a refund of the English tea duties. As a consequence it might undercut also the illegal trader since its tea would be cheaper than the undutied Dutch tea. Moreover, other observers foresaw disaster for everyone if the East India Company proved the practicability of the project. There would be nothing to prevent the ministry from authorizing similar ventures in other lines of trade. Since fair trader

---

[2] Harrington, *The New York Merchant,* p. 344; Schlesinger, *The Colonial Merchants,* pp. 249-51.

[3] The act of 1773 conferred upon the East India Company a monopoly of tea exportation to the American colonies. Schlesinger, *The Colonial Merchants,* pp. 262-64.

and smuggler would suffer alike, or as a contemporary drily commented, "virtue and vice being thus united," both groups had common ground on which to unite in their opposition to the plan.[4]

If this situation in 1773 had involved only these economic considerations, a tea party might not have occurred in New York. It was precisely because the affair fused the economic and political variables that it produced volatile combustibles. Impending large-scale importations of the commodity which itself was the focus of an attenuated constitutional conflict revived the complex controversy over colonial taxation and regulation. Although Bostonians and others imported and paid the three-pence duty on tea from 1770 to 1773, they saw that the Tea Act fundamentally altered their commercial relationships. If the colonies consumed annually an estimated one to one and a half million pounds of tea leaves, if they bought their beverage from the East India Company, they would pay from £12,500 to £18,750 in import duties on this product.[5] Having paid these duties, the colonials would no longer be able to argue that they did not acquiesce in parliamentary taxation. Indeed, there were Yorkers who accused the North ministry of seduction in this matter, of

---

4 *Ibid.*, pp. 249-51, 272-73; William Smith's Memoirs, quoted in Wertenbaker, *Father Knickerbocker Rebels*, p. 32; Abbott, *New York in the American Revolution*, p. 99. For a contrary view see Benjamin W. Labaree, *The Boston Tea Party* (New York, 1964), pp. 76-77.

5 Since there are no reliable tea consumption statistics, this total derives from crude calculation. Contemporary reckoning placed legal and illegal importations at three million pounds. Import statistics for 1768-1774 show that peak consumption in these years was 873,744 pounds but naturally this does not include the smuggled tea. However, the gap might be filled by calculating the average annual per capita consumption from later import data. From 1790 to 1798 annual importations of tea averaged two million pounds, which indicates an average annual per capita consumption of 0.51 pounds. If the population is computed at 2.1 to 2.5 million and per capita usage at 0.51 pounds, the result is a total consumption of one to one and one-half million pounds. Lawrence A. Harper, *The English Navigation Laws: A Seventeenth Century Experiment in Social Engineering* (New York, 1939), p. 269, n. 125; U.S. Bureau of the Census, *Historical Statistics of the United States, Colonial Times to 1957* (Washington, D.C., 1957), ser. Z254-261. See Labaree, *Boston Tea Party*, pp. 7-8.

providing cheap tea in order to lure Americans into payment of the tax.[6] Thus opened the great drama which con-
vulsed New York for the next decade.

Although there were signs of strain in the political structure of New York in the 1760's, it did not reveal any grave
defects that threatened to disrupt it. Through most of the
ten years from 1763 to 1773 the political game was a triangu-
lar affair involving two factions and the governor. Each
faction, the De Lancey and the Livingston, was intent upon
domination of assembly, council, and governor. When the
factions could not control the governor, they sought to influence and use him to gain their ends. The governor,
naturally, strove to maintain his independence, to play off
one group against the other. All three acted out their roles
with one eye on London; this was especially true for the
governor since he was dependent on the ministry and
needed to maintain good relations in Britain in order to protect his possession of the governorship. It was not enough
for the governor to concern himself with the appearance of
his record in Whitehall; he perforce took into his calculations the fact that members of both factions kept up a constant correspondence with friends in Britain, that their
hostile depiction of events in New York would find its way
to the attention of the ministry. On the other hand, an astute
governor employed the official minutes of his council meetings as a club over the heads of the members since he
transmitted these to England and since councilors were
removable by the crown.[7]

The anatomy of a faction illuminates the fluid state of
politics. Family kinship, symbolized by the factional titles,
was a material element in the nucleus of the political group.

---

[6] Schlesinger, *The Colonial Merchants*, pp. 246-49; Becker, *The History of Political Parties*, pp. 99, 104.
[7] *Ibid.*, pp. 7-8, 11-12; Harrington, *The New York Merchant*, p. 43; William H. W. Sabine, ed., *Historical Memoirs from 16 March 1763 to 9 July 1776 of William Smith* (New York, 1956), *passim*.

Nonetheless, large families and intermarriage among the wealthy weakened the kinship factor except in primary relationships. Other adherents flocked to the family standard from varied motivations. Some were simply place-seekers; patronage was a magnet which strongly attracted all ranks of society. The desire for personal gain, particularly in the form of land, drew many to one faction or the other. Still others sought political and legal influence to further business matters. There were some, also, who entered politics from a sense of *noblesse oblige* or to acquire prestige. Finally, there were those who sought power to gratify ambition. A faction, then, was a collection of interest groups having no organizational framework, no platform, and no proclaimed principles. Shifts from one faction to another, springing on occasion from personality clashes as well as quarrels over pelf and place, were neither unusual nor infrequent.[8]

The composition of each faction cut across social lines. Both groups of leaders contained modest gentry as well as great landed proprietors. Although both factions numbered merchants among their ranks, the De Lanceys appear to have had the greater lure for the commercial class. There was one difference between the parties to which contemporaries attached special meaning. The De Lanceys apparently enjoyed a greater affinity with the Anglicans than did the Livingstons, who seemed to hold a greater attraction for the dissenting denominations. Therefore, there were those who saw the factional antagonism in religious terms and labeled the Livingstons the Presbyterian party, the De Lanceys the Church party. The religious distribution between the

---

[8] Sabine, *Memoirs of William Smith, passim;* Becker, *The History of Political Parties,* p. 13; Harrington, *The New York Merchant,* pp. 11-13, 140-42. For the contention that organization and principles did count in politics see Milton M. Klein, "Democracy and Politics in Colonial New York," *New York History,* XL (July, 1959), 221-46.

factions partly mirrors the frictions which arose from the establishment of the Anglican church in some of the counties in the colony.[9]

The mingling of the political and religious strife sometimes produced blunt exchanges at the topmost level of government. Such a clash took place at a meeting of the governor and the council in January, 1774. The dispute concerned a petition of the Schenectady Dutch Reformed Church to increase the amount of funds that its congregation might raise. William Smith, a Presbyterian and arch-foe of the De Lanceyites, pointedly compared this Schenectady request for a revenue of £1,000 with the £5,000 authorization for the small Albany Anglican Church. Smith jotted down in his private notes that Oliver De Lancey, one of the faction leaders, "upon my mentioning the Albany Church Revenue said, that was *because they were Christians.* What said I are not the Dutch of Schenectady, Christians? *Not such Christians* says he. How do you mean not Episcopalians? Do you mean that? Ay says he. That we all know said I."[10]

Although the De Lanceyites gained and held the upper hand in politics from 1769 to 1773, their superiority was neither overwhelming nor stable. On paper at least the De Lancey position was formidable. They had a long-standing preponderance in the council where the subtle and

---

[9] Harrington, *The New York Merchant*, pp. 37-41; Becker, *The History of Political Parties*, pp. 12-13, 18-19; Sabine, *Memoirs of William Smith*, pp. 146, 169, 207, 235; Thomas Jones, *History of New York during the Revolutionary War, and of the Leading Events in the Other Colonies of that Period*, ed. Edward Floyd de Lancey (2 vols.; New York, 1879), I, 2, 18n.; II, 291n.; Dorothy R. Dillon, *The New York Triumvirate*, pp. 44-53; Peter Force, ed., *American Archives* (9 vols.: Washington, D.C., 1837-1853), 4th ser., I, 300-301; Peter Van Schaack to Henry Van Schaack, January 27, 1769, in Henry C. Van Schaack, *The Life of Peter Van Schaack* (New York, 1842), pp. 10-11.

[10] Sabine, *Memoirs of William Smith*, p. 169. See also Peter Van Schaack's analysis of the 1769 election in terms of religious enmity. Van Schaack, *Peter Van Schaack*, pp. 10-11.

supple William Smith was their minor but frequently effective opponent.[11] Since there were no colonywide political organizations and since there was no party discipline, the De Lancey sway in the assembly was less firm than in the council but they did put together majorities with which to pass legislation.[12] The De Lancey political future was apparently assured when that faction evolved a modus vivendi, first with Acting Governor Cadwallader Colden, 1769-1770, and then with the new governor, Lord Dunmore, 1770-1771.[13] This satisfactory state of affairs for the De Lanceys ended with the arrival in July, 1771, of a successor for Dunmore, William Tryon. Tryon rejected the "leading strings" of the dominant faction and trod an independent path with the encouragement of the Livingstons.[14] Although their in-

---

11 Oliver De Lancey was the leader in the council, having most consistent support from John Watts, Joseph Reade, Henry Cruger, Roger Morris, and Charles W. Apthorpe. Other councilors who voted most frequently with De Lancey were Daniel Horsmanden, Hugh Wallace, William Axtell, and Henry White. Cadwallader Colden commonly had differences with De Lancey. Smith, though he had connections with the Livingstons, often pursued an independent path. If Smith's notes are any guide to his motivation, he apparently aspired to be chief justice and perhaps to be lieutenant-governor. Sabine, *Memoirs of William Smith, passim.*

12 Although the question of who possessed the suffrage in New York is a moot one, recent research has tended to demonstrate that a broad electorate existed. Estimates range from 50 to 80 percent of the adult white male population. See Chilton Williamson, *American Suffrage from Property to Democracy, 1760-1860* (Princeton, N.J., 1960), pp. 27-28; Klein, *New York History*, XL, 236-37; Nicholas Varga, "Election Procedures and Practices in Colonial New York," *New York History*, XLI (July, 1960), 252-53.

13 Smith claimed that Colden and the De Lanceys framed a "bargain" under which the De Lanceys guaranteed approval of the Acting Governor's salary by the assembly and promised to seek the assembly's modification of its reproach of Colden for his conduct in the Stamp Act troubles. In return for these services Colden was not to dissolve the assembly until the end of its seven-year life nor to veto whatever legislation his allies enacted. Although Smith initially made some impression on Dunmore, the councilor soon concluded from his conduct that the Governor had no political perspicacity, that he had fallen under De Lancey influence, and that he was a "fool." Sabine, *Memoirs of William Smith*, pp. 67, 83-103.

14 Governor Tryon, surmising himself to be in a strong position in 1773, declared his independence of the factions. He is reported to have told his council: "I wish to promote the Interest of the Province, and find it very disagreeable to me to be crossed by your Parties. . . . I will take no sides myself, and desire that I may not be dealt with or crossed for Party Purposes. If you will maintain Parties keep Party Spirit to yourselves." *Ibid.*, p. 143.

ability to yoke the Governor did not break the De Lanceyites, their difficulties mounted and in early 1773 they met
with a severe mauling at the hands of the Livingstons and
the Governor. Not only did the De Lanceys lose bills in the
assembly and council but they also incurred the enmity of
some of their erstwhile supporters at the polls. Smith
exulted at "the Abatement if not the Ruin of the Power of
the De Lancey Family" and happily proclaimed that "the
old Despotism was broke. . . ." The obituary was, however,
premature.[15]

Local politics in the fall of 1773 gave promise of generat-
ing high temperatures, but the quarrels over patronage were
only the brief prelude to a cataclysm. The Livingstons and
De Lanceys were hard at it, scrambling for leverage with
which to convince Governor Tryon that he should appoint
their aspirants to a number of posts. Although these matters greatly roiled political relations, they receded quickly
into obscurity in late September when the ship *Lord Dunmore* out of London docked in New York. Captain Lawrence
brought information that the East India Company had
chosen agents in New York for its tea, that it was shipping
600 chests of tea to the city, that the New York, Boston,
and Philadelphia shipmasters declined to load the tea, and
that the consignees would pay the duty upon entry.[16]

Reactions to the East India Company project differed and
some weeks elapsed before opinion jelled sufficiently to
permit leaders to reach a consensus. Among the steersmen
of the inactive Sons of Liberty there were men who saw
clearly what to do, but even these firebrands were tempor-

15 For the intricate details of these events see *ibid.*, pp. 136-48.
16 *Ibid.*, pp. 152-55, 156; Becker, *The History of Political Parties*, pp.
103-4. Smith prophetically recorded in his notes for October 13, 1773: "A
New Flame is apparently kindling in America. . . . Our Domestic Parties will
probably die, and be swallowed up in the general Opposition to the Parliamentary Project of raising the Arm of Government by Revenue Laws."
Quoted in Wertenbaker, *Father Knickerbocker Rebels* (copyright 1948 by
Charles Scribner's Sons, reprinted by permission of the publishers), pp. 31-32.

arily impotent.[17] Their greatest accomplishment, apparently, was the initiation of correspondence with Boston and Philadelphia. Some of them also may have participated in the propaganda campaign assailing the East India Company, its agents, and Parliament, a campaign which accelerated during October. A break in the passivity of the town occurred when unknown persons summoned a meeting of merchants on October 15 for the purpose of congratulating the New York captains who had refused to load their ships with cargoes of tea. Since there were not only many merchants but also other citizens at this gathering, it was likely that Liberty Boys were present. The assemblage, however, did not engender momentum for further action. When action did erupt, as on November 5, it was peripheral and presumably under the direction of Isaac Sears and John Lamb.[18]

Perhaps one source of the indecision in New York was the difference of opinion over the tax sections of the Tea Act. Some interpreted the statute to mean that the East India Company would not pay the three-pence import duty in America, while others contended that the company was liable for the tax. If the company was not subject to the duty, importation of the tea had no bearing on the constitutional problem of taxation. It therefore would not be necessary to prevent the entry of the tea.[19] Since the merchants were at odds with each other, it was impracticable to

---

17 Isaac Sears, Alexander McDougall, and John Lamb played prominent roles in the organization in the 1760's.

18 Becker, *The History of Political Parties,* p. 104; Wertenbaker, *Father Knickerbocker Rebels,* p. 32. A street demonstration hanged William Kelley, New York merchant, in effigy because he had urged the East India Company to ship to Manhattan. Isaac N. P. Stokes, ed., *The Iconography of Manhattan Island* (6 vols.; New York, 1915-1928), IV, 841.

19 Both Tryon and Abraham Lott, one of the tea agents, implied the existence of this division of opinion. Edmund B. O'Callaghan, ed., *Documents Relative to the Colonial History of the State of New York* (15 vols.; Albany, N.Y., 1856), VIII, 400-1; Becker, *The History of Political Parties,* p. 105.

Those merchants who did not purvey tea may have emphasized the possibility of untaxed tea and have opposed the taking of any steps to block the landing of the commodity.

obtain agreement on a course of action. Even though it was a matter of public record that Philadelphia in October had forced the resignation of its tea agents and had resolved against the entry and landing of the tea, these events seemed to have no appreciable impact upon affairs on the Hudson.[20]

It was the Sons of Liberty who broke the log jam and set in motion the machinery of opposition. However, the Liberty Boys, disagreeing among themselves over what policy to adopt, did not arrive at a decision until the third week in November. They sought to have the tea consignees acknowledge the "general sense" of the inhabitants that the agents ought not receive or sell the tea. Secondly, the Sons demanded a pledge that the tea commissioners would not receive or sell the tea.[21] The reply of the agents the next day was only partially satisfactory since it stipulated that they would not accept the cargo if it was "liable to the payment of the American duty." Unwilling to assume at this time the onus for illegal action, the Sons of Liberty did not respond to this note, but a pseudonymous broadside, November 27, threatened that "The Mohawks" would wreak their anger on anyone who dared to import India tea. Rather than mount a campaign to obtain an unqualified resignation of the tea commissioners, the Sons of Liberty prepared a statement of association with which to launch a boycott movement. The weakness of the association was the lack of sanctions with which to enforce its provisions; the associators covenanted to publish the names of violators as "enemies to their country." The most effective method of enforcement was to prevent the landing of the tea, since, once it was ashore, merchants might sell it as Dutch tea. Nevertheless, the association skirted the problem, limiting

---

[20] The pot in Boston, simmering much as it did in New York, came to a boil in early November. Schlesinger, *The Colonial Merchants*, pp. 281-84; Labaree, *Boston Tea Party*, chap. vi.

[21] One of the Liberty Boys, "Brutus," published a statement of these events in May, 1774. See Force, *American Archives*, 4th ser., I, 253n.

itself to a resolution to employ "all lawful means to defeat the pernicious project."[22] The activists hardly began to distribute copies of their association when they learned that the tea ship *Nancy* was on the high seas for New York and that the consignees were responsible for payment of the duty.

Although this intelligence swept away some confusion, it thrust upon New Yorkers the pressing problem of what to do with the tea when it arrived. The Sons of Liberty lost no time in calling upon Messrs. White, Lott, and Booth, agents for the John Company, and bidding these gentlemen to resign their commissions. The merchants promptly complied and apprised the Governor that they could not accept the shipment of tea.[23] Tryon and his council were already exploring the ramifications of the circumstances and on December 1 they concurred in a proposal to store the tea either in the fort or in the barracks.[24] When the government unofficially disseminated its decision, the townspeople displayed no antipathy to the policy. Unlikely though it was that Sears would acquiesce in this disposition of the matter, the Sons of Liberty did not protest until December 10. Having had a letter from Boston which asserted the determination of that town to prevent the landing of tea, a committee of the Liberty Boys visited William Smith to acquaint him with the opposition of the society

---

22 *Ibid.;* Becker, *The History of Political Parties,* pp. 105-7; Wertenbaker, *Father Knickerbocker Rebels,* p. 32.

23 Their declination seems to be directly connected with Governor Tryon's attitude. One of the consignees, Henry White, was a member of the council. In a council meeting with White in attendance, November 30, Tryon asserted that he would protect the cargo if the commissioners "cast it into his care." The next day the agents announced their resignations. Sabine, *Memoirs of William Smith,* p. 157.

The Sons of Liberty included in their leadership Livingstons, De Lanceys, and the activist element as represented by Sears. Control of the society seems to have been in the hands of a coalition of the Livingstons and De Lanceys. Smith mentions a visit to him of some of the leaders: Philip Livingston, Isaac Low, Sears, McDougall, and Samuel and John Broome. *Ibid.*

24 Smith did not differ on this matter with his opponents on the council. He noted that "the De Lanceys wait to see the Disposition of the People." *Ibid.*

to government intervention.[25] Isaac Low, spokesman for the group, told Smith that the governors of Massachusetts and Pennsylvania had declined to take possession of the tea, that if Tryon stood aside the unbroken cargo would retrace its path to Britain. Furthermore, if the Governor unloaded the tea, it would "not be safe." Therefore, the committee entreated Smith to advise Tryon to reverse his position. Low, vindicating this view, argued that admission of the tea would open the door to its sale and arouse the hostility of the other colonies.[26] In conclusion the Liberty Boys offered to guarantee the safety of the tea so long as it remained aboard ship. Smith assented only to pass on to Governor Tryon the sentiments of the group.

The stand taken by the Governor may have inflamed discord within the Sons of Liberty and paralyzed the society. Sears and McDougall might well have viewed with alarm the sweep of events in Boston and Philadelphia, since New York lagged behind in public resolutions and spirited mass meetings.[27] On the other hand, the Low-Livingston clique wished to avoid action that would stir up the inhabitants and wished to minimize the possibilities of a clash with the government. The disposition of the tea clearly was a vital question. Therefore, the December 10 conversation with Smith

---

[25] The letter reached New York December 7. Since the Liberty Boys did nothing for three days, it is possible that they were quarreling among themselves over what to do.

The committee consisted of Philip Livingston, Isaac Low, Sears, McDougall, David Van Horne, and the Broomes. *Ibid.*

[26] Smith, privately, did not accept this explanation; he speculated that the change of front by the Liberty Boys arose from other causes: "their chief Motive was an Apprehension, that the Populace would change their present Sentiments and call for the Tea. They had Reason for these Suspicions (1) because the Subscription to an Association Paper printed and set on Foot the 30 Inst, proceeded slowly and second, because there was but little Tea in the Port, third, the two old Insurance Offices hung back in the Subscriptions, and have not yet signed the Association Paper. . . ." *Ibid.*; Becker, *The History of Political Parties*, p. 107.

[27] Philadelphia through mass meetings had unequivocally refused to permit the landing of the tea. Word had come from Boston of the developing clash with the government over the disposition of the tea. Schlesinger, *The Colonial Merchants*, pp. 278-81, 285-87, 290-91; Sabine, *Memoirs of William Smith*, p. 157.

represented a retreat by the cautious element which shortly
turned into a defeat. After speaking to Smith, Low broached
the subject to other members of the council, but their replies were unsatisfactory. One of the councilors, John
Watts, went so far as to deny that there was any potential
danger if the Governor stored the tea. This rebuff by the
councilors apparently caused a reaction among other members of the liberty club, because the organization sent its
committee to Smith to retract the promise of protection for
the tea ship. Smith seized the occasion to expostulate with
his visitors against their attitude, but only Low and Livingston displayed any sign of approval. McDougall threw a
bombshell into the circle when he asked, "What if we prevent the Landing, and kill [the] Gov[erno]r and all the
Council?" Philip Livingston "started and said I won't think
half so far."[28] The conversation terminated on this grim
note.

The subsequent conduct of the Sons of Liberty connoted
a serious rift in the ranks of the society. Since the tea ship
was due momentarily, the activists had to prod the club into
motion; any delay would enable the Governor to carry
through his plan without effective opposition. In the face
of Tryon's insistence the use of force was the most likely
alternative open to the activists; otherwise they would have
to accept the landing and storage of the tea. It was one thing
for Sears to advocate opposition but it was quite another
matter for him to find the means of executing the policy.
The outcome was a call for the citizens' rally at the City
Hall on December 17. The meeting would fulfill a number
of major prerequisites. The leaders would use this opportunity to nerve the populace to the task before them. It was
essential to the Liberty Boys to procure some expression of
mass approval before they undertook to prevent the unload-

---

28 Smith ended his notes at this point, so the reply, if any, is unknown.
Ibid., p. 158.

ing of the tea. Moreover, the rally would afford the leaders an opportunity to secure general approval of the boycott association. Lastly, the occasion would be right for concordance in the creation of a city committee of correspondence. The new organ would constitute an effective center for the direction of the opposition; a general committee rather than a Sons of Liberty committee would command greater respect and wield broader authority. Although the prudent members would not concur in the proposal for a rally, the activists plunged ahead without them.[29]

The proceedings at the City Hall on December 17 were a resounding triumph for the activists but the Governor deserved credit for inadvertent assistance. The large throng who gathered in spite of the inclement weather listened to the reading of several letters from Boston and Philadelphia and elected a standing committee of correspondence.[30] Hav-

---

[29] The extent of the disagreement in the Sons of Liberty is unknown but certain external events point to its existence. Although Sears and Mc-Dougall received correspondence from Boston on December 7, the notice of the meeting did not appear until December 16; there were no ostensible reasons for the time lag. The conversation with Smith on December 13 revealed the difference in outlook between Low and Livingston on one side and Sears and McDougall on the other. Furthermore, the advertisement of the meeting was in the name of "a committee of the association" rather than in the names of any officers of the Sons of Liberty or in the name of the organization itself. When the rally took place, John Lamb was chairman. This was unusual, since Lamb was a secondary leader and the importance of the event warranted a chairman of reputation and prestige. In this connection of course, Philip Livingston or Isaac Low, both of them wealthy merchants, would have chaired the meeting precisely because they would have had a positive impact on the audience. The fact that they did not serve suggests that they rejected the proposal for a meeting. Smith tells us also that Low, Abraham Walton, and others refused to serve on the committee of correspondence which the assemblage elected. Finally, on December 20 Low and Walton circulated a petition which condemned efforts to prevent storage of the tea. *Ibid.*, pp. 157-58, 159-60, 162; Becker, *The History of Political Parties*, pp. 106-8.

[30] Estimates of the size of the convocation ranged from 800 to 3,000. Force, *American Archives*, 4th ser., I, 254n.; Sabine, *Memoirs of William Smith*, pp. 161, 162.

It is probable that Sears and McDougall had selected the fifteen nominees before the meeting. All the names are not known but among them were Isaac Low, Abraham Walton, Leonard Lispenard, Francis Lewis, David Van Horne, Sears, McDougall, John Broome, John Morin Scott, and perhaps Philip Livingston and John Lamb. *Ibid.*, p. 162; Dillon, *The New York Triumvirate*, p. 126.

ing disposed of this business, the chairman, John Lamb,
read the November 29 association and asked the audience
whether they assented to the resolutions contained in the
declaration. There was no dissenting vote. It was at this
juncture that the meeting took an unexpected turn that
yielded large dividends to its sponsors. Responding to the
potential danger that might arise from the assemblage, Governor Tryon summoned his council into emergency session to obtain its advice. The council unenthusiastically
thrashed over several ideas, one of which was a proclamation
to disperse, and at last settled on the dispatch of the mayor
and recorder with a message from the Governor to the concourse.[31] Tryon promised to disburse no tea except with the
consent of the council, or on the orders of the King or the
East India Company; he exhorted the citizenry to behave
with moderation; he expressed his intention to use no force;
he concluded that he could "do no more nor less" and hoped
the people would "neither disgrace their Gov[erno]r nor
themselves by any imprudent violent & intemperate Behavior." The maneuver miscarried, however, because Mayor
Hicks in the City Hall confined his relation to a bare-bones
statement of the pledge not to dispense the stored tea, omitting any mention of the earnest plea of duty and for moderation. When the mayor compounded his blunder by asking,
"Gentlemen, is this satisfactory?" there was a general cry
of "No! No! No!" Lamb, snatching this golden opportunity,
read aloud the text of the Tea Act, which he embroidered
with a suitable commentary. When he completed his cri-
tique, Lamb posed a crucial question to the crowd. "Is it
then your opinion, gentlemen, that the tea should be landed

---

[31] Smith urged the Governor to go before the meeting but De Lancey and
Watts rejected the idea, proposing that either one of the council or the
mayor be sent. Tryon was unreceptive to Smith's advice. Since the Governor
was popular, it was possible that he might sway part of the multitude and
thus divide the meeting. Although Smith counted on this result, his plan
involved considerable risk of failure. Sabine, *Memoirs of William Smith*,
pp. 159, 160.

under this circumstance?" So loud was the negative oral reply that no one demanded a division.[32] Nailing down the last loose scantling, the chairman secured acceptance of a resolution in which the "spirited and patriotic conduct" of Philadelphia and Boston was "highly" commended.[33] This concluded the rally.

Subsequent events confirmed the victory of the Sears-McDougall group. Although Isaac Low and Abraham Walton set out on December 20 to obtain pledges of nonviolence in the tea boycott, the absence of support caused them to abandon the project the next day.[34] Simultaneously, intelligence arrived from South Carolina that Charleston had resolved to block the admission of the tea and to return it to Britain.[35] The most telling stroke, though, was the news of the Boston Tea Party; the information generated the currents of opinion that moved Tryon to reverse his position.[36] There followed a series of conferences between the

---

32 Force, *American Archives*, 4th ser., I, 254n.; Sabine, *Memoirs of William Smith*, pp. 160, 161; Becker, *The History of Political Parties*, pp. 106-7.

If Smith was a reliable reporter, the reader may accept his statement that a number of prominent people attended the affair because they anticipated a vote in opposition to the storage of the tea. However, at the critical moment James Jauncey and John H. Cruger, major De Lancey leaders, did not request a division but complained that the form of the question did not allow the people a true choice of alternatives.

Smith also reported that he encountered Sears and McDougall at Simmons Tavern the next evening and discussed the meeting with them. He inferred that they had not expected the decisive majority vote, that had they anticipated it, they would have demanded a division be made on the question.

Perhaps there was an undercurrent of local politics present, since Smith speculated that "the De Lanceys rather fell in with the Multitude to save Interest and out of Pique to the Governor who is too Independently spirited for them." Sabine, *Memoirs of William Smith*, p. 162.

33 Force, *American Archives*, 4th ser., I, 254n.

34 Becker, *The History of Political Parties*, pp. 107-8.

35 Sabine, *Memoirs of William Smith*, p. 163; Schlesinger, *The Colonial Merchants*, pp. 295-96. Smith on December 20 stated that the news "greatly influences" the town.

36 It is difficult to decide whether Smith derived his narration of this episode from firsthand knowledge or hearsay. He wrote that "the Boston News astonished the Town . . . those who were for storing it seem most disposed to intreat the Govr. to change his Resolutions for Fear of the Multitude." Sabine, *Memoirs of William Smith*, p. 163.

Governor and several prominent persons in which Tryon made it clear that he was quite willing to forgo storage of the tea but that he was anxious to keep his skirts clean and his reputation untarnished with the ministry in London. The upshot of this intricate maneuvering was a design by which the consignees would stop the tea ship at Sandy Hook, inform Captain Lockyer of the *Nancy* of the menacing situation in town, advise him to depart forthwith, and furnish him with provisions at the Hook. Although Governor Tryon did not wish to publicize his change of front, Captain Ayscough of the warship *Swan,* a "Blab Tongue," let the word slip out and Rivington printed it in his newspaper. The Governor was "in great Wrath" but the townsfolk approved of the executive retreat. Henry White and the other agents sent the letter of advice to Sandy Hook for delivery to the *Nancy* when Captain Lockyer entered the Lower Bay. So the city, confident that it had escaped a clash, settled down to await the tea ship.[37]

The next three months were relatively calm and politics subsided into their customary channels. The legislature sat in these months and devoted much time to quarreling over local problems. One of the features of this legislative session was a tendency of the Livingstons to lend aid to the Governor in order to embarrass the De Lanceys.[38] On the whole, the De Lancey faction lost ground; it suffered the defection of the Jauncey family interest when a squabble arose over the appointment of James Jauncey, Jr., as master

---

[37] *Ibid.*, pp. 163-66; Becker, *The History of Political Parties,* p. 108. Smith explained Tryon's conduct in this manner: "He is afraid of losing Popularity & yet must be hurt at being obliged to drop his high Tone. If he can make the Agents his Instruments, & get the Ship away privately, his Credit will be saved on both sides of the Water; unless he has revealed himself too far to Capt. Ayscough as I think he has—for White says—Some (he means the DeLanceys) sneer & taunt with a What! all this Hauteur come to Nothing!"

Henry White persuaded Smith to draft the consignee's letter to Captain Lockyer. Sabine, *Memoirs of William Smith,* pp. 165-66.

[38] *Ibid.*, p. 176.

of the rolls.[39] Neither faction exhibited any pronounced alterations as a consequence of the imperial dispute; this quarrel had not yet become the touchstone of politics.

The first third of spring had almost elapsed before the suspense in New York ended. Captain Lockyer hove to at Sandy Hook on April 18, twelve days after Governor Tryon took ship for Britain.[40] The shipmaster, having read the communication from the consignees, did not choose to challenge the authority of the committee of correspondence, but he traveled to Manhattan in the pilot boat to arrange for provisions and for an explicit declination by the tea agents to accept the cargo.[41] Lockyer completed his arrangement under the watchful eye of the committee while an observational sloop maintained surveillance over the *Nancy* at the Hook. Determined to impress upon British officialdom the magnitude of the opposition to the Tea Act, the committee of correspondence published the departure date of the captain and bade the citizenry be on hand April 23 to give him a rousing send-off. Although New York was on the verge of conforming to the pattern set by Philadelphia, an unexpected variable disrupted the proceedings.[42]

New York had its tea party not because the committee of correspondence planned it but because a brash shipmaster chose to gamble that he could outwit the committee. Since the tea did not appear on the master's bills of lading, the only evidence of its existence was in the cargo's customs certificates of which those for the tea the captain concealed.

---

39 *Ibid.*, pp. 174-79.

Smith was extremely sanguine about the DeLancey losses: "The De Lancey Party are so broken to pieces out of Doors, that a new Election would bring an independt. Sett of People at least for the City." *Ibid.*, p. 176.

40 Storms delayed the ship's arrival and dealt the vessel some hard blows. Becker, *The History of Political Parties*, p. 108; Wertenbaker, *Father Knickerbocker Rebels*, p. 33.

41 Lockyer needed evidence with which to defend in Britain his failure to deliver his cargo.

42 Force, *American Archives*, 4th ser., I, 249-50; Becker, *The History of Political Parties*, pp. 108-9; Wertenbaker, *Father Knickerbocker Rebels*, p. 33.

However, Captain James Chambers, who arrived with the *London* on April 22, underestimated his opponents; more specifically, he did not know that the committee possessed advices which informed it of the tea aboard his ship.[43] Although a committee paid a visit to the *London* at the Hook and searched through the cockets of the captain, it did not find any for tea. When the observers apprised Chambers of the information that they had, he still insisted that he had no tea in his cargo. Chambers, upon docking, submitted to another examination and maintained that there was none of the vile stuff aboard. Only when his interrogators threatened to open "every package" did he break down and produce the cockets for the tea. Taken with the ship's owners before the committee of correspondence, Captain Chambers explained that he had laded the tea on his private account. By his conduct in New York the master of the *London* thrust a bouquet of thorns into the hands of the committee. Under normal circumstances owners or consignees of goods paid the customs duties within twenty days of entry or officials might seize the vessel.[44] Furthermore, in order to depart, a ship needed a permit from the governor which was usually contingent upon clearance from customs. The owners of the *London* were in a fair way to lose their whole lading even though they had no part in the importation of the tea; either customs would take the ship or the committee would compel it to depart. Having determined not to allow the landing of the tea, the committee of correspondence deliberated over two alternatives. One, the members could demand that Chambers procure from Acting Governor Colden the necessary leave to sail, or two, they could destroy the tea.[45] It was ironical that the destruction of the

---

[43] The Philadelphia committee forwarded detailed data which one of its captains obtained from customs records in London. Secondly, Captain Lawrence docked in New York April 20 and passed on to the committee details which confirmed the Philadelphia intelligence. Force, *American Archives*, 4th ser., I, 249; Becker, *The History of Political Parties*, p. 109.

[44] Schlesinger, *The Colonial Merchants*, pp. 286-87.

tea would protect the investment of the owners in their freight. The committee, "after the most mature deliberation," communicated "the whole state of the matter" to the crowd that had assembled on the wharf near the *London*.[46] Although the "Mohawks" bore the responsibility for removing the tea, the "thousands" on the dock chafed at the inaction and about eight o'clock some of them went aboard the vessel to seize the tea.[47] Diligent labor in two hours dispatched the contents of eighteen boxes of tea into the waters of the harbor; an untold number of spectators carted the empty wooden containers to the Merchants Coffee House where a bonfire consumed them.[48] Presumably there was some hue and cry against Chambers at the completion of the party "and it was not without some risk of his life that he escaped."[49]

The city participated in the last act of the drama on the next morning when all the church bells summoned the citizenry to witness the departure of Captain Lockyer. "Many Thousands" watched and cheered, a band played "God Save the King," and ships' cannon fired as the hapless

---

[45] Since Colden was the bête noire of the Stamp Act proceedings in 1766 and had shown no sign of changed political sentiment since then, there was little to hope for in that quarter.

Colden later repeated hearsay, May 4, that the people particularly resented the "duplicity" of Chambers because he claimed credit previously for being the first New York captain to reject the East India Company's offer of tea. Force, *American Archives,* 4th ser., I, 249; Becker, *The History of Political Parties,* p. 109; Schlesinger, *The Colonial Merchants,* p. 294.

[46] The phraseology of this contemporary newspaper account suggests that the committee itself took no specific decision to destroy the cargo but acted according to a prearranged scheme. The communication of information to the crowd was the signal for the activists to take the initiative. Smith recorded in his notes of December 22, 1773, the discovery "by Hints" that Sears, McDougall, *et al.* were meeting with mechanics in the pubs "to concert Measures for the Day of the Shipp's Arrival." The parallel with Boston is too close to be coincidental. Force, *American Archives,* 4th ser., I, 250; Sabine, *Memoirs of William Smith,* p. 163.

[47] This is Smith's report of the numbers on the docks. *Ibid.,* p. 185.

[48] Smith said the value of the tea was £2,000. The raiders did not damage any other portion of the cargo. *Ibid.*

[49] Force, *American Archives,* 4th ser., I, 250; Becker, *The History of Political Parties,* pp. 109-10; Wertenbaker, *Father Knickerbocker Rebels,* pp. 33-34.

captain took leave of the town aboard the pilot boat. Although there was shouting for Captain Chambers, that worthy, abandoning his command, was preceding Lockyer to the *Nancy*. The trials of Lockyer, however, were not quite over. The crew of the *Nancy* had strong objections to departing without shore leave and set about constructing a raft with which to jump ship. The captain with the aid of the picket sloop put an end to the plot and the ship stood out to sea on April 24.[50]

An aftermath of the tea party was the emergence of the imperial dispute as a salient ingredient of New York factional politics. The tea affair was a catalyst which jolted some party associates into a realization that quarrels with the British ministry might lead to the generation of partisan capital for an alert leadership. Symptoms of this reappraisal appeared in the press shortly after the departure of the *Nancy*.[51] Although the story of the transactions of the past week which the *Gazette* printed was a factual, anonymous piece, by implication it placed credit for the successful outcome of the tea incident on the shoulders of the committee of correspondence. Since the De Lanceyites had dissociated themselves from the committee whereas John Morin Scott and perhaps Philip Livingston had remained on it, the Livingstons would pluck the fruit of the committee action.[52] The De Lancey reaction to the committee account was swift; an anonymous writer ridiculed the whole affair, closing his diatribe with a veiled assault on the Livingstons. He not only attributed the narrative to "party relations" but also

---

50 The phrase "Many Thousands" is Smith's. Sabine, *Memoirs of William Smith*, p. 185; Becker, *The History of Political Parties*, p. 110; Wertenbaker, *Father Knickerbocker Rebels*, p. 34.

51 The committee of correspondence, apparently as a means of informing the urban residents and other citizens of the colony, sent an anonymous relation of the preceding events to the *New-York Gazette and Weekly Mercury* (hereinafter cited as *N.Y.G.*). It appeared in the April 25, 1773 issue; it is also in Force, *American Archives*, 4th ser., I, pp. 249-51.

52 See above, p. 15, n. 30.

sought to identify the Livingstons with "Coblers and Tailors" by professing that tradesmen held "the power of directing the loyal and 'sensible' inhabitants of the city and Province. . . ."[53] The objective of the author was to arouse among the merchants apprehension of the mechanics by raising a bogey and so to reduce mercantile attachment to the committee of correspondence.

Although the targets of these taunts did not suffer them to pass unchallenged, two weeks elapsed before the defenders mounted their counterattack. Writing under the pseudonym "Brutus," one of them retorted with a lengthy relation of the December and April occurrences.[54] When he disposed of these matters, "Brutus" shifted his fire to partisan politics. He warned his readers against those "who are well known to excite sedition, or countenance a suppression of the laudable spirit of liberty alternately. . . ." There were those, he went on, "who ever wear two faces; one to recommend them to ministerial favour, another to beguile the sons of liberty into bondage. . . ." These accusations were not riddles; they were specific characterizations of the De Lancey-

---

53 The reference to party relations was to the Livingstons since the committee nominally was not linked to the factions. *Rivington's New-York Gazetteer,* April 28, 1773 (hereinafter cited as *Riv. Gaz.*) and Force, *American Archives,* 4th ser., I, 251n.

This letter has special importance because historians have seen in it a reflection of the fears of the wealthy at the interference of the poorer classes in politics. However, this interpretation does violence to the context of the letter. After all, it was common knowledge to contemporaries that the committee of fifteen consisted of merchants and lawyers rather than mechanics, that the committee rather than the mechanics directed the events of April 19-23, that the mechanics had played a supporting role in politics at least since 1765. Cf. Becker, *The History of Political Parties,* pp. 110-11; Alexander, *Revolutionary Conservative: James Duane of New York,* p. 97; Flick, *History of New York,* III, 225.

The anonymous writer's phrase, "Coblers and Tailors," perhaps was a reference to individuals of these trades who led in the dumping of the tea or who were close associates of Sears. For example, John Lasher, a cobbler, was a member of the Committee of Mechanics. Jones, *History of New York During the Revolutionary War,* I, 101.

54*Riv. Gaz.,* May 12, 1773, and Force, *American Archives,* 4th ser., I, 251n.-258n.

ites with which many townspeople were familiar.[55] "Brutus" declined to name these insidious foes because, he said, "their persons and their threadbare system of politics are well known. . . ."[56] The polemicist closed his peroration with a thinly disguised reference to the De Lanceys: "if they do not alter their measures, incapable as they now must appear to lead this Colony, they must lose all credit with Government. . . ."[57]

After the news of the British coercive acts hit New York on May 11, factional bickering over the tea party gave way to "heats" of a more serious order. Parliament in effect sealed the port of Boston and deprived Massachusetts of some of its powers of self-government. Confusion and division reigned in New York in reaction to the legislation, confusion and division which stemmed partly from the severity of the ministerial measures. The prior experience with Parliament in 1766 and 1769 encouraged expectation of British concessions to the colonials; the coercive acts were a fearful shock. Opinions among the De Lanceys seemed to run the spectrum from those who contended that Boston had only to pay for the tea to find relief to those like Oliver De Lancey who insisted upon opposition to the acts. Although sentiment among the Livingstons was unclear, there was no uncertainty among the Liberty Boys. Sears and McDougall not only condemned the laws but also expounded the necessity for the institution of a nonimportation policy.[58]

---

55 Smith wrote of the De Lanceys in similar vein. Sabine, *Memoirs of William Smith*, pp. 47, 48, 60, 69, 95, 96, 97, 103, 141, 162.

56 Perhaps the writer, if it was not McDougall himself, recalled McDougall's arrest and indictment in 1770 on charges of seditious libel. Since De Lancey leaders were officeholders, publication of their names in this form was open to a charge of seditious libel of the government. On McDougall's affair see Leonard W. Levy, *Legacy of Suppression: Freedom of Speech and Press in Early American History* (Cambridge, 1960), pp. 79-85.

57 Force, *American Archives*, 4th ser., I, 258n.

58 Roger J. Champagne, "The Sons of Liberty and the Aristocracy in New York Politics, 1765-1790" (unpublished Ph.D. dissertation, University of Wisconsin, 1960), p. 316; Wertenbaker, *Father Knickerbocker Rebels*, pp. 34-35.

Anxious conferences of faction leaders and their henchmen were the order of the day but it was the Liberty Boys–Livingston coalition which sparked the protest movement.[59] Since a major aim of the Sears leadership was the imposition of an embargo on purchases from Great Britain, it was essential to have the wholehearted cooperation of the merchant community. Collaboration of the economic elite with the existing committee of correspondence was highly unlikely because most of the merchants were De Lancey adherents. Set against these relationships, the problem appeared to be most susceptible of solution by the organization of a committee of merchants. Furthermore, the formation of this committee tied in with another related aim of the activists, that of stimulating a call for an intercolonial congress to grapple with the current discord.[60] Sears on May 14 hammered out a compact with the drygoods merchants whereby the latter summoned the merchants to a meeting on May 16.[61]

---

[59] It took the Sears-Livingston committee of correspondence three days to iron out its differences and agree on a policy. It was not until May 14 that the group opened transactions with the merchants. Champagne, "The Sons of Liberty," pp. 315-16.

[60] The collapse of the last commercial boycott in 1769-1770 underscored the need for intercolonial cooperation as the best means of achieving an effective embargo. The proposal for a colonial congress would best come from a committee of merchants rather than from a minority committee of correspondence.

[61] There were important implications in the strategy of Sears and McDougall. The decision to found a merchants' committee as the key agency of the protest movement implied relinquishment of any aspiration by the Sons of Liberty to sole control of the organization. The Sons were too weak to win dominance in a merchant group. The other implication was the continuation of the alliance with the Livingstons as the device by which the Sons might influence the committee. *Ibid.,* pp. 317-18. The May 16 rally was for the purpose of choosing a committee of correspondence, of adopting a policy of nonimportation vis-à-vis Britain, of embargoing the shipment of lumber products to the British West Indies, and of calling a colonial congress. Since the third item was aimed at squeezing the powerful sugar interests, it was odd that the group singled out only lumber. The inclusion of provisions, flour, meat, and fish would have greatly increased the pressure on the islands but perhaps these commodities were shipped mainly in the fall after the harvests whereas timber cargoes were mostly made up in the spring and summer. *Ibid.,* p. 317; Wertenbaker, *Father Knickerbocker Rebels,* p. 35; Schlesinger, *The Colonial Merchants,* pp. 327-28.

When the gathering terminated its deliberations on May 16, the outcome of the debates was not what the Sears-Livingston leadership had anticipated. Although the De Lanceys did not inaugurate any action, the advertisement of the May 16 meeting galvanized them into strenuous exertion to insure a large turnout of their supporters. Their perturbation had its roots in their fear of the potential application of the Boston Port Act to New York as well as in narrower partisan objectives.[62] Their numerical preponderance enabled the Church party to place Isaac Low, a wealthy merchant, in the chair. Having carried a motion to establish a committee of correspondence, the assemblage wrangled over the size of their committee. Sears and McDougall contended for a unit of fifteen or twenty-one members but the opposition advocated and obtained a fifty-member committee.[63] Taking up the business of nominations, the factions bickered hotly over the composition of the committee. When the dust settled, the slate of fifty nominees reflected the numerical superiority of the De Lanceys. That faction won a large majority on the ticket but the Sears-Livingston alliance refused to accept the results as final.[64] Although this was

---

[62] Although the De Lanceys did not approve of the rigorous Lord North policies, neither did they wish to have the Sears-Livingston combine drive a new committee to "extremities" as it had driven the committee of correspondence in April. Perhaps the Church party would have preferred to do nothing except through the legislature but the excitement was such that inactivity for the leadership was impracticable. Finally, as a political interest group the De Lanceyites could not afford to permit the Presbyterian party to reap future good will from their leadership of a new committee. Harrington, *The New York Merchant*, p. 347; Wertenbaker, *Father Knickerbocker Rebels*, p. 36; Becker, *The History of Political Parties*, p. 111; Sabine, *Memoirs of William Smith*, p. 186; Colden to Dartmouth, June 1, 1774, O'Callaghan, *Documents, Colonial, New York*, VIII, 433.

[63] Perhaps the objective in the dispute was the relationship of attendance to control. The coalition wanted a small committee because its members were apt to attend faithfully and so win dominance by perseverance. The De Lanceys desired a large committee in which they would have an overwhelming majority in order that their members might absent themselves without endangering a De Lancey majority. See Smith's comment on the merchants' fear of a small committee. Sabine, *Memoirs of William Smith*, p. 186.

primarily a committee of merchants, both factions desired a formal expression of approval of the nominations by the townfolk and agreed upon a general meeting for this purpose on May 19.[65]

An unwonted component obtruded itself into political affairs at this juncture. Isaac Sears and Alexander McDougall either contrived the formation of a committee of mechanics or joined forces with a recently founded mechanics organ in order to have a counterpoise for use against the De Lancey majority on the Committee of Fifty.[66] McDougall and Sears persuaded the mechanics, if persuasion was necessary, to prepare a rival ticket of twenty-five which they drew mostly from the list of fifty.[67] Armed with this slate, the leaders prepared to enter the lists again the next day in spite of the fact that some of the Livingstons were

---

[64] A correlation of the subsequent voting record of the committee and Becker's analysis of members who became loyalists indicates that the De Lanceys numbered thirty-seven and the Livingstons fourteen. The De Lanceys included Isaac Low, John De Lancey, James Jauncey, John Jay, William and Abraham Walton, James Duane, John Alsop, and Alexander Wallace. Some of the Livingstons were Philip and Peter Van Brugh Livingston, Sears, McDougall, and Leonard Lispenard. Force, *American Archives*, 4th ser., I, 294-321; Becker, *The History of Political Parties*, p. 116, n.16.

[65] Champagne, "The Sons of Liberty," pp. 318-20; Becker, *The History of Political Parties*, pp. 113-15. There is no record of a decision on the embargo question.

[66] The first notice of the new organ is in the records of the Committee of Fifty; the committee received a letter from the Committee of Mechanics on May 23, 1774. However, William Smith noted a meeting of "Mechanics" on May 18 to consider the nominees of May 16. If Sears and McDougall did not create the Committee of Mechanics, its formation was an important declaration of political independence by the craftsmen who heretofore were content either to align themselves with one of the factions or to accept the leadership of a Sears or McDougall. This committee, therefore, was not a continuation of the Sons of Liberty which was in the hands of the merchants. When Sears, McDougall, and John Lamb went their separate ways, mechanics led the Committee of Mechanics. *Ibid.*, p. 120 and n.23; Sabine, *Memoirs of William Smith*, pp. 186, 187.

[67] The list is in Becker, *The History of Political Parties*, p. 113, n. 4. The ticket contained eleven men who were Livingstonians, three whose politics are unknown, and eleven who were De Lanceyites. Two of the twenty-five, Francis Lewis and John Aspinwall, were not among the original fifty. The De Lanceys on May 19 added Lewis to the slate, bringing the committee total to fifty-one. A surprising facet of the ticket of the mechanics is the omission of Philip Livingston.

apparently unwilling to renew the battle of nominees.[68]

A "great concourse" thronged the Royal Exchange on May 19 in preparation for the decisive engagement. Low again chaired the meeting and spoke at length on the need for "unanimity" and an end to "party distinctions, feuds and animosities."[69] The exact strength of each side is unknown but the De Lanceys carried the day on the vital question of nominations.[70] However, the victors threw a crumb to the vanquished by adding merchant Francis Lewis, a Livingstonian, to the committee as member fifty-one. Sears, before the disruptions which the nominations engendered, endeavored to maneuver the De Lanceys into formal discussion of the question of nonimportation. Low and others managed to stifle the attempt, although some speakers did give vent to ideas which disturbed the elite before the chair cut them off.[71] These events consummated the defeat of the

---

[68] William Smith, for example, argued extensively with McDougall, urging him to drop the issue and not to dabble with the idea of employing force to prevent importations. Presumably Smith anticipated that the activists would use the Committee of Mechanics to intimidate the importers. Sabine, *Memoirs of William Smith*, pp. 186, 187.

[69] Becker, *The History of Political Parties*, p. 115; Wertenbaker, *Father Knickerbocker Rebels*, pp. 36-37.
Although the appeal for unity meant unity on De Lancey terms, the dangers inherent in disunity at this stage of events were very real. Smith was also fearful of disunity. Sabine, *Memoirs of William Smith*, p. 187.

[70] The De Lanceyites won over the cartmen and some of the craftsmen, thus depriving the Livingstons of considerable strength. *Ibid.*
Precisely what was decided at the meeting is difficult to discern. There were rabid speeches, disorders on the floor, and the people did not vote on the two tickets. Low at the height of the confusion proposed a division of the audience so that an actual count of the votes might be taken. Sears, for reasons unknown, rejected this procedure; perhaps he was unsure of his votes. "There was such an Uproar, that it was agreed to take the Voices of the Citizens by Subscription," Smith noted in his memoirs. Actually the antagonists compromised on this suggested canvass of the city but they did not execute the compromise. The negotiations between the two parties broke down over the mechanics of the balloting. The consequence was that the De Lanceys announced in the press that the meeting "confirmed" the slate of fifty-one. Gouverneur Morris "confirmed" the confirmation when he wrote on May 20 an account of these events to a friend. "We have appointed a Committee," he said, "or rather we have nominated one." Nonetheless, whether nominated only or elected, thereafter the Fifty-One wielded unchallenged authority. Force, *American Archives*, 4th ser., I, 342; Sabine, *Memoirs of William Smith*, p. 187; Champagne, "The Sons of Liberty," pp. 321-22.

activists and the Livingstons but they also set the stage for the further development of illegal opposition to the crown.[72]

Both factions desired the formation of a committee and, as it turned out, both initially sought to use the committee for the same purpose, to promote an intercolonial congress. Although Sears and McDougall primarily stressed the non-importation proposal, their defeat at the May 19 meeting caused them to shunt aside the embargo idea and accept the priority of an intercolonial conference.[73] Having grasped the reins of the Committee of Fifty-One, the De Lanceyites pondered over the direction which the committee should take. These men did not approve of the measures of Lord North but neither could they stomach commercial retaliation, or at least they could not abide it if the boycott were to be the result of the unilateral decision of each colony. Never-

---

71 A clue to the content of the remarks of the speakers is in the letter of Morris to Penn, May 20, 1774: "[the citizens] fairly contended about the future forms of our Government, whether it should be founded upon aristocratic or democratic principles." The contention over "aristocratic or democratic principles" might have arisen out of criticism of the fact that a very large majority of the Fifty-One were very wealthy, were the "gentry." Morris himself depicted the Fifty-One as a "committee of patricians." A possible remedy for this condition was the ticket which Sears proposed since it proportionately reduced the number of very wealthy and increased the weight of the less affluent merchants. If this were true, Morris was not describing a debate in which the central question was rule by an elite or rule by all the people; rather he was characterizing contention in which the central question was rule by an elite or rule by the small propertyholders. There was still another context into which the description of the gentleman from Westchester might have fitted. Argument over nonimportation might have touched upon the right of an illegal body, the Fifty-One, to dispose of the property of the merchants. "Brutus" expounded one approach to this problem in his defense of the tea party: "when individuals . . . will risk their property in the cause of despotism, or for the sake of sordid and flagitious profit, no good member of society will hesitate to pronounce, that private interest falls a just sacrifice to public utility." Since "public utility" took precedence over the right of private property, in a sense "aristocratic" values gave way to "democratic" values. Force, *American Archives,* 4th ser., I, 258, 342.

72 Sears and McDougall and the Committee of Mechanics resigned themselves to their defeat and accepted De Lancey control of the Fifty-One. Sabine, *Memoirs of William Smith,* p. 187; Champagne, "The Sons of Liberty," pp. 322-24.

73 In a letter to Samuel Adams, May 15, 1774, Sears and McDougall espoused a commercial embargo under the direction of a continental congress. Stokes, *The Iconography of Manhattan Island,* IV, 853.

theless, relentless pressures were accumulating which would not permit the De Lanceys to obstruct endlessly committee action. Since the ministry, unlike its legislative action in 1766 and 1768, was employing physical suasion against the colonies, New York could not close its eyes to the plight of Boston. It was also highly unlikely that the Livingston-Mechanics coalition would accede to the abandonment of Massachusetts without vociferous and vigorous opposition. Another consideration for the De Lancey leaders was the impact of their tactics on the electorate, since the life of the current general assembly would expire in early 1776 and the governor would issue writs for elections to the new legislature. There was in addition to the foregoing matters a sphere of action over which the New Yorkers had no control but about which they manifested great concern. Passivity in New York would not insure passivity among the other colonies; indeed, it was probable that the other provinces would hasten to the aid of Massachusetts and move in the direction of the formation of an association. Having mulled over these affairs, the De Lanceyites fastened on the convocation of an interprovincial parley as the least objectionable alternative. This decision, risky though it was, did not surrender the De Lancey faction's freedom to maneuver, since the York delegates to a continental assemblage might employ their parliamentary skill in efforts to block the adoption of a nonimportation resolution.[74]

When the Committee of Fifty-One met in May and June, the worst fears of the Livingstons and activists that the De Lancey faction would dominate the new organ were not realized. Whatever differences arose between the factions, the Livingstons might have regarded the conduct of the committee as a vindication of their position on the quarrel with Britain. A consensus in the matter of a congress materialized quickly in the course of the first session of the

---

[74] Becker, *The History of Political Parties,* pp. 117-19.

Fifty-One and on the same day the members easily transformed this sentiment into a formal proposal to Boston.[75] Awaiting a commitment from the New England entrepot, the activists neither pressed for committee adoption of nonimportation nor presented resolutions in condemnation of the Coercive Acts. Meanwhile, Sears and McDougall were advising Samuel Adams: "Be firm & prudent & a little time will effect your Salvation. . . ."[76] However, the harmony dissolved when the Massachusetts acceptance of the New York suggestion of a congress arrived in the last week of June.

Although the members of the Committee of Fifty-One could not have foreseen it, their meeting of June 27 opened a month-long period of protracted debate and maneuvering over the selection of the delegates to the Continental Congress in Philadelphia. There were two central issues about which all others tended to circumvolve. One of these two questions was the composition of the continental delegation; the other was the problem of a committee statement on the Coercive Acts. The Livingston allies, conscious of their minority status in the committee, strove to secure a majority of the mission to Philadelphia by insisting on the right of the Committee of Mechanics to approve the nominations by the Fifty-One.[77] Even though the De Lanceyites triumphed in the Fifty-One and nominated Low, John Alsop, James Duane, John Jay, and Philip Livingston,[78]

---

[75] The committee proposition was stronger than that of Sears and McDougall because it suggested a conference of deputies from the provinces whereas the activists recommended a meeting of deputies from the port committees of correspondence. Adherence to the former plan would automatically commit the rural population to the support of the congressional program and would make possible effective enforcement of that body's policies.

[76] Force, *American Archives*, 4th ser., I, 295-307; Stokes, *The Iconography of Manhattan Island*, IV, 857.

[77] The Mechanics, under the influence of Sears and McDougall, would have demanded candidates for whom these two activists had striven in the meetings of the Fifty-One.

[78] Alsop and Livingston were merchants; Jay and Duane were lawyers.

the activists carried the battle to the public. All their efforts, including the promulgation of a rival slate by the Committee of Mechanics, were unavailing.[79] After McDougall gave up the struggle, the opposition, except for a splinter group, collapsed on July 25.[80] An election on July 28 confirmed the victory of the De Lanceys.[81]

The second core question, one which split the committee, was the matter of a public statement on the British ministry's treatment of Massachusetts. Defeat within the Committee of Fifty-One on the matter of the candidates for the Continental Congress may have provoked the Livingstonians to a reconsideration of their role in the committee and of their objectives. Two days later, on July 6, the activists held a mass meeting at which McDougall presided and at which the organizers obtained approval of a series of resolutions on the Boston Port Act.[82] Although the last of these

---

[79] The Mechanics retained Low, Livingston, and Jay on their ticket but substituted McDougall and Leonard Lispenard for Alsop and Duane.

Although the encounter of the De Lanceys with the Mechanics began over candidates, it spread quickly into areas of voting procedures and qualifications. The merchants reluctantly agreed to a canvass of each ward by a team of merchants and mechanics as well as to an extension of the ballot to taxpayers. Becker, *The History of Political Parties*, p. 133.

[80] The diehards seem to have been a fraction of the Committee of Mechanics and included Abraham Brasher, Theophilus Anthony, Francis Van Dyck, Jeremiah Platt, and Christopher Duyckinck. Whether Sears was one of them is problematical. This group hauled down its flag too, but only after it won a significant concession from the De Lancey candidates. It threatened to support a rival ticket unless the candidates promised to work in Congress for a nonimportation agreement. Although the committee slate would not bind itself in this fashion, it published a statement in which the signatories declared that they believed in the efficacy of an embargo as a means of exerting pressure on Britain. Force, *American Archives*, 4th ser., I, 319; Becker, *The History of Political Parties*, pp. 134-35.

[81] The intricate details and a dissimilar interpretation of this fray over the candidates are in *ibid.*, chap. v.

[82] There were nine resolves: (1) that the Port Act is "oppressive" and "unconstitutional"; (2) that "any attack" on the liberties of "any of our sister Colonies" is an attack on all; (3) that "shutting up" any port to "exact" taxation is "highly unconstitutional"; (4) that if "principal" colonies enter into nonimportation from and nonexportation to Britain, they will preserve the liberties of all; (5) that New York deputies to the Continental Congress are instructed to enter nonimportation agreements with other colonies; (6) that this meeting will obey all of Congress's resolutions; (7) that each county send deputies to a provincial convention in order

statements directed the Committee of Fifty-One to carry the propositions into execution, that organ at its session of July 7 emphatically denounced the rally as "calculated to throw an odium upon this Committee. . . ."[83] The De Lanceys, notwithstanding their disavowal of the public proceedings, yielded to this pressure and adopted a motion to constitute a committee to draft resolves on the Port Act.[84] A surprise motion by the De Lanceys at the close of the meeting to publish the previously adopted censure resolution carried and the Livingstonians departed from the hall in a rage.[85] Promptly resigning from the Committee of Fifty-One, the Livingstons publicly vindicated their behavior on the ground that the committee's disclaimer of the July 6 meeting proclaimed both at home and abroad the

to choose delegates to the Continental Congress or that the counties approve the city's choices; (8) that money be raised for the relief of Boston's poor; (9) that the city Committee of Fifty-One be instructed to carry out these resolves. Force, *American Archives*, 4th ser., I, 312-13.

[83] *Ibid.*, p. 311.

[84] The De Lanceys even permitted Sears and McDougall to be on the drafting committee. *Ibid.*, p. 312.

[85] The precise nature of the incident is not clear. Apparently the timing of the motion was deliberate, since a move to publish ordinarily would be raised immediately after the adoption of the relevant resolve. The Livingstonians alleged that McEvers presented his motion after the session ostensibly ended and eight members had left the chamber. Whereas 30 votes were cast on prior motions that evening, only 22 were recorded for this ballot. The tally was 13 to 9. Later the De Lanceys did not deny that eight men left before McEvers took the floor. *Ibid.*, pp. 311-12, 313-14; Becker, *The History of Political Parties*, pp. 126-27 and n.42. When both parties aired their explanations of the affair in print, they adverted to their motivation and illumined an important aspect of factional politics. The statements of both sides indicate that the leaders were acting with one eye on Britain. Charles McEvers, in the course of the discussion on his motion to print the censure, justifying his maneuver, said that the activists published the July 6 rally's resolutions because they knew someone would transmit them to London. The speaker was implying that the ministry would interpret the news as a demonstration of the unity of the people and the Committee of Fifty-One in opposition to the Boston Port Act. Therefore, McEvers declared, the committee must make public its disavowal of the July 6 proceedings in order that it "might be sent home by the packet." Consequently, the British government would not only see that the fractious opposition did not control New York but also would understand that the De Lanceys did not engage in sedition or treason. The Livingstons by implication admitted their desire to flaunt the united opposition of the colony to the Port Act in the face of Lord North. Force, *American Archives*, 4th ser., I, 313-14.

existence of grave dissension in New York.[86] Perhaps the
unspoken rationale in this situation was more important
than the spoken. The practical significance of the motion
to print the repudiation was that the Livingstons could not
remain on the committee and mobilize the citizenry to reverse their defeats by the De Lancey majority. The tug
of war between the De Lanceys and Livingstons over the
resolves went on, even though the Livingstons were no
longer on the Committee of Fifty-One.[87] After both sides

[86] The Livingstons may have regarded the McEvers motion as treachery.
When the committee proposed to draft its propositions on the Port Act, it
tacitly conceded to the Livingstons the necessity of such procedure, but
when it voted to publish a disavowal of the rally and those resolutions,
it created a public impression of its opposition to the adoption of any
proposals. This was partisanship with a vengeance. Since the De Lanceys
acted deceitfully, the Livingstons could not hope for any future advantage
from their labors in the committee.

Three of the Livingstons did not resign, nor has anyone explained their
action. They were Philip Livingston, Peter T. Curtenius, and Abraham
Duryee. Those who withdrew were Peter Van Brugh Livingston, Sears,
McDougall, Francis Lewis, Joseph Hallett, Thomas Randall, Abraham P.
Lott, Leonard Lispenard, John Broome, Abraham Brasher, and Jacobus
Van Zandt. *Ibid.*, 310-14; Becker, *The History of Political Parties*, p. 127.

[87] On July 13 the Committee of Fifty-One drew up and printed its first
set of propositions, which differed materially from the statement of the
July 6 rally (see *ibid.*, p. 129, n.47, for July 13 resolves). The most significant difference between the two declarations was the July 6 call for
immediate nonimportation and an explicit pledge of obedience to any congressional policies. Desiring an expression of popular approval of their
resolutions, the De Lanceys summoned a meeting for July 19 but the rally
was a fiasco for the Church party. Under the leadership of John Morin
Scott the Livingstons won control of the gathering, Scott slashed the De
Lanceys' "pusillanimous" affirmation to ribbons, and the assemblage rejected the document and chose a committee to draft a new bill of particulars. The Livingstons, probably according to preconceived plans, placed
ten of their coalition on the drafting committee of fifteen. These were
P.V.B. Livingston, McDougall, Sears, Lispenard, Randall, J. M. Scott, James
Van Varck, William Goforth, John Lamb, and Theophilus Anthony. There
were five De Lanceys: Low, Duane, Jay, John Moore, and Henry Remsen.
Although the De Lanceyites did not serve on the new committee, the ten
Livingstonians on July 20 and 21 put together a statement which they
modeled on the Fifty-One's handiwork. Meanwhile, jolted by the events of
July 19, the Fifty-One stiffened the verbiage in their resolves but there
was still a gap between the ideas of the two groups. Principally, the conflict centered on the question of obedience to the decisions of the Continental
Congress. The Livingstons were unequivocal in their asseveration of
compliance but the De Lanceys were evasive. The two factions seem to have
attempted between July 21 and 24 to end their disagreement but the effort
was fruitless. A stalemate prevailed. *Ibid.*, pp. 130-33; Sabine, *Memoirs of
William Smith*, pp. 188, 189; Force, *American Archives*, 4th ser., I, 315-18.

modified their positions, they remained deadlocked until July 25.[88] Possibly, the question of the Port Act and that of the candidates for the Philadelphia delegation merged here and as part of a compromise the Livingstonians dropped their insistence upon the adoption of their resolutions.[89] No further mention of the matter occurred; the city accepted the Committee of Fifty-One's declaration of grievances against the North ministry.

The clamor of political strife hardly stilled in the streets of New York in August, 1774, when echoes of a more distant din disturbed the city. Through September and into October the colonials who met in Philadelphia to concert a common defense of American rights poured oratory into each others' ears in Carpenters Hall, argued earnestly over thorny questions in committee, and tactfully probed for weaknesses over food and drink in the city's taverns.[90] Out

---

[88] When the committee of ten Livingstonians completed their work, they bade the people to attend at the City Hall, July 25, to approve the drafters' labors. The transactions at this meeting have not come to light except for the brief newspaper account which noted that "nothing decisive was resolved upon." Perhaps a vigorous opposition by the De Lanceys and the presence of a large number of their adherents deterred the Livingstons from driving matters to a conclusion. Under these circumstances any vote would have revealed serious differences and since both factions saw the need for unity, both were reluctant to shoulder the responsibility for initiating an open break. Becker, *The History of Political Parties*, p. 133 and n.60.

[89] Perhaps the key to the secret lies in the relationship between the City Hall rally and Committee of Fifty-One meeting on the same day, July 25. Although nothing materialized from the public assemblage, the Fifty-One opened their meeting at 6 P.M. with the unanimous adoption of a plan for the election of the congressional delegates in cooperation with the Committee of Mechanics on July 28. Whereas such motions in the past paired the balloting with the Port Act resolves, this prescription was silent on the latter subject. Negotiations in the intervening hours between the sessions may have broken the deadlock. Some opinion certainly pressed for the kind of settlement which the parties made. A broadside, signed "An Honest American," on July 25 stressed that the "Resolves are not material; whether we approve of a one Set or the other, is of no Consequence . . . a Reconciliation of Parties . . . is really essential, in order to procure a proper Delegation. . . ." Stokes, *The Iconography of Manhattan Island*, IV, 861; Becker, *The History of Political Parties*, pp. 133-34.

[90] See the accounts in Jensen, *The Articles of Confederation*, chap. iii; Edmund C. Burnett, *The Continental Congress* (New York, 1941), chap. iii; Becker, *The History of Political Parties*, chap. vi; Schlesinger, *The Colonial Merchants*, chap. x.

of the welter of words came a design which was to have a major impact on New York politics. Despite its tinkering, the Continental Congress bolted together an effective boycott machine, the Continental Association, and sanctioned the use of compulsion to obtain compliance with the provisions of the embargo. Since the provincials did not wish to trigger immediate economic chaos, they elaborated a timetable for the cessation of trade with Britain. They set December 1, 1774, as the opening of the nonimportation phase of the association; March 1, 1775, as the commencement of nonconsumption of tea; September 10, 1775, as the inauguration of nonexportation to Great Britain, Ireland, and the West Indies.[91] The association recommended the formation of county, city, and town enforcement committees and empowered these committees to seize goods which merchants imported in violation of the terms of the boycott. The committees were to publicize the names of those who flouted any of the association's stipulations and the people were not to purchase from those merchants. There was little consolation in all this for the De Lanceys but the association was not an unqualified disaster for them. All merchants were under the same restrictions; merchants in other towns would not be able to capture the New Yorkers' markets. Secondly, there was a period of grace before the nonexportation stage became operative, whereas in New York in the preceding May and June, 1774, the Livingstonians had sought an instant suspension of commerce.[92]

When the De Lancey representatives returned home from the Continental Congress, they brought with them a problem that caused considerable anguish among that faction.

---

[91] The association banned the importation of all goods from Great Britain and Ireland, of smuggled tea, of molasses, coffee, pimento, syrups, and paneles from the British West Indies, of wines from Madeira and the Western Islands, of foreign indigo, and of slaves. The nonexportation article placed an absolute ban on both direct and indirect shipments to Great Britain, Ireland, and the West Indies, except rice for Europe. *Ibid.*, pp. 421-27.

[92] Becker, *The History of Political Parties*, pp. 152-55.

By signing the Continental Association, they bound their colony to observe the conditions of the boycott. However, many of the leading merchants thought that it was a "wrong measure."[93] A conflict over what policy to pursue seems to have supervened among the De Lanceys but the differences did not lead to the dissolution of the Committee of Fifty-One.[94] Since the Low-Duane-Jay group among the Church party accepted the association, its knotty problem was how to apply the boycott without losing control of the machinery to the Livingstons. As a factor in the relative strength of the two factions, the association was a vindication of the views of the Livingstons and a consequent blow to the prestige of the De Lanceyites.

Any potential political advantage for the Livingstons in this situation remained hypothetical until the party hit upon the means by which to transmute their vindication into power. Since the Presbyterian party had read itself out of the Committee of Fifty-One, its record militated against its reentry into the committee. A practical alternative was the formation of a new committee to enforce the boycott, but the initiative lay in the hands of the Fifty-One because that body was still the titular leader of the city. The Livingstons did not act until the Fifty-One announced its plans and then the Presbyterians chose to challenge the De Lanceys through the medium of the Committee of Mechanics.[95]

---

93 Colden to Dartmouth, October 5, 1774, *Letterbooks of Cadwallader Colden,* (New-York Historical Society *Collections,* Vol. X), (New York, 1877), II, 368; Sabine, *Memoirs of William Smith,* p. 203; Becker, *The History of Political Parties,* p. 163.

94 The Fifty-One met three times in November after the publication of the decisions of the Continental Congress. De Lancey attendance at these meetings did not decline, since it was fifteen, seventeen, and nineteen, respectively, approximating that group's range of nineteen to twenty-seven in June and July, thirteen to twenty in August, September, and October. Force, *American Archives,* 4th ser., I, 300-12, 328, 329, 330.

Becker interprets this internal conflict of the De Lanceys as centering on the fear that the Livingstons might assume direction of the opposition to Britain if the Church party withdrew. *The History of Political Parties,* pp. 163-64.

95 *Ibid.,* p. 165; Sabine, *Memoirs of William Smith,* p. 203.

Although the Committee of Fifty-One proposed a modus operandi for the enforcement of the association, the Livingstons' opposition compelled that junto to abandon its project. When the Fifty-One published a plan on November 7 for the election of ward committees of inspection to supervise the terms of the association, the Committee of Mechanics objected and on November 14 organized a protest meeting which condemned the Fifty-One's proposition. If the De Lanceyites were as confident of their political strength in November as they were in July, they would have spurned the Mechanics' objections and permitted a stalemate to evolve. Their action was indicative of their apprehension; they heeded the Mechanics. On the evening of November 14 the De Lanceys invited the Mechanics to hold a joint session on the morrow with the Fifty-One in order to smooth over the differences between them. Apparently there were two bargaining conclaves, November 15 and 16, from which the Livingstons came away with a major victory.[96]

The dimensions of the Livingstonian triumph clearly illumined the shift in power relationships. Not only did the De Lanceys agree to the formation of another committee but they consented also to the dissolution of the Committee of Fifty-One. Another revealing facet of the situation was the composition of the new Committee of Sixty. The De Lanceys accorded 43 percent of the seats to their opponents, which sharply contrasted with the Livingstons' 27 percent of the membership of the Fifty-One.[97] Moreover, the joint

---

[96] For a different interpretation of the De Lanceys' motivation, see Becker, *The History of Political Parties*, p. 165; Force, *American Archives*, 4th ser., I, 330.

[97] The division of the membership is conservative but conjectural. What it amounts to is this. In addition to the sixteen De Lancey holdovers, there were six who became loyalists and twelve whose affiliations are unknown. This combination gives the De Lanceys thirty-four members. One might argue that perhaps four of the unknowns (John White, Francis Bassett, John Anthony, and Jacob Van Voorhees) belong in the Livingston camp. If the De Lancey share is reduced by four, one has evenly divided the Sixty. Such an arrangement would accentuate, of course, the scope of the Livingston victory. Becker, *The History of Political Parties*, p. 168nn.

nominations for the succession organ contained ten of the eleven Livingstons who had resigned from the Fifty-One as well as six members of the Committee of Mechanics.[98] In addition, the De Lancey share of the slate denoted that the faction retained sixteen and dropped twenty-one of its adherents on the Fifty-One, substituting eighteen other men for the latter.[99] Circumstantial evidence suggests that pressure by the Livingstons forced the Low-Duane-Jay group to jettison twelve of those twenty-one whom it discarded.[100]

---

[98] Jacobus Van Zandt was not among the ten Livingstons.

The six men from the Committee of Mechanics were Abraham Brasher, Hercules Mulligan, Victor Bicker, Theophilus Anthony, William Goforth, and Jeremiah Platt. *Ibid.*, p. 198, n.23; Force, *American Archives*, 4th ser., I, 319.

[99] The sixteen carryovers were Alsop, Bull, De Lancey, Duane, Hoffman, Jay, Johnston, Laight, Low, Ludlow, Nicholl, Remsen, Shaw, Van Schaack, and A. and W. Walton.

The eliminated were Bache, Bayard, Beekman, Booth, Browne, Desbrosses, Duyckinck, Goelet, Jauncey, McAdam, McEvers, Marston, Moore, Pearsall, Sharpe, Sherbrook, Thurman, Van Horne, Wallace, Yates, and Young.

The eighteen new men were J. Anthony, F. Bassett, J. Berrien, L. Burling, L. Embree, W. W. Gilbert, T. Ivers, G. Janeway, F. Jay, S. Jones, W. W. Ludlow, J. B. Moore, L. Murray, J. Roome, J. Totten, W. Ustick, J. Van Voorhees, and J. White. Becker, *The History of Political Parties*, pp. 168, 197 and nn.

[100] Perhaps there were two factors which motivated the De Lancey leadership: Livingston pressure and De Lancey attendance at meetings. Possibly it was coincidence but these twelve members voted for the censure of the Livingstons on July 7. This was the meeting which induced eleven Livingstons to resign from the Fifty-One. There is the possibility that some De Lanceys withdrew because they could not accept the association. This is unlikely, however, since the attendance pattern of these dozen men was quite consistent. Their best record at meetings of the Fifty-One was from May through July 7 when their average was 66 percent. From July 19 through October 4 their attendance was an average 33 percent. There were no other meetings until November, at which time there were three. The group's attendance then averaged 28 percent. Even at the climax of the struggle with the Livingstons on July 7, only 57 percent of this De Lancey dozen were present. The attendance record of the sixteen De Lanceys who remained on the committee was much better than that of their factional colleagues. The comparable averages were 81, 62, and 62 and for July 7 it was 62 percent. Finally, four of the twelve who were purged appeared on the newly formed Committee of One Hundred in April, 1775. Pressure rather than dislike of the association seems a more plausible explanation of the change in De Lancey personnel.

The attendance factor rather than Livingston antagonism may explain the case of eight of the remaining nine De Lanceys. There are records for twenty-seven committee meetings between May and November. Four of this group of eight members were not present at any of these sessions and the other four went to fewer than 40 percent of the meetings. A possible ex-

Therefore, acceptance by the De Lanceys of the Committee
of Sixty with which to enforce the association was a signal
stride forward for the Livingstons.

The people consummated this compromise between the
factions on November 22, 1774. Since there was no opposition ticket, there was little interest among the electorate.
Contemporaries estimated that from 30 to 200 voters participated.[101] The city thus preserved its facade of unity in
opposition to imperial policies but the facade concealed
serious antagonisms that were becoming less and less
amenable to conciliation.

Subtly but surely the grounds of factional hostility were
shifting from the traditional arena of legal power and place
to that of illegal power and place. The catalytic agent in
this trend was imperial relations. As the colonial crisis

---

planation of their elimination is that the faction leaders hoped to replace
eight shirkers with more active partisans.

One other facet of this intrafactional strife demands clarification. Since
there were thirty-seven De Lanceyites on the Committee of Fifty-One, one
might well wonder how a minority of sixteen managed to purge a majority of twenty-one. The answer lies in the attendance at the committee
meeting of November 15 at which the Fifty-One arranged their compromise
with the Mechanics. There were nineteen De Lanceys and three Livingstons
at this session; twelve of these were among the survivors, seven were among
the purged. The combination of twelve De Lanceys and three Livingstons
supplied a majority vote of 15 for motions on whom to eliminate. William
Smith who probably had the information from a Livingston leader suc-
cinctly summarized these maneuvers in this fashion: "You'll not wonder
therefore to learn that by the interest of the [Continental Congress] delegates the committee of Fifty-One is to be dissolved and a new committee
to be appointed to execute the decrees of Congress, which is to consist of
the [Continental Congress] Delegates and such a set as the most active of
the Liberty Boys approve, and had (through the mechanics, who were consulted) chosen in conjunction with the Fifty-One, from which a set [i.e.,
the twenty-one] who formerly dictated all their movements, have retired,
outwitted and disgusted, and, as they think, betrayed." For the attendance
record of the Fifty-One see Force, *American Archives,* 4th ser., I, 293-330;
Smith to Philip Schuyler, November 22, 1774, quoted in Becker, *The History
of Political Parties,* p. 164, n. 24, and in Sabine, *Memoirs of William Smith,*
p. 203; Jones, *History of New York During the Revolutionary War,* I, 488-89.

101 William Smith implied that the De Lancey–Livingston agreement on
the membership of the Sixty removed the stimulus to vote: "Not above 200
Electors attended, the Committee of Merchants & Mechanics having concerted the Nomination some Days before." Becker, *The History of Political
Parties,* p. 167, n. 33; Sabine, *Memoirs of William Smith,* pp. 202-3.

sharpened in 1775, more and more De Lanceyites drifted out
of illegal committees into the ranks of the Friends of Government, or, as the revolutionaries called them, Tories.
The formation of rural committees of safety accentuated
this direction of events since the De Lanceyites frequently
refrained from joining these committees. Furthermore, the
legislature which was a major center of De Lancey puissance
atrophied in response to the deepening hostility to royal
government. De Lancey influence waned gradually, while
that of the Livingstons waxed. The Livingstons were building a broader party base than they had ever had.[102]

There were other factional permutations which also had
their origins in the quarrel with Britain. Those who be-
labored the British ministry and their supporters increas-
ingly denominated themselves Whigs and their opponents
Tories. These appellations were naturally broader in their
connotations than the party entities, but the Livingstons
tended to assume that Whig was synonymous with Livingston. However, the application of these labels did not
and does not imply the materialization of two political
parties, each of which possessed a specifically defined program. There were no party programs but the factions
espoused a line of conduct on sundry issues, issues which
centered on colonial ties with Great Britain. Moreover, it
does not clarify the relationship of the two factions to tag
them as conservative or radical courses of action. Nevertheless, the Whig faction's conduct was more ambivalent than
that of the Tories because the Whigs included an articulate
group of mechanics who did not always concur in the
policies of the leadership and who sometimes demanded
substantial political reform.[103]

---

102 Becker, *The History of Political Parties,* pp. 155-57, 160-61.
Some of the De Lanceyites moved into the Livingston or Whig camp.
Duane and Jay were prominent examples of this minority trend.
103 For another interpretation of the events of 1773-1774 see Roger J.
Champagne, "New York and the Intolerable Acts, 1774," *New-York His-
torical Society Quarterly,* XLV (April, 1961), 195-207.

TWO

Royal Influence in New York

ALTHOUGH the Continental Congress adjourned October 26, 1774, and published the Continental Association, the people of New York, except in the metropolis, reacted uncertainly and slowly to the general policies which that document set forth. Hesitation, indifference, and opposition became manifest in the rural counties when the Fifty-One circularized them in November to organize county committees of inspection. Only three counties—Albany, Ulster, and Suffolk—complied with the recommendation from their brethren in Manhattan. The Whigs in five counties, if they bestirred themselves at all, made no impression on the countryside; neither county committees nor district committees were forthcoming. The Tories in the other five counties checkmated the Whigs, although the Whigs did mobilize some district committees in Tryon and Queens.[1]

Disturbed by these setbacks, the Whigs cast about for a means of invigorating the association movement. The Whig leaders transferred the weight of their efforts from the rural districts to the legislative halls, but their parliamentary tactics in the provincial assembly were no more successful than their county campaigns. Laboring assiduously, the De Lancey faction mustered the requisite majorities with which to beat down the three key Whig motions.[2] These three resolutions were a proposal to approve the policies of the Continental Congress, a statement of gratitude to the merchants for their cooperation in the execution of the association, and a recommendation that the assembly appoint delegates to the Second Continental Congress. When the session closed, the Whigs took some comfort in the fact that the assembly adopted a petition to the King, a remonstrance to the House of Commons, and a memorial to the House of Lords. However, the Tories hailed the conduct of the legislature as a great victory for constitutional government.[3]

Although the Whigs had no other alternative but to call for the election of a provincial convention, they had to reach a difficult decision on what measures to propose to that body. Their inability to form strong county committees and their defeat in the assembly were factors in their decision not to strive in convention for an expression of approval of the Continental Association. If the motion of approval had carried in the assembly, it would have committed the colony to the policies of the Continental Congress and would have commended the city Committee of Fifty-One for their enforcement of nonimportation. This latter commitment by implication would have placed the imprimatur of the assembly on the extension of committees throughout the colony. Since none of these possibilities

---

1 Becker mistakenly notes that there was no record of any action in Cumberland. Cumberland elected a county committee but the Tories prevented it from functioning. Carl L. Becker, *The History of Political Parties in the Province of New York, 1760-1776* (Madison, 1909), pp. 169-73: Peter Force, ed., *American Archives* (9 vols.; Washington, D.C., 1837-1853), 4th ser., II, 218-22.

2 See below, p. 52.

3 The British government interpreted these events as a serious setback for the Whigs. General Gage congratulated Colden on the conduct of the assembly. Becker, *The History of Political Parties*, pp. 177-78; Arthur M. Schlesinger, Sr., *The Colonial Merchants and the American Revolution, 1763-1776* (New York, 1939), p. 452; Thomas J. Wertenbaker, *Father Knickerbocker Rebels: New York City During the Revolution* (New York, 1948), p. 45.

had materialized and since these county elections were of purely local relevance and could not be affected by external concerns, the Whigs would find it very difficult at this juncture to circumvent the veto of the assembly. Therefore, the only feasible course for the Whigs was to summon a convention in order to choose delegates to the Continental Congress. This was not likely to be opposed by other than Tories, because the New Yorkers understood that Congress would meet with or without delegates from the Hudson. Since the Continental Congress might function without a New York representation, the province might lose out or suffer embarrassment through the lack of a voice in the continental proceedings.[4]

The climax of these months of maneuvering was the convocation of a provincial convention in April, 1775. The recently chosen city General Committee of Sixty, initiating the convention movement in March, circularized the counties, asking them to send deputies to New York City on April 20 for the purpose of selecting delegates to the Continental Congress. Although nine counties responded favorably to the appeal from the city, five did not comply. Forty-one men met April 20-22 and chose a delegation of twelve to represent the province in Continental Congress.[5] Thus the Whigs managed to maintain intact the ranks of the intercolonial opposition to the North ministry but their

---

4 For a contrary analysis of these events see Schlesinger, *The Colonial Merchants,* pp. 453-54.

If Whig Alexander McDougall may be believed, the Friends of Liberty reached a consensus in early February on the question of holding a provincial convention. "We have not yet chosen Delegates to meet the next Congress, waiting till we know whether the Assembly will do it or not. If they don't we shall be able with more Ease to bring about a Provincial Congress." McDougall to William Cooper, February 9, 1775, Alexander McDougall Papers, NYHS.

5 Richmond, Charlotte, Cumberland, Tryon, and Gloucester did not respond. Becker, *The History of Political Parties,* pp. 186-92; *Journals of the Provincial Congress, Provincial Convention, Committee of Safety and Council of Safety of the State of New York, 1775-1777* (2 vols.; Albany, 1842), I, 5 (hereinafter cited as *Jour. Prov. Cong.*).

activity faltered because they did not have a viable county committee network.

The halting progress of revolutionary organization in the colony of New York in 1774 and 1775 was partly the consequence of royal authority. Although critics in neighboring colonies often harshly criticized the Yorkers for their dilatoriness, some critics permitted their ardor to override their knowledge of that colony's complex state of affairs, a state of affairs that compelled the revolutionaries to tread warily. The British government sought to block every move of the Whigs and its influence in the colony was widespread. The province had special significance for the British for both political and military reasons. The continued attachment of New York to the crown would split the continental union and multiply the pitfalls in the path of those who persisted in opposition. Since 1763 the city had been the headquarters of His Majesty's Forces in North America, a strategic center from which to direct the assembling and transposition of troops. Moreover, in critical days to come, it would afford a secure base from which to launch an offensive to split the rebels, or from which large-scale operations could be directed against the whole continental seacoast.[6]

One source of royal authority was the considerable administrative machine that permeated the province.[7] Some

---

6 Edmund Burke to James De Lancey, March 14, 1775, in Ross J. S. Hoffman, *Edmund Burke, New York Agent with His Letters to the New York Assembly and Intimate Correspondence with Charles O'Hara 1761-1776* (Philadelphia, 1956), pp. 262-63; General Gage to Lord Dartmouth, August 20, 1775, Dartmouth to Gage, April 15, August 2, 1775, Clarence E. Carter, ed., *The Correspondence of General Thomas Gage with the Secretaries of State and with the War Office and the Treasury, 1763-1775* (2 vols.; New Haven, 1931, 1933), I, 413-14, II, 194, 205. See also the discussion of the importance of the commander-in-chief by C. E. Carter, "The Office of the Commander in Chief," in Richard B. Morris, ed., *The Era of the American Revolution* (New York, 1939), pp. 170-213.

7 See the civil list reported by Governor Tryon in Edmund B. O'Callaghan, ed., *Documentary History of the State of New York* (4 vols.; Albany, 1850-1857), I, 521-22. Extensive as the list is, it omits such county and town officials as county judges, coroners, sheriffs, county clerks, justices of the peace, and mayors.

The Road to Independence

of these officials had imperial responsibilities; some had primarily local duties; others combined both. At the head of the administration stood the governor whose power in varying degrees reached down through the council, assembly, courts, sheriffs, mayors, and county and town officials. In another area functioned the customs, Indian, and post office departments. Standing behind civil officialdom, more and more obtrusively by 1775, loomed the armed forces under the control of the commander-in-chief. The South Carolina General Committee illustrated the contemporary comprehension of these relationships when that organ wrote to the New York Committee of Sixty: "We are not ignorant of that crowd of placemen, of contractors, of officers, and needy dependents upon the Crown, who are constantly employed to frustrate your measures. We know the dangerous tendency of being made the Headquarters of America for many years."[8] Despite the imposing outlines of the provincial machine, no one would contend that a strong and vocal opposition did not exist. Within the provincial government, however, only a minority would join the revolutionaries.

More particularly, a point of complaint arose over the administration's influence in the assembly, which represented the freeholders and freemen. An anonymous New York correspondent of the *Pennsylvania Journal,* after listing the elected members of the legislature, their occupations, their social connections, and in many cases their crown offices held during pleasure, asked:

First, Whether the great number of crown officers, or their near relatives in the Assembly, is not a proof either of our extreme negligence of our Liberties, or of the vigilance of government for biassing our Members?

---

8 Letter dated March 1, 1775, *New York Journal,* April 6, 1775 (hereinafter cited as *N.Y.J.*); Force, *American Archives,* 4th ser., II, 1-2. In the pamphlet *The Farmer Refuted* Alexander Hamilton says: "How great an influence, places, pensions and honours have upon the minds of men, we may easily discover by contrasting the former, with present conduct of some

Second, Whether though the highest honour is due to the integrity of so many gentlemen, who have nobly risked their offices by their fidelity to the country, it is not nevertheless a scandal to the province, that we have as yet no place bill to exclude such from the House of Assembly as after an election render themselves dependent upon the Crown for offices held during pleasure, and Third, Whether from the arbitrary project of the late Parliament for introducing a council into the Massachusetts Bay, at the pleasure of the Crown, it does not appear to be an indispensible duty firmly to insist upon a law utterly to exclude the dangerous influence of his Majesty's Council, at all elections for representatives of the People.[9]

The unappropriated lands of the colony gave to the British a potentially persuasive instrument, especially in a tense period, since the possession of land seems to have been an almost universal aspiration among both the lesser and greater propertied classes.[10] Issuance of the letters patent for land grants depended upon approval of the governor and council, who tended to favor the supporters of administration. Those who lacked the requisite political or social connections had to resort to other methods which might entail partial loss of the grant. "Rough Hewer" referred to this practice when he wrote that one "could not obtain a patent, except through the interest of . . .[government] favorites, and that often at the expense of part, if not the half of his right."[11] In the case of the Vermont lands some men even managed to secure patents from the New Hampshire government. Henry Franklin and Frederick and William Rhinelander inserted an advertisement in the newspapers, warning that they had obtained recently

---

among ourselves." Harold C. Syrett and Jacob E. Cooke, eds., *The Papers of Alexander Hamilton* (8 vols.; New York, 1961-), I, 141.

[9]*Pennsylvania Journal*, February 22, 1775 (hereinafter cited as *Pa. Jour.*). Perhaps some of the radical members of the New York City Committee of Sixty sent the letter to the Philadelphia committee.

[10] For British use of this device see below, pp. 49-50.

[11] This was the pseudonym of Abraham Yates, Jr. "Rough Hewer," *N.Y.J.*, January 24, 1784; Virginia D. Harrington, *The New York Merchant on the Eve of the Revolution* (New York, 1935), pp. 140-41, 142.

a New York grant of 63,000 acres in Charlotte County on the east side of Lake Champlain but that they would share it with those who held these lands under a prior New Hampshire patent. The new patentees demanded the sharing of all costs and the procurement of a New York title. Among those named as holding from New Hampshire were Isaac Sears, Isaac Sears, Jr., William Smith, William Smith, Jr., Philip French, Philip French, Jr., David Matthews, Cornelius Low, Jr., Benjamin Blagge, John Blagge, Peter Ten Eyck, and Andrew Ten Eyck.[12]

Although the home government sought to revise the system, the governor and council perpetuated it by granting land to those who would uphold the royal prerogative. From April, 1775, to July, 1776, Colden and Tryon approved grants totaling 423,064 acres, of which 328,216 acres lay in Vermont. More than 64 percent of the total, 273,121 acres, went to prominent Tories: the Rhinelanders, Franklins, Apthorpes, Edmund Fanning, the Rapaljes, Robert Rogers, and William Smith, agent for Governor Martin of North Carolina.[13]

The merchants presented another possible channel for the diffusion of royal influence. Many Yorkers had strong commercial ties with the mother country; either they relied on British credit for their operations or they traded wholly within the empire. Still others functioned as factors for English houses or sold goods on a commission basis for British correspondents. A small group profited as contractors for the British military and naval establishment.[14]   In

---

12 *New York Packet,* March 7, 1776 (hereinafter cited as *N.Y.P.*).

13 New York, *Calendar of New York Colonial Manuscripts Indorsed Land Papers in the Office of the Secretary of State of New York* (Albany, 1864), pp. 625ff.; Harrington, *The New York Merchant,* pp. 142-43; Irving Mark, *Agrarian Conflicts in New York, 1711-1775* (New York, 1940), p. 48, nn. 137 and 138.

14 Barrack Master General Brigadier General James Robertson told some merchants he had spent £260,000 in New York. Presumably this covered the period as B.M.G., 1765-1775. William H. W. Sabine, ed., *Historical Memoirs from 16 March 1763 to 9 July 1776 of William Smith* (New York, 1956), pp. 219-20; Carter, *Correspondence of General Gage,* II, 310.

addition to these, the Indian traders under the supervision of the government had long conducted a profitable business. Economic considerations, however, by no means predominated in the web of bonds with Britain. A number of merchants had emigrated only recently to America or had maintained close ties back home. Another group of merchants served on the council or held office on the local level in Albany and the capital. Finally, intermarriage between merchants and officials drew a number of leading families into the circle of government supporters.[15]

When colonial affairs deteriorated critically in 1773 and 1774, the British ministry turned to good account its position in New York. Employing a combination of persuasion and pressure, the ministry sought to mobilize enough strength to split New York from the Continental Association. Certainly the landholding aristocracy and speculators, involved in major boundary disputes with New Hampshire, Massachusetts, and New Jersey, would have welcomed a Privy Council decision in their favor. The Secretary of State for the Colonies, Lord Dartmouth, intimated the rewards that awaited the faithful when he discussed the state of the Vermont controversy with Lieutenant-Governor Colden at the close of 1774: "Their [i.e., the Yorkers'] Pretensions will meet with every Countenance and Support that can be shewn consistent with Justice; for I can with Truth say that the Conduct of that Province in general . . . has been such as justly intitles its well disposed and peaceable Inhabitants to His Majesty's particular Favor and Indulgence."[16] Colden himself pressed the Secretary to conduct policy along these lines, expressing the hope that he "will encourage this good and singular disposition by such

---

[15] Harrington, *The New York Merchant*, pp. 350-51. See also the marriage relations of the council listed in *Pa. Jour.*, February 22, 1775.

[16] Dartmouth to Colden, December 10, 1774, Edmund B. O'Callaghan, ed., *Documents Relative to the Colonial History of the State of New York* (15 vols.; Albany, 1856), VIII, 514.

instances of indulgence and favor, as shall be wisely calculated to render most evident the good effects of the conduct
of this Province."[17]

Governor William Tryon's instructions of May, 1775,
containing several important proffers, bore out the continuance of these tactics. Dartmouth offered a blanket
assurance᾽ to give "every reasonable satisfaction" to His
Majesty's faithful subjects in New York. A second example
of the royal indulgence and favor manifested itself in con-
ditional approval of the Totten and Crossfield Indian purchase. This tract comprised an extremely large area in the
Adirondacks and involved many of the colony's leading
personages. Royal confirmation of the transaction hinged
upon New York's repudiation of the Continental Association. Even education had its political application. The
Colonial Secretary had no objections to the draft of the
new charter for Kings College and did not anticipate difficulties for it in the Privy Council. In addition, the instructions held out the prospect of the council's assent to charters
of incorporation for the Dutch Reformed and Presbyterian
churches.[18]

The British did not neglect the power of the purse, although no evidence of open bribery has come to light.
Nonetheless, the Whigs circulated charges that Dartmouth

17 Colden to Dartmouth, February 1, 1775, *ibid.*, VIII, 532. Those in high
places in London assured the Friends of Government in New York of the
royal esteem for that colony: " 'Pursue the same path, and your province
will be honoured with every mark of distinction from this country. His
Majesty is already disposed to grant you every honourable favour that can
be proposed.' " Dr. Samuel Auchmuty to Captain Montresor, April 19,
1775, quoting from a letter to himself from London, *Pa. Jour.*, May 31, 1775.

18 Major Philip Skene and Rev. John Vardill urged Dartmouth to grant
the charters since it would lead the Presbyterians "to cooperate more zeal-
ously in support of government." Skene and Vardill to Dartmouth, March,
1775, Great Britain, Historical Manuscripts Commission, *Fourteenth Report,
Appendix Part X* (Manuscripts of the Earl of Dartmouth) (London, 1895),
p. 284 (hereinafter cited as *Hist. Mss. Com.*). Dartmouth to Tryon, May 4,
1775, O'Callaghan, *Documents, Colonial, New York*, VIII, 573. See William
Smith's comment, Historical Memoirs of the Province of New York, V, June
28, 1775, William Smith Papers, NYPL (hereinafter cited as Memoirs).

had large sums to expend in America. Some "Citizens of New York" published a broadside in November, 1774, warning the people that the ministry intended to buy up the newspaper printers.[19] Early in 1775 the press carried an extract of a letter from London which asserted that "it is currently said here and with much confidence, that a good deal of public Money, has been put in the Hands of a Mr. ——— one of the ——— and some of your other great Men, in order to buy their Influence in Favour of the Ministerial Measures. . . ."[20]

By far the most sensational allegation of bribery came to hand in May, so sensational that the New York Committee of One Hundred[21] tried to suppress it, but the *Pennsylvania Journal* frustrated the committee's design. The *Journal* of May 17 reproduced an extract of a London letter which asserted that several members of the New York assembly had pocketed bribes of more than £1,000 each for their votes in January, 1775. The writer went on to allege that a group of De Lancey party leaders would be rewarded with places of "honor, profit and pensions."

The source of this information seems to have been a letter from London alderman William Lee to Samuel Adams, who, in turn, edited the letter for publication. Lee charged that "the Ministry now openly boast of their having last year sent large sums to New York to bribe the Members of that Assembly and the names of De Lancey, Phillips and Rappalje are frequently mentioned as having each of them received one thousand guineas for their conduct in the Assembly respecting the late Continental Congress and for refusing

---

[19] *To the Public* by "Citizens of New York," November 16, 1774, Broadsides, NYPL.

[20] *N.Y.J.*, February 9, 1775. A similar warning appeared in *ibid.*, March 16, 1775. This letter seems to have been from Thomas Lane, Chairman of the London Merchants to Francis Lewis. See the comment of William Smith, Sabine, *Memoirs of William Smith*, p. 213.

[21] For the creation of the Committee of One Hundred, see below, pp. 69-75.

to send Delegates to the May Congress." Lee set forth a
number of other grave imputations. For example, he alleged that Lieutenant-Governor Colden would resign with
a pension, that Councilor John Watts would succeed Colden,
that Watts's son would take his father's place on the governor's council. Lastly, Lee declared that Philip Skene
would receive a land grant of 120,000 acres and a commission as governor of Crown Point and Ticonderoga.

Later events substantiated some of the allegations. Skene
did secure both the office and the land. Moreover, the De
Lancey party did move as a subterfuge to petition the King
and Parliament in order to forestall approval of the Continental Congress by the New York assembly.[22]

A passage in Smith's memoirs tends to give a shadow, but
no more, of credibility to the bribery charges. Smith records
a meeting of the key De Lancey faction leaders on January
9 at which they discussed the probable division of the assembly on the question of approving the acts of the First
Continental Congress. The leaders agreed that the administration could count on eleven votes against approval, but
they calculated Whig strength at fourteen votes, which
meant there were six uncommitted members. When the
January vote came, it went 11 to 10 in favor of the De
Lancey faction. Later votes on the colonial dispute ran
15 to 9, 15 to 10, and 17 to 9 for the government's position.[23]

22 There were two letters, April 4 and 10, 1775, Bancroft Transcripts:
Samuel Adams Papers, NYPL. Lee apparently prepared the first one for
publication, signing it "L.L." The New York copy of the extract, which
Adams probably sent to a number of committees, is printed in New York,
*Calendar of Historical Manuscripts Relating to the War of the Revolution,
in the Office of the Secretary of State* (2 vols.; Albany, 1868), I, 1-2 (hereinafter cited as *Cal. Hist. Mss.*).

Adams, prior to receipt of the Lee letter, believed the assembly to be
corrupt. Adams to Arthur Lee, March 4, 1775. Arthur Lee had warned
Adams also that the North ministry was spending lavishly and offering con-
cessions in order to maintain New York's allegiance to the crown. Arthur
Lee to Adams, March 2 and 4, 1775, Bancroft Transcripts: Samuel Adams
Papers, NYPL.

On Skene see Carter, *Correspondence of General Gage*, I, 354, II, 158;
Hist. Mss. Com., p. 269.

The De Lancey leaders' gross underestimation of Tory strength suggests that the administration applied powerful pressure to change some votes.[24]

Although nothing in the preceding material proves the Whig charges of bribery, it is true that some men did receive special inducements. The Colonial Department notified Drs. Myles Cooper and Thomas B. Chandler, able Tory penmen, that the Treasury would pay them £200 per annum "from a consideration of your merit and services."[25] James Rivington, printer of *Rivington's New-York Gazetteer,* having won favor in the ministry's eyes, became the recipient of £100 per year and the title of His Majesty's Printer within the Province of New York.[26]

Rivington had earned his £100 salary. Although he had not begun publication of his newspaper until 1773, he had surpassed his competitors, Hugh Gaine and John Holt, and circulated his *Gazetteer* through many of the colonies.[27] As political differences multiplied, Rivington's paper emerged as the bulwark of established government. Equally important, the printer functioned as a publisher of Tory tracts.[28] It is not surprising that the Whigs detested him. Bitter denunciation of his press spread through the colonies

---

23 The difference among the totals of votes cast reflects the absences of members. There were thirty-one members of the assembly.

24 Becker, *The History of Political Parties,* p. 176; Sabine, *Memoirs of William Smith, p.* 208. See below, pp. 79-80, for discussion of these affairs in the assembly.

25 Secretary Pownall to Drs. Cooper and Chandler, April 5, 1775, O'Callaghan, *Documents, Colonial, New York,* VIII, 569.

26 Sidney I. Pomerantz, "The Patriot Newspaper and the American Revolution," in Morris, *Era of the American Revolution,* p. 316. That this was an unusual appointment may be seen from the source of the money. The Lords Commissioners of the Treasury were to pay him "out of such fund as their Lordships shall think proper." O'Callaghan, *Documents, Colonial, New York,* VIII, 568.

27 Pomerantz, "The Patriot Newspaper," in Morris, *Era of the American Revolution,* p. 315. Gaine published the *New-York Gazette and Weekly Mercury;* Holt printed the *New-York Journal.*

28 In 1775 Rivington printed approximately twenty-eight political tracts, most of which were Tory. Charles R. Hildeburn, *Sketches of Printers and Printing in Colonial New York* (New York, 1895), p. 117.

from South Carolina to Rhode Island, taxing him with the publication of "glaring falsehoods."[29]

One of his stories brought him a reprimand from the New York City Committee of Observation[30] in March, 1775. Sponsoring the most debatable recommendation of the day, participation by the province of New York in the Second Continental Congress, the Whigs maneuvered to win popular approval of their proposal.[31] On March 2, *Rivington's Gazetteer* carried this item without any qualification: "Last Monday the committee of observation met; it was proposed that they should nominate delegates, to the continental congress, for the approbation of the city and county, but being opposed, the final resolution of the committee was deferred until the next meeting." To the reader the story bore the implication that those who advocated sending delegates to Congress comprised only a minority of the committee and so avoided a vote on their proposal. Fearing an adverse reaction to the report, the committee formally repudiated it as false and voted to have two members pay Rivington a call in order to learn its origin. The delegation apprised their colleagues that Rivington had stated the source of his news as "common report" and, under pressure, had agreed to print a retraction. Having heard the presentment, the committee resolved then that Rivington should not present "common report" to the public as news.[32]

After the startling news of Lexington and Concord had aroused the city on April 23, the Tory printer abruptly

---

29 Quoted in Pomerantz, "The Patriot Newspaper," in Morris, *Era of the American Revolution*, p. 316: Arthur M. Schlesinger, Sr., *Prelude to Independence: The Newspaper War on Britain, 1764-1776* (New York, 1958), pp. 223-27.

30 The Committee of Sixty.

31 See below, p. 81.

32 *Riv. Gaz.*, March 2, 1775; *N.Y.G.*, March 20, 1775. Rivington challenged the accuracy of the delegation's summary of their interview: he asserted he told the committeemen the news was "credited" not "common report." *Riv. Gaz.*, March 16, 1775.

revised the tone of his paper. The numerous letters from Tories vanished; the partisan news reporting diminished; however, the reformation did not result in the publishing of the pseudonymous political letters of the printer's antagonists.[33] Although Rivington in the issue of May 4 denied any intent to injure American liberty, six days later he fled from a group of angry Whigs to a British vessel in the harbor. By promising to reform and promising not to violate the association, Rivington won the permission of the Provincial Congress to continue publishing.[34]

Shortly thereafter the *Gazetteer* showed signs of trimming even more closely to the prevailing wind but once more changed course with the arrival of Governor Tryon. Before Governor Tryon, returning from Britain, reached the city June 25, this newspaper carried two installments of Alexander Hamilton's pamphlet which attacked the Quebec Act.[35] The reappearance of the Governor seems to have emboldened Rivington, and the *Gazetteer* took on a more pronounced Tory flavor. Even though the Rivington press had begun printing Hamilton's *Remarks on the Quebec Bill*, the newspaper not only discontinued further installments but also ceased to advertise it. The June 29 number, furthermore, while containing a description of Tryon's reception by the town, had nothing to say about the simultaneous arrival of Washington in New York and only a few words that noted his departure for Boston. Having changed

---

33 *Ibid.*, April 27, May 4, 11, 18, 25, 1775.
34 Pomerantz, "The Patriot Newspaper," in Morris, *Era of the American Revolution*, pp. 317-18; Hugh Finlay to his brother, New York, May 29, 1775, Great Britain, *Calendar of Home Office Papers of the Reign of George III, 1773-1775* (London, 1899), pp. 365-66 (hereinafter cited as *Cal. H. O. Papers*); "Case of Mr. James Rivington, Printer at New York" by Coriolanus, *Gentleman's Magazine*, November, 1776, quoted in J. Shannon, comp., *Manual of the Corporation of the City of New York, 1868* (New York, 1868), p. 825; Robert C. Livingston to Colonel Robert Livingston, May 13, 1775, Livingston Redmond Papers, FDRL. Despite Rivington's absence from his shop, the paper continued to appear.
35 *Riv. Gaz.*, June 15, 22, 1775. Rivington had published previously two other Hamilton pamphlets, although not serializing them in the *Gazetteer*.

his publishing policy, Rivington persistently filled his columns with pro-Tory news stories until the demise of the paper in November, 1775.[36]

Rivington was so successful in presenting the Tory view of events in America that the Whigs destroyed his newspaper in November, 1775. The most widely accepted interpretation of the wreckage of Rivington's shop is that Isaac Sears conducted the foray to satisfy his personal animus against the printer. The basis for this viewpoint is an acrimonious exchange of letters in 1774 between the two men. An examination of the letters, however, does not reveal any threat, overt or implied, by Sears.[37]

Early in January, 1775, Rivington and the Tories utilized a minor incident to seek to discredit Sears. The *Gazetteer* carried a statement by John Case which charged that Sears had threatened and roughly handled him in a political dispute. "A Friend to Constitutional Liberty" rebutted the accusation in detail with supporting statements from witnesses and stated that Case was a dupe of the "anti-American club" that met at Rivington's. Although he might have done so, Sears did not turn his anger on Rivington.[38]

If the accusation of a personal feud were true, the radical leader certainly did not have a consuming desire to wreak vengeance on his adversary. He waited eight months to strike a blow. With the city in turmoil the week after the

---

36 *Ibid.,* June 29–November 23, 1775. On Washington and Tryon see below, p. 78.
37 Pomerantz, "The Patriot Newspaper," in Morris, *Era of the American Revolution,* p. 318; Henry B. Dawson, *Westchester County, New York, During the American Revolution* (Morrisania, 1886), pp. 127-40; Thomas Jones, *History of New York During the Revolutionary War, and of the Leading Events in the Other Colonies at that Period,* ed. Edward F. de Lancey (2 vols.; New York, 1879), I, 66; Becker, *The History of Political Parties,* pp. 245-46; Hildeburn, *Sketches of Printers,* p. 120; Victor H. Paltsits, "James Rivington," and Charles H. Vance, "Isaac Sears," *Dictionary of American Biography,* XV, 638, XVI, 539; George H. Sargent, "James Rivington, the Tory Printer," *Americana Collector,* II (Metuchen, 1926), 336-41; Schlesinger, *Prelude to Independence,* p. 240. The letters are in Jones, *History of New York During the Revolutionary War,* I, 561-66.
38 *Riv. Gaz.,* January 12, 1775; *N.Y.J.,* February 2, 1775.

news of Lexington arrived, Sears could have very easily organized a mob to destroy the Rivington press. Moreover, when a band did visit the Rivington shop in May, 1775, apparently seizing the sheets of a Tory pamphlet in press, it did not molest the newspaper, which was published regularly during the temporary exile of the printer.[39]

Why then did Sears hold his grudge in abeyance another six months before putting an end to the printing activities of Rivington? Governor Tryon did not mention personal feelings when he apprised Dartmouth of the November incident. Tryon attributed the catastrophe to "the freedom of Mr. Rivington's publications, & especially in his last paper."[40] Since the last number of the *Gazetteer* bore the date November 23, Sears could not have seen it before setting out on his expedition from New Haven on the twentieth.[41] The Governor, however, may have been partly correct.

A comparison of the *Gazetteer* for November 2, 9, and 16 points to the issue of the ninth as likely to have offended the Whigs most. The volume of pro-Tory news in that day's paper far overshadowed the other numbers; indeed, the final issue of the twenty-third was quite mild in contrast. Rivington devoted three and a half columns of the front page of the November 9 issue of the *Gazetteer* to the August 8 proclamation of Governor Martin of North Carolina

---

39 Hildeburn, *Sketches of Printers,* p. 120. See above, p. 55. The pamphlet, *The Republican Dissected,* was "A. W. Farmer's" reply to Hamilton's *The Farmer Refuted.* Advertisement, *Riv. Gaz.,* April 13, 1775.

40 Tryon to Dartmouth, December 6, 1775, O'Callaghan, *Documents, Colonial, New York,* VIII, 646.

41 Sears apparently quitted New York in a huff after he quarreled with the Provincial Congress in early November, 1775. He urged the seizure of some British army blankets and hospital stores but the Provincial Congress would have nothing to do with it. "Sears I'm told is so highly offended with this Congress for acting so that he is set out for Connecticut and swears he wont return—meaning to *punish* the City by absenting himself from it. All people seem to wish he may persevere in such a punishment." John Patterson to Colonel Robert Livingston, November 6, 1775, Livingston Redmond Papers, FDRL.

which labeled the provincial convention of that colony as treasonable and its members traitors, ordered the arrest of its leaders, placed prices on the heads of the leaders, and held out pardon to those who would ask for it.[42] Page two presented the address of the Boston Tories to Gage on his departure and the reply of the latter. Page three contained more Boston items, three proclamations of General Howe, and a proposal to form an association of Boston Tories. Page four reproduced the Quaker address to the Pennsylvania General Assembly, an address which was strongly Tory in tone.[43]

Radical Whigs seem to have maintained a sharp eye on the press and reacted strongly. "An Occasional Remarker" attacked the *Gazetteer* in the *New-York Journal* on the sixteenth, exhorting the Committee of Safety[44] and other "friends of liberty" to make Rivington reveal the names of the persons who contributed the offensive pieces. Alarmed by the quantity of Tory news, "Remarker" also pressed for the creation of a special committee that would write replies to these stories. It may be that "Remarker" reflected the growing alarm among the more radical rebels at the increasing boldness of Rivington.

There is still another aspect of this picture that deserves notice. Governor Dunmore of Virginia may have unwittingly played a part in the ruin of Rivington. On October 7 he directed the seizure of the Norfolk press of John H. Holt and two of his workmen, provoking even the Tory mayor and town council to protest unavailingly.[45] It is highly

---

[42] Rivington copied the text from the *Pennsylvania Journal,* November 1, 1775, but the latter also printed the North Carolina Convention's indignant reply to Martin which the New Yorker omitted.

[43] Of the other New York newspapers, the ardent Whig *Journal* did not carry any of the North Carolina, Boston, and Philadelphia items, but the *Gazette* did publish the Boston stories November 6 and 13.

[44] See Becker, *The History of Political Parties,* chap. ix, for the chronological narrative of these months.

[45] John H. Holt was the nephew of printer John Holt of New York. Schlesinger, *Prelude to Independence,* p. 57.

probable that Sears read of this event since the story appeared in both the New Haven and New York papers.[46] There is, furthermore, a more direct link between the Virginia and New York proceedings. According to the contemporary account of the Rivington incident, as Sears and his men carried out the printing types, "they offered to give an order on Lord Dunmore [for them]."[47] It may be that the combination of the content of the *Gazetteer* and confiscation by Dunmore of the printing equipment of Holt led to the drastic action against Rivington.

The foray of Sears from New Haven reflected careful planning which involved two other Yorkers, Samuel Broome and John Woodward. The leaders had two major objectives: the seizure of three Westchester Tories and the destruction of the Rivington press. Sears suspected the intended Westchester victims of planning to waylay him and put him aboard the British warship *Asia*. Assembling approximately ninety-seven mounted men, Sears departed for New York on November 20. In Westchester the troop secured Samuel Seabury, Judge Jonathan Fowler, and Mayor Nathaniel Underhill of Westchester Borough without incident and dispatched them to New Haven under strong guard. At Mamaroneck they burned a small sloop which the British had purchased to supply the *Asia*. They paraded down the "main street" of Manhattan at noon, November 23, and drew up in front of the Rivington shop. It took a small detachment about three-quarters of an hour to smash the printing press and package the type. As they rode off with the type the "vast concourse" of spectators, estimated at 1,500, "gave them three very hearty cheers." On their eastward journey the raiders disarmed all the Tories whom

---

46 *Connecticut Journal,* October 25, 1775; *Riv. Gaz.,* October 26, November 2, 1775.

47 *Connecticut Journal,* December 6, 1775; Schlesinger, *Prelude to Independence,* p. 240.

they encountered. The last leg of the trip through Connecticut assumed the proportions of a triumphal procession and New Haven welcomed them with a salute from two cannon. The loss of *Rivington's Gazetteer* deprived the British of a major channel of communication with the people of the province in this critical period and contributed to the diminution of the influence of the government.[48]

British patronage and the hesitant policy of the New York Provincial Congress in 1775 inspired ugly suspicions in the other colonies.[49] Holt's *Journal* published a warning to its readers on how New York looked to the outside world, when it printed part of a letter from the familiar "gentleman in London to his friends": "The duplicity of New York will ever render them suspected. The many, repeated assurances given to the Ministry by their quondam leaders, will justify a suspicion, which the conduct of some of the merchants and traders confirms, that they would adopt any means to break through or elude the association."[50] Closer to home, General Wooster of Connecticut was protesting to Governor Trumbull his subordination to the control of the New York Provincial Congress as a "disgrace" to himself and a "dishonour" to his own colony. "Your Honour well

---

48 The *Connecticut Journal,* November 29, 1775, has a narrative of the raid. The same version also appears in the *Connecticut Courant,* November 29, 1775 and *Pa. Jour.,* December 6, 1775. Briefer stories were published in the *Constitutional Gazette,* November 25, 1775 (hereinafter cited as *Const. Gaz.*), *Connecticut Gazette,* December 1, 1775 and *Pennsylvania Gazette,* December 29, 1775. Jones, *History of New York During the Revolutionary War,* I, 66; Proceedings of the General Committee of New York, November 23, 1775, Shannon, *Manual of Corporation of New York, 1868,* p. 815.

49 See below, chap. iv.

50 *N.Y.J.,* August 31, 1775, letter from London to his friend in Philadelphia, June 4, 1775. *Pa. Jour.,* April 19, 1775, had printed an extract which stated that the ministry expected New York to desert the continental union. For similar sentiments see the broadside, *To the Inhabitants of New York and . . . America,* New York, April 20, 1775, NYPL which contains extracts of several letters from London. Franklin said the ministry expected the 4,000 troops being dispatched to New York would be received with cordiality. *Extract of a Letter from Philadelphia to a Gentleman in this City, Dated the 6th Inst.,* New York, May 8, 1775, Broadsides, NYPL.

knows," he wrote, "the suspicious light in which the New-York Congress are viewed by the rest of the Continent. . . . I have no faith in their honesty in the cause."[51] After having encountered New York reluctance at first hand, General Charles Lee had much the same opinion of the rebel leadership.[52] Although John Jay confessed anxiety for the "Honour of our caluminated Colony," he hastened to add, "I can assure you the Province stands well with the [Continental] Congress. . . ."[53] Jay to the contrary notwithstanding, a committee of Congress that had visited New York in February, 1776, privately voiced skepticism of New York loyalty to the cause.[54] These misgivings persisted until the colony accepted the Declaration of Independence.[55]

In spite of the far-reaching authority of the government, a rising opposition to royal policies gradually broke down the government's supremacy. The province divided into two major groups, Tory and Whig, that cut across social and class lines.

---

[51] Wooster to Trumbull, August 24, 1775, Force, *American Archives,* 4th ser., III, 263.
[52] Curtis P. Nettels, *George Washington and American Independence* (Boston, 1951), pp. 207, 211-12.
[53] Jay to McDougall, March 27, 1776, McDougall Papers, NYHS. Jay said, "it would give me Pleasure to see them [New York] distinguished by vigorous Exertion."
[54] Nettels, *George Washington,* p. 212.
[55] Becker, *The History of Political Parties,* p. 272.

THREE

Division into Tory and Whig

WHEN General Thomas Gage set his troops in motion for Lexington and Concord in April of 1775, he had no notion, of course, that he was constructing a species of *deus ex machina* for the New York Friends of Liberty. The spur of the military confrontation enabled the Whigs to solve the internal problem of revolutionary committee organization and to elaborate a provincial system of district and county committees. This linkage of external and internal affairs was to recur in New York at critical moments in 1775 and 1776 and was to give a fillip to the revolutionary movement.

Events in New York moved swiftly in April in direct response to word of the encounter in Massachusetts. Amid the excitement which this information generated, the city General Committee on April 26, seizing the initiative, entreated the counties to elect a provincial congress, which would convene May 22. The General Committee, reorganizing itself to meet the new conditions, expanded its membership to one hundred.[1] Well might the Tories have gnashed their teeth in frustration over the trend of affairs, especially since Lieutenant-Governor Colden had received a copy of Lord North's conciliatory resolution. However, so intense was the agitation in the city that Colden and the council reluctantly declined to permit the colonial assembly to resume its adjourned session and consider this gesture of the British ministry.[2]

The focus of revolutionary power in the next few months swung to the First Provincial Congress, which assembled May 23. The passage of a recommendation to the laggard counties to create county and district committees was one of the first measures which the Provincial Congress undertook. Concomitantly, the deputies agreed unanimously to have the local committees canvass their districts for signatures to the Defense or General Association. This General Association, not to be confused with the Continental Association, was in effect a pledge of allegiance to the Provincial Congress, since the signer resolved "in all things [to] follow the advice of our [Provincial Congress] respecting the purposes aforesaid, the preservation of peace, and good order, and the safety of individual and private property."[3] All problems, however, paled into insignificance beside the crucial one of defense, and the congressmen devoted most time and energy to placing the colony in a military posture. Two transactions in Philadelphia confirmed the Yorkers in the wisdom of their military preparations: the Continental Congress assumed jurisdiction over the colonial units that were besieging Boston, appointing George Washington in June as command-in-chief of all continental forces, and then, in July, administered the *coup de grâce* to the conciliation proposal of Lord North.[4] Although the Whigs wielded authority in these weeks, they acted so hesitantly on numerous occasions that they gave contemporaries an impression of weakness rather than of strength.

---

1 See below, pp. 69-75.

2 Carl L. Becker, *The History of Political Parties in the Province of New York, 1760-1776* (Madison, 1909), pp. 194-99.

3 *Jour. Prov. Cong.*, I, 15.

4 Becker, *The History of Political Parties*, pp. 201, 212, 216; Edmund C. Burnett, *The Continental Congress* (New York, 1941), pp. 76, 95-96; John R. Alden, *The American Revolution, 1775-1783* (New York, 1954), pp. 29-31.

The slow maturation of the New York revolutionary party and the tortuous course of the Whigs generated a deceptive image of political relationships in the colony. The unwary observer might have inferred from an uncritical examination of these factors that the Whigs were a minority, but a searching probe of these elements exposes the falsity of this conclusion. It is the contention of the subsequent pages that the Friends of Liberty constituted a majority of the population.

It is impossible to determine with exactitude the division of the people into Tory and Whig. British rule in the province enjoyed its most loyal support among the De Lancey faction, who composed the core of Toryism. The faction drew its leaders from the landed aristocracy and the principal merchants of the province, a group largely in support of the administration.[5] Moreover, the Tories possessed a numerous following among the middle landholders and tenantry, the professional classes, the smaller merchants, mechanics and tradesmen, and among the urban laborers.[6]

---

[5] Alexander C. Flick, *Loyalism in New York During the American Revolution* (New York, 1901), p. 33; Virginia D. Harrington, *The New York Merchant on the Eve of the Revolution* (New York, 1935), pp. 74, 349; E. Wilder Spaulding, *New York in the Critical Period, 1783-1789* (New York, 1932), p. 121; Harry B. Yoshpe, *The Disposition of Loyalist Estates in the Southern District of the State of New York* (New York, 1939), pp. 121-53; Samuel Adams to Arthur Lee, March 4, 1775, Bancroft Transcripts: Samuel Adams Papers, NYPL.

[6] William H. Nelson, *The American Tory* (Oxford, 1961), p. 86; Flick, *Loyalism*, pp. 32-33; Alexander C. Flick, ed., *A History of the State of New York* (10 vols.; New York, 1933-1937), IV, 151; Irving Mark, *Agrarian Conflicts in New York, 1711-1775* (New York, 1940), pp. 91, 201; Paul M. Hamlin, *Legal Education in Colonial New York* (New York, 1939), pp. 135-55; Spaulding, *New York in the Critical Period, 1783-1789*, p. 127; Henry B. Dawson, *Westchester County, New York, During the American Revolution* (Morrisania, 1886), p. 83; Yoshpe, *The Disposition of Loyalist Estates*, pp. 187-209. In June, 1775, *ca.* one-third of the Livingston manor tenants were Tory. Judge Robert R. Livingston to Robert R. Livingston, Jr., June 17, 1775, Robert R. Livingston, American Art Association Catalogue, *Revolutionary Letters of Importance: The Unpublished Correspondence of Robert R. Livingston* (New York, 1918), No. 46; Staughton Lynd, "The Tenant Rising at Livingston Manor, May, 1777," *New-York Historical Society Quarterly*, XLVIII (April, 1964), 163-77.

Among the Tory middle landholders and tenantry were Alpheus Avery,

The colony was indeed a house divided. As for the revolutionary opposition, it attracted a minority of the great landed families and rich merchants but enlisted strong popular support among the middle-class farmers and tenantry and the lesser merchants, mechanics, and laborers. Furthermore, it is possible to obtain an approximate idea of the relative strength of the contending parties through an examination of some of the events of these days and of the opinions of contemporaries.

New York City faithfully performed its role in 1775 as the storm center of the province. The Friends of Government challenged the Liberty Boys to a test of their popularity in February when they sought to break the Continental Association against imports from Britain. The arrival of the *James,* Captain Watson commanding, from Glasgow the morning of February 2 became the occasion for a contest between the defenders of the established order and the government's critics. A few members of the Committee of Sixty leaned toward granting Watson permission to unload, but at a meeting that same night only three or four members of the approximately forty present voted for it. The committee, therefore, ordered the *James* to depart without registering at customs or breaking cargo, although it granted the captain time to obtain supplies and necessary papers. At the special request of Buchanan, consignee of the cargo, the committee conferred again the evening of the third to reconsider but adhered to its original decision. Although the consignee declined to invoke governmental aid, the Friends of Government, with Watson's approval, planned to organize a posse to protect the unloading of the goods, a species of tea party

---

John Bates, and James Beyea, farmers of Westchester; John Brown, William Brown, Abraham, Henry and John Bulyea, and James Crawford, tenants of Westchester. Among the professional classes and merchants, for example, were Samuel Clossy of Kings College and Isaac Bennet, merchant of New Rochelle. Among mechanics, tradesmen, and laborers were Thomas Austin, blacksmith, John Bennett, ship's carpenter, and Frederick Brantigan, baker.

in reverse. Learning of these intentions, the radicals spread the alarm and mobilized so many people to oppose the landing that it could not be carried through; the crowd dispersed the posse.[7]

Checkmated, but not willing to concede defeat, the Tories now turned to official measures. Lieutenant-Governor Colden convened his council to determine a course of action and, after a three-hour debate without Colden's presence, the councilors ordered the man-of-war *King's Fisher* to provide an armed escort for the *James*. When the *James* reappeared at the wharves with a naval complement aboard, a large Whig crowd stood ready to prevent the ship's unloading. Deterred by this show of popular sentiment, the Tories yielded. So great was the hostility of the people that even Tory leaders denounced Captain Watson. Oliver De Lancey exclaimed to Philip Livingston and Francis Lewis, "What does that dam'd Rascal come up here again for? Why don't he quit the Port?"[8] And quit the port Captain Watson did, with cargo unbroken.

The very day, February 10, the De Lanceys strove to mollify public opinion, a grand jury drew up an address to the city Court of Quarter Sessions. The message expressed opposition to parliamentary taxation and termed "oppressive" those acts of Parliament which extended the powers of the Admiralty and Vice Admiralty courts. The ideas and

---

7 Arthur M. Schlesinger, Sr., *The Colonial Merchants and the American Revolution, 1763-1776* (New York, 1939), p. 490; *N.Y.J.*, February 9, 16, 1775; *To the Freeholders, Freemen, and Inhabitants of the City and County of New York,* February 6, 1775, Broadsides, NYPL.

8 Quoted by William Smith. John De Lancey went about declaring to all and sundry that Colden had not solicited the captain to remain. William H. W. Sabine, ed., *Historical Memoirs from 16 March 1763 to 9 July 1776 of William Smith* (New York, 1956), pp. 209, 210.

Colden defended his conduct to Lord Dartmouth by distorting the actions of the participants. Smith saw Colden's role in the affair as an effort to cast the blame for governmental failure on the council. *Letterbooks of Cadwallader Colden,* New-York Historical Society *Collections,* Vol. X (New York, 1877), II, 389; Sabine, *Memoirs of William Smith,* p. 210.

terminology followed the fourteenth section of the Continental Association.[9]

The government's position continued to deteriorate and suffered a further shock in the middle of April. Whereas in October, 1774, the Fifty-One had disapproved interference with shipping supplies to Gage in Boston, in April, 1775, the Committee of Sixty resolved to forbid such shipments. Although two merchants fell victim immediately to the ban, two others, Ralph Thurman and Robert Harding, determined to defy the committee. Sears, John Lamb, and Marinus Willett rallied the people to compel the two merchants to abide by the committee's resolution. Alarmed by the threats of the British Barrack Master General to take himself and his contracts elsewhere, the mayor and petty merchants importuned the government to intervene.[10] Although the council voted to have Colden issue a proclamation against interference with commerce, William Smith prevailed upon his colleagues to launch an inquiry into the matter in order to "know the Truth, & have solid Grounds to act upon."

The council lost its opportunity to investigate the matter because some councilors underestimated the hostility of the people. After hearing the testimony of Barrack Master General Brigadier General James Robertson, some members of the council implied to Mayor Hicks that the governor and council wished him to arrest Sears and Willett. The Mayor obligingly had the two men brought before him. Willett gave bail, but Sears refused to do so on the ground that the arrest was "a violation of liberty." When the officers of justice arrived at the jail with their prisoner, they had to

---

[9] *N.Y.J.*, February 16, 1775 and *Pa. Jour.*, February 20, 1775. A squib in the *N.Y.G.*, February 20, 1775 stated that the jury foreman did not present the address to the court nor read it to the court. The association text is in Schlesinger, *The Colonial Merchants*, p. 612.

[10] *Ibid.*, p. 388; Becker, *The History of Political Parties*, pp. 162-63. General Robertson said he had spent £260,000 in his department, presumably since 1765. Sabine, *Memoirs of William Smith*, pp. 219-20.

surrender him to a party of his friends who had gathered hurriedly to rescue him. The release became a triumphal procession, with colors flying, through the town to the Liberty Pole. According to prior notice, a multitude of people had assembled at the Pole to adopt a decision on the violation of the exportation interdict. Although Mayor Hicks and all the bailiffs had come to this meeting, Sears underscored their helplessness when he asked the audience "whether a Son of Liberty ought to give bail or not?" Upon hearing the question carried in the negative, the assemblage gave three huzzas. The intended show of authority ended in defeat for the government and exposed it to the contempt of the people.[11] Although Anglican churchman Dr. Samuel Auchmuty could declare disgustedly that "our magistrates have not the spirit of a louse," there was little else they could do.[12] The British had reduced the garrison to slightly more than 100 men in order to reinforce Gage in Boston and could not rely upon the city militia, as coming events would soon prove. In Tryon County the Tory Johnson family depended upon their Highlander tenantry to intimidate and overawe the Whig farmers, but in the city to whom could the administration look for aid?[13] The Sears incident dramatically revealed how public opinion had shifted since the preceding December.

At the close of December, 1774, however, an incident occurred which exposed the Whigs' weakness. Andrew Elliot, Collector of the port, seized a shipment of British manufactured arms imported in the *Lady Gage*.[14] As the customs

11 *Ibid.;* "Anti-Licentiousness" to the Printer, *Riv. Gaz.,* April 20, 1775; *To the Inhabitants of the City and County of New York,* April 13, 1775, Broadsides, NYPL; Berthold Fernow, ed., "Calendar of Council Minutes, 1668-1783," New York State Library *Bulletin 58* (March, 1902), p. 505.

12 Auchmuty to Captain Montresor, April 19, 1775 in *Pa. Jour.,* May 31, 1775. Auchmuty hopefully predicted "That it will not be long before he [Sears] is handled by authority."

13 Becker, *The History of Political Parties,* p. 202; Flick, *History of New York,* III, 335; Samuel L. Frey, ed., *The Minute Book of the Committee of Safety of Tryon County* (New York, 1905), pp. 7, 11.

officers carted the arms to the custom house, a small party of Whigs fell on the officials and carried off the wagons. Before they could secrete the weapons, however, a larger body of royal officials recovered them and eventually put the cargo aboard a man-of-war. A broadside, appearing over the pseudonym "Plain English," arraigned Elliot for acting arbitrarily and exhorted the people to assemble and demand the arms. The Collector denied the charge and challenged "Plain English" to come to the Coffee House to present a bill of particulars. The Tories rallied a considerable number of people, including merchants, shipmasters, seamen, and citizenry, to Elliot's defense. When the Collector demanded that the broadside's author step forward, there was no response and the crowd gave three cheers for Elliot. The Whigs could not win enough support to regain the arms.[15] But between December and April the change in public sentiment might have stimulated forebodings about the future. Further inflammatory acts or news might lead to a crisis.

The crisis immediately followed the Sears affair. The grim tidings of Lexington reached New York about 2 P.M. Sunday, April 23, 1775, by an express rider from Connecticut and two ships from Newport. Hastily convening in response to the emergency, the Committee of Sixty met at 4 P.M. amid the general confusion and took important preliminary steps.

---

14 The destination of the arms was Rhode Island. Elliot confiscated the weapons when they were being loaded aboard a coasting vessel because the *Lady Gage's* captain had no cockets for the shipment. Furthermore, a British order-in-council forbade the colonial importation of arms and ammunition without a license from the Privy Council. Just prior to this incident Colden transmitted to Elliot Dartmouth's instructions on such matters. Colden to Elliot, December 15, 1774, Colden to Dartmouth, January 4, 1775, *Letterbooks of Cadwallader Colden,* New-York Historical Society *Collections,* X (New York, 1877), II, 376, 377-78; A Short Detail of the Conduct of the Collector of New York from December 1774 to March 1776 . . . , Andrew Elliot Papers, NYSL.

15 Isaac Q. Leake, *Memoir of the Life and Times of General John Lamb* (Albany, 1857), pp. 95-96; *Riv. Gaz.,* January 5, 1775.

An unknown person or persons filed suit against the Collector in 1775 but the closing of the courts blocked the action. A Short Detail . . . of the Collector . . . , Andrew Elliot Papers, NYSL.

They dispatched the express to Philadelphia with the news, ordered the unloading of two sloops with provisions for the British troops in Boston, sent after a ship that was in motion down the harbor for the same destination, prepared a broadside containing the advices from Boston, and notified the citizenry of a public meeting in the fields at 2 P.M., Monday, the following day.[16] The Committee of Sixty gained control of the situation, but the tremendous upsurge of hostility to the British ministry caused many of the committee to reassess their position.

The outpouring of the people on April 24 played a part in the shift of the committee from the enforcement of a boycott to the usurpation of authority. An estimated 8,000 of the city's population responded to the call for a meeting. The rally approved proposals to organize a militia, to draw up a new defense association (a draft of which the committee read), and to authorize the committee "with full & unlimited Power to consult upon and determine & direct the means" for the city's preservation. By voting unanimously for the last of these proposals the people had in fact created a revolutionary government for the city.[17] The size and enthusiasm of the crowd and the policies approved may have aroused the committee to a realization of the need for a new approach.

---

[16] Activist leaders had broken into the city's arsenal to secure arms but McDougall persuaded them to cease their distribution for a day. McDougall's notations, n.d., *The Following interesting Advices were this Day received here, by two Vessels from Newport, and by an Express by Land,* New York, April 23, 1775, Broadsides, NYPL; New York, *New York City During the American Revolution. Being a Collection of Original Papers (Now First Published) from the Manuscripts in the Possession of the Mercantile Library Association of New York City* (New York, 1861), pp. 54-55; Roger J. Champagne, "New York's Radicals and the Coming of Independence," *Journal of American History,* LI (June, 1964), 21-40; Roger J. Champagne, "New York Politics and Independence, 1776," *New-York Historical Society Quarterly,* XLVI (July, 1962), 281-303. For a contrary view of these and the subsequent events, see Becker, *The History of Political Parties,* pp. 193-99.

The "fields" are now City Hall Park. New York, *New York City During the American Revolution,* pp. 25-26.

[17] *Pa. Jour.,* April 26, 1775; McDougall's notations, *Following interesting Advices . . . by Land,* April 23, 1775, Broadsides, NYPL. McDougall opposed the appointment of officers for the militia.

The British conduct in Massachusetts was not only a shattering blow to many of the De Lanceys but also it was another one of those actions which diminished old party differences and tended to convert people into Whigs and Tories. Perhaps in response to the electric atmosphere as well as to personal indignation against the British many De Lanceys openly espoused defensive preparation and supported the tacit assumption of power in the city by the Committee of Sixty.[18] Within the Committee of Sixty these trends forced a realignment in which some Livingstons and the De Lanceys allied against other Livingstons. The coalition consisted of erstwhile opponents who wished to pursue a cautious opposition to the British ministry but who disagreed among themselves over the nature of their circumspect resistance. Basically there were among them many who would carry their hostility up to that point which in their minds led to rebellion and independence. When they thought this stage had arrived, they would submit to Great Britain. These men were conservatives. There were others who as a last resort reluctantly took up arms as the least objectionable of twin evils, submission or rebellion. These were the moderates. The minority who fought the conservative-moderate combine were the activists, men who would settle for nothing less than complete retreat by Britain, who would willingly embrace rebellion and independence.[19] These were the radicals.[20] Although this process of division was far from complete, it shaped the occurrences of April and May.

---

18 Judge Robert R. Livingston informed his wife on April 27, "the Tories turn Whigs so fast that they will soon be as much united as they are in the Massachusetts colony." William Smith observed on the same day that "all Parties here . . . cry out for committees and Congresses. . . ." Isaac N. P. Stokes, *The Iconography of Manhattan Island* (6 vols.; New York, 1915-1928), IV, 883; Sabine, *Memoirs of William Smith,* p. 222.

19 For different usage of the same terminology see Becker, *The History of Political Parties, passim.*

20 The touchstone which underlies the usage of these terms (conservative, moderate, radical) is the question of rebellion-independence. These words are not intended to denote general values, nor do they imply that each category is monolithic. For example, there are perhaps as many variants of

When the Committee of Sixty on April 26 recommended to the city its enlargement in function and numbers and the summoning of a provincial congress, the new political affinities quickly made themselves felt. Although the committee declared that it unanimously adopted these proposals, the unanimity rapidly dissolved in a conflict over the personnel of the projected city Committee of One Hundred and the city delegation to the Provincial Congress. Since the conservatives and moderates dominated the Sixty, they filled the nomination lists with men of similar stripe.[21] There were

---

conservatism as there are conservatives and this qualification applies also to the other two categories. Obviously, some in one group are closer to persons in the adjacent classification than they are to others who bear their label. Moderate John Jay illustrates this point. His views of the imperial conflict in 1774-1775 were more nearly similar to those of conservative Isaac Low than they were to those of moderate Philip Livingston. Furthermore, there were many men whose opinions gradually changed, who were conservatives in 1774 but who were moderates in 1776. James Duane exemplifies this process of almost invisible transition, moving from condemnation of vigorous resistance in 1774-1775 to acceptance of independence. Since contemporaries did not consider themselves as being conservatives, radicals, and moderates, the preceding categorization is an artificial imposition of present ideology on the past. However, it serves the purpose of facilitating the grouping of people in relation to one issue in order to clarify their political differences.

[21] A tentative analysis of the two slates suggests the existence of a *quid pro quo* by means of which the conservatives and moderates cemented their union. The ticket for the Committee of One Hundred contained forty-five known to be De Lanceys and thirteen others who perhaps were of that faction; of the remaining forty-two men, there were thirty-six Livingstons (including activists) and six possible Livingstons. The list of twenty candidates for the Provincial Congress is made up of nine known De Lanceys and one who perhaps was of the same persuasion; of the remaining ten men, nine were known Livingstons and one was possibly a Livingston. It seems that the De Lanceys traded an even division or a numerical majority of the congressional delegation for a majority of the city committee.

On the Provincial Congress ticket the following were Livingstons: L. Lispenard, I. Roosevelt, A. Brasher, A. McDougall, P.V.B. Livingston, J. M. Scott, T. Smith, J. Hallett, J. Van Cortlandt, and possibly David Clarkson.

On the city committee slate the following were Livingstons: Philip Livingston, P.V.B. Livingston, Sears, McDougall, T. Randall, L. Lispenard, J. Broome, J. Hallett, P. T. Curtenius, A. Brasher, A. P. Lott, A. Duryee, F. Lewis, H. Mulligan, V. Bicker, T. Anthony, W. Goforth, W. Denning, I. Roosevelt, J. Platt, C. Sands, R. Benson, N. Roosevelt, R. Ritzema, J. Lasher, J. Van Zandt, D. Beekman, E. Bancker, R. Ray, J. Lamb, D. Phoenix, and D. Dunscomb. Additional possible Livingstons were: D. Clarkson, G. Keteltas, C. Clopper, J. Lefferts, A. Brinckerhoff, and P. Byvanck. *Ibid.*, pp. 197-98 nn.; Thomas Jones, *History of New York During the Revolutionary War, and of the Leading Events in the Other Colonies at that Period*, ed. Edward F. de Lancey (2 vols.; New York, 1879), I, 488-89; John A. Stevens, Jr., ed., *Colonial*

perhaps twenty radicals on the ticket for the One Hundred and three to six out of the twenty for the congressional deputation.[22] Responding to criticisms of its nominations, the moderate-conservative group frankly explained that it sought to add "many of weight and consequence" in order to reduce opposition to committee measures. Some of the nominees, the coalition admitted, were "objects of distrust and suspicion" but Whigs ought not to exclude them unless they rejected the Whigs. Lastly, this broadside warned of "tumult, anarchy and confusion" if the populace did not elect an enlarged committee.[23]

The moderate-conservatives' maneuvers put the radicals in a difficult position. On the one hand the radicals objected to many of the candidates but on the other hand the slates bore the official imprimatur of the Sixty, who had popular backing. If the radicals offered opposition nominations, in whose name could they be put up? The radicals resolved their dilemma by sponsoring a meeting Thursday afternoon, April 27, in the name of the Sons of Liberty; at that meeting they obtained approval of their own nominees for the Committee of One Hundred and the Provincial Congress.[24] On

---

Records of the New York Chamber of Commerce, 1768-1784 (New York, 1867), *passim;* Harrington, *The New York Merchant,* pp. 338, 348-51.

[22] The twenty radicals on the city committee slate were: P.V.B. Livingston, Sears, Randall, Lispenard, Broome, Hallett, Brasher, Lott, Duryee, Lewis, Mulligan, Bicker, Anthony, Goforth, Platt, Lasher, Scott, Van Zandt, Lamb, and Dunscomb. Of these men, there were a number whose views were not clear. McDougall, for example, began to move toward a center position. The radicals on the congressional ticket were Lispenard, Brasher, Mc-Dougall, P.V.B. Livingston, Scott, and Hallett. This classification is uncertain, since the radicals struck Brasher and Hallett from their congressional list of candidates. See below, note 25, the slate of the Sons of Liberty. Becker, *The History of Political Parties,* pp. 197-98nn.

[23] Peter Force, ed., *American Archives* (9 vols.; Washington, D.C., 1837-1853), 4th ser., II, 400, 427-28.

[24] *Sons of Liberty, New York,* April 28, 1775, Broadsides, NYPL. An earlier broadside implied the continued existence of the Sons: *The Following Anonymous Letter was some Nights Ago thrown in among the Sons of Liberty,* 1775, *ibid.;* Richard B. Morris, ed., *The Era of the American Revolution* (New York, 1939), pp. 287-88; Philip Davidson, *Propaganda and the American Revolution, 1763-1783* (Chapel Hill, 1941), p. 79, n. 41.

Revival of the name of the Sons of Liberty seems to have had the objective of broadening the appeal of the radical ticket since merchants were prominent

the list of one hundred that the Sons of Liberty offered, only twenty-one differed from the moderate-conservative ticket, but these were substitutes for men who had not served on previous committees.[25] On the Provincial Congress list, the radicals backed only eight of the Sixty's choice, substituting twelve of their own choosing.[26]

Confronted with an opposing slate, the moderates and conservatives took to the press to justify their selection. Thus on Friday, the twenty-eighth, New Yorkers were reading the handbills both of the Sons of Liberty and of the Committee of Sixty which drew the lines of political strife. The Sixty had set Friday for the election, but apparently as a consequence of the opposition, their Friday broadside postponed the voting to Monday, May 1.

These political debates became even more complicated after the arrival of the *Pennsylvania Journal* on Friday. The newspaper contained an extract of a letter from London which stated that Oliver De Lancey, John Watts, Myles Cooper, Henry White, and Colden had requested the North government to dispatch troops to New York to regain control

participants in the old organization. If the radicals offered their slate in the name of the Committee of Mechanics, they could hardly hope to attract many votes from the merchants.

25 The twenty-one substitutes were: T. Van Wyck, J. Woodward, John W. Smith, W. Keteltas, J. Pell, L. Van Ranst, P. Vandervoort, P. Clopper, J. Imlay, G. Abeel, P. P. Van Zandt, Capt. W. Heyer, T. Tucker, J. Le Roy, R. Deane, Capt. Nicholas Bogart, W. Bedlow, W. Post, I. Stoutenburgh, A. Marschalk, and P. Messier. Since it is likely that most of these men were radicals, the number of radicals on the Sons of Liberty ticket was between thirty and forty. If all of the twenty-one substitutes were Livingstons, the factional division of the radical slate was fifty-one Livingstons, forty-nine De Lanceys. *Sons of Liberty, New York*, April 28, 1775, Broadsides, NYPL.

26 The twelve substitutes were: G. W. Ludlow, P.V.B. Livingston, J. Broome, W. Bedlow, Sears, J. Woodward, Hugh Hughes, J. W. Smith, P. T. Curtenius, P. Vandervoort, S. Broome, and P. Clopper. Perhaps eight to thirteen of the twenty-man list were radicals. Thirteen of the slate are clearly Livingstons (Lispenard, Roosevelt, P.V.B. Livingston, J. and S. Broome, McDougall, Sears, T. Smith, Scott, H. Hughes, J. Van Cortlandt, Curtenius, and Van Zandt) and one (G. W. Ludlow) is clearly a De Lancey. The other six (D. Clarkson, W. Bedlow, J. Woodward, J. W. Smith, P. Vandervoort, and P. Clopper) are probably not De Lanceys but are assignable to both factions. *Sons of Liberty, New York*, April 28, 1775, Broadsides, NYPL.

of the colony. A furious crowd gathered which threatened "to proceed to execute them immediately." White and De Lancey did their utmost to assure the people of the falsity of the letter, but without notable success. So high did tempers rise that the Committee of Sixty summoned a meeting on that day in the fields with two of the accused in attendance. Denials from White and De Lancey and their pledge to swear out affidavits attesting their innocence satisfied the crowd and averted the threat of violence. The next day the Sixty promulgated the new form of association and De Lancey, White, and Watts produced the promised affidavits. The excitement over the association eased the tension and the Tories heard no more threats.[27]

Publication of the new association by the Committee of Sixty dealt the radicals a shrewd political blow. The firm tone of the oath not only reassured the Whigs of the committee's steadfastness but also demonstrated the adroitness of the conservatives and moderates. The moderates carried the election. The caution with which the new committee moved can be attributed to the natural prudence of the coalition. Although the committee contained a diversity of political views, to assert that it was an instrument of party rather than of a large proportion of the people is to ignore the foregoing events.[28]

Impressive testimony of the minority position of the Tories in the city comes from the Tories themselves.[29] The gov-

---

[27] *Pa. Jour.*, April 26, 1775; Sabine, *Memoirs of William Smith*, p. 222. White went to the trouble of having his statement and affidavit printed as a broadside and distributed. *To the Public* by Henry White, New York, April 29, 1775, Broadsides, NYPL.

[28] Becker sees this as a party measure; *The History of Political Parties*, p. 196.

[29] However, McDougall had quite accurately predicted how the people would react in a crisis: "from the Knowledge I have of the State of this Colony, I am morally certain, they will not fly to Arms as a Colony; but by the Influence of one of these Contingencies Vizt: The Attack of the Troops on your People [i.e., Massachusetts]. . . ." McDougall to W. Cooper, February 9, 1775, McDougall Papers, NYHS.

ernor's council, meeting Monday, April 24, to assess the situation, called in various officials to inform them on specific points. The councilors first considered turning to the militia, but Leonard Lispenard, commander of the city's regiment, said no aid would come from that quarter since the men counted themselves as Liberty Boys. The Major then remarked that the authority of the magistrates had vanished. Councilor Thomas Jones, nevertheless, advocated calling out the militia, reading the riot act, and imprisoning the ringleaders. William Smith, opposing Jones, argued that the government would have to deal with the general population and not just a few rioters. To this, Jones had no rebuttal. "We were thus unanimously of Opinion," Smith recorded in his memoirs, "that we had no power to do anything & the best mode of proceeding for private Safety and general Peace was to use Diswasion from Violence."[30]

Colden also confessed to the complete collapse of the government's authority. In his report to the Colonial Secretary, Colden attributed the lack of popular support for the government to the magistrates' timidity and the depletion of the garrison. A month later, however, he declared that government authority would have withstood the storm if the garrison had been at its normal strength.[31] Captain Montague of the *King's Fisher* wrote with something akin to astonishment that "the major part of the people here are almost in a state of rebellion. . . ."[32] One of the numerous letters from New York printed in a London newspaper commented that "in this city it is astonishing to find the most violent

---

[30] Sabine, *Memoirs of William Smith*, p. 221; Jones, *History of New York During the Revolutionary War*, I, 41; Fernow, "Calendar of Council Minutes," p. 505.

[31] Colden to Dartmouth, May 3, June 7, 1775, O'Callaghan, *Documents, Colonial, New York*, VIII, 571, 582; Colden to Captain Vandeput, May 27, 1775, *Letterbooks of Cadwallader Colden*, II, 413.

[32] Montague to Admiral Graves, April 26, 1775, *Cal. H. O. Papers*, p. 358. See also the comment of a post office official, Hugh Finlay to his brother, May 29, 1775, *ibid.*, p. 366.

proposals meeting with universal approbation."[33] Merchant James Richardson explained the latest developments to his business correspondent in London with these words: "Friends of government in this city in danger and business suspended; port now re-opened and the whole city entered into an association to abide the measures recommended by the next Congress. All unanimous for the American cause."[34]

Even a fully manned garrison might have had difficulty in maintaining the government, particularly in view of the revolutionaries' relations with the soldiers. The Whigs effectively utilized the press to appeal to the soldiery to desert and join the cause of liberty. Although only four men deserted from May 1 to May 23, in the next three days four more went over to the rebels. Major Isaac Hamilton expressed to Colden his fear of losing the whole garrison. Ten days later Hamilton confessed to Colden that his position was untenable: "The Loss of our Men by Desertion is so great, and [due to] the Apprehension of losing more, I therefore think it necessary for the good of the Service to retreat on Board his Majesty's Ship the Asia...." The British withdrew the troops, about 100 in all, to the *Asia* on June 6. The retreat, therefore, did not constitute a peaceful gesture to avoid an armed clash between the soldiers and citizenry.[35]

The same month, June, which saw the garrison's evacuation, also witnessed another incident of some significance.

---

[33] Letter from New York, May 4, 1775., Margaret W. Willard, ed., *Letters on the American Revolution, 1774-1776* (Boston, 1925), p. 101. See also similar letters, May 1, 4, 1775, *ibid.*, pp. 97, 99-100.

[34] Richardson to Alexander Gordon, May 4, 1775, *Hist. Mss. Com.*, p. 299. For a similar comment see Smith Ramadge to Johnston and Canning, May 3, 1775, *ibid.*, p. 298.

[35] As stated in Becker, *The History of Political Parties*, pp. 218-19; Gage to Barrington, May 13, 1775, Clarence E. Carter, ed., *The Correspondence of General Thomas Gage with the Secretaries of State, and with the War Office and the Treasury, 1763-1775* (2 vols.; New Haven, 1931, 1933), II, 678-79; Major Isaac Hamilton to Colden, May 26, June 5, 1775, *Letters and Papers of Cadwallader Colden*, New-York Historical Society *Collections*, LVI (New York, 1922), VII, 297, 299-300; Colden to Dartmouth, June 7, 1775, O'Callaghan, *Documents, Colonial, New York*, VIII, 582; *To the Regular Soldiery of Great Britain*, New York, May 1, 1775, Broadsides, NYPL.

As noted above, Tryon returned from England on the same day Washington reached the city on his way to Massachusetts. Not wishing to offend either party, the Provincial Congress detailed militia escorts for both. Ostensibly, the same people who greeted the General enthusiastically in the afternoon "huzzaed for Tryon in the evening." Smith clarified this apparently contradictory action when he put it down as a personal tribute to the Governor rather than a manifestation of attachment to the crown. The citizens "hate his commission," Smith recorded in his notes, "& would certainly have insulted any other in that station."[36]

Demographic statistics contribute a final bit of evidence to this examination of the city's political sympathies. Although population statistics for 1776 are only estimates, they do give some clue to the political temper of the people. Driven by fear of the cannon's thunder, thousands of the inhabitants streamed out of the city. Some of them returned after the danger had seemed to abate, but by February, 1776, perhaps 11,000 had settled elsewhere.[37] When news of the impending descent of the British spread through the streets, a wholesale evacuation of the populace got under way, leaving approximately 5,000 behind. After the fighting had halted in the environs, the tide of migration reversed itself. Of the esti-

---

[36] Smith says that an "immense crowd" gave Tryon a warm sendoff when he sailed in April, 1774. Smith, Memoirs, V, April 7, 1774. Becker, *The History of Political Parties*, p. 218; Smith, Memoirs, V, June 25, 1775.

[37] William Axtel, council member, placed the remaining population at 16,000. Smith, Memoirs, V, February 11, 1776.
Calculations of the city's population in 1776 have used the rate of increase between the censuses of 1756 and 1771 as their basis. Their estimates ranged from 22,000 to 25,000 people, white and Negro. However, this study has employed a figure of 25,000 whites and 2,000 Negroes which in turn derived from an estimated state total of 208,000 whites. Since the port maintained a fairly constant ratio of *ca.* 12 percent of the total population of 1756 and 1771, this ratio has been applied to the calculation of total white population. For the computation of the total white population, see below, pp. 92-93. Evarts B. Greene and Virginia D. Harrington, *American Population Before the Federal Census of 1790* (New York, 1932), p. 91; Carl Bridenbaugh, *Cities in Revolt: Urban Life in America, 1743-1776* (New York, 1955), p. 216.

mated 22,000 who had fled, some 4,000 made their way back
through the British lines into the city.[38] General Robertson
calculated the city's inhabitants in February, 1777, at 11,000,
but this figure probably included loyalists from upstate and
other states as well as a number of slaves who thought to find
freedom with the British.[39] Far from remaining overwhelmingly loyal, considerably more than half of New York City's
residents opposed the crown.[40]

To argue that the capital was a center of revolutionary
activity is not to conclude that a majority of the province
chose independence rather than British dominion. As in the
case of the city there are no election returns to demonstrate
how many supported the revolutionary cause and how many
opposed it throughout the colony. Expressions of Tory
opinion and indirect evidence, however, corroborate the
existence of a Whig majority.

As the year 1774 drew to a close the government faced the
unpleasant fact that the Whigs would move to have the
colony nominate representatives to attend the Second Continental Congress. If the provincial assembly met, it would
take into consideration the resolutions of the First Congress
and the choice of a delegation to the Second. If the governor
prorogued the assembly, the Whigs would win by default.
The government, therefore, had no alternative but to permit

---

38 Oscar T. Barck, Jr., *New York City During the War for Independence*
(New York, 1931), p. 76. On the basis of the number who signed the loyalist
welcome to Howe, Barck estimated the loyalist following in the city at 9,000.
Ibid., p. 77, n. 10. See also Flick, *History of New York*, IV, 261; Edward P.
Alexander, *A Revolutionary Conservative: James Duane of New York* (New
York, 1938), p. 156; Thomas J. Wertenbaker, *Father Knickerbocker Rebels:
New York City During the Revolution* (New York, 1948), p. 99.
39 An undated, unidentified sheet in the Andrew Elliot Papers contains
what seems to be a census return for perhaps 1779 or 1780 which approxi-
mates Robertson's statement. The city contained 4,686 white males and 5,771
white females, none of whom were under fourteen years of age, and 1,951
Negroes; the total was 12,408. Elliot Papers, NYSL; Barck, *New York City*,
p. 77; Wertenbaker, *Father Knickerbocker Rebels*, p. 103; Flick, *History of
New York*, III, 346; Jones, *History of New York During the Revolutionary
War*, I, 322-23.
40 See Flick, *Loyalism*, p. 181.

the assembly to meet and to seek to win through parliamentary maneuver. Although the issue hung in the balance, the De Lancey party leaders regarded the prospect with foreboding, while the Whigs maintained an optimistic outlook.[41] At a private conference summoned to devise strategy, leading Tories first discussed whether they should block assembly approval of the acts of Congress. Tactics of this sort, however, would lay the government open to a charge of arbitrary conduct. Convinced that they could muster only 11 votes to the Whigs' 14 on the question of congressional endorsement, the Tories prepared to concede to the Whigs on another question in order to detach votes from the opposition. They would move for a petition to the King for a redress of grievances. "The Generality [was] for this Measure as the only Scheme to prevent voting in Favor of the Congress."[42] If the government could win this test, they could go on to defeat a motion to choose delegates to the Second Congress.[43] It is an instructive comment on the state of opinion in the colony that a De Lancey assembly elected by a limited suffrage should be expected to take a stand in opposition to the crown.

At this critical juncture of affairs Colden decided to take

[41] For a differing interpretation, see Becker, *The History of Political Parties*, pp. 174-75. The radicals did have a keen interest in the assembly's action. Sabine, *Memoirs of William Smith*, p. 208; McDougall to Samuel Adams, January 29, 1775, same to W. Cooper, February 9, 1775, McDougall Papers, NYHS.

[42] It is curious that party leader James De Lancey opposed the proposal to make the petition to the King the first order of business, although he approved the petition. Moving the petition immediately would prepare the ground for defeating the Whigs. Sabine, *Memoirs of William Smith*, p. 208. Merrill Jensen, *The Articles of Confederation* (Madison, 1940), p. 76, cites the assembly's disapproval of the Congress as evidence of strong opposition to the Congress.

[43] Even though the Tories moved the petitions to King and Parliament, the drafts produced in committee proved to be too forceful for their taste. The Whigs charged the Tories with withholding emasculating amendments until some Whig members had left the session to return home. The subsequent addresses, they asserted, differed materially from the drafts approved in committee. McDougall to Josiah Quincy, April 16, 1775, McDougall Papers, NYHS; Becker, *The History of Political Parties*, p. 177. For the assembly votes, see above, p. 52.

an aggressive tone in his message to the legislature and drew up a strong, provocative address in which he condemned the Continental Congress and insisted upon the supremacy of the royal prerogative. After receiving persistent criticism from the council, Colden modified the draft, but Smith said it shocked the assembly nevertheless. This incident points up Colden's willingness to act boldly, but Smith's memoirs make clear the complexity of the interplay between council and governor. A governor could not cavalierly disregard the council's advice. Colden's and the council's failure to act decisively on various occasions reflected more an acknowledgment of their lack of power with which to execute firm policies than personal timidity.[44]

In the middle of March, 1775, instructions from Dartmouth came to hand directing Colden to prohibit the province from sending delegates to the Second Continental Congress. Since the assembly had voted against doing so, the Whigs set out to call a provincial convention to choose the continental deputies. In fact, the Whigs had scheduled an election for March 15 to approve the convening of the convention. Two days prior to this election, Colden met with the council to consider the Colonial Secretary's orders. Although normal procedure entailed the issuance of a proclamation conveying the Secretary's instructions, neither Colden nor the council relished the idea. "All agreed that it would excite the People to be more zealous for Delegates." At Smith's suggestion they determined to have Colden show the letter to the assembly and to inform others that a congress displeased the King and that Dartmouth had forbidden it.[45] Although the Friends of Government had exulted only recently over their victory on this question in the assembly, they watched it turn into a paper triumph. So little effect

44 See Becker, *The History of Political Parties,* p. 193 and n. 3; Sabine, *Memoirs of William Smith,* pp. 205-6; Fernow, "Calendar of Council Minutes," p. 503.
45 Sabine, *Memoirs of William Smith,* pp. 212-13.

did Dartmouth's letter have on colonial opinion that the government did not dare to take the next logical step and forbid the assumed minority to select representatives for the Continental Congress.

When Tryon resumed the reins of government in June, 1775, he perceived he could do little directly to reestablish British authority. As he disclosed to the Colonial Secretary, "to attempt coercive measures by the civil aid would hold up government to additional contempt by the exposure of the weakness of the executive and civil branches. . . ." Moreover, he added, even the provincial legislature would not accept the parliamentary measure for conciliation.[45] By October the Governor seemed to have relinquished hope that Tory sentiment could ever again command a majority in New York; he read and approved a letter from William Smith to General Frederick Haldimand which quite frankly outlined the political atmosphere: "There is no more Hope from Intrigue & Diversity of Sentiment, no further Dependance upon antient Prejudice and Habits. The Americans are voluntary Subjects to Congresses and Armies of their own forming, who are systematically supporting a Principle, which no man dare any longer to controvert on this Side of the Water."[47]

---

45 Tryon to Dartmouth, July 4, 7, 1775, O'Callaghan, *Documents, Colonial, New York,* VIII, 589, 593; same to same, December 7, 1775, *Hist. Mss. Com.,* p. 402.

The fact that the Governor with council concurrence refused to let the assembly meet during 1775 implies admission of the government's minority position.

47 Smith, Memoirs, V, October 6, 1775. Smith declined a seat on the bench in December, 1775, because he considered the administration "a falling house." *Ibid.,* December 19, 1775.

A correspondent of émigré Isaac Wilkins made the following interesting observation on political polarization: "The people of desperate fortunes, and those who are sure to swing for what they have done, are as violent as ever, as are most of the ignorant, who are led by the others, but those of prosperity are afraid of their estates, and are coming about fast." V. Pearse Ashfield to Wilkins, November 4, 1775, *Cal. H. O. Papers,* p. 482. For other comments on Tory weakness see Hugh Finlay to his brother, May 29, 1775, John De Lancey to Oliver De Lancey, Jr., October 3, 1775, same to Ralph Izard, October 5, 1775, *ibid.,* pp. 366, 439, 443.

The employment of troops to suppress the Whigs in the province received extensive consideration by local officials, but Colden warned the ministry to dispatch a large enough number "as might deter any Opposition to them." When the military proposed to march troops through New York to recapture Ticonderoga from the Allens, the Lieutenant-Governor advised Gage that "the Spirit and Phrensey of the People is such that it may be questioned whether one Regt could now prudently venture thro' the Country."[48] Tryon's estimate of the number of soldiers necessary to pacify the colony furnished a further clue to the state of political sympathies. He thought that more than 6,000 regulars aided by three or four regiments of loyalists would have to be utilized.[49]

Although the Whigs had taken the initiative in evolving suitable forms to oppose the policies of the home government, the Tories had not countered effectively. In the contest for men's loyalties the Tories did not manage to set up an active organization that could command a numerous following.[50] When the occasion demanded it, they engaged the

---

[48] Colden to Gage, May 31, 1775, *Letterbooks of Cadwallader Colden*, II, 415.

By August, 1775, both Gage and Dartmouth thought New York lost to the government as a consequence of the Tories' minority position. Gage to Dartmouth, August 20, 1775, Dartmouth to Gage, August 2, 1775, Carter, *Correspondence of General Gage*, I, 413-14, II, 205.

[49] Tryon to Dartmouth, August 7, 1775, O'Callaghan, *Documents, Colonial, New York*, VIII, 598. See also John Weatherhead to Charles Williamos, July 5, 1775, *Hist. Mss. Com.*, p. 327.

The North government ordered four regiments, *ca.* 2,800 men, to New York, but Gage intercepted the ships and diverted them to Boston. Vandeput to Colden, June 1, 1775, *Letters and Papers of Cadwallader Colden*, VII, 299; Gage to Lord Barrington, June 6, 1775, Carter, *Correspondence of General Gage*, II, 682; Smith, Memoirs, V, June 28, 1775.

[50] Becker argues: "In defining their position the loyalists were strong; it was in giving practical effect to their views that they were weak. They never had any party organization worthy of the name, and in the nature of the case it was difficult for them to have one. Their position was essentially one of negation: they denied the authority of Congress; they denied the expedience of non-intercourse; their organization was the English government itself, and upon it they relied to do whatever was necessary. To attempt to suppress the extra-legal committees by force would involve the very illegal methods

dissidents vigorously in several spheres of battle. They raked
the Whigs heavily in the newspapers and in pamphlets; they
battered them in the assembly. They obstructed the formation of local and county committees; they voted against holding a provincial convention.[51] They fought against the selection of delegates to the Continental Congress and opposed
the enforcement of the Continental Association and the Defense Association. They stood for the established order of
things and obedience to the law.[52] When words and ballots
seemed inadequate, the Tories did not hesitate to try
suppression.[53]

Reverend Samuel Seabury participated in this phase of the
contest. In a pamphlet directed to the colonial assembly, he
called upon the legislature to denounce the Continental
Congress and the Continental Association and to refuse to
cooperate further with the other colonies. Majority approval
of this policy, he declared, would be forthcoming from the
people when the assembly delivered them from the tyranny
of committees, from the fear of violence and the dread of
mobs. However, he gave no hint how the assembly could

---

against which they protested." Reprinted with permission of the copyright
owners, the Regents of the University of Wisconsin, from Carl L. Becker,
The History of Political Parties in the Province of New York, 1760-1776
(Madison: the University of Wisconsin Press, 1909), pp. 160-61.

51 *Ibid.*, pp. 201-3.

52 A protest in Orange County against signing the Defense Association
presents an interesting commentary on the extent to which the debate over
political rights had spread through the countryside. Thirty-two recalcitrants
drew up a substitute statement in which they reaffirmed their loyalty to the
King but protested their love of liberty, "disallowing texation in any wise
contrary to the Charter, and shall neaver consent to texasation without being
fully represented with out consent." See also a similar espousal of no taxation
without representation by a district committee in Tryon County in 1774.
Cal. Hist. Mss., I, 9; Frey, *The Minute Book*, p. 1.

53 See above, pp. 65-69, 81-82, the ship *James* incident in February, Dart-
mouth's order of March re delegates to the Congress, the arrest of Sears in
April, and the actions of the Johnsons in May. Set on foot by Dr. Myles
Cooper, a move began in March to ban a Whig meeting in the city, but gov-
ernment leaders seem to have divided on the proposal and did nothing. *To
the Freemen and Freeholders of . . . New York*, September 23, 1775, by
"The Remembrancer," Broadsides, NYPL; Sabine, *Memoirs of William
Smith*, p. 211.

accomplish these objectives. A statute forbidding committees would have entailed the use of force to suppress them. Perhaps Seabury intended this, since he pleaded with the legislature to "break up this horrid combination of seditious men."[54]

These events do not disprove, however, the contention that the Tories by the very nature of their position did not need nor could not have had an extensive party structure. The conduct of the Friends of Government in other circumstances will demonstrate whether they did try to rally the people to their side.

When the Whigs plunged into the task of obtaining local approval of the Continental Association in the first months of 1775, they stirred the Tories into brisk opposition. In some districts the adversaries drew up loyalist declarations, in others they signed counterassociations. The latter usually contained a pledge to assist the magistrates in the execution of the law.[55] Under the leadership of the Johnsons and Butlers, the grand jury and magistrates of the Tryon County Court of Quarter Sessions published a loyalist declaration. Shortly thereafter, in early May, the Palatine District committee denounced the declaration as unrepresentative of the county.[56] The loyalist associations marked a new phase in Tory tactics, the attempted formation of a popular bulwark.

The Tories seem to have concentrated their efforts in Westchester and Dutchess counties, but after three months they claimed a maximum of only 600 signatures to their association in Dutchess County. The lack of spirited response and Whig countermeasures apparently stalled the drive and the Friends of Government never revived it.[57] A similar fate

54 Samuel Seabury, *An Alarm to the Legislature of the Province of New York* (New York, 1775), pp. 83, 88, 89.

55 Becker, *The History of Political Parties*, pp. 170-72; Schlesinger, *The Colonial Merchants*, p. 493; Dawson, *Westchester County*, pp. 43-45; *N.Y.G.*, February 13, 1775; *Riv. Gaz.*, February 16, March 2, April 6, 1775.

56 Frey, *The Minute Book*, pp. 4-5.

overtook the Westchester campaign. Their rebuff is all the more surprising, since the county's greatest manorholder, Frederick Philipse, played a leading part among the Tories. On the other hand, Pierre Van Cortlandt of Cortlandt Manor aligned himself with the Whigs. "An Inhabitant" of this manor happily informed the public that "some lovers of Loyalty and Liberty" had "disconcerted" the loyalist association drive there.[58] Thus the Tory association movement lost momentum and died.

If the Tory measures to build a popular base did not succeed, neither did the Whigs, according to some writers, attain that objective.[59] Two key tests supply the criteria for the latter judgment: the election in April, 1775, for the provincial convention and the election in May, 1775, for the First Provincial Congress. Unfortunately, the surviving fragmentary evidence of participation in the balloting renders any conclusions tentative ones. However, a reexamination of certain contests suggests that the Whig influence predominated, although previous studies have given the primacy to the Tories.

The cases in point in the provincial convention elections are Dutchess and Westchester counties. After the election in Dutchess, the Tories attacked the victorious Whig delegates as representatives of a minority. An anonymous correspondent set down the Tory estimate of the county's sentiment, but gave figures for only one of the eleven Dutchess precincts. He said that the Poughkeepsie precinct balloted 110 to 77 against sending delegates, that a "great majority" in Charlotte precinct voted similarly, that in five other precincts the

---

57 "One of the Associators of Dutchess County," *Riv. Gaz.*, March 30, 1775. The Tories circulated their association among all male inhabitants, not simply the freeholders. According to the 1771 census the county had 21,000 whites.

58 Becker, *The History of Political Parties*, p. 189 and n. 51; Dawson, *Westchester County*, p. 47; "An Inhabitant," Cortlandt Manor, *N.Y.G.*, June 19, 1775.

59 Becker, *The History of Political Parties*, pp. 187-91; Dawson, *Westchester County, passim.*

people "almost unanimously opposed" the convention. These supporters of royal administration approved a "Protest" against holding a provincial convention and denied that the remaining four precincts, which had voted Whig, spoke for the county. The writer of this letter felt so confident of his case that he offered to produce proof: "If any of the Minority entertain the least Doubt that the Protest does not express the Sense of the Precincts therein mentioned, formal and ample Testimonies of its Authenticity shall be sent you." "A Freeholder of Dutchess County" retorted that the Tories never read the "Protest" publicly, nor did any one of the seven precincts approve it before it appeared in print. Furthermore, this Whig "Freeholder," maintaining that 1,200 of the 1,800 county freeholders favored a provincial convention, challenged the Friends of Government to print their list of names with precincts appended in order to prevent fraud. After a two-week pause a Tory rejoinder appeared, declining further disputation on the grounds that "every Alteration that may tend to promote Divisions and Animosities ought carefully to be avoided; and . . . a Coalition of Parties in the County of Dutchess will probably very soon take place, and a proper Union between its Inhabitants established. . . ." It is possible that the Whigs did not have enough time to organize their support throughout the county but, even so, the Tories seemed to have strength with which to counter only in Charlotte and Poughkeepsie. However, the news of the fighting at Lexington may have dissipated the previous indifference and deprived the Tories of much of their popularity. Therefore, the Tories declined to produce proof of their strength.[60]

As it did in Dutchess, a sharp skirmish developed in Westchester over participation in the provincial convention. When the Whigs circulated an appeal to the freeholders to

---

60 *N.Y.G.*, April 24, May 1, 15, 1775.

meet at White Plains to select a county representation, the Tories rallied their adherents, freeholder and nonfreeholder alike, to oppose them. "A White Oak," writing in *Rivington's Gazetteer,* pressed the Tories "to give your votes" against the convention. Led by Colonel Frederick Philipse, Assemblyman Isaac Wilkins, and Reverend Samuel Seabury, some 250 gathered at White Plains on the appointed day to cast their ballots. Although the two opposing factions comprised approximately an equal number, an important difference existed between them. The Whigs seemed to be freeholders, a fact which the Tories never disputed, whereas almost 50 percent of the opposition fell into the nonfreeholding class. Consequently, half the Tory votes would be challenged and the Whigs would carry the day. Possibly this is the explanation of the Tory withdrawal from the meeting without voting.

The importance of the White Plains incident lies in the determination of the representative character of the two parties. The evidence, however, is inconclusive. Since the Whigs claimed freeholds, it is possible they represented a larger section of the county population than the Tories.[61] On the other hand, a comparison of the list of Philipsburg Manor occupants with the signers of the loyalist statement shows that Philipse tenants constituted about one-third of the group that accompanied the Colonel to White Plains. In an attempt to recoup the loss at the county courthouse, an anonymous writer, perhaps Wilkins or Seabury, alleged that two-thirds of the county disapproved the provincial convention and promised to prove it with the publication of certain resolves then signing. However, the Friends of Government did not fulfill this promise.[62]

---

[61] Since the Whigs expected the Tories to challenge nonfreehold voters, they had not sought to mobilize these lessees at will and, therefore, Whig strength was potentially much greater than the number present at White Plains.

[62] "A White Oak," *Riv. Gaz.,* April 6, 1775; Lewis Morris to the Printer,

The chief point of interest in the First New York Provincial Congress election is the contention that in at least five of the counties only a small minority participated in the voting.[63] In two of these, however, Tryon and Dutchess, there are indications to the contrary. Tory influence in Tryon seems to have centered in Mohawk District, the Johnson bailiwick, but the Whigs dominated the other four districts. The key factor lay in the tardy organization of the county committee. The Palatine District Committee notified the Albany County Committee of Correspondence on May 19, 1775, that it could not hold an election early enough to be in time for the congressional meeting. Nevertheless, the committee assured Albany, a majority of the county were Whigs. Five days later thirty delegates from all districts, except Mohawk, met to form a county committee. Despite threats by the Johnsons, the Mohawk people chose four persons to represent them on the county committee. When the Johnsons threatened to imprison some of the Whig leaders, the county committee resolved to use force to free them unless the Tories abided by legal procedures. Undeterred by the Johnsons' armed tenantry, the Whigs could report by June 2 that all districts had met to sign the congressional association and had completed the choice of full delegations to serve on the county committee. In response to the urgent letters of May 31 and June 3 from the First New York Provincial Congress, the committee voted promptly to delegate two members to represent Tryon County in that body. With this action Judge Robert R. Livingston could

---

April 11, Anonymous, Westchester County, April 13, Lewis Morris to the Printer, May 7, 1775, *N.Y.G.*, April 17, May 15, 1775; Memorial of Samuel Seabury, Philipsburg Rent Roll, in American Loyalists, Transcripts of the Manuscript Books and Papers of the Commission of Enquiry into the Losses and Services of the American Loyalists . . . , XLI, 562, 581-92, NYPL; M. K. Couzens, *Index of Grantees of Lands Sold by the Commissioners of Forfeitures of the Southern District of the State of New York Situate in the Manor of Philipsburg, Westchester County, New York* (Yonkers, 1880), *passim.*
[63] Becker, *The History of Political Parties*, p. 201.

advise his son that "the Whigs are predominated at last in Tryon. . . ."[64]

In Dutchess the postelection conflict over the provincial convention still roiled the waters when the New York city committee's circular, soliciting a provincial congress, reached the inhabitants in early May. The Whigs campaigned energetically to establish committees in every precinct and to have the citizenry sign the association. The Tories fought back vigorously, but the tide ran against them. In mid-June the Whigs said with assurance that "Committees either have or will be chosen in every part of Dutchess. . . ." Considered in the context of this activity, the election of delegates to the Provincial Congress would seem likely to have aroused more than a minority of the freeholders to participate.[65]

The clash of arms in the spring of 1775 sharpened the tensions in the colony and the subsequent deepening of hostility to the administration turned the Tories from words to guns. Shortly before Lexington and Concord, Dartmouth approved a plan to raise an armed loyalist association from the Highlanders of New York to oppose all illegal combinations and insurrections and to give the utmost aid in suppressing all such practices as were contrary to the law and to the King's authority. The project seems to have contemplated the settlement of associators on a strategically located tract of land in the province, awarding to each family head who took the oath of association 100 acres free of quitrents for five years. Although Dartmouth had commended Colden to secrecy, Gage reemphasized the necessity of stealth, "for the Friends of Government appear every where to be so subdued, as not to admit of its being done openly." When the association's sponsor, Colonel Allen Maclean, reached

---

64 *Ibid.,* pp. 202-3; Frey, *The Minute Book,* pp. 9, 12-19; Judge Robert R. Livingston to Robert R. Livingston, Jr., June 17, 1775, Livingston, *Revolutionary Letters of Importance,* No. 46.
65 *Ibid.;* Becker, *The History of Political Parties,* p. 203.

New York, the omnipresent hostility to the government sent him rushing off to Boston to confer with Gage. Apparently fearful of arousing the Whigs' anger, he dropped the association scheme, but made his way cautiously to Johnstown. There he arranged with Sir John Johnson to recruit Highlanders for him from among his tenantry and to dispatch them to Montreal where he intended to organize a regiment.[66] Toward the close of the year, Sir John Johnson also undertook the formation of a battalion of his own, but, he wrote to Tryon, "we must however not think of stirring till we have a support. . . ." That support never came, however, even though Johnson raised 500 to 600 men. Schuyler disarmed them in January, 1776.[67] If the Tories had the numerous adherents claimed for them, Tryon and Maclean would have succeeded in founding the loyalist association.

The last link in the chain of evidence relating to the division of political loyalties is military service in the respective armies. There can be no more severe test of political beliefs than to call upon the people to defend them with their lives. That the people did so is a gauge of the profundity of their attachment.[68] Determination of the numbers

---

[66] Colden to Dartmouth, June 7, 1775, *Letterbooks of Cadwallader Colden,* II, 426; Dartmouth to Colden, April 5, 1775, *Letters and Papers of Cadwallader Colden,* VII, 281; Gage to Dartmouth, May 25, July 24, September 20, 1775, Dartmouth to Gage, April 15, 1775, Carter, *Correspondence of General Gage,* I, 401, 409-10, 414-15, II, 193, 195; Warrant to Colonel Maclean to Raise a Regiment, April 3, 1775, Oath of Association, Colden to Dartmouth, July 3, 1775, O'Callaghan, *Documents, Colonial, New York,* VIII, 562-63, 564, 588; Force, *American Archives,* 4th ser., III, 552.

[67] Sir John Johnson to Tryon, n.d., Tryon to Dartmouth, January 5, February 7, 1776, O'Callaghan, *Documents, Colonial, New York,* VIII, 651, 663. Tryon directed his energies toward the military organization of the Queens County Tories, an act which provoked the Provincial Congress to request troops from the Continental Congress. The Tories published a declaration, averring that they were arming for self-defense only. New Jersey troops disarmed about 600 in January. Becker, *The History of Political Parties,* pp. 238, 244-45; *Queens County,* December 6, 1775, Broadsides, NYPL.

[68] A rebuttal to this argument is that many Tories, confronted with the alternatives of fleeing and surrendering lands or leases or serving in Whig militia, chose to endure militia service. Their duty with their units did not

who served, however, is a very difficult task. The investigator is beset by obstacles of many kinds, some of which are insoluble for the present. For example, the American lists of soldiers do not distinguish men who enlisted as paid substitutes, deserted, and then reenlisted for someone else. Nor is it possible to tell how many fictitious names are in muster rolls, nor how many names there are of those who deserted at a propitious moment to join the British.

Since available military statistics are incomplete and even conflicting, one method of evaluating them is a comparison with population figures. The Continental Army drew 19,793 New Yorkers into the regiments of the line, the levies, and the privateers. Another 23,852 served in the militia and an additional 8,327 prepared for duty, but the termination of the war spared them. The total is 51,972. Furthermore, fragmentary documents suggest that this figure is incomplete, that units existed whose records have disappeared.[69] Ap-

---

make these men Whigs. However, one might compare this hypothesis with the case of American prisoners on the British prison hulks. In the face of an extremely high mortality rate large numbers of prisoners refused to take advantage of a British offer of freedom in return for enlistment in His Majesty's forces. In the one case land was hypothetically more important than political principle, in the other life itself was less important than political belief. One might also ask why pseudo-Whig militia who fell into British hands did not promptly disavow the Revolution and enlist in the royal forces. See below, pp. 94-96. Richard B. Morris, "Class Struggle and the American Revolution," *William and Mary Quarterly*, 3rd ser., XIX (January, 1962) 15.

Inspiration for the preceding viewpoint seems to come from contemporary Whig comments relative to Tory strength in Dutchess County. If the statements of some Whigs on this matter were accepted at face value, posterity would have wondered whether there were any Whigs in the state. Although the tendency to see Tories behind every tree often stemmed from defeatism and fright, there were other reasons for the phenomenon. Whig leaders not only sometimes identified criticism and complaint with disloyalty but they also considered the grumblings of the tenantry as toryism. Staughton Lynd, *Anti-Federalism in Dutchess County New York: A Study of Democracy and Class Conflict in the Revolutionary Era* (Chicago, 1962), pp. 59-61; George Dangerfield, *Chancellor Robert R. Livingston of New York, 1746-1813* (New York, 1960), pp. 60, 81; Nelson, *The American Tory*, p. 101. For other examples of Whig fears of Tories, see *Jour. Prov. Cong.*, I, 606, 687, 700, 919, 1039; Force, *American Archives*, 4th ser., I, 355, III, 458, VI, 1415, 1442; *Cal. Hist. Mss.*, I, 525.

proximately 23,500 fought for the British, of whom 15,000 were in the army and navy and 8,500 in the loyalist militia.[70] Thus the total number of men under arms is 75,472. Herein lies a contradiction. The sixteen to sixty age group supplied the pool from which the armies drew their recruits.[71] According to the censuses of 1756, 1771, and 1786, this bracket comprised 23.8 percent, 25 percent, and 24 percent respectively of the total white population.[72] Therefore, *if* 75,472 men bore arms, and if 25 percent was the age-bracket percentage, the total white population must have been at least 301,888. Since the 1771 census counted only 148,124 whites, it is highly improbable that the population could have doubled by 1783. Even if it is assumed that the rate of growth was the same for 1771-1776 as for 1756-1771, the total white population would have been only 169,148 and the military age group only 42,287. It is possible that the estimates of men in arms are erroneous and that the census understated the size of the population. Application of the 25 percent military age bracket to a *suggested* total white population of 208,000 would yield a pool of 52,000 fighting men.[73]

---

[69] James A. Roberts, comp., *New York in the Revolution as Colony and State* (2nd. ed.; Albany, 1898), p. 15. A year-by-year breakdown of regulars and levies furnished the Continental Army is in the Hamilton Papers, L.C., V (microfilm, 1st ser., reel 3, courtesy of The Papers of Alexander Hamilton, CUL).

[70] Flick, *Loyalism*, p. 112; Claude H. Van Tyne, *The Loyalists in the American Revolution* (New York, 1902), pp. 182-83. Van Tyne agrees with Flick's estimate, but an analysis of some of the sources employed by Flick raises a question as to their reliability and their interpretation. The detailed presentation is in Flick, pp. 95-112. For the most part figures of troops are drawn from general statements and commissions to recruit specific numbers. Flick used very few unit records. The difficulties to which the use of this material can lead receive illustration in the Appendix, pp. 254-257.

[71] In August, 1776, the Provincial Congress ordered all white males aged sixteen to fifty to enroll in the militia. Since the state was under almost incessant attack from 1776 to 1782, it is unlikely the government released the able bodied from militia duty after they reached the age of fifty. *Jour. Prov. Cong.*, I, 566.

[72] Greene and Harrington, *American Population*, pp. 101, 102, 104; *Daily Advertiser*, December 26, 1786.

Although the Continental Army compilations derive from an actual computation of names on payrolls and muster rolls, it is obvious that they are unreliable. On the other hand, the state of the evidence does not permit an accurate reevaluation.[74]

An analysis of loyalist statistics reveals much the same situation as that of the American. First, the total number of loyalists in arms from all colonies seems to be less than Flick thought. An early computation, which had the merit of drawing upon muster rolls, placed the overall figure at 15,000, although the author warned that he could not find some unit records.[75] Troop returns by Howe and Clinton reveal that provincial forces from all colonies ranged from 3,000 to 8,200 in any one year, while those in Canada fluctuated around 2,400.[76] A maximum of 25,000 would seem to

---

73 There are signs that there was a substantial immigration to New York. One contemporary assessment was that twenty-two vessels discharged immigrants between August, 1773, and August, 1774. Stokes, *The Iconography of Manhattan Island*, IV, 862. Estimates of the New York population in 1776 vary from 190,000 to 200,000, including slaves. Although the Continental Congress had accepted the latter figure, the former figure is an estimate based on the rate of increase between 1756 and 1771. Robert R. Livingston thought the total to be 190,000 in 1775. Greene and Harrington, *American Population*, pp. 7, 91; Livingston to de la Luzerne, April 24, 1787, Robert R. Livingston Collection, NYHS; U.S. Bureau of the Census, *Historical Statistics of the United States, Colonial Times to 1957* (Washington, D.C., 1957), ser. Z 1-19.

If the greater validity of the American figures is granted, it would be necessary to reduce them drastically to tailor them to fit into a white population of 169,000. On the other hand, if the total white population is increased much beyond 208,000, the growth between 1771 and 1776 tends to become less credible.

74 Nevertheless, a very general approximation might be made on an arbitrary basis. Such an approximation might allow an error of 15,000 for all factors. Subtraction of this number from the American computation of 51,972 would leave 36,000. The loyalists on this basis would have 16,000.

75 W. O. Raymond, "Loyalists in Arms," New Brunswick Historical Society *Collections*, II (St. John, 1904), 220-21; Paul H. Smith, *Loyalists and Redcoats: A Study in British Revolutionary Policy* (Chapel Hill, 1964), pp. 60-61.

76 After a year's occupation of southern New York Howe could only list 3,257 provincials from all colonies. Troyer S. Anderson, *The Command of the Howe Brothers During the American Revolution* (New York, 1936), p. 314; Sir William Howe, *A Schedule of Sir William Howe's Correspondence as Produced to the House of Commons* (Extracted from the *Parliamentary Register*, XI, 1779) (London, 1779), p. 390; Great Britain, Historical Manuscripts Commission, *Report on the Manuscripts of Mrs. Stopford-Sackville of Drayton House, Northamptonshire* (2 vols.; London, 1904-1910), II, 65, 212

be a reasonable appraisal of the total loyalist contribution. When assessed against this figure, it is highly improbable that New York's share is 23,000.[77] Second, many New York units consisted of men from other colonies as well as from New York. For example, one battalion of De Lancey's brigade drew its recruits from Connecticut.[78] Third, an unknown number joined the British army involuntarily. Howe himself admitted that his officers sought recruits among prisoners of war, offering such inducements as "pay, liberty

(hereinafter cited as *Stopford Mss.*); General Sir Henry Clinton, *The American Rebellion*, ed. William B. Willcox (New Haven, 1954), p. 548; Ernest A. Cruikshank, ed., *The Settlement of the United Empire Loyalists on the Upper St. Lawrence and Bay of Quinte in 1784: A Documentary Record* (Toronto, 1934), pp. 30-31; Alden, *The American Revolution, 1775-1783*, p. 88.

[77] Flick thought that the New York total was about half of all loyalists in British units. *Loyalism*, p. 113; Smith, *Loyalists and Redcoats*, chap. v.

[78] On De Lancey see Arthur W. Eaton, "New York Loyalists in Nova Scotia," *The Grafton Magazine*, February, 1910, p. 174. Roger's King's Rangers included enlistees from Quebec, New Hampshire, Connecticut, Nova Scotia, and other colonies, although the British regarded it as a "New York" corps. Simcoe's Queen's Rangers began with *ca.* 100 from Westchester, but the majority of the unit were Europeans. Although Maclean raised one battalion of his Royal Highland Emigrants in New York, the other battalion comprised Nova Scotians. Indeed some of the men came out of Quebec's prison. The New York Volunteers first came from New England refugees and later from New York. Another Yorker regiment, the Royal Fencible Americans, had its origins in Boston in 1775. The King's Royal Regiment of New York numbered men from Canada, New Hampshire, and Vermont. Wilbur H. Siebert, "The American Loyalists in the Eastern Seigniories and Townships of the Province of Quebec," Royal Society of Canada, *Proceedings and Transactions*, Series 3, VII (Ottawa, 1913), Section II, 15, 16; *Jour.' Prov. Cong.*, II, 317; H. M. Jackson, "Queen's Rangers and Their Contribution in the Years 1776 to 1784," Canadian Historical Association, *Annual Report*, 1950, p. 13; Harold M. Jackson, *Roberts Rangers: A History* (Ottawa, 1953), pp. 183-88; Jonas Howe, "The Royal Emigrants," *Acadiensis*, IV (St. John, 1904), 50-51; C. T. Atkinson, "British Forces in North America, 1774-81," *Journal of the Society for Army Historical Research*, XVI (1941), 6, 9, 14, n. 26.

Not all loyalists came from the revolting thirteen colonies. Some had just arrived from Europe, some lived in Canada and Nova Scotia. Howe stated that a large number of his 3,609 provincials in May, 1778, were not Americans. There are indications that Scottish emigrants reached America only to be inducted into loyalist regiments. Sir William Howe, *Narrative of Lieutenant-General Sir William Howe in a Committee of the House of Commons on 29 April, 1779 Relative to His Conduct During His Late Command of the King's Troops in North America: To Which are Added, Some Observations Upon a Pamphlet Entitled, Letters to a Nobleman* (London, 1780), pp. 52-53; W. O. Raymond, "Roll of Officers of the British American or Loyalist Corps," New Brunswick Historical Society *Collections*, II (St. John, 1904), 225, 226; *Const. Gaz.*, December 30, 1775.

and pardon."[79] The British employed another kind of inducement of which the Continental Congress took note. The American Board of War reported that the British commonly held new prisoners for three to five days without food, then tempted them to enlist in order to avoid starvation.[80] There is profuse testimony of British compulsion, particularly among the prisoners aboard the prison hulks in New York harbor where thousands died.[81] Lastly, contemporary correspondence indicates that some loyalists deserted from the British. Unfortunately no figures are available and the scope of the movement is indeterminate.[82] For these reasons the calculations of New York loyalist soldiers are tentative until someone evaluates these factors accurately.

---

[79] Howe, *Narrative*, p. 52. Since the King had declared the Americans rebels, they might be threatened with execution. Howe's statement on "pardon" implies that the British did so threaten the prisoners.

[80] *N.Y.P.*, February 26, 1778. John Adams threw this charge at the British during the peace negotiations in 1782. He said the British starved the American prisoners taken at Fort Washington in order to force them to enlist in the British army. Extract from John Adams's Journal, November 17, 1782, *American Daily Advertiser, Extra.*, February 12, 1794. See also the references to 1,821 privates in "dispute," presumably the Fort Washington prisoners, in David L. Sterling, ed., "American Prisoners of War in New York: A Report by Elias Boudinot," *William and Mary Quarterly*, 3rd ser., XIII (July, 1956), 382, 384.

[81] Depositions of Robert Troup, January 17, 1777 and Adolph Myer, February 5, 1777, *Jour. Prov. Cong.*, II, 411, 412; testimony of Peter Wood, February 19, 1777 and deposition of Garret Luyster, May 13, 1777, *Minutes of the Committee and of the First Commission for Detecting and Defeating Conspiraicies in the State of New York, 1776-1778*, New-York Historical Society *Collections*, LVII (New York, 1924), I, 135, 283.

On the prison hulks, see David Ramsay, *The History of the Revolution* (2 vols.; Trenton, 1811), II, 372; William Gordon, *History of the Rise, Progress, and Establishment of the Independence of the United States of America* (3 vols.; New York, 1801), II, 172; Henry Onderdonk, *British Prisons and Prison Ships at New York, 1776-1783* (Jamaica, 1863), n. p., "recollections of General Jeremiah Johnson"; *Minutes, Commission, Conspiracies, New York*, I, 89; *American Citizen*, February 22, 1803; Albert G. Greene, *Recollections of the Jersey Prison-Ship* (Morrisania, 1865), pp. 70-71 and n. 1.

Hobart relayed disturbing news about Tryon's recruiting tactics in Suffolk. The British governor threatened Huntington that "unless the young men do voluntarily take up arms against their country, an inveterate and disappointed soldiery will be let loose upon them." *Jour. Prov. Cong.*, I, 671.

[82] John Henry to President, Council of Safety, May 31, 1777, *Jour. Prov. Cong.*, II, 444; Assistant Commissioners for Conspiracies to Council of Safety, December 4, 1777, *Minutes of the Committee and of the First Commission for Detecting and Defeating Conspiracies in the State of New York, 1776-1778*, New-York Historical Society *Collections*, LVII (New York, 1925), II, 445.

There is still another element in any consideration of Tory strength. If the loyalists counted such large numbers of supporters as they themselves so frequently maintained, why did they not rally to the British standard when Howe arrived? Howe, for example, described the energetic, but futile, efforts of De Lancey to bring his brigade to its authorized level of 1,500. Brigadier General De Lancey scoured not only the occupied counties, but also the American-held areas for volunteers. Despite these vigorous exertions, at the commencement of the 1777 campaign De Lancey's brigade numbered only 597 men.[83] As a matter of fact, General Howe quickly perceived the fatal weakness of the Tories, for in September, 1776, he wrote to Lord George Germain from New York: "We must also have recruits from Europe, not finding the Americans disposed to serve with arms, notwithstanding the hopes held out to me upon my arrival at this port."[84]

Burgoyne put the loyalists to the acid test in 1777 and found them wanting. Some historians think he acquired a few thousand reinforcements from the Tories, but reliable statements place the number at 682 to 830.[85] Burgoyne extensively solicited loyalist aid before marching south from Canada. The General sent agents into New York to collect provincials. When the campaign began he issued proclamations appealing to the loyalists to enlist and promising to support them if they rose against the Whigs.[86] By August

83 Howe, *Narrative,* p. 52.

84 *Stopford Mss.,* II, 41. For a contrary view see Smith, *Loyalists and Redcoats,* chap. iv, v.

85 Flick opines "several thousand," but Siebert reduced this to *ca.* 2,000. There is a difference in the official statement of the British lists, but Fortescue mentions the larger number, 830. The inconsistency of Siebert's estimate is his demonstration that the five loyalist units which had not surrendered with Burgoyne amounted to only 485 men in the winter of 1778-1779. Flick, *Loyalism,* p. 110; Siebert, Royal Society of Canada, *Proceedings and Transactions,* ser. 3, VII, 11, 14; Sir John W. Fortescue, *A History of the British Army* (14 vols.; New York, 1899-1930), III, 234n.; Jones, *History of New York During the Revolutionary War,* I, 678 (ed. notes on Burgoyne).

86 Siebert, Royal Society of Canada, *Proceedings and Transactions,* ser. 3,

Burgoyne became convinced of the minority status of the loyalists. In a communication to Germain, he complained: "The great bulk of the country is undoubtedly with the Congress, in principle and zeal; and their measures are executed with a secrecy and dispatch that are not to be equalled."[87] Subjected by Parliament to examination on his defeat, Burgoyne was called upon to explain why he did not attempt a rapid advance to reach Albany. He retorted: "Would the Tories have risen? Why did they not rise round Albany and below it, at the time they found Mr. Gate's army increasing . . . ? Why did they not rise in that populous and as supposed well affected district, the German Flats at the time St. Leger was before Fort Stanwix? A critical insurrection from any one point of the compass within distance to create a diversion would probably have secured the success of the campaign."[88] There can be no doubt that a rising of several thousand loyalists would have created a critical situation for the Americans.

A comparison of the loyalist reaction with the American at this time reveals the validity of Burgoyne's strictures. Governor Clinton advised Washington of the alacrity with which the militia responded to the mobilization order.[89]

VII, 7; *A Broadside by John Burgoyne, Esq.*, July 2, 1777, Broadsides, NYHS; Proclamation, June 29, 1777; [N.Y.] *Diary*, January 17, 1794; Philip Skene to Dartmouth, August 30, 1777, Benjamin F. Stevens, ed., *Facsimiles of Manuscripts in European Archives Relating to America, 1773-1783* (25 vols.; London, 1889-1898), XVIII, No. 1665; Morris to Council of Safety, July 16, 1777, *Jour. Prov. Cong.*, II, 511.

87 Burgoyne to Germain, August 20, 1777, General John Burgoyne, *A State of the Expedition from Canada as Laid Before the House of Commons* (London, 1780), Appendix, xlvi.

88 *Ibid.*, pp. 151-52. However, see Smith, *Loyalists and Redcoats*, pp. 50-59. Sir Henry Clinton also complained of loyalist indifference: "It will not be out of place here to express my regret at seeing the incomplete state of the provincial corps. So many attempts to raise men have always totally failed of success, and some corps which at first promised to be of importance have remained notwithstanding in so very weak a state that there is little encouragement to undertake anything more in that line." Clinton to Germain, December, 1779, quoted in Wertenbaker, *Father Knickerbocker Rebels*, p. 227.

89 August 9, 1777, George Clinton, *Public Papers of George Clinton, First Governor of New York* (10 vols.; Albany, 1899-1914), II, 195-97.

90 *Ibid.*, II, 323-25, 333, 334-35, 344, 347, also 402, 409, 411. Nickerson put

At the height of the campaign in September, Clinton related to Duane that New York had eleven militia regiments from the region south of Poughkeepsie and New Paltz on active duty and had dispatched to Gates every other regiment in the state except two in Tryon and one in Schoharie.[90]

The testimony of two other men strongly sustained the preceding evidence. Joseph Galloway, when questioned in Parliament, conceded that the New York loyalists could not defend themselves without the British army, even though the British might fully arm and organize them. General James Robertson, who had served in New York from 1765 to 1777, made a similar admission.[91]

Although the Tories possessed the advantage of an extensive governmental machinery, they lacked the capability of halting the burgeoning revolutionary sentiment and in 1775 went down to a series of political defeats throughout the colony. Tryon, Gage, and Dartmouth admitted the loss of royal control in New York as the consequence of the unpopularity of the government. Endeavors to form loyalist associations and to arm the friends of government proved fruitless in the long run. So long as the Tories constituted a minority of the populace, they had little chance of regaining a position of supremacy.[92]

---

the total number of militia with Gates at 12,000; some were from New England. Both Patterson and Ward understate the militia units. Hoffman Nickerson, *The Turning Point of the Revolution* (Boston, 1928), pp. 326-37, graph opp. p. 384; Samuel W. Patterson, *Horatio Gates* (New York, 1941), p. 167, n. 5; Christopher Ward, *War of the Revolution,* ed. John R. Alden (2 vols.; New York, 1952), II, 529.

A recent computation which is based on fragmentary militia records indicates the strength of the New York units at more than 2,000. Charles W. Snell, "Report on the Organization and Numbers of Gates' Army, September 19, October 7, and October 17, 1777, Including an Appendix with Regimental Data and Notes," pp. 18-19, 76-77, Files of the Saratoga National Historical Park.

[91] Anderson, *The Command of the Howe Brothers,* pp. 311, 315.

[92] Hamilton, writing to John Jay about the impending assembly election early in 1776, commented, "for the Whigs, I doubt not, constitute a large majority of the people." Hamilton to Jay, December 31, 1775, John Jay Papers, Iselin Collection, CUL; Henry P. Johnston, ed., *The Correspondence and Public Papers of John Jay* (4 vols.; New York, 1890-1893), I, 41.

FOUR

Crystallization of the Revolutionary Spirit

WHEN the fall and winter of 1775-1776 had run their course, the Whig leaders possessed a double reason for congratulating themselves. Elections in November registered approval of the First Provincial Congress and eliminated some of its less vigorous men.[1] And, military forces disarmed the menacing Tories in Queens, Richmond, and Tryon, who became more submissive to congressional authority.[2] However, there were other circumstances that prevented the appearance of complacency among the Whigs.

Lowering transatlantic skies during these months induced growing anxiety among the Friends of Liberty. It was the season for harsh pronunciamentos from Whitehall as the ministry reacted vigorously to the dispatches from America. The first of these chilling advices, reaching New York in early November, was the royal proclamation of August, 1775, which pronounced the colonies to be in a state of rebellion and fulminated against the misleaders of His Majesty's subjects. Hardly had the shock of this information begun to subside when word came that George III had refused to receive the Olive Branch petition from the Continental Congress. January, 1776, brought copies of the royal speech to Parliament in October in which the King called for suppression of the rebellion by armed force. The

last of these ill tidings, arriving in February, was the Pro-
hibitory Act, which declared a blockade of the colonies and
ordered the impressment of colonial seamen from captured
merchant vessels.[3]

As the year 1776 opened, New York seemed about to
become the scene of major military operations. Washington,
worried over the slow progress of military preparations on
the Hudson, commanded General Charles Lee to repair to
New York City to fortify it. Lee marched into town just as
General Henry Clinton sailed into port with three ships.
A panic ensued; "away flew the women, children, goods and
chattels."[4] Although the inhabitants did not give credence
to the statement, Clinton averred that he had no hostile
intentions; his objective was the Carolinas. Meanwhile,
there was widespread hardship and privation as thousands
of people in the depth of winter sought shelter on Long
Island and in Jersey.[5] The departure of Clinton was simply
a temporary reprieve because in March Washington, antici-
pating an assault by Sir William Howe, began the transfer
of his army from Boston to New York.[6]

Amid these alarms and the swelling martial turbulence
the Second Provincial Congress, or its alternate, the Committee of Safety, ran out the remainder of its allotted life-

1 See below, p. 181.

2 See below, pp. 99, 131, 141, 198.

3 Edmund C. Burnett, *The Continental Congress* (New York, 1941), pp.
115, 116, 138; John R. Alden, *The American Revolution, 1777-1783* (New
York, 1954), pp. 65, 75; Arthur M. Schlesinger, Sr., *The Colonial Merchants
and the American Revolution* (New York, 1939), p. 579.

4 Shewkirk Diary, quoted in Thomas J. Wertenbaker, *Father Knickerbocker
Rebels: New York City During the Revolution* (New York, 1948), p. 70.

5 "The Fears of the Multitude made them forget the Mayor's Message concerning the expected Ship & conceiving that they were betrayed Mr. Clinton
& the Governor were calumniated as false Villains, Liars and Decievers—The
River was full of Ice and the Cold intemperate and yet the Inhabitants
flew into the Country with their Effects." William H. W. Sabine, ed., *Historical Memoirs from 16 March 1763 to 9 July 1776 of William Smith* (New
York, 1956), p. 263.

6 Carl L. Becker, *The History of Political Parties in the Province of New
York, 1760-1776* (Madison, 1909), pp. 246, 248, 251; Wertenbaker, *Father
Knickerbocker Rebels*, pp. 70-71, 77. See below, pp. 105-7.

span. Although the congressmen early in this session had designated April for elections to a third provincial assembly, they had not foreseen the circumstances in which the balloting would occur. Tory manipulations in local contests largely disappeared; those Tories who had hoped for an accommodation with Britain despaired and withdrew into passivity or armed opposition. The Continental Congress caused a stir when on April 6 it flung open the colonial ports to the ships of nations other than Great Britain. Upon receiving this intelligence, the New York Committee of Safety urgently summoned a meeting of the Provincial Congress for May 1 in order to execute the instructions of the Continental Congress in relation to trade.[7] The conduct of the Second Provincial Congress from December, 1775, to May, 1776, rendered no satisfaction to men of a radical stamp like Isaac Sears. Indeed there were many far from the North River who looked askance at the Provincial Congress because they thought that body dragged its collective feet in the opposition to Britain.

Although opposition to the measures of the North ministry had proceeded on the premise that the Whigs could compel Great Britain to yield the desired reforms, the events of the latter half of 1775 and early 1776 made that premise more and more untenable. The increasing resort to muskets and cannon had a dispiriting effect upon the moderate and conservative leaders in New York. Furthermore, the campaign against the imperial government posed a delicate internal problem for the revolutionary party. Slogans of no taxation without representation and demands for constitutional liberties had a dangerous potential in a province where the great landholders frequently manipulated their tenants' votes. Notwithstanding the caution of the great landholders, some of the revolutionary ferment seeped down to the tenantry,

---

[7] Becker, *The History of Political Parties*, pp. 253, 256; Burnett, *The Continental Congress*, pp. 139-40; *Jour. Prov. Cong.*, I, 410.

expressing itself in pressure for more favorable land leases. Writing from Dutchess County, Henry B. Livingston conveyed the attitude of the aristocracy when he condemned the renters: "The Tenants here are Great Villains. Some of them are resolved to take advantage of the times and make their Landlords give them Leases forever. . . ."[8]

The sharpening lines of conflict and the consequent Whig loss of vigor have given rise to the view that a loyalist reaction had set in.[9] This interpretation rests on several considerations: the delays in the election of deputies to the Second New York Provincial Congress and in the attendance of the members, and Tryon's maneuver to convene a new provincial assembly. However, there is another pertinent but overlooked fact: Whig timidity.

Vacillation appeared among the Whigs in consequence of events in July and August, 1775. In July the Continental Congress published its justification for taking up arms and virtually rejected Lord North's conciliatory motion. Immediately thereafter word came from Britain that both the King and Parliament had rejected the New York provincial assembly's conciliatory overture. After the engagement occurred in Massachusetts and units of the Continental Army gathered at Albany for an invasion of Canada, the prospect of peace receded visibly. The practical meaning of these occurrences came home literally with the crash of cannon when the warship *Asia* in New York Harbor clashed with a party removing cannon from the fort on the night of August 23. Fear of the cannonading set in motion a general exodus of the population that continued in sporadic fashion until the practical evacuation of the city in June, 1776. Haunted by their fear of loss of life and property, many Whig leaders became visibly less belligerent when Tryon and the Tories

---

[8] H.B. to R.R. Livingston, May, 1775, Robert R. Livingston, American Art Association Catalogue, *Revolutionary Letters of Importance: The Unpublished Correspondence of Robert R. Livingston* (New York, 1918), No. 30.

[9] Becker, *The History of Political Parties*, pp. 221-52.

reminded them of the possibility of a general bombardment of the city.

In fact, some radicals had anticipated such an eventuality back in July and had proposed the seizure of the Governor as hostage for the good behavior of the ships. The plan did have much to commend it. It would have spared the people. It would have mitigated the growing fear within the Provincial Congress and reduced the spread of confusion among the general populace. It might very well have put a halt to the arming of the Tories on Long Island. However, seizing the King's personal representative would have put New York in the same position as Massachusetts and placed the members of its congress in the same category as the Adamses and Hancock.[10] The plan had its inception when Isaac Sears returned to the city from a visit to the Continental Congress and conferred with General Philip Schuyler. Schuyler, characterizing the idea as "rash" and "unjustifiable," argued that the Continental Congress would disapprove. Sears replied that he had discussed the proposal with a number of the continental delegates, who had approved it. Only when Schuyler stated that he had written orders from General Washington against it did Sears reluctantly agree to drop the matter. Schuyler hastened to inform Councilor William Smith of the affair and to assure him that he supported the "Magistracy in all cases but where they opposed the Common Defence." The General, while refusing Smith permission to warn the Governor, did have the Councilor draw up a proclamation for the protection of Tryon. Schuyler incorporated it in a letter of orders to General Wooster, commander of the Connecticut detachment in the city.[11]

---

10 Tryon transmitted at this time lists of names of Whigs and Tories to Dartmouth. Tryon to Dartmouth, January 5, 1776, Edmund B. O'Callaghan, ed., *Documents Relative to the Colonial History of the State of New York* (15 vols.; Albany, 1856), VIII, 651.

11 William Smith, Memoirs, IV, July 3, 1775; Schuyler to Wooster, July 3, 1775, Benson J. Lossing, *The Life and Times of Philip Schuyler* (2 vols.; New York, 1873), I, 346.

The Governor essayed a psychological maneuver in order to heighten the tension that the *Asia* incident aroused. It is likely that the Provincial Congress, temporarily handing over power to a Committee of Safety on September 2, was partly responding to the previous week's cannonade.[12] Tryon discomfited the Whigs when he arranged to have Mayor Hicks inform the Committee of Safety that Tryon had word from Dartmouth pertaining to fresh orders for naval commanders. British captains would adjudge towns to be in a state of rebellion where they raised troops, erected fortifications, or removed His Majesty's stores.[13] Actually, Admiral Graves sent Captain Vandeput of the *Asia* similar but more limited orders at the same time. If the city prohibited intercourse with the ships or molested them, Graves ordered Vandeput to open fire. The Admiral directed the Captain to destroy Sears's house, the houses of other known rebels, and burn all shipping in the harbor.[14] Although the committee strove to obtain an extract of the letter from the Governor or its "exact purport," their *Journal* did not refer to the matter again. Two days later, however, *Rivington's Gazetteer* carried the substance of a part of the letter that conveyed the same information Hicks had given the Committee of Safety.[15] If Tryon intended to immobilize the Provincial Congress, he very nearly succeeded.

Although the Whigs did not take the threat of bombardment lightly, nevertheless, there is strong ground for believing it to have been a bluff. As long as the Governor remained in the city, he was, in effect, a hostage who guaranteed the peaceable behavior of the warships. Moreover, the Tories

---

[12] Congress's mood was not necessarily the people's mood. The indignant reaction of the populace to the August 23 incident caused the Provincial Congress to arrange an alternative method of supplying the ships which would keep the crews out of the city. *Jour. Prov. Cong.,* I, 126.

[13] *Ibid.,* I, 152, 153; Dartmouth to the Lords of Admiralty, July 1, 1775, *Cal. H. O. Papers,* p. 362.

[14] Admiral Graves to Vandeput, September 10, 1775, *Cal. H. O. Papers,* p. 464.

[15] *Riv. Gaz.,* September 21, 1775.

and their property would suffer as much as the Whigs in a general cannonading. The British weighed other factors. A pitched battle in the port might very well raise the political temperature of the province to fever pitch, rendering the position of the Tories impossible. The Yorkers would appeal to the Continental Congress and neighboring colonies, and troops would pour into the city. The combination of these factors would drive the ships out of the harbor, and the destruction wrought by the cannon might end the city's usefulness to the British as their headquarters.[16]

News of the impending arrival of continental troops commanded by General Charles Lee stirred new fears in the city. Tryon in mid-December, underscoring his September warning, distributed a handbill that reprinted a letter from the captain of the *Phoenix* to the Governor. Captain Parker stated that he had orders to treat the town as in open rebellion against the King if the people resorted to violent acts. When General Lee prepared to march into New York in January, 1776, to fortify the city against an expected British attack, the Committee of Safety reacted with alarm. Eliphalet Dyer, Connecticut delegate to the Continental Congress, described the atmosphere as he passed through the town homeward bound: "New York appears empty and desolate; you would scarce see any person or but few in the streets carts and waggons all employed in carrying out goods and furniture, the men-o-warr lying broadside against the town and near the wharfs sails bent and prepared at a moment's warning. Their present constirnation in New York arises from the near approach of Gen'l Lee. . . ." Nonetheless, a broadside signed "Sentinel" urged the people to isolate the British ships. The city, declared the author, "becomes more and more the scoff and wonder of America." He concluded with an appeal to the people's patriotism: "Are you

---

[16] Curtis P. Nettels, *George Washington and American Independence* (Boston, 1951), chap. xi; Wertenbaker, *Father Knickerbocker Rebels,* p. 62.

so callous and dead to every sense of honour, as to disregard the taunts and scoffs of your brethren in the neighbouring Colonies?"[17]

During his brief tenure in New York, Lee sought to checkmate the British and thereby alarmed the Whig leaders. He countered the menace of bombardment with a threat to retaliate against the Tories; it was a challenge the British did not choose to accept. The General charted a bold course when he ordered all communication with the ships halted and removed cannon and stores from the fortifications. Even though Tryon had advance information concerning Lee's plans, the ships did not intervene when the people hauled away the cannon in broad daylight. Complaints from the cautious Yorkers, however, forced Lee's transfer, but in April Washington rebuked the Provincial Congress for tolerating contact between the people and the ships. The Provincial Congress thereupon interdicted the traffic and the British made no move to retaliate. Tryon, informing the Colonial Secretary, George Germain, of the interdiction, wrote: "The destruction therefore of the city where there were so many friends to Government, with the loss of all their property, & the consideration of preserving the town for the King's army was thought to be too great sacrifices to make for only retarding the removal of the artillery and stores which even after such sacrifices could have been carried off by the Jersey and Connecticutt troops."[18]

The Committee of Safety did little more than to further the measures already set in motion by the parent body. At

---

[17] Nettels, *George Washington,* chap. xi; Becker, *The History of Political Parties,* pp. 246-50; Parker to Tryon, December 18, 1775, *N.Y.G.,* December 25, 1775; Dyer to Samuel Adams, January 28, February 27, 1776, Samuel Adams Papers, NYPL; New York, *New York City During the American Revolution. Being a Collection of Original Papers (Now First Published) from the Manuscripts in the Possession of the Mercantile Library Association of New York City* (New York, 1861), pp. 85-87; *To the Inhabitants of New York,* January 27, 1776, Broadsides, NYPL.

[18] Smith, Memoirs, V, February 11, 1776; Tryon to Germain, April 6, 1776, O'Callaghan, *Documents, Colonial, New York,* VIII, 674.

one point, indeed, when a combination of some moderates
and radicals sought to move vigorously against the Tories,
the committee lost its nerve. Driven by the critical shortage
of arms, the committee had voted to impress all weapons and
recompense their owners. Word from Queens soon reached
the committee not only that the Tories had refused to hand
in their arms but also that they had disarmed Whigs and that
the Colden family had directed these proceedings. McDougall presented a motion to dispatch to Queens a battalion
from his regiment, which was then raising, to compel
acquiescence in the impressment action. After considerable
discussion the committee defeated the proposal.[19] Hesitancy
of this kind was characteristic of the committee.

The committee's timidity in dealing with the Tory problem provoked disgust within the army. Colonel Rudolph
Ritzema demanded that the Provincial Congress "confiscate
their estates and banish them from the country." Since the
colonel wrote from Montreal two days after its capture, his
subsequent vehemence may be understood. "Such miscreants
ought not to breathe the same air with men resolved to be
free. From their machinations in & out of Congress have
arisen the hardships we have endured and are further to
undergo."[20] If the Committee of Safety heard these grumblings, it gave no sign.

Additional difficult problems harassed the committee
throughout September. September 28, three days after the
rebuff to McDougall on the Queens affair, the committee had
an urgent message from the commissioners who had been
detailed to construct fortifications along the mid-Hudson.
Information had reached them that Tryon and a party had

---

[19] *Jour. Prov. Cong.*, I, 156. Tryon praised the obstructionist activities of
the Coldens. Tryon to Dartmouth, December 6, 1775, O'Callaghan, *Documents, Colonial, New York*, VIII, 646.

When the Provincial Congress reconvened, it disapproved the impressment
resolution. McDougall dissented. *Jour. Prov. Cong.*, I, 184.

[20] Ritzema to McDougall, November 19, 1775, McDougall Papers, NYHS.

landed at Haverstraw where they questioned closely one of the commissioners about the fort and its strength. The commissioners expected the Governor to put in an appearance upriver and asked for a guard. When the committee answered the letter, it ignored both the news of Tryon's movements and the request for troops.[21] The next day the officers of the city's militia petitioned the committee to revise the training regulations so that the companies would train once a week and the battalions once a month. The present routine of once a month, they complained, lacked efficacy. The committee did not reply; the *Journal* tersely recorded, "Read and filed."[22] Both moderate Alexander McDougall and radical Hugh Hughes complained of the militia situation. The former told Jay that "men of rank and consideration refused to accept of commissions as field officers of the militia; so that these commissions have gone a beging for six or seven weeks." Hughes ascribed the lack of drilling among the militia to the fact that the officers without their commissions could not compel them to turn out. "These circumstances," he added, "have a very bad effect, as they encourage the Tories, who exult at it, and discourage the timid Whigs." Just before its collapse the Provincial Congress finally issued the commissions.[23]

When the New York Provincial Congress reassembled in early October, it sat hardly a week before ill tidings reached it. Washington warned that no prospect of conciliation existed and that all the evidence indicated the British would prosecute the war with the utmost vigor. The next day the Provincial Congress examined Captain Lawrence, a recently arrived shipmaster who had sailed from London August 2

---

21 Peter Force, ed., *American Archives* (9 vols.; Washington, D.C., 1837-1853), 4th ser., III, 914-15, 919-20.
22 *Jour. Prov. Cong.*, I, 159-60.
23 McDougall to Jay, October 30, 1775, John Jay Papers, Iselin Collection, CUL; Hughes to Samuel and John Adams, October 17, 1775, Samuel Adams Papers, NYPL; *Jour. Prov. Cong.*, I, 192.

and who brought news that more than sustained Washington's interpretation of the situation. Informed sources in London said that the ministry planned to hire 16,000 Hessians and Hanoverians for the American campaign and that they intended to increase the army in America to 30,000 over the winter. Within twenty-four hours the delegates listened to the reading of three letters from London, dated July 31 and August 7, which concurred in the fact that the government had determined to recover New York, control the Hudson, and open direct communication with Canada.[24] Scarcely had the members comprehended this intelligence when Tryon demanded that the Provincial Congress guarantee his safety. Dissatisfied with the subsequent assurances, the Governor shifted his quarters October 19 to one of the vessels in the harbor.[25] Tryon's flight seemed to denote the imminence of bombardment, and the seizure of three vessels in the lower harbor and their escort to Boston by the British sloop *Viper* tended to confirm it.[26] Many congressmen now found it urgent to attend to their personal affairs and the Provincial Congress, lacking a quorum October 28 and 29, adjourned until November 2.

When it reconvened on November 2, it heard more grim reports. Dispatches from the Continental Congress contained interrogations of captured British officers who had secretly recruited loyalists in New York. The bait offered to enlistees included a promise of 200 acres of *forfeited* lands in settled areas of the province, a promise authorized by Dartmouth.[27] That same afternoon the Provincial Congress listened to a letter from Washington which contained an eye-witness account of the burning of Falmouth by the British. Furthermore, the correspondent continued, the British commander

---

24 *Ibid.*, I, 170-71, 172-73.
25 Becker, *The History of Political Parties,* p. 225.
26 *Riv. Gaz.,* October 26, 1775.
27 *Jour. Prov. Cong.,* I, 188-90; Captain M. Maclean to Major John Small, December 13, 1775, Force, *American Archives,* 4th ser., IV, 312-13.

reportedly told the inhabitants of Falmouth he had orders to burn all towns between Boston and Halifax and he expected that his compatriots had put New York to the torch.[28]

Two actions of the New York Provincial Congress reflected the impact of this disconcerting news. On November 2 it rejected a request of the Continental Congress to appropriate the shirts, blankets, and sheets in the King's stores. Since some persons had carted them to the provincial commissary's house without the provincial organ's authority, the New Yorkers declared that they had ordered them returned because they feared retaliation by the warships. The next day the provincial body disposed of another delicate matter, which related to Westchester. Whigs of Rye and Mamaroneck, writing to New York in alarm, had charged the Tories with plotting to seize a number of leading committeemen and to put them aboard a British tender for transport to Boston. Although the Provincial Congress had provided by its resolutions of September 1 for the arrest, trial, and imprisonment of dangerous opponents by the district and county committees or by itself, it turned its back now on its former directive and voted to instruct the Westchester County committee to investigate the affair. If the plot were real, then the committee would furnish protection to those threatened. The Provincial Congress recommended that any culprits taken be handed over to the civil magistrates for prosecution. This last proposition proved too weak not only for Isaac Sears but also for John Thomas, Jr., Dr. Robert Graham of Westchester, and Melancton Smith of Dutchess, all of whom dissented.[29] By November 4 so many representatives had absented themselves that the Provincial Congress ceased functioning without formal adjournment. McDougall complained to Schuyler that this hasty dissolution endangered

---

28 *Jour. Prov. Cong.*, I, 191.
29 *Ibid.*, I, 190, 192-4.

the colony since Provincial Congress had not established a committee of safety.[30]

Tory comment not only accurately reported this vacillation but also revealed one of its sources. V. P. Ashfield, a Tory merchant, noting the influence of property on the political situation, advised Isaac Wilkins that "those of prosperity are afraid of their estates, and are coming about fast. They say they have gone too far."[31] Jacob Walton, another Tory, spoke of the leaders' "growing very timid," and added significantly, "but now they have raised the devil amongst them they do not know how to lay him."[32]

The Second Provincial Congress, which assembled in December, was in the eyes of contemporaries just as timid as its predecessors. Hughes wrote Sam Adams that "the people [are] constrained, disappointed and discouraged here by the timidity or treachery of their leaders."[33] A writer in the *New York Journal* berated the cowardly, the do-nothings, and called for "activity, vigilance and resolution."[34] The hesitancy of some Whigs led them to urge Holt not to reprint Thomas Paine's *Common Sense*. In describing this incident Hughes wrote:

"Another anecdote I must trouble you with, is, that Col. McDougall waited on Mr. Holt and desired that he would not reprint 'Common Sense'; the people's minds not being prepared for such a chance &c. Somebody else, I forget who, waited on him for the same purpose. The contrary is so much the case, that the people are constantly treading on their leaders heels, and, in a hundred

---

30 McDougall to Schuyler, November 14, 1775, McDougall Papers, NYHS and Schuyler Papers, NYPL.

31 Ashfield to Wilkins, November 4, 1775, *Cal. H. O. Papers*, p. 482. See also the similar comments of John Cruger to Henry Cruger, November 1, 1775 and Harris Cruger to Henry Cruger, November 3, 1775, *ibid.*, pp. 479, 481.

32 Partially quoted in Becker, *The History of Political Parties*, p. 226, n. 205; *Cal. H. O. Papers*, p. 478.

33 Hughes to Adams, December 19, 1775, same to same, January 8, 1776, Samuel Adams Papers, NYPL.

34 "The Monitor", No. 7, *N.Y.J.*, December 21, 1775.

cases, have taken the lead of them. But his patrons don't approve of it, and he must beat time with them. Phil [Livingston] says it was written by some Tory &c. However, let them say and do what they please, the people are determined to read and think for themselves. It is certain, that there never was any thing published here within these thirty years, or since I have been in this place, that has been more universally approved and admired."[35]

None of the foregoing events came as a response to an upsurge of Tory sentiment among the people; rather, they reveal the working of the powerful emotion of self-preservation.

At first glance the polling for the Second Provincial Congress and the laggardness of the deputies in assembling for its opening seem to lend credence to the idea of a royalist reaction, but a closer scrutiny will disclose the fallacy of this view.[36] One author pointed out that the people went to the polls in only nine of the fourteen counties, that, of the nine, in Orange only one precinct voted, and that in Tryon a newly chosen deputy resigned and his successor did not appear until February.[37] Therefore, the people in only seven counties supported the Second Provincial Congress.

However, in Orange County factionalism may have complicated the situation. Although two precincts had voted on November 7, Goshen precinct complained that the county committee, "through some unhappy mistake," had failed to notify the people of the election. Goshen hastened to rectify the omission, leaving Orange Town as the only precinct in which no balloting had taken place. The two precincts of Orange Town and Haverstraw had a joint precinct committee, but Haverstraw chose delegates November 7, whereas Orange Town did not. The freeholders and tenants held

35 Hughes to Samuel and John Adams, February 4, 1776 [?], Samuel Adams Papers, NYPL. John Anderson, publisher of a new gazette, the *Constitutional Gazette*, reprinted *Common Sense* in pamphlet form.
36 Becker, *The History of Political Parties*, pp. 229-38.
37 *Ibid.*

several meetings in Orange Town prior to election day, but on the vital day, owing to "some misapprehension" as the precinct chairman said, no polling occurred. Two days later, November 9, Chairman Thomas Outwater of Orange Town entreated the Provincial Congress to set aside another day for the precinct to vote, but that body did not read the letter until December 1; the delay did not wholly lie with the township. When Orange Town cast its ballots December 7, completing the precinct voting, the whole county, therefore, had taken part in the electoral process.[38]

The Whigs seem to have organized the election in Tryon as well as in New York and Albany. The county committee notified each district of the impending election but confined the vote to freeholders.[39] Although the electors chose two deputies, one, Isaac Paris, resigned shortly after to assume the chairmanship of the county committee. On November 25 the county committee selected William Wills to replace Paris and dispatched him immediately to New York. Wills's failure to arrive in the city became the subject of correspondence between the Provincial Congress and the county committee. The committee expressed its astonishment at Wills's dereliction, mentioning that it had information that Wills had departed as instructed. Furthermore, the committee did not know what had happened to him. The delinquent delegate appeared at the Provincial Congress two months later.[40] Whatever reason caused the delay, the promptness with which the committee held the election and the alacrity with which it picked Paris's successor refute the idea of any cooling toward the revolutionary cause. It may be that this incident illustrates the difficulties inherent

[38] *Jour. Prov. Cong.,* I, 213, 214, 225, II, 95; Force, *American Archives,* 4th ser., III, 1762, IV, 385, 399, 402.
[39] The First Provincial Congress had extended the suffrage to tenants having realty assessed at £80. Becker, *The History of Political Parties,* p. 227.
[40] Samuel L. Frey, ed., *The Minute Book of the Committee of Safety of Tryon County* (New York, 1905), pp. 89-90; *Jour. Prov. Cong.,* I, 212, 213, 293, II, 142; Force, *American Archives,* 4th ser., IV, 400.

in operating a revolutionary organization in the isolated rural areas of the province.

Of the five counties (Richmond, Queens, Cumberland, Charlotte, and Gloucester) in which the people supposedly did not elect deputies,[41] the situation in the last three was a compound of communication difficulties, factionalism, and the Vermont controversy between New York and New Hampshire.[42] Through some miscarriage of the correspondence the Cumberland committee did not receive the Provincial Congress's notice of election nor did it hear of it from its delegate in New York. The first intimation of it came through the *New-York Journal* of October 19, which printed the text of the congressional resolution. Some of the committeemen desired to hold the election on the newspaper's authority, but most wished to have official word. When they wrote the Provincial Congress for advice, they affirmed the steadfastness of the county: "the people in general among us, want to choose new members; and are always ready to adhere strictly to the resolves of . . . Congress. . . ." Since the Provincial Congress had already adjourned, Cumberland waited in vain for a reply. Finally, the committee, acting on its own authority, appointed two delegates.[43]

---

41 Becker, *The History of Political Parties*, pp. 234, 236-37, treats this occurrence in confusing fashion. The delegates in New York dispatched the letter of December 1, which posed the drastic consequences of a congressional collapse, to three counties (Tryon, Cumberland, and Charlotte), not to six. Although the letter writers could not have known it, their warning was unnecessary. As the material on the preceding and subsequent pages shows, the people of these counties did not deliberately drag their feet. The letter did not produce the delegates from these three counties as Becker contends. Furthermore, the arrival of Dr. John Williams from Charlotte on February 13, 1776, reduced the number of unrepresented counties to two, Gloucester and Queens, not three. *Jour. Prov. Cong.*, I, 199, 297.

42 For the complexities of the dispute between New York and New Hampshire over the "Grants" (Vermont) see Chilton Williamson, *Vermont in Quandary: 1763-1825* (Montpelier, 1949), chaps. ii-v.

43 Writing to Provincial Congress at the beginning of February, 1776, the committee declared that the people were "heartily disposed" to American liberty. Force, *American Archives*, 4th ser., IV, 426n.; *Jour. Prov. Cong.*, I, 331, II, 99. Factionalism reared its head in matters relating to the organization of the militia and the choice of militia officers. Force, *American Archives*, 4th ser., IV, 309; *Cal. Hist. Mss.*, I, 195-98, 204.

Similar delays occurred in Charlotte and Gloucester. Despite the friction with Yankee settlers over land rights, Charlotte in an election on January 25, 1776, chose two representatives for the Provincial Congress.[44] Although Gloucester had established district and county committees by July, 1775, and had chosen a deputy to the First Provincial Congress, the fear of an attack from Canada deterred Congressman Bayley from attending. Undeterred by the uncertainty of communication with New York, the county committee took the initiative in circulating the Continental Association, which everyone signed. Furthermore, Bayley complained in October that notwithstanding the silence from the Provincial Congress, the people had commenced the organization of their militia, using the form suggested by the Continental Congress. Under the illusion that the First Provincial Congress was still sitting, Bayley promised to attend that winter, "if health permit." In view of this isolation, it is not surprising that the county seems not to have held an election for the Second Provincial Congress; probably the people did not hear of it until late in the spring. The wonder is that the county created an effective Whig organization.[45]

Kings County may, or may not, have held an election. Eight days after the opening of the Second Provincial Congress, the members present, lacking a quorum, wrote a letter to the "members chosen to represent Kings County," pressing them to attend. The next day, November 23, a Kings deputy appeared, but when deliberations began on December 6, only one Kings member attended. Although the house read and formally recorded all election certificates, they did not mention Kings County. Moreover, even though Orange could

---

44 *Jour. Prov. Cong.*, I, 297. On the land dispute and factionalism see Duer to Peter V. B. Livingston, June 2, 1775, *ibid.*, I, 71-72 and Judge R. R. Livingston to R. R. Livingston, Jr., May 18, 1775, Livingston, *Revolutionary Letters of Importance*, No. 44.

45 John Taplin to P. V. B. Livingston, July 15, 1775, Jacob Bayley to Provincial Congress, October 20, 1775, *Jour. Prov. Cong.*, I, 95, II, 96.

claim only one delegate from Goshen precinct, the house seated him, but with the provision that he have no vote until his county had a quorum. The meticulous action in relation to Orange renders the silence on Kings even more puzzling. When a second Kings representative arrived in the city on December 8, the county cast its vote in the first formal division entered in the *Journal,* but the official record does not refer to the seating of the delegation nor to receipt of its election certificate. The reference of the Provincial Congress's letter of November 22 does seem to indicate that the county did have an election, but there is no explanation for the omission in the *Journal.* Possibly it was the result of clerical oversight. For example, although William Smith's memoirs contain a brief summary of Thomas Smith's aecount of the proceedings of the afternoon of December 13, 1775, the *Journal* does not record Thomas Smith as present.[46]

Of the fourteen counties, then, only two (Richmond and Queens) refused to choose deputies, and since they had always been strongholds of Tory sentiment, their refusal did not represent any shift in political loyalty. No doubt the equivocation of the Provincial Congress in regard to the Tories during the preceding months had fatally affected the weak Whig organization in both counties. Nevertheless, the action of two Tory counties cannot be construed as evidence of a general loyalist reaction. McDougall's explanation of the Provincial Congress's predicament largely confirms the foregoing: "This [bare quorum] is owing to the tardiness of the Deputies of the New Counties [Tryon, Charlotte, Cumberland, and Gloucester], who are not come down. And to the machinations of the Tories, who have so wrought on the Fears and Jealousies of the Counties of Richmond and Queens, that the Former has not chosen any deputies: and the Latter has Voted against any being Sent. . . ."[47]

---

46 *Ibid.,* I, 198, 199, 205-6, 207-8.

Those who see evidence of a rising loyalist tide also point to the circumstances surrounding the complicated Tory stratagem of having the Provincial Congress approve a meeting of the general assembly. The irresolution of the Whigs in the fall of 1775 cost them the political initiative and exposed them to the possibility of a major political defeat. Perspicacious William Smith evolved a two-pronged maneuver which ostensibly aimed at conciliatory negotiations with Britain but which substantially sought to break the continental union and to reestablish the government's control over New York. The first step envisaged instructions by the Provincial Congress to the New York representatives at the Continental Congress to move new conciliatory proposals. In preparing these proposals for presentation to the Provincial Congress, Smith sought to attract enough moderate and conservative votes to secure the adoption of the recommendations by the New Yorkers, but he also sought to insure either their rejection by the Continental Congress or New York's freedom of action. The result of approval or disapproval by the "grand Congress" would be a meeting of the New York provincial assembly to debate Lord North's motion of February 20. Smith cannily incorporated a provision which he had suggested in June to the First Provincial Congress, to have the Continental Congress initiate negotiations.[48]

---

47 McDougall to Schuyler, December 7, 1775, McDougall Papers, NYHS. McDougall's reference to machinations and fears may not have been imaginary. A letter to the *New York Journal* early in the year had described the tactics used by the Tories to prevent the formation of a Whig committee in Jamaica. The Tories circulated a statement to which they solicited signatures, opposing the election of the committee. "A Lover of Liberty" charged that the Tories told people the proposed committee would be authorized to break open their houses in search of tea, that the committee would break their molasses jugs, that if they did not sign the statement, they would be adjudged enemies to the King and might be hanged. *N.Y.J.*, February 9, 1775.

Even after the crushing defeat of the Queens Whigs in the election of November, 1775, printer John Holt still insisted that the Tories did not number one-third of the Queens population, that those who voted for them were "dependant upon, or under the influence" of their social superiors. *Ibid.*, December 28, 1775.

Smith's suggestion of June had centered on the formation of a permanent continental congress to apportion the colonies' shares of funds requisitioned by Great Britain. Elaborating on this idea now, he proposed that Britain consider such monies as a gift, that Parliament account for their expenditure for national defense, and that Parliament also report on the expenditure of the funds which came from the regulation of commerce. While the colonies sustained the costs of civil government, no official of the province might receive "any other pension or provision." Smith recommended as immediate steps that the Continental Congress urge that all the colonial assemblies convene to petition the crown and Parliament and avoid "as much as possible everything that tends to irritate or offend in asserting the essential Rights and Privileges of His Majesty's American Subjects" and that it declare what parts of the parliamentary resolution of February 20 it would accept.[49] Once the disputants resolved the question of taxation, Congress would rescind the Continental Association and Parliament would

---

[48] Dorothy R. Dillon, *The New York Triumvirate: A Study of the Legal and Political Careers of William Livingston, John Morin Scott, William Smith, Jr.* (New York, 1949), pp. 139-40. The June instructions to the New York delegates included: repeal of the obnoxious legislation; limitation of colonial assemblies to three years; Parliament's surrender of its right to interfere in colonial religious affairs; complete internal colonial autonomy subject to the crown's veto; all duties raised by regulation of trade to be paid to the colonies; all funds to be raised for defense to be voted by a continental congress. The deputies from New York never presented the plan. Becker, *The History of Political Parties*, pp. 214-15; Sabine, *Memoirs of William Smith*, pp. 224-25, 228b.

Smith formally described his purpose to Tryon after these events had occurred: "I confess that I flattered myself with hopes that this Province might have been induced by Your advice to set an example to the rest, for a return from their wanderings in that wide field of discontent opened by the Continental Congress in 1774." O'Callaghan, *Documents, Colonial, New York*, VIII, 653.

[49] Since the Continental Congress had rebuffed Lord North's proposition in July and had learned in November of the King's refusal to receive their Olive Branch petition, it was highly improbable that they would consider another petition. Inasmuch as Smith's ideas represented a retreat from Congress's statement of July 31, the likelihood of a cordial reception for them was extremely remote. Burnett, *The Continental Congress*, pp. 95-97; Worthington C. Ford and Gaillard Hunt, eds., *Journals of the Continental Congress* (34 vols.; Washington, D.C., 1904-1937), II, 224-27.

pass a general act of "oblivion and indemnity." The colonists
would express their readiness "to place an intire confidence
in parliament" for the redress of their other grievances. The
last provision of the plan revealed Smith's major intent, for
it reserved to each colony the liberty to pursue any "measure
. . . that may facilitate the designed Reconciliation not inconsistent with the Plan of Contract to be concerted and recommended to them by the Continental Congress." Since the
sole power and authority of the Continental Congress would
consist of matters of taxation, New York would have a free
hand to make her own peace with the ministry.[50]

If the Continental Congress defeated a New York motion
on conciliation, Smith might plausibly appeal to the Whigs
to call for a meeting of the provincial legislature. The assembly would consider Lord North's motion.[51] An independent
memorial from the colony on this matter after its rejection
by the Continental Congress would stir up dissension among
the colonies, discredit the Provincial Congress, and open the
door to restoration of the governor's authority. Smith's plan
owed its inspiration to a letter from delegate John Alsop,

---

[50] Smith, Memoirs, V, November 30, 1775; Sabine, *Memoirs of William
Smith*, pp. 244-47. Smith admitted indirectly that this was the case when his
plan failed. Upon learning that the Provincial Congress had repudiated
any separate negotiation, Smith wrote: "for it was resolved that the latter
[i.e., Continental Congress] only should declare upon all terms of Reconciliation & thus the former [i.e., Provincial Congress] became meer executive
Instruments." Smith, Memoirs, V, December 14, 1775.

[51] Smith's sincerity in advocating another petition by the assembly is a
moot point in view of the preceding events. It will be recalled that the
administration's supporters had made a great deal of noise over their decent
and constitutional appeal to the King and Parliament in the spring, practically acting upon the unofficial invitation of the ministry. The refusal of
the British, therefore, even to receive the assembly's petitions came as a
sharp slap in the face not only to the Tories but also to the conservative and
moderate Whigs. On what basis did Smith expect a different reaction now?
Lord North's resolution did not offer negotiation; it required submission on
specific terms. Moreover, by December the whole atmosphere had altered.
In August the King had proclaimed the Americans to be in rebellion. The
succeeding months had witnessed the rejection of the Olive Branch petition
and the acceleration of measures designed to crush the rebellion by arms.
Since Smith possessed acute political perception, it is difficult not to conclude
that the petition was secondary to the aim of reasserting the government's
authority. On the moderate attitude, see Jay to McDougall, December 8,
1775, McDougall Papers, NYHS.

conservative and future loyalist, which suggested that the New York Provincial Congress instruct its representatives in Philadelphia to introduce pacificatory measures.[52]

The arrival of Alsop's letter presented William Smith with his opportunity. Smith and his brother Thomas, a member of the Provincial Congress, had striven for some time without notable success to persuade John Morin Scott to moderate his views. When Scott informed Thomas Smith of the receipt of Alsop's letter, Deputy Smith exhorted him to move at the opening session of the Second Provincial Congress for new instructions for the Philadelphia delegation. Scott consented conditionally, insisting that Smith prepare the draft. William Smith, however, composed the resolves which Thomas Smith gave to Scott.[53] Councilor William Smith ran into strong opposition when he broached his plan to Tryon and some of the executive council on December 1. In his memoirs Smith discreetly avoided disclosing the substance of the talk but recorded that the opposition subsided when he placed his formulation on this basis: "Suppose says I it procures a constitutional application to Parliament upon the controverted subjects in a more moderate tone." The "constitutional application," of course, was an assembly petition. Shortly thereafter Smith handed Tryon the draft of a letter to the people in which the Governor intimated his desire of having the assembly examine Lord North's resolution. Dated December 4, Tryon's letter appeared in the newspapers in modified form.[54] The Tories had launched their trial balloon, and William Smith busily guided it.

---

52 Apparently Smith was already thinking along these lines. Under date of November 25 he recorded counseling Tryon to make public his permission to return to England. Smith, Memoirs, V, November 25, 28, 1775; Sabine, *Memoirs of William Smith*, pp. 242, 243.

53 Smith, Memoirs, V, December 1, 1775; Sabine, *Memoirs of William Smith*, p. 243.

54 Smith, Memoirs, V, December 1, 1775; Sabine, *Memoirs of William Smith*, p. 243; *Const. Gaz.*, December 6, 1775. Tryon explained to Smith that he could not use the letter as drafted because he feared the other governors might accuse him of being in league with "the People."

On the one hand, William Smith consolidated opinion among the city magistrates for having another meeting of the colony's assembly, while on the other, his brother sounded out feeling in the Provincial Congress for new instructions to the colony's representatives at Philadelphia. Having obtained a favorable response, Thomas Smith arranged a private meeting of ten members of the Provincial Congress and his brother at Simmons Tavern on December 7.[55] Before attending the meeting, William Smith submitted the draft instructions to Colonel Edmund Fanning, Tryon's son-in-law, who read and approved them. Most of the discussion at the tavern revolved around the terms of the conciliatory proposals. When some members suggested that Alexander McDougall would never consent to the presently constituted provincial assembly's taking up the North resolution, William Smith assured them that the Governor would not insist upon it, but he, nevertheless, argued against the election of a new assembly. Encouraged by the expressions of support, Thomas Smith declared he would introduce the resolutions in the Provincial Congress the next day.[56]

Instead of moving for new instructions to the delegates at the Continental Congress, Thomas Smith presented four resolves to the Provincial Congress: (1) that Gage had begun hostilities without waiting for colonial consideration of Lord North's motion and that New York had borne arms in self-defense; (2) that New York boasts the "most unshaken loyalty," the "warmest attachment" to the crown, and "an ardent desire to maintain the ancient union of the two countries"; (3) that the Provincial Congress "conceive it highly necessary and expedient" for the King to have the

---

55 Smith, Memoirs, V, December 5, 7, 1775. The ten deputies were Nathaniel Woodhull, John Sloss Hobart and Ezra L'Hommedieu of Suffolk, John J. Bleecker, Leonard Gansevoort, Jacob Cuyler, Francis Nicoll, and Robert Van Rensselaer of Albany, John Van Cortlandt of New York, and Gilbert Livingston of Dutchess.
56 *Ibid.*, December 6, 7, 1775.

colony's opinion on the North resolution "in such a way as his Excellency may conceive to be most constitutional" and that the Provincial Congress consider the Governor's letter as "proceeding from an anxious desire for a reestablishment of . . . harmony"; (4) that the Provincial Congress desire Tryon to return to his residence in the city and guarantee his safety.[57] Since these resolves were preliminaries to the instructions, they were presumably intended to create favorable sentiment among the members for conciliation, to lay the basis for convoking the legislature should the Continental Congress reject conciliation, and to reassure the Governor as to the attitude of the Provincial Congress.

Thomas Smith erred seriously when he neglected to assure himself of Scott's support before introducing his resolves.[58] The introductory motion precipitated an acrimonious debate, in the course of which Scott teamed with McDougall and Hobart to oppose Smith. Scott severely castigated Governor Tryon for accusing the people in his December 4 letter of withholding "their allegiance from their sovereign and their obedience" from Parliament. The trio also criticized the assembly and demanded its dissolution.[59] It is likely that the house would have defeated Smith's motion, but the delegates from Albany, Dutchess, and Ulster took refuge in the rules of procedure which enabled them to postpone further debate for five days.[60]

Thomas Smith sought to repair the damage the next day,

---

57 Becker, *The History of Political Parties*, pp. 239-40; *Jour. Prov. Cong.*, I, 210-11.

58 Although Scott was a key figure in the Provincial Congress and had possession of a copy of William Smith's draft, Thomas had not invited him to the consultation at Simmons Tavern. William noted noncommittally that Thomas had not consulted Scott on the introductory motion. Smith, Memoirs, V, December 8, 13, 1775; Sabine, *Memoirs of William Smith*, pp. 252, 253, 256.

59 Smith, Memoirs, V, December 4, 8, 13, 31, 1775; Sabine, *Memoirs of William Smith*, pp. 252, 253, 256.

60 Rule 10 stated: "That no question shall be determined on the day that it is agitated if three counties shall request that it be deferred to the next day." *Jour. Prov. Cong.*, I, 206, 211.

December 9, by presenting a motion to appoint a committee
to draft a letter to the representatives at Philadelphia that
would instruct them on measures to be taken "in this alarming state of our affairs." The general nature of the motion
won unanimous approval and the deputies referred it to a
committee of Scott, Hobart, Smith, Gansevoort, Gilbert
Livingston, and Abraham Brasher.

When the Provincial Congress reopened the debate on
Smith's resolves on December 13, Hobart proposed an amendment to Smith's motion which rebuked the Governor and
placed the responsibility for the crisis on the ministry's
shoulders. The amendment contained five resolves: (1) that
none of the people have renounced their allegiance to the
King or desire independence; (2) that the colonies have
taken up arms to defend their rights and privileges against
"the arbitrary and tyrannical encroachments of His Majesty's
Ministers"; (3) that though "this colony" had recourse to
committees and Provincial Congress to secure redress of their
grievances, the people do not desire to oppose the colonial
legislature but insist upon their right to continued representation therein; (4) that the government's failure to convene the assembly this season has caused uneasiness among
the people; (5) that the Provincial Congress thinks there
is no danger of "insult or interruption" to either of the
branches of the legislature and that it would be extremely
agreeable to the people to have the assembly meet to consider the "present unhappy controversy."[61] The debate on
Hobart's amendment produced heated exchanges. Smith remarked that the first part of the fifth resolution was similar
to his own motion for guaranteeing the Governor's safety,
whereupon Hobart answered that the Provincial Congress
might arrest Tryon without breach of faith. Since Colden

[61] Becker, *The History of Political Parties,* p. 240; *Jour. Prov. Cong.,* I, 212,
217. The committee appointed December 9 to draft the letter to Philadelphia
never reported.

could legally replace the Governor, the Suffolk delegate stated, the legislature could proceed without "interruption." The speaker declared "impudently" that he had drawn the clause in that form to trap the Governor.[62] The vote on the amendment overwhelmed Smith, for only one county, Kings, voted against it and one, Orange, divided. The house then held the amendment for detailed consideration, voting on it paragraph by paragraph. When the voting ended, Smith had won his major point: it would be extremely agreeable to the people to have the assembly sit. On all the other resolves Smith suffered a sharp reverse, and the volleys of invective had so exacerbated tempers that the ultimate fate of the motion remained in doubt.

Indeed the following day's session demonstrated how the struggle over the amendment had fused the radicals, moderates, and most of the conservatives into a determined opposition. This temporarily united group deprived Smith of his partial victory in the previous day's debates. Reflecting this new vigor, Isaac Roosevelt, a conservative from New York City, offered further amendments to the first two resolutions that broadened in harsh tones their scope to include Parliament. His motion charged that the sole sources of the supposed present turbulence were the "oppressive acts" of Parliament, "devised for enslaving His Majesty's liege subjects," and the "hostile attempts of the Ministry to carry those acts into execution." Roosevelt's amendment carried unanimously, for all counties voted for it. John M. Scott and Alexander McDougall opened the assault on the next resolve. When Scott and McDougall finished obliterating and transposing words in the third resolution, they barely left the door ajar for another session of the assembly. They declared that the people do not wish "to disuse . . . the ordinary course

---

[62] Smith, Memoirs, V, December 13, 1775; Sabine, *Memoirs of William Smith*, p. 253. Scott dissociated himself from Hobart's "trap the governor" remarks.

of legislation, but . . . highly esteem their right of being represented in General Assembly." This, too, carried unanimously. Hobart moved that the fourth resolve be expunged; his motion carried with no county dissenting. The fifth resolve met the same fate, although its demise spanned two motions. Haring of Orange, seconded by Sands of New York, proposed to delete the latter half of the fifth, which welcomed a meeting of the legislature. When put to a vote, only Kings opposed it, but Roosevelt recorded his dissent from the New York City ballot. Sands then spoke for the disposal of the rump and only Kings voted against it.[63] Having administered a stinging admonition to the Governor and the Tories, the house proceeded to other business.

The dinner intermission that day must have seen further conversation on the debates because when the Provincial Congress reconvened in the afternoon, the moderates reopened the subject. Scott took the floor to present an additional proposition: "that nothing of a salutary nature can be expected from the separate declaration of the sense of this Colony on the Resolution of the House of Commons on the 20th February last; and that as the motion whereon the scheme was grounded was confessedly framed to disunite the Colonies, it would be highly dangerous and totally inconsistent with the glorious plan of American Union, should this Colony express their separate sense on the above-mentioned supposed conciliatory proposal. . . ." All the counties voted in the affirmative except Orange, which divided.[64] McDougall concluded the business by moving "that this Colony is fully and effectually represented in the Continental Congress for the purpose of expressing the sense of its inhabitants on any overtures for a reconciliation, and that the Continental

---

[63] Becker, *The History of Political Parties*, pp. 240-41; *Jour. Prov. Cong.*, I, 217-18. Although William Smith states that his brother quitted the Provincial Congress in disgust on the fourteenth, the *Journal* does not record him present either the afternoon of December 13 or at any time on December 14.

[64] Becker, *The History of Political Parties*, p. 241; *Jour. Prov. Cong.*, I, 219. Roosevelt, Cuyler, and Hay entered their dissents to their counties' votes.

Congress has fully and dispassionately expressed the sense of the inhabitants of this Colony on the above-mentioned Resolution. . . ." All the counties approved this resolution, but Roosevelt and Cuyler registered their disapproval. When the resolutions passed their third reading on December 15, the conservatives cast their last negative votes. Van Zandt, Roosevelt, and Beekman of New York, Van Derbilt and Covenhoven of Kings, and Cuyler of Albany voted against the fourth and fifth resolutions and opposed the publication of any of them.[65]

William Smith officially attributed the defeat of his proposals to the machinations of Scott, McDougall, and Hobart who, seeing "a spirit of moderation would be inauspicious to their private aims, of gaining seats in the new Assembly, and" who, "by working upon the general jealousies of the main Body, and the ambitions of some members who had ends similar to their own," defeated the resolves.[66] In his private notes Smith ascribed the defeat to the arrival of news from Philadelphia and Canada on the evening of December 8. From Philadelphia had come the Continental Congress's acerbic response to the royal proclamation on rebellion, a response denying that the Americans were rebels and opposing the "exercise of unconstitutional powers, to which neither the Crown nor Parliament were ever entitled."[67] The reports from Canada spoke of further military successes after the fall of Montreal.[68] Although the news of these events may have stiffened the opposition, as Smith thought, the information arrived in New York after intemperate argument had already occurred in the Provincial Congress.

There is, however, another relevant factor in this affair

---

[65] *Jour. Prov. Cong.*, I, 219 and 220. See the comments of McDougall to Jay, December 14, 18, 1775, Jay Papers, CUL and Jay to McDougall, December 8, 1775, McDougall Papers, NYHS.

[66] Smith to Tryon, December 17, 1775, O'Callaghan, *Documents, Colonial, New York*, VIII, 653.

[67] Quoted in Burnett, *The Continental Congress*, p. 117.

[68] Smith, Memoirs, V, December 13, 1775; Sabine, *Memoirs of William Smith*, p. 253.

which Smith glossed over in his letter to Tryon. He referred
to his brother's resolutions as "incautiously framed," and a
comparison of them with Tryon's letter to the people will
demonstrate the truth of this understatement. Although the
Governor had expressed the wish to have the people's opinion
of the North resolution and to have peace, he had concluded
his letter with the implication that the Whigs had indulged
in treason. In this context Thomas Smith's propositions
possibly evoked the image of the dangling halter in the minds
of some Whigs.

Thomas Smith phrased his motion in more than conciliatory language. His first resolution ignored the North policies
of 1773-1775 as the cause of the American unrest and sought
to create the impression that Gage's expedition was the
origin of the troubles. If this view were correct, what would
Smith say about those who advocated the formation of a
committee and a provincial congress before April, 1775?
Would the government treat them as restless and turbulent
characters? The second resolution conceded that the conduct
of some "would countenance a charge of withholding their
allegiance from their Sovereign," although it added, "it must
be attributed to an apprehension that all protection was
withdrawn from them." Nevertheless, the resolve did lend
color to Tryon's accusation of treason. The third resolution
praised the Governor's initiative as indicating both his affec-
tion for the people and his "anxious desire for a reestablishment of that harmony that has been so long interrupted by
the misrepresentations and artifices of evil and designing
men."[69] Did these last words refer to the De Lancey faction
or to the moderates and radicals? As phrased, these proposals
seemed to bear the aspect of an invitation to approve Tryon's
judgment of the Whigs. Furthermore, since Scott and Hobart
had either read or heard the gist of William Smith's draft

---

[69] *Ibid.*, p. 252; *Jour. Prov. Cong.*, I, 210-11.

instructions, these unrelated and unexpected resolves must have aroused suspicions as to Thomas and William Smith's objectives. It was not surprising that "Congress was thrown into great heats" and that it rejected the plan.[70]

Although the radical and moderate Whigs might well have congratulated themselves upon their resounding victory on the floor of the Provincial Congress, William Smith was not yet ready to concede the battle. Since the resolutions provided at least indirectly for a meeting of the assembly, Smith counseled Governor Tryon to act upon the hint. Taking into account the congressional diatribes against the prorogued legislature, William Smith advocated the election of a new assembly: "The dissolution will enable men of temper, to testify their disapprobation of the present violence, under a popular and safe cloke form a confederacy to correct and undermine the tyranny erected over the colony, turn the eyes of the multitude to a power that is constitutional, and favor future overtures for the restoration of harmony. . . ."[71] When Tryon put the issues to his council, a majority favored a dissolution.[72] Although the Governor tried to conceal his termination of the legislature, not even informing his council, he failed to deceive the Whigs.[73] They took prompt steps to wage an energetic campaign to insure the election of a Whig assembly.[74]

[70] Smith, *Memoirs*, V, December 13, 1775; Sabine, *Memoirs of William Smith*, p. 253.

[71] Smith to Tryon, December 17, 1775, quoted in Becker, *The History of Political Parties*, p. 241; Smith, *Memoirs*, V, December 17, 1775.

[72] *Ibid.*, V, December 23, 26, 1775. De Lancey, Cruger, and Horsmanden opposed dissolution, at least until the legal life of the assembly had expired. In the face of this opposition the Governor declared he would use his own discretion as to the precise date of dissolution.

[73] Smith records that Tryon had not informed the council of his action on December 30. The secrecy would have hampered the organization of an effective campaign by the Whigs in the rural districts and a small vote would have enhanced the odds of a Tory victory. *Ibid.*, V, December 31, 1775.

[74] Becker, *The History of Political Parties*, p. 242, states the election aroused "little interest," but the Whig activity belies such an interpretation. Robert R. Livingston, expressing his surprise and mystification at the

By means of handbills and the newspapers the Whig propagandists warned the people of the consequences of the election of a corrupt legislature and against Tory guile to divide the colony. "A Citizen," urging vigilance by the people, maintained that the administration had prepared the election as a trap. Avoid the snares, elect independent men of integrity, he concluded. "A Poor Man" wrote that a corrupt assembly would make dangerous concessions to the North ministry and that the people therefore should unite to choose "Good, steady friends" to their liberties. "Philo-Demos" asked the citizens to examine carefully the candidates' principles and warned that secret enemies were worse than avowed opponents.[75]

On another front the provincial Committee of Safety warned the county committees not to be "taken unaware & surprized into an Election without Time to Consult & prepare for it," to hold caucuses of "leading friends to liberty" to choose candidates of "zeal, spirit and integrity," and to spare no "care & pains" to elect them.[76] Desiring to leave as little to chance as possible, the Committee of Safety in a second circular to the counties emphasized the necessity of prompt attendance at the meeting of the Provincial Congress February 1 so that it could "awe a corrupt Assembly."[77]

The election resulted in an overwhelming victory for the Whigs, who won twenty-four seats to four for the Tories.[78]

Governor's action, pressed Philip Schuyler to stand for the assembly. Livingston to Schuyler, January 11, 1776, Livingston Redmond Papers, FDRL.

[75] *To the Freeholders and Freemen of New York* by "A Citizen," December 29, 1775, *To the Citizens of New York* by "A Poor Man," December 30, 1775, *To the Electors of New York* by "Publicola," January 6, 1776, Broadsides, NYPL; "Monitor," No. 10, *N.Y.J.*, January 11, 1776; "Philo-Demos," *Const. Gaz.*, January 6, 1776; Schuyler to McDougall, January 11, 1776, McDougall to Schuyler, January 17, 1776, McDougall Papers, NYHS; Hamilton to Jay, December 31, 1775, Jay Papers, CUL.

[76] *Jour. Prov. Cong.*, I, 236; Committee of Safety to Chairman, Tryon County Committee, January 2, 1776, Schuyler Papers, NYPL; Force, *American Archives*, 4th ser., IV, 1020-21.

[77] Becker, *The History of Political Parties*, p. 242.

In the capital, the Tories had not even put up a slate.[79] Whigs won the two seats in Queens, but the Jersey troops probably had cowed the Tories when they disarmed several hundred in late January.[80] The dampening of Tory ardor in Queens did not affect Richmond where the two leading Tories retained their assembly seats. Similarly, in the Borough of Westchester in the southern part of that county a De Lancey gained the victory, but Whigs captured the two other seats for the county. Although the Whigs won an impressive victory, moderates and conservatives would compose the new assembly and the Tories might sway the Whigs if they pursued a policy of indirection.[81]

Having committed themselves to the election of the new

---

[78] Thirteen of the Whigs were members of the current Provincial Congress. The previous assembly had thirty-one seats, but the newspapers reported the names of only twenty-eight victors. There was no report from Cumberland and only one name from Orange. There was no mention of Charlotte and Gloucester counties.

The four Tories were Oliver De Lancey of Westchester, Seaman and Billop of Richmond, and John Alsop of New York. The Whigs nominated the latter as a conciliatory gesture.

The Whigs were Philip Livingston, Jay, and McDougall of New York, John Leffertse and Covenhoven of Kings, Blackwell and Samuel Townsend of Queens, N. Woodhull and William Smith of Suffolk, John Thomas, Jr., and Lewis Morris of Westchester, Pierre Van Cortlandt of Manor of Cortlandt; P. R. Livingston of Manor of Livingston; R. R. Livingston, Jr. and Dirck Brinckerhoff of Dutchess; Abraham Yates, Jr. and Robert Van Rensselaer of Albany; Abraham Ten Broeck of Manor of Rensselaer; Christopher Yates of Borough of Schenectady; Paris and Moore of Tryon; George Clinton and Charles DeWitt of Ulster; and John Haring of Orange. *N.Y.P.*, February 22, 1776.

The account of the Whigs' victory in New York City triumphantly concluded: "What think ye of our New York Tories now?" *Const. Gaz.*, February 3, 1776.

[79] Becker, *The History of Political Parties*, p. 242. The Whigs had called in the newspapers for a meeting of the freemen and freeholders on January 17 to choose a ticket. It was this meeting that nominated the victors. *Const. Gaz.*, January 17, 1776; Smith, Memoirs, V, February 2 and 3, 1776.

[80] Becker, *The History of Political Parties*, pp. 244-45. When the Tories surrendered their weapons, they took an oath to support the Provincial Congress and not to aid the British. Force, *American Archives*, 4th ser., IV, 858; *N.Y.G.*, January 29, 1776.

[81] The inability of the Tories to win a majority in the assembly under the conditions of restricted suffrage is striking testimony of their loss of influence among the electorate. This is all the more astonishing in the countryside where the great landholders could sway the votes of their lessees.

assembly, the Tories had to make the difficult decision whether they would permit the legislature to convene. Certainly the Tory defeat at the polls had not induced the Governor to prorogue the assembly. What gave Tryon and his council pause was not the election but the state of public opinion. Early in January New York papers carried the text of the King's October speech to Parliament in which he declared his intention of ending the rebellion quickly by the "most decisive exertions."[82] William Smith remarked that the news "greatly inflamed the multitude, upon the certain prospect of a new [military] campaign."[83] When the council met before the election on January 29 to lay plans for the coming legislative session, the members were gloomy concerning the administration's prospects.[84] They divided over the question of how long to postpone the opening of the assembly; one faction favored a month's delay, the other a fortnight. They resolved the difference by agreeing to permit the meeting on February 14 as stipulated in the writs of election, if good news came from Britain to soothe the "popular ferments." Otherwise, the Governor would prorogue the legislature for a month.[85] Not only did expectations of good news from Britain prove illusory, but the threat of war increased with the arrival of General Charles Lee to erect defenses against an expected British assault.[86] Consequently, the council approved the prorogation of the legislature and the assembly never again sat in the colony.

Although the Whig leaders had wavered and hesitated in the latter half of 1775, they had consolidated support among the people for the revolutionary cause and had consolidated the revolutionary organizations throughout the province.

---

82 *Ibid.,* January 8, 1776.
83 Smith, Memoirs, V, January 6, 1776.
84 *Ibid.,* V, January 29, 1776.
85 *Ibid.*
86 Nettels, *George Washington,* pp. 209-13.

The February prorogation of the assembly signaled the end of Tory efforts, without the employment of an army, to regain supremacy in the province. Their defeat within and without the Provincial Congress underlined the fact that they were a minority.

FIVE

The Tide Sets for Independence

THE irresolution of the First and the Second Provincial Congresses often tends to obscure the hardening of the opposition to Britain and the growth of sentiment for independence. Even in the dismal days of November when the First Provincial Congress collapsed, the press carried letters which expressed determined resistance to British measures. "Philo Patriae," lecturing his readers on patriotism, heaped scorn on those who sold their talents to the ministry and on those who drew back in fear.[1] Although "The Monitor" confidently asserted that Britain would weary of fruitless endeavors and ultimately would concede, he also warned his country men that they must prepare to die in defense of their liberties.[2] "An Occasional Remarker" warned against the increasing boldness of the Tories and said that he was prepared to make the final sacrifice in defense of American rights.[3] "A Poor Man" remonstrated with those of the "industrious" poor who favored the government. Contrasting the condition of the American farmer and laborer with his European counterpart, he wrote: "Here, a poor man, can get his bread, and eat it in comfort and peace. There, the greatest part of his earnings are taken from him, to fatten and feed the pride of the rich and lazy; who instead of thanking him for it, only insult and despise him. He hardly dares to say his soul is his own. . . . I would rather die ten thousand deaths, than to see this country enslaved, and ruined by a venal wicked, blundering parliament."[4] When news of Governor Dunmore's depredations in Virginia reached New York, "Minos" proposed that he be tried and hanged for his crimes.[5]

Among those who sought to counteract the effect on public opinion of the Whig leadership's timidity was "The Monitor." When the Tories attempted to beguile the Second Provincial Congress into calling for a meeting of the assembly to act on Lord North's proposition, "The Monitor" wrote a detailed dissection of the offer which exposed its damaging consequences.[6] This same writer drove home sharp attacks on the frightened congressmen and on those who had opposed Britain in 1774 but who now sided with the ministry.[7] In his seventh number "The Monitor" differentiated nicely between timidity and prudence:

When the former qualities prevailed in the conduct of affairs, we see none but weak and irresolute councils, productive of plans and measures, slow in their execution, and insignificant in their consequences. Every proposal, whether trivial or important, is preplexed with endless debates; however obvious its propriety, still it must be examined in every light, must undergo the nicest dissection, and each member of it be viewed with the most scrupulous precision. . . . In a word, nothing wise, provident, manly or decisive is to be expected; a scandalous remissness, imbecility and inaction, characterise the general current of affairs. . . . When the latter ingredients

---

1 *N.Y.J.*, November 2, 1775.
2 *Ibid.*, November 9, 1775.
3 *Ibid.*, November 16, 1775.
4 *Const. Gaz.*, November 25, 1775.
5 *N.Y.J.*, December 7, 1775.
6 "The Monitor," No. 6, *ibid.*, December 14, 1775. He concluded on a note of open hostility: "The resolution in question is at such an infinite distance from anything we can embrace, and is clothed in such a menacing garb, that it clearly evinces the most unfriendly disposition, and claims nothing from us, but the most contemptuous inattention."
7 "The Monitor," Nos. 7 and 8, *ibid.*, December 21, 28, 1775.

preponderate, we see bold designs concerted with becoming resolution, and executed with answerable firmness and success. . . . Deliberation is indulged within proper bounds. . . . Activity and fortitude are the very life of great exploits, and can alone produce security in perilous and stormy times.

As the January, 1776, assembly election campaign approached its climax, "The Monitor" called for the rejection of "those whose conduct has been ambiguous and wavering" and urged the electors to extract a promise from every candidate to espouse legislative reform.[8] He concluded with proposals for triennial assemblies and laws against "every species" of bribery and corruption.

Correspondents defended vigorously the colonial position on the political and constitutional issues of the day. In a special plea "To the Inhabitants of Queen's County, Long Island," "A plain man" reviewed the major irritants in imperial relations. Emphasizing no taxation without representation and quoting Locke on the right to possess property, the writer observed "that representation should accompany taxation is an eternal law of nature, and inseperable from the very idea of property, so that no property can exist without it: whatever is a man's own, no other person can have a right to take from him, without his consent, expressed by himself, or his representative."[9] Although "The Monitor" essayed a comprehensive analysis of the disputes, he devoted more argument to the tax question than to any other single subject.[10] The changing tone of these

<hr>

8 *Ibid.,* January 11, 1776.

9 He specified the other grievances in this order: the prohibition on making steel· the importation of Spanish and Portuguese wines through England; restrictions on the marketing of hats; the prohibition on building plating and slitting mills and tilt hammers; limitations on the marketing of wool and woolen textiles; trial of causes in Admiralty courts. *Const. Gaz.,* November 29, December 2, 6, 1775.

10 *N.Y.J.,* November 23, 30, 1775, January 4, 18, 1776. There is some ground for suspecting "The Monitor" to be Alexander Hamilton. Professor Broadus Mitchell subscribes to this viewpoint of Hamilton. The known Hamilton pamphlets of this period provide a basis for comparison. The

articles connoted the stiffening of public opinion. Writing in November, the author discerned the intent of the ministry to be the "subjugation" of the colonies to parliamentary supremacy. By January "The Monitor" saw in the government's policies a consistent effort "to impose and rivet the chains of America."[11] Notwithstanding the frequent recurrence of the taxation theme, this author also touched upon home rule and claimed the "exclusive right to regulate our internal police."[12] Moreover, "the power of legislation," he argued, "is so necessary to preserve that of taxation, that the one cannot long exist without the other." These ideas, appearing in November and December, preceded the publication of Paine's *Common Sense* and their appearance suggested that they had obtained considerable currency.

Until September, 1775, the Whigs focused their criticism on the North ministry and Parliament but in that month they broadened their attacks to include the King. The Whigs proclaimed themselves the champions of constitutional monarchy as opposed to Parliament, whom they accused of enacting illegal statutes. Since George III reigned as a constitutional sovereign, he must reject unconstitutional laws. When the King sought to enforce these unlawful statutes, he acted unconstitutionally and in "very iniquitous" fashion. By opposing the royal measures, with force if necessary, the Whigs defended the Hanoverian crown, while the Tories sought to alter the constitutional basis of monarchy and to restore absolutism.[13] "Amicus

---

similarity of style, method of argument, and references to Hume are suggestive. Perhaps most persuasive of all is the similarity of content in "The Monitor" No. 4 on the tea tax and the Hamilton pamphlet, *The Farmer Refuted*.

11 *N.Y.J.*, November 30, 1775, January 18, 1776.

12 *Ibid.*, February 8, 1776.

13 "Obadiah," *ibid.*, September 21, 1775; "Lucius," *Const. Gaz.*, September 27, 1775.

Constitutionis" went so far as to assert that the King had deposed himself constitutionally by his conduct and could not be deemed lawful ruler until he stopped the war and repealed the "cruel" acts against the colonies.[14] Although "The Monitor" wrote in similar vein about King and constitution in his second number, his twelfth production presented powerful reasons for breaking the tie to George III.[15] This last philippic set out to destroy "superstitious veneration for dignified names," but went on to attack the institution of monarchy. "The Monitor" wrote: "the black catalogue of royal malignities would rather stimulate their [i.e., the people's] disgust than feed their admiration. They would discover that the ambition and avarice, the pride, caprice and cruelty of monarchs have been the most fruitful sources of havoc, devastation and ruin among men. They would be sensible, that those attributes of perfection they are wont to ascribe to the British sovereign, as they have no sufficient foundation in his own particular character, are altogether fancies and visions." Appearing fifteen days after Paine's *Common Sense,* this piece by "The Monitor" reflected perhaps growing public sentiment in its disillusionment with monarchy.

Letters opposing surrender to the British continued to appear in the press throughout the spring of 1776. Writers, warning against the "insidious wiles" of the North government, denounced the peace commissioners' mission as an attempt to divide and conquer. One anonymous penman, refusing to accept a British offer to repeal the "detestable" acts, questioned the faith of the ministry. He recalled to his readers the fate of those Dutch provinces in the sixteenth century that had submitted to the Spanish. Having disarmed the rebels, the Duke of Alva hanged "upwards of 15,000 of their principal gentlemen."[16]

---

14 *N.Y.J.,* October 19, 1775.
15 *Ibid.,* November 23, 1775, January 25, 1776.

While the newspapers reflected one facet of revolutionary thought, they were not the only guides. Other observers testified more directly to the popular enthusiasm for the American cause. In spite of the backwardness of the Whig leaders in fortifying the port against the probable British attack, William Thompson could still write: "I am happy to find the Inhabitants of the place so far exceed the character I had of them. I never knew people so willing to assist in every military manoevre, and every thing that can be set on foot for the defence of the City is carried on with the greatest attention and spirit."[17] Eliphalet Dyer attributed "pannick" to "Mr Duane &c &c," but praised Isaac Sears for his role in the defensive preparations.[18] So confident was Jay of the popular strength of the revolutionary party throughout the colony that he exhorted McDougall to have the Provincial Congress levy taxes.[19]

During the first four months of 1776 the thinking of the moderate Whigs moved perceptibly closer to that of the radicals. Men like Jay and Robert R. Livingston, driven by the current of events, slowly shifted position.[20] Jay ac-

---

16 "An Observer" and "The Monitor" No. 15, February 22, 1776, anon. on the British commissioners, *ibid.*, April 25, 1776; anon. on arbitrary rule and laying down arms, *Const. Gaz.*, February 24, 28, 1776; "American Patriot" and anon. on British commissioners, *N.Y.P.*, April 11, 25, 1776; "H.Y.," *N.Y.G.*, April 29, 1776; "Americanus," March 30, 1776, Peter Force, ed., *American Archives* (9 vols.; Washington, D.C., 1837-1853), 4th ser., V, 548.

17 Thompson to Schuyler, March 28, 1776, Miscellaneous Papers: Philip Schuyler, NYPL. For similar comments, see General Charles Lee to Washington, February 14, 1776, quoted in Curtis P. Nettels, *George Washington and American Independence* (Boston, 1951), pp. 211-12; R. H. Lee to General Charles Lee, April 1, 1776, *Papers of Charles Lee*, New-York Historical Society *Collections,* IV (New York, 1871), 367-68; Hugh Hughes to Samuel and John Adams, February 4, 1776, Samuel Adams Papers, NYPL.

18 "I trust that City is now pretty well secured & can assure you it is much owing to that crazy Capt Sears which Y——k Delegates would affect to call him." Dyer to Samuel Adams, February 27, 1776, *ibid.*

19 Jay to McDougall, March 27, 1776, McDougall Papers, NYHS.

20 Jay placed himself among the moderate group which included McDougall. He frowned on those who "observe no medium and are either all Flame or all Frost." *Ibid.*

Tryon's March proclamation, offering forgiveness to the penitent and promising armed support for the Tories, did nothing to reverse the trend:

knowledged that "from the present Appearance of Things it
is natural to suppose that the Sword must decide the Controversy—and with a View to that object our Measures
should in a great Degree be taken."[21] Livingston predicted
"that another year of war and devastation will confirm me a
republican. . . ."[22] While accepting the inevitability of war,
the moderates were also disturbed by the lack of "good and
well ordered Governments" to counteract "that Anarchy
which already too much prevails."[23] Hugh Hughes had
prodded Jay and McDougall in January on the "absolute
necessity . . . for adopting some rational system of government" but it took three months for the latter to accept that
necessity.[24] The moderates' and conservatives' reaction to
Lord North's plan to send commissioners to negotiate with
the colonies delineated the growing divergence in their
views. Jay doubted that they would have any effective power
to treat and therefore acquiesced in the requirement of more
vigorous armed resistance." Conservative James Duane,
who disagreed with Jay, wrote Livingston: "I am unwilling
that while Commissioners are daily looked for, we should

"It is generally a matter of laughter and surprize, that he could do anything so weak and ill-judged. The friends of government were provoked at
being so distinguished, and the friends to liberty hung him in effigy and
printed a dying speech for him." Quoted in Alexander C. Flick, *Loyalism
in New York During the American Revolution* (New York, 1901), p. 51
from "a Letter from New York," April 12, 1776, *The Remembrancer*, p. 86.
  21 Jay to McDougall, April 11, 1776, McDougall Papers, NYHS.
  22 Livingston to Duane, February 16, 1776, Bancroft Transcripts: Livingston Papers, NYPL. A month previously he had written Schuyler, "it is
time we sh'd act decisively, heaven & our own vigor must support us."
January 16, 1776, Philip Schuyler Papers, NYPL.
  23 Jay to McDougall, April 11, 1776, McDougall Papers, NYHS. See also
McDougall to Schuyler, March 7, 1776, Schuyler to McDougall, March 14,
1776, *ibid.*
  24 Hughes to Samuel Adams, January 8, 1776, Samuel Adams Papers,
NYPL.
  25 Jay to McDougall, April 11, 1776, McDougall Papers, NYHS. See also
William Floyd to John McKesson, May 9, 1776, Force, *American Archives*,
4th ser., V, 395; speech of Gouverneur Morris, May 24, 1776, Gouverneur
Morris Papers, CUL and Jared Sparks, *Life of Gouverneur Morris with
Selections from His Correspondence and Miscellaneous Papers* (3 vols.;
Boston, 1832), I, 106-7.

by any irrevocable measure tie up our hands, and put it out of our power to terminate this destructive war."[26]

When the election of the Third Provincial Congress in April, 1776, is contrasted with the election of the Second Provincial Congress in November, 1775, the scope of the changing political mood becomes readily apparent. As compared with 80 delegates chosen to the Second Provincial Congress, the people sent 101 to the Third.[27] Most of the counties had fully established a network of district committees in which each district had a proportionate share of the county congressional representation.[28] The numerical increase, therefore, indicated in part widespread voting within the districts.[29] In part also it signified the participation for the first time of all fourteen counties in the electoral process; Queens and Gloucester counties had not been represented in the Second Provincial Congress. The sterner treatment of the Queens Tories in January and February enabled the Whigs there to put together a county committee and several district committees.[30] Finally, even though all the congressmen did not attend the session, enough did so to satisfy the quorum needs; the lack of a quorum had operated as a constant obstacle in the work of the Second Provincial Congress.[31] All of these factors pointed toward a Third Provincial Congress that would be amenable to the adoption of firmer policies when it convened in May. However, this lay in the future.

Meanwhile, the Second Provincial Congress and its Com-

---

26 Duane to R. R. Livingston, March 20, 1776, Bancroft Transcripts: Livingston Papers, NYPL.

27 Carl L. Becker, *The History of Political Parties in the Province of New York, 1760-1776* (Madison, 1909), pp. 232, 238, places the deputies for ten counties at 76, but two other counties chose a total of 4 men. See above p. 114.

28 Queens and Richmond lacked committees for most districts.

29 Becker, *The History of Political Parties,* p. 258.

30 *Ibid.,* p. 259, n. 33; Provincial Congress to Queens County Committee, March 7, 1776, *Jour. Prov. Cong.,* I, 345.

31 Becker, *The History of Political Parties,* p. 260.

mittee of Safety pursued a general course of temporization, although they did adopt some aggressive measures. Alarmed by General Lee's endeavors to interdict communication with Governor Tryon and the men-of-war, the Provincial Congress did consent reluctantly to a stricter regulation of the traffic after March 8. Resumption of the intercourse depended upon British nonmolestation of the city's supplies coming from Jersey.[32] Furthermore, the Committee of Safety strove to check on the quantities of supplies delivered to the British vessels in order to prevent them from accumulating reserve stores.[33] Taking advantage of congressional hesitancy, Tryon and the naval officers planned a partial blockade of the port. They fitted out two armed ships to prey on merchantmen that plied the waters between the Delaware River and Sandy Hook and to stop shipping from sailing out of the harbor. The congressional reaction to this challenge mingled new resoluteness with past fear. The Provincial Congress ordered the arming of a vessel to protect the trade lanes to Philadelphia, but it did not protest the interference with departures.[34]

When Washington's army commenced its transfer to New York in April, the Committee of Safety acknowledged that intercourse with the enemy would have to cease. The committee told the New Jersey Provincial Congress: "As the ships of war in our harbour are daily committing acts of piracy and depredation on vessels and property of the inhabitants of the United Colonies, we apprehend orders will soon issue for stopping all farther supplies to them." It would not assume, however, the responsibility of putting the ships under a ban even though it charged the British with bad faith. The committee preferred to await the com-

---

32 *Ibid.*, p. 249. For the details see *Jour. Prov. Cong.*, I, 346.
33 *Ibid.*, I, 372.
34 The New Yorkers asked the Continental Congress to provide a ship to patrol the southern half of the threatened area while they guarded the northern sector. *Ibid.*, I, 354, 380.

mander-in-chief's orders. When Washington in mid-April prohibited the communication between ships and shore, the committee complied willingly.[35]

Although the Continental Congress had authorized the colony to raise four regiments for the Continental Army in anticipation of a British attack upon the city, the Second Provincial Congress had neglected the task. Since the Continental Congress had not assigned these troops to the invasion of Canada, Schuyler had left them under the command of New York. When Washington arrived, a delicate question of jurisdiction arose. The General's application for information on the status of the units not only posed the problem of their command but also embarrassed the Committee of Safety, since it revealed its negligence in recruiting and arming the units. The committee admitted Washington's prior authority and spurred the campaign to enlist and equip the troops.[36]

The need for the formation of a general antiloyalist policy grew in urgency as hostilities spread. Neglect of the loyalists would permit the growth of a party that might wreck the revolutionary organization. The Provincial Congress's request in December, 1775, for continental troops to disarm the Tories in Tryon, Queens, and Richmond constituted a tacit admission of the critical nature of the problem. An armed confrontation with the Tories was a task from which the moderates and conservatives shrank. On the other hand, if the Whigs adopted a stern policy of

---

[35] Becker, *The History of Political Parties*, p. 249; Nettels, *George Washington*, pp. 284-85; Committee of Safety to New Jersey Provincial Congress, April 2, 1776, *Jour. Prov. Cong.*, I, 397.

[36] Nettels, *George Washington*, pp. 285-87; *Jour. Prov. Cong.*, I, 420-21. Washington also prodded the committee on the organization of the militia for emergency mobilization. He asked the committee how long it would take to gather 2,500 men in a "sudden emergency" and pressed them to cooperate with him in planning for such an eventuality. The committee's state of mind may be seen in its comment that "we do not at present foresee that emergency." Conceding the possibility of the contingency, however, the committee readily set to work to fabricate the needed machinery. *Ibid.*, I, 419-20.

imprisoning those suspected of hostile intentions, they would take another long stride down the road to revolution. When in March the Continental Congress passed a resolution to disarm all nonassociators, it thrust upon the New York Whigs the necessity of a decision on the Tory problem. The Committee of Safety first learned of Congress's action when General Lord Stirling passed on to it a copy of the congressional resolve. Having read and filed the copy, the committee received its official transcript from the Congress two days later. For five days nothing happened; then on March 26 the Committee of Safety appointed a committee "to report a plan" to give effect to the Continental Congress's decision. Having taken the first step, the committee the following day presented its proposal which the Committee of Safety unanimously approved. The resolution ordered the local committee "forthwith" to disarm all known "disaffected" persons and those who refused to sign an association which pledged them to defend the colonies by arms. If it is true that the committee advocated the use of "prudence and moderation," it is also true that it gave the district committees a blank check to call out the militia and minutemen to assist them in carrying out the resolution. The Committee of Safety required an inventory of the arms gathered, since it contemplated the equipping of four new regiments with them.[37]

Although a month later the Committee of Safety complained to the county committees about their failure to forward the arms inventories, the local organizations did carry out their instructions.[38] For example, Washington

---

[37] *Ibid.*, I, 375, 379, 386, 389.
[38] Becker, *The History of Political Parties*, p. 262, interprets this letter as evidence that "the order had scarcely been attended to at all." However, comments in the *Journal* and other evidence indicate that arms had been seized in New York City, Queens, Dutchess, Ulster, Westchester, Suffolk, and Albany. Moreover, the lack of inventories is no proof of committee inaction as the heretofore cited cases show. *Jour. Prov. Cong.*, I, 411, 415, 417, 420; Force, *American Archives*, 4th ser., V, 1469, 1487; J. Sullivan, ed., Minutes of the Albany Committee of Correspondence, *1775-1779 and Minutes*

acquired some of the guns in Ulster. The uncertainties of the communications system probably affected the committee's plans. The committee had entrusted the Albany County Committee of Correspondence's copy of its March 27 order to member Peter R. Livingston for delivery, but Albany never saw it. Instead the Albany committee, taking the initiative, wrote to New York that it had seen a resolution of the Congress for disarming Tories and solicited instructions on executing it. Meanwhile, Albany had lost more than a month.[39] However halting, this step represented the first consistent effort to lay down a general anti-Tory policy.[40] Beyond this, however, the Second Provincial Congress would not go.

The Provincial Congress moved cautiously in two other Tory matters. The question of confiscation arose in connection with the case of Henry Lloyd of Queens Village, Queens. Lloyd went to Boston to join General Howe, leaving his property in the hands of his nephew, John Lloyd. The Committee of Safety ordered an accurate inventory of all his property. Although the committee entrusted the property's care to John Lloyd, it forbade the nephew to transfer or sell any part of it unless by order of the Provincial Congress. While acting gingerly, the committee had exercised sovereign power in placing limits on the use of the property.[41]

The second matter came to the reconvened Provincial Congress's attention the day before its life expired. A committee recommended the levying of a fine on all male disarmed Tories between the ages of sixteen and fifty. Since

---

of the Schenectady Committee, 1775-1779 (2 vols.; Albany, 1923, 1925), I, 403.

39 Exhorting Albany to carry out the resolution without delay, the committee complained that it "expected" that Livingston had delivered their resolve "long since." *Jour. Prov. Cong.*, I, 424, 425.

40 Becker, *The History of Political Parties*, p. 262 concludes that the Second Provincial Congress did not make "any serious effort to deal with loyalist opposition in a systematic or effective fashion."

41 *Jour. Prov. Cong.*, I, 428-29.

these Tories could not serve now in the militia, the committee proposed to penalize them five shillings for every mustering of the militia. Instead of rejecting the plan outright, the congress voted to refer it to the Third Provincial Congress, which would meet in five days.[42]

Factors outside the colony could precipitate distasteful dilemmas for the New York Provincial Congress notwithstanding its caution. The Continental Congress posed a knotty problem for the New Yorkers when it recommended in May the suppression of the crown's authority and the formation of new governments. However much the provincial body might have preferred to defer consideration of the topic, it could not escape its own constituents.

Since January widespread public debate had occurred over the cognate questions of independence and a new internal government. "Salus Populi" in February declared that in the face of the crisis the people practically had abolished the old forms of government and substituted temporary ones. This fact was a potent argument for more permanent change: "Does not this shew evidently, that the forms we have hitherto lived under are by no means equal to the task of preserving our liberties, and that without such reforms as will enable them to withstand attacks we can never be safe?" Pointing in admiration to Connecticut and Rhode Island which had an elected executive, he wrote: "That form of government alone can give us security which puts all the servants of the public under the power of the people."[43] A handbill in the form of a petition to the Committee of Safety signed by "A Free Citizen" first appeared on the city's streets and then reappeared in one of the news-

---

42 *Ibid.*, I, 440.
43 He warned, "He who has the giving of all places in a government will always be master, if the constitution were in other respects the most perfect in the world." *Const. Gaz.*, February 14, 1776. Another unnamed author urged Connecticut's form as a model. "To the Freeborn Sons of America, in General, and of Connecticut in Particular," *N.Y.P.*, March 21, 1776.

papers. Motivated by fear of military government on the
one hand and the "ungovernable fury of a mob" on the
other, "A Free Citizen" pleaded with the Committee of
Safety to apply to the Continental Congress "for liberty"
to establish a suitable government.[44] An unsigned piece in
May dismissed reconciliation as a "painted dream" and
made the question of government one of timing. Which
would be more advantageous, to draw up a constitution
amidst the confusion of war or to wait until peace is won?
We must choose the former alternative because "there is
nothing so conducive to vigor, expedition, foresight, secrecy,
and everything advantageous in war, as a well regulated
government." Moreover, after we have triumphed over
Britain, if we have no sound government, we may have to
face the twin evils of a Caesar (or Cromwell) or "mobile
frenzy." Read diligently England's history after 1649, he
admonished his readers, so we may not "run the risk of
having our constitution finally determined by the sword."[45]

Moderate opinion in the revolutionary party in April
veered toward the idea, one which radicals had long espoused, of a more stable government. Jay confided to Mc-
Dougall that the colony must look to the establishment of a
firm government and suggested that the Second Provincial
Congress begin to think about the problem. Having committed himself thus far, Jay hastened to remark that the
expectation of British peace commissioners would probably
delay the matter of a constitution.[46] Citing the drafting of
governments in the Carolinas, William Floyd expected
New York to take similar action soon.[47] Writing to Jay
from Philadelphia in May, R. R. Livingston voiced the hope

---

[44] "A Free Citizen" still hoped for a reconciliation "upon constitutional
principles." *Const. Gaz.*, April 24, 1776.
[45] *N.Y.L.*, May 9, 1776. See also "Spartanus," *ibid.*, May 30, 1776.
[46] Jay to McDougall, April 11. 1776, McDougall Papers, NYHS.
[47] Floyd to McKesson, May 9, 1776, Force, *American Archives*, 4th ser.,
V, 395.

that the New York Provincial Congress understood the necessity of erecting a new government.[48] Congressman Ezra L'Hommedieu of Suffolk assured his colleague General Nathaniel Woodhull that "most people" approved the idea of a new governmental form.[49] On the other hand, conservatives like Duane contended that the defeat of most of the New York City radicals in the April elections for the Third Provincial Congress and the city committee demonstrated the lack of popular support for experiments in government. Therefore, Duane declared, the provincial body should not be "too precipitate" in raising the constitutional issue; rather, it should delay and see what course the other middle colonies adopted before it moved.[50]

Duane's interpretation of the April balloting, if correct, is of considerable importance. It meant that public opinion opposed any effort to supplant the revolutionary committee system. An examination of the city elections, therefore, is necessary to determine the validity of Duane's claim. Four tickets were submitted to the inhabitants. The four slates carried many of the candidates in common, but the exceptions gave the election its tone. The city committee headed its list of April 13 with the men who represented New York in the Continental Congress (Jay, Philip Livingston, Francis Lewis, and John Alsop), but it excluded the fifth delegate, Duane.[51] That same day a broadside by

---

48 Livingston to Jay, May 17, 1776, John Jay Papers, Iselin Collection, CUL; Henry P. Johnston, ed., *The Correspondence and Public Papers of John Jay* (4 vols.; New York, 1890-1893), I, 60.
49 L'Hommedieu to Nathaniel Woodhull, June 2, 1776, Force, *American Archives*, 4th ser., VI, 684.
50 Duane to Jay, May 18, 1776, Johnston, *Correspondence of John Jay*, I, 61. Duane also miscalculated the situation in Virginia in this letter. He implied that Virginia would be against changing the government, but at that very moment word was on the way to Philadelphia instructing the Virginia representatives to move for independence.
51 The ticket included five radicals (J. M. Scott, John Broome, Samuel Prince, Peter Pra Van Zandt, and James Alner), five conservatives (John Alsop, Comfort Sands, Isaac Stoutenburgh, William Denning, and Isaac Roosevelt), and eleven moderates (Jay, Livingston, Lewis, J. Van Zandt, J. Hallett, A. Brasher, J. Van Cortlandt, J. Beekman, Anthony Rutgers, E. Bancker, and T. Randall). Becker, *The History of Political Parties*, p. 257.

"Sentinel" circulated about town which substituted seven new choices (Alexander McDougall, Thomas Marston, John Ray, Adrian Rutgers, Robert Ray, Abraham P. Lott, and Henry Remsen) for an equal number of the committee's ticket. "Sentinel" deleted the names of the four continental delegates and three radicals (John Broome, Peter Pra Van Zandt, and James Alner).[52] Two other tickets appeared in rapid succession.

On April 16 the Committee of Mechanics produced a modified slate. It approved "Sentinel's" excision of the continental delegates' names but did not accept his substitutes for them. It would not permit the loss of Broome, Van Zandt, and Alner whom it added to its ticket, sacrificing "Sentinel's" selection of McDougall, Marston, and John Ray. In addition the Mechanics ruled out Comfort Sands and Thomas Randall, both of whom appeared on the other two lists, to make room for Isaac Sears and William Malcolm.[53] All three slates had one thing in common; none of them named Duane. Still another handbill appeared, this time without signature, which adopted the whole city committee bloc but substituted Duane for Alner, who was a member of the Committee of Mechanics.[54]

At the height of the campaign a broadside by "A Sober Citizen" presented what was practically an ultimatum to the voters. He stated as if it were fact that the continental delegates, if defeated, would withdraw from the revolutionary movement and would seek pardon from the British to save

---

[52] The political complexion of the "Sentinel" ticket was almost the same as the committee's slate: five radicals, four conservatives, thirteen moderates. The deletion of the continental delegation may have reflected a desire to elect a bolder group of men as well as personal ambitions. *Ibid.*, pp. 257-58; "Sentinel," April 13, 1776, Broadsides, NYPL.

[53] The Mechanics' ticket consisted of ten radicals (Malcolm, Ray, Sears, Lott, Rutgers, Scott, Broome, Prince, P. P. Van Zandt, and Alner), three conservatives (Roosevelt, Stoutenburgh, and Denning), eight moderates (J. Van Zandt, Hallet, Brasher, Van Cortlandt, Beekman, Anthony Rutgers, Bancker, and Randall). Becker, *The History of Political Parties,* pp. 257-58; "Mechanics in Union," April 16, 1776, Broadsides, NYPL.

[54] Becker, *The History of Political Parties,* pp. 257-58.

themselves. Facing the probability of an invasion, the city could not afford the possible disruption of the revolutionary organization which might ensue from the defection of these leading Whigs. "A Sober Citizen" accompanied this advice with a diatribe against the Mechanics' candidates whom he regarded as the principal opponents of the continental delegates. The Mechanics' nominees, he warned, possessed no property or virtue and, if elected, would bring both colony and continent into contempt.[55]

The election results indicate that the electorate heeded the admonition of "A Sober Citizen," for the continental delegates and Duane won seats. Indeed, almost the whole of the city committee's ticket of twenty-one ran successfully. Alner and Prince, the exceptions, lost out to Duane and Remsen. Therefore, the principal men on the Mechanics' ballot, with one exception, suffered defeat. Henry Remsen, alone of their substitutes, won a seat, but he also had "Sentinel's" support. Furthermore, two radicals on the city committee's and Mechanics' slates, Broome and Van Zandt, defeated two of "Sentinel's" moderates. Even McDougall did not win.[56] The balloting, therefore, did not so much express a rejection of the moderates and radicals as it did a fear of disunity in the face of the enemy. Duane's interpretation of these events perhaps reflects more his desire to prevent change than it does factual evaluation.

The Whigs transformed opinions into deeds on May 24 when the New York Provincial Congress took up the subject of government as recommended by the Continental Congress. Unable to evade the issue, some deputies sought refuge in further delay, advocating another polling of the people. Taking a different tack, Gouverneur Morris pleaded in a lengthy speech for the election of a special constitutional convention.[57] Since this would have meant bypassing

---

55 "A Sober Citizen," April 16, 1776, Broadsides, NYPL.
56 Becker, *The History of Political Parties*, pp. 257-58.

the Provincial Congress in which the moderates and conservatives prevailed, one author has said that "Morris undoubtedly represented the more radical views. . . ."[58] No
doubt many moderates and conservatives wished to prevent
the writing of a radical charter and they believed the Provincial Congress to be the means of maintaining their political supremacy. Morris, however, had carefully reassured
the members on this point, when he said: "Nor do I think
it quite proper for us all to abandon the Senate House and
leave the business to entire new men, while the country
continues in its present dangerous situation."[59] Thus the
election of a convention would not open the floodgates to
the radicals. Practically, of course, Morris's procedure guaranteed postponement of any labor on a draft constitution
until June or July, since the election would consume a
month or more.[60]

Actually Scott's plan represented the radical approach.
His proposition would have served radical ends because it
proposed that the Provincial Congress should draw up the

[57] *Jour. Prov. Cong.*, I, 460; Sparks, *Life of Gouverneur Morris*, I, 97-106;
Gouverneur Morris papers, CUL.
[58] Becker, *The History of Political Parties*, p. 267. This judgment was
probably influenced by Sparks's quotations from the speech which argued
that the colonies were independent in fact and congress should acknowledge
that fact. Despite this plea Morris's subsequent behavior was at variance
with these ideas. For example, when the Committee of Mechanics presented
a petition to the Provincial Congress on June 4, urging it to instruct the
continental delegates to move for independence, it rejected the plea without
recorded dissent. Although Morris was present, there is nothing to indicate that he favored such instructions or even that he raised the subject of
independence during the discussion of the petition. Again, when on June
5 the Provincial Congress entertained the Virginia Provincial Convention's
crucial letter on independence, Morris did not attempt to compel a debate,
even though the Provincial Congress named him and Jay a committee to
draft a reply to the Virginians. The committee's draft, which the Provincial
Congress approved without dissent, was polite but evasive. If Morris disagreed with these sentiments, he did not bother to express his disapproval.
Moreover, even after his return from a visit in the middle of June to
Philadelphia where the fateful debate had begun and been postponed
to July 1, Morris did not raise the matter on the floor of the Provincial
Congress. *Jour. Prov. Cong.*, I, 474ff.
[59] Sparks, *Life of Gouverneur Morris*, I, 106.
[60] Under the modified plan actually adopted, the colony held elections in
June and the new Provincial Congress met in July.

constitution and, once having the matter under consideration, it could not shunt a question of such major importance into obscurity and forget it. This procedure, therefore, would minimize delay. The united mechanics' association welcomed Scott's interpretation of the Provincial Congress's authority and expressed "astonishment" that any doubt should arise about the power of the house to frame the charter.[61] The record does not show that any disagreement existed over the basic question of whether the Whigs should form a government; rather, both groups assumed the necessity of so doing but differed over timing and, thereby, procedure.

Morris's speech and motion on May 24 opened the proceedings on the great question.[62] Although Scott delivered a long counterargument, he closed his speech on an indecisive note that weakened his position. When he argued for the Provincial Congress's constitution-drafting power, he put it negatively: "at least, it is doubtful whether they have not that power. . . ." Having conceded the existence of doubt, Scott recommended that the house refer this point to committee. Since Morris had moved previously for the appointment of a committee to draw up instructions for the election of a constitutional convention, Comfort Sands submitted an amendment that the suggested committee "take into consideration the Resolutions of the Continental Con-

---

61 *N.Y.G.*, June 17, 1776; Force, *American Archives*, 4th ser., VI, 895-98.

62 According to the *Journal* Morris made two long speeches, the latter of which was his rejoinder to Scott. Sparks copiously quoted a fragment of one of them in *Life of Gouverneur Morris*, I, 97ff. Unfortunately, Sparks omitted sections and altered phraseology without indicating the changes. The printed portion is in the Gouverneur Morris Papers, CUL, and may represent one-half the original, since its pages are numbered five through eight. Their theme is that New York is already independent in everything but name, that the Provincial Congress is in fact a legislature and that only an open avowal of independence can guarantee peace and security. Since the nature of the argument is such, it is questionable that Morris could have intended it as a rebuttal to Scott's contention on the Provincial Congress's powers. It is more likely a part of the first address which preceded Scott's.

gress of the 15th May instant, and report thereon with all convenient speed." This substitute motion, which Scott seconded, carried with only two counties and Morris voting against. The Provincial Congress chose Scott, Jay, John Haring, Francis Lewis, Henry Remsen, John Broome, and Jacob Cuyler as the committee.[63]

Referral of the motion transferred debate on the general question to the committee. If Scott expected the committee to limit itself to the single formulation he had proposed, he misinterpreted Sands's amendment. The general phraseology of the motion placed no stipulations on the committee's labors. In the committee the opposing viewpoints accepted a compromise which sacrificed Morris's special convention but salvaged the all-important time element. Perhaps the congressmen's desire to be both legislators and constitution-drafters may have figured in the abandonment of the constitutional convention. If they adopted Morris's plan, the Provincial Congress would have to recess until after the convention had completed its work. That might entail the absence of any legislative body for several months in a period of rapidly increasing danger. If the Provincial Congress remained in session, the members could not serve in the convention. In order, therefore, to keep the reins in their own hands and to still the misgivings they themselves had raised, they recommended the election of a new congress whose members would specifically have the people's mandate to form a new government. Naturally the polling process would delay any constitutional action until the end of June or early July.

In its report to the house on May 27, the committee presented a series of conclusions on which it based its recommendations that new elections be held. This report is of the utmost importance because there is a major difference

---

63 *Jour. Prov. Cong.*, I, 460.

between it and the final resolutions. The fourth clause of
the report summarized the events that dissolved the royal
government and concluded: "whereby, it hath become absolutely necessary for the good people of this Colony to
institute a new and regular form of internal Government
and Police. . . ." The seventh and eighth clauses repeated
this clear and unequivocal determination to replace the
government. The seventh called on the people to declare
the present members "competent for the purpose of establishing such new form of internal police and government"
or to choose others "with express authority to institute and
establish such new and internal form of government." The
eighth reiterated the phrase, "with express authority to
institute" a new government.[64] Having approved the report
without any modification, the Provincial Congress accepted,
therefore, the concept that the mode of governing *must*
be changed; it would not debate *whether* any change should
be made. The house committed the report to Scott, Jay,
and Haring to convert it into formal resolutions.[65]

When the report emerged from the committee on May
31, the key ideas expressed in the fourth, seventh, and eighth
sections had undergone subtle but substantial modification.
The resolves consolidated these sections into a single resolution which ran:

That it be recommended to the electors . . . either to authorize
(in addition to the powers vested in this Congress) their present
Deputies, or others . . . or either of them, *to take into consideration the necessity and propriety of instituting such government*
as in and by the said resolution of the Continental Congress is
described and recommended. *And if the majority of the Counties by their Deputies in Provincial Congress, shall be of opinion that such new government ought to be instituted and established, then to institute and establish such a government as*

64 *Ibid.*, I, 462-63.
65 *Ibid.* Becker, *The History of Political Parties,* p. 269 incorrectly places
Remsen on this committee.

they shall deem best calculated to serve the rights, liberties and happiness of the good people of this Colony. . . .[66]

Did the resolution mean that the newly elected congress would proceed immediately to the task of drafting a constitution? Or did it mean that the newly elected congress would proceed immediately to debate whether or not they should draft a constitution?[67] The phraseology implied that congress would consider first whether it ought to establish a new government. The drafting committee, therefore, had reopened the question, but the Provincial Congress passed the resolution without discussion and without a recorded vote.[68] In whatever manner the people interpreted this recommendation, they seem to have assumed that a new government would replace the committee system.[69]

After the Provincial Congress published these resolves, public protest arose, but it did not strike out against the authority requested nor the procedure laid down. The sole organized criticism came from the Committee of Me-

---

[66] *Jour. Prov. Cong.*, I, 469. Italics mine.

[67] Becker, *The History of Political Parties*, p. 269, considers the ambiguity to be in the sentence beginning "And if the majority of the Counties" and implies that this election was to be a referendum in which the possibility of a "no" vote existed. Taking the phrase in the context of the preceding sentence, it is apparent that the "majority of the Counties" referred to is the majority of county delegations voting on this question in the Provincial Congress. It is not a majority of the electors instructing their deputies. William Smith understood the resolution to mean that the deputies in the Provincial Congress would discuss the necessity for instituting a new government. Moreover, Jay, for example, had no doubt whatsoever that the people would grant the requested power to the Provincial Congress. William H. W. Sabine, ed., *Historical Memoirs from 16 March 1763 to 9 July 1776 of William Smith* (New York, 1956), p. 282; Jay to R. R. Livingston, May 29, 1776, Robert R. Livingston, American Art Association Catalogue, *Revolutionary Letters of Importance: The Unpublished Correspondence of Robert R. Livingston* (New York, 1918), No. 25; Johnston, *Correspondence of John Jay*, I, 65.

[68] *Jour. Prov. Cong.*, I, 469.

[69] Two penmen, "Spartanus," letter II, and "Columbus," *N.Y.J.*, June 13, 1776, exhibited no doubts. The former commented, "As we are to assume a new mode of Government, I think it ought properly to be new." The latter said, "The subject upon which we are now to deliberate . . . is the election of proper persons to form a new mode of Government for this Colony."

chanics, which sent to the Provincial Congress a discursive but provocative letter that throws some light on the political thinking of the lesser merchants, tradesmen, mechanics, and laborers.[70] Admittedly, the communication stated, open opposition to the resolutions by the Mechanics might offer a lever to the "indefatigable" emissaries of the British or might confuse numbers of the people and dangerously weaken popular support of the revolutionary cause. But, the Mechanics explained, they risked these consequences because they conversed daily "with numbers who have been deceived" by the misinterpretation of the resolutions. Many believed that the Provincial Congress would not submit a new charter to the people for ratification. "They are terrified at the consequences, although a sincere zeal for the general cause inspires them to suppress their remonstrances, lest the common enemy should avail himself of that circumstance to undermine your [i.e., the Provincial Congress's] authority."[71] "Impressed with a just fear of the consequences" which flowed from this misconception, the Mechanics pleaded with the Provincial Congress for a "full and timely explanation" to put an end to the "groundless jealousies" of their "patriotick Resolve."

Having justified their right to evoke the question, the Mechanics entered into a detailed exposition of the people's "inalienable right" to ratify a constitution. This was the "birthright of every man" which God had given to him. Although every individual did not possess the prerequisites for constitutional labors, God-given common sense would enable him to determine "what degree of safety and what advantage he is likely to enjoy, or be deprived of" under any proposed constitution. Should the people delude them-

---

[70] See Becker, *The History of Political Parties,* p. 270; Staughton Lynd, "The Mechanics in New York City Politics, 1774-1788," *Labor History,* V (Fall, 1964), 225-46.

[71] *N.Y.G.,* June 17, 1776; reprinted in *Jour. Prov. Cong.,* II, 241-43; Force, *American Archives,* 4th ser., VI, 895-98.

selves into a renunciation of their right to ratification, such an "impious and frantick act of self-destruction" would cast them into "absolute slavery" and would destroy the Provincial Congress's "lawful power" over them. Of this dual outcome the committee observed: "It might probably accelerate our [i.e., the people's] political death; but it must immediately cause your own."

The Mechanics also took cognizance of the empowering clause in the congressional resolutions. The ambiguity of the language did not trouble the Mechanics, but the implication that the Provincial Congress would establish the new government without submitting it to the people for confirmation did. The committee chose to believe, however, that since the Provincial Congress had stated the right of the people to determine existing doubts of constitutional authority, it could not have intended to obtain a surreptitious renunciation of that right: "Human nature, depraved as it is, has not yet, and we hope never will, be guilty of so much hypocrisy and treachery." On the contrary, the Mechanics deemed the questionable resolution to be "perfectly consistent with the liberal principles on which it is introduced." In support of their interpretation they quoted a much-elided version of the clause: "if the majority of the Counties shall be of opinion that such new Government ought to be instituted, then to institute and establish such a Government." Although this was quoting out of context with a vengeance, it presented the Provincial Congress with an acute dilemma. If it denied this meaning of the passage, then the people could accuse it of "promoting the selfish views of . . . oligarchy." On the other hand, if the Provincial Congress accepted the Mechanics' explication, the people would regard its acceptance as a pledge to refer the constitution to the people for ratification.[72]

---

72 They warned the Provincial Congress: "Posterity will behold that Resolve as the test of your rectitude. It will prove that you have fully restored

By implication the Committee of Mechanics raised the question of class power and condemned rule by an elite. Expounding on the necessity and propriety of reliance upon the "sound judgment, integrity, and moderation of a free people," the letter confuted emphatically the idea that any man or men could draft a constitution to which a majority of the people would have no objections whatsoever. The people's free assent constituted the "only characteristick of the true lawfulness and legality that can be given to human institutions."[73] Any other procedure smacked of the "illegal and tyrannical" and proceeded "from the selfish principles of corrupt oligarchy." Furthermore, fundamental law derived in this arbitrary fashion "could be lawfully binding on none but the legislators themselves."

There was a bold but ambiguous statement on the consequences of British rule and this might have suggested to the elite that their worst fears of the "licentiousness" of the people were about to materialize. Asserting that the British had deprived the colonists of the right to determine their own laws, the Mechanics argued that existing laws "have but a relative legality, and that not one of them is lawfully binding upon us." They added, however, that most of these laws should be "tolerated" for "common convenience" until a new government "shall have been freely ratified by the co-legislative power of the people, the sole lawful Legislature of this Colony." Allegations of this nature suggested

---

to us the exercise of our right finally to determine on the laws by which this Colony is to be governed: a right of which, by the injustice of the British Government, we have till now been deprived. . . ." Force, *American Archives*, 4th ser., VI, 895-98.

73 These passages implied a concept of majority rule, a concept which the committee did not adequately define. Speaking of the ratification process, the Mechanics argued for submission of a constitution "to the collective judgment of all the individuals who might be interested in its operation." The words "interested in" are used in the sense of affected by. This interpretation is supported by a prior passage in which the authors spoke of the God-given right of the "inhabitants at large" to accept or reject the constitution. *Ibid.*

that Mechanics would not accept a return to the *status quo ante* and perhaps that they had changes to propose in political and economic relations.

Finally, the power to ratify connoted the power to amend the fundamental law whenever the majority should choose. Associated with this authority was the right of the people to recall their deputies to committees and congresses when a majority in such "district shall think fit."

Despite these strictures the communication welcomed the resolutions and extended to the Provincial Congress "that tribute of esteem and respect to which you are justly entitled for your zeal in so nobly asserting the rights which the people at large have to legislation, and in promoting their free exercise of those rights."[74] At the same time the Mechanics pledged their continued support for the Provincial Congress.[75]

Its reaction to this letter was extraordinary. The Provincial Congress customarily read its correspondence and entered it in the *Journal*. Indeed, a previous Mechanics' letter of May 29 did receive this treatment, but the congressmen did not adhere to the precedent.[76] There is no notation in the *Journal* of the receipt of the letter or of any discussion of it.[77] Since the Provincial Congress did not ultimately submit the constitution to the people for ratification, it is perhaps possible that some of the deputies never intended to have the people affirm it and, therefore, managed to bury the letter of the Mechanics.[78] Failing to obtain any response

---

74 *Ibid.*

75 They maintained, likewise, their right to express their opinions "with propriety" and to rely "on public indulgence for any imperfection." The defensive and apologetic tone of the letter is an interesting expression of a consciousness of social inferiority.

76 *Jour. Prov. Cong.*, I, 474.

77 The Provincial Congress must have received the letter, since it was found among that body's papers and published with its papers along with the *Journal*. Moreover, it is quite likely that a group of leaders of the Committee of Mechanics presented their letter in person, since they had followed this procedure with their first letter on May 29. *Ibid.*, II, 241-43.

from the Provincial Congress, the Mechanics presumably
sent their letter to the newspapers to place the issue before
the people. In the city's military atmosphere in June, 1776,
and with most of the populace evacuated, the Mechanics
aroused little response from the people on the ratification
dispute.

Both inside and outside the Provincial Congress men
saw the interrelationship of the issues of a new government
and independence. It was impossible to discuss the one
without implying the other; they were two sides of the same
coin.

Although the people read occasionally about some aspects
of the government question in the newspapers, they read
about, and probably discussed, even more frequently the
correlative issue of independence. Even though no formal
debate on this question had occurred in the Third Provincial Congress, New Yorkers had read the pros and cons
of the subject in the newspapers for five months. "Lycurgus"
introduced the topic in the press in late December, 1775,
when he castigated the Pennsylvania Assembly for forbidding their delegates to the Continental Congress to vote
for independence.[79] He did not espouse the opposing position, but contended that the blank prohibition bound the
delegation when no one could foretell what would be necessary in the future. Although "Lycurgus" discussed independence obliquely, "Memento" confronted it squarely and
unhesitatingly advocated separation rather than submission
to the British "yoke."[80] Paine's *Common Sense* inspired

---

78 Subsequent events gave the advantage to the Mechanics' opponents.
The rapid exodus of the population in June would have hampered any
large-scale effort to bring pressure to bear on the Provincial Congress. Also
the appearance of the British at the end of the month threw everything
into turmoil; the Provincial Congress adjourned hurriedly and left the city.

79 *N.Y.J.*, December 21, 1775.

80 *N.Y.P.*, January 25, 1776. This appeared before publication of Paine's
piece in New York. See also the anonymous piece quoted in John C. Hamilton, *The Life of Alexander Hamilton: A History of the Republic of the
United States of America, as Traced in His Writings and in Those of His
Contemporaries* (10 vols.; Boston, 1879), I, 112.

other letters which advocated an end to colonialism. "Independent Whig" saw nothing to lose and everything to gain by separation. The North administration is convinced we mean to be independent, he reasoned, and we shall lose no friends by asserting our intent. As for those in Parliament who have opposed the North measures, we shall experience small loss by their alienation. For all their friendship for America they have proved incapable of blocking the policies of the government.[81] "Candidus," assailing British regulation of land, commerce, and manufactures, concluded that the colonial system sought to "milk rather than to suckle" the colonies.[82] Turning his wrath on colonial officialdom, he accused them of carrying on "their oppressions, vexations and depredations" under the color of royal authority.

Hardly a week passed from late February through June in which the newspapers did not carry at least one contribution to the great controversy. The writers reviewed the causes of the crisis and the constitutional relations of the colonists to crown and Parliament.[83] One of the authors disclosed the progress of the sentiment for independence by elaborating the stages which public opinion had traversed. Events compelled the people to abandon these positions as illusory:

That the King can do no wrong; that the interests of Great Britain and the colonies were the same, reciprocal and inseperable; . . . that the King was imposed upon by his ministers; that a change in administration would rectify the evils complained of; . . . that our friends throughout the nation would return a better parliament than the last; that the act declaring

---

81 *N.Y.J.*, February 22, 1776. See also anon., *ibid.*, March 7, 1776; "Z. F.," *N.Y.P.*, March 7, 1776.
82 *Ibid.*, March 21, 1776. See also anon., *ibid.*, April 18, 1776; Force, *American Archives*, 4th ser., V, 974-77.
83 Anon., *N.Y.J.*, April 4, 1776; anon., anon. "Queries," "Amicus Patriae," and anon., *Const. Gaz.*, March 9, 30, June 5, July 3, 1776; "Speech of A Farmer," "A. B.," "To the Freeborn Sons of America in General and of Connecticut in Particular," "Hector," anon., "Independent Whig," *N.Y.P.*, March 14, 21, April 11, 18, 1776; "Cato" No. 3, April 20, 1776, Hamilton, *Life of Alexander Hamilton*, I, 113.

their right to tax us in all cases whatsoever, would not be carried into execution, . . . that the several repeals and seeming alterations in their plan of conduct, proved a relinquishment of any evil intentions; . . . that we have no resources to carry on a war; that jealousies and opposition of interests would ever prevent a junction of the colonies.[84]

A notable alteration of content in these polemics occurred toward the close of April. No writer any longer questioned the propriety of independence. When differences cropped up, they revolved around the timing of the separation. The letter writers pronounced the present as most propitious for independence and warned against delay.[85]

Notwithstanding the inaction of the Provincial Congress, the Tories feared the worst. "There is a great talk of independence, and the unthinking multitude are mad for it; but how matters will terminate, I cannot judge, but believe great will be the opposition [in the Provincial Congress] to such a declaration. A pamphlet called Common Sense, has carried off its thousands; an answer thereto is come out, but instantly seized in the printer's shop, and burnt in the street, as unfit to be read at this time. I fear, from this line of conduct, the people here will shake you off, and, once gone, will never be regained."[86]

Try as some deputies might, they could not avoid the issue of independence. Gouverneur Morris spoke at length

---

[84] Anon., *Const. Gaz.*, March 9, 1776.

[85] "Serious Questions Addressed to the Congress," Force, *American Archives*, 4th ser., V, 1078-79; anon., *Const. Gaz.*, May 8, 1776; "Hermina," "Columbus," *N.Y.J.*, May 16, June 13, 1776.

There is some evidence for believing that the prevalence of these pro-independence letters was directly proportional to the general sentiments of the populace. Britisher Ambrose Serle expressed amazement at the "incredible influence" of the newspapers in New York. "One is astonished to see with what avidity they are sought after, and how implicitly they are believed, by the great bulk of the people." Serle to Dartmouth, November 26, 1776, Benjamin F. Stevens, ed., *Facsimiles of Manuscripts in European Archives Relating to America, 1773-1783* (25 vols.; London, 1889-1898), XXIV, No. 2059.

[86] Anon., Letter from New York, March 22, 1776, *The Remembrancer*, 1776, p. 85. See also Joseph Bull to Henry Remsen, June 1, 1776, Force, *American Archives*, 4th ser., VI, 672.

upon the topic in May in the course of the debate on creating a new government, but the question of independence was not on the order of the day. The Committee of Mechanics, however, raised the question when it drew up an address to the Provincial Congress urging that body to instruct the delegates at Philadelphia to work for independence.[87] Although the letter of the Mechanics bore the date of May 29, the committee did not present it to their representatives until June 4. Presumably, the Mechanics delayed delivery until they had word of the decision of the Provincial Congress on the matter of government. If so, an item in the *New York Gazette* of June 3, in which also appeared the government resolutions of the Provincial Congress of May 31, must have stirred them. The news was the text of the Virginia resolutions, which instructed the continental delegates of that colony to move for independence.[88]

The reaction of the Provincial Congress to the letter of the Mechanics revealed clearly the sensitivity of that body to the question of independence. When the delegation from the Mechanics in Union, led by its chairman, Lewis Thibou, entered the house and presented the address, the Chair first cleared the house of all spectators so that it might be determined whether it was "proper" to receive the memorial. Having "inspected" the document, the congressmen opened the doors and invited Thibou to read it to the house. Although the *Journal* neither mentioned any time lapse in the inspection process nor described what the Provincial Congress did, the house handed Thibou a formal, detailed reply when he finished reading the letter of the Mechanics.[89]

---

87 Becker, *The History of Political Parties*, p. 270.
88 *N.Y.G.*, June 3, 1776.
89 *Jour. Prov. Cong.*, I, 474. The vagueness and brevity of the record suggest abnormal procedure. Normally all motions and resolutions were entered in the *Journal*. The Provincial Congress could not have drawn up the reply without some motion or order which it ought to have recorded, but none appears in the *Journal*.

The answer betrayed resentment at the political activity of the Mechanics: "We flatter ourselves, however, that neither that association, nor their Committee, will claim any authority whatsoever in the public transactions of the present times; but that, on the contrary, they will ever be ready to submit to that constitutional authority which, by a free election, has been vested in Congress and Committees."[90] The point was wholly gratuitous, since the Mechanics not only had not claimed such authority, but had been very deferential: "We as part of your constituents . . . beg leave in a dutiful manner at this time, to approach unto you our Representatives, and request your kind attention to this our humble Address . . . should you . . . think proper to instruct our most honourable Delegates . . . it would give us the highest satisfaction; and we hereby sincerely promise to endeavour to support the same with our lives and fortunes."[91] The Provincial Congress then declined to accede to the Mechanics' plea:

We are of opinion that the Continental Congress alone have that enlarged view of our political circumstances, which will enable them to decide upon those measures which are necessary for the general welfare; *we cannot presume, by any instructions, to make or declare any resolutions, or declarations, upon a so general and momentous concern; but are determined patiently to await and firmly to abide by whatever a majority of that august body shall think needful.* We therefore cannot presume to instruct the Delegates of this Colony on the momentous question to which your address refers, until we are informed that it is brought before the Continental Congress, and the sense of this Colony be required through the Congress.[92]

---

90 *Ibid.* Since these remarks were completely irrelevant, they may have served the dual function of inhibiting the Mechanics' political aggressiveness and of obscuring the key issue, which was not any Mechanics' claim to authority but the Provincial Congress's refusal to move on the question of independence. The Mechanics later asserted their right to speak up when they saw fit. Mechanics to Provincial Congress, June 14, 1776, *ibid.*, II, 243.

91 *N.Y.J.*, June 6, 1776; *Const. Gaz.*, June 5, 1776; Force, *American Archives*, 4th ser., VI, 615.

The Third Provincial Congress's disinclination to act on independence seems to have dashed the hopes of the enthusiasts, who began to look toward the election of the Fourth Provincial Congress to remedy the colony's laggardness.[93]

Meanwhile the Virginia Provincial Convention, taking steps to win support for its decision to introduce an independence resolution in Philadelphia, posted off a letter to New York which solicited the latter to give the Virginia resolves due "consideration." The New York Provincial Congress received this letter June 5, two days after the resolves had appeared in the *Gazette*. Drafted by Jay and Morris, the answer constituted a polite evasion. The firmest commitment in the message was a pledge that the resolves "will be considered . . . with all the deliberation due to the importance of the subject." Perhaps to offset the indefiniteness of its response, the Provincial Congress concluded in a tone of affirmation: "the Congress of this Colony will invariably adopt and pursue every measure which may tend to promote the union and secure the rights and happiness of the United Colonies."[94]

---

92 Italics mine. The italicized passage does not appear in the letter as published in the press, but appears only in the *Journal's* version. This passage and the following sentence are in fact mutually exclusive. Since the Continental Congress delegates could not act without instructions from their provincial congresses, a decision on independence could not be taken until colonies like New York instructed their deputies for it. It is inconceivable that the Provincial Congress could have thought that the people did not know this fact. It is not unlikely that these words were the consequence of the haste with which it drafted its reply to the Mechanics. Perhaps some members noticed the inconsistency when they prepared copies of the letter for the newspapers and deleted the clause. *Jour. Prov. Cong.,* I, 474; *N.Y.J.,* June 6, 1776; *Const. Gaz.,* June 5, 1776.

93 Colonel Jedediah Huntington wrote Governor Trumbull of Connecticut, June 6, 1776. "The mechanicks of the city have voted independence; it is expected the new Congress will follow suit. There will be, I am told, a majority of Presbyterians, which will probably give the representation a different guise from what it has heretofore had." Force, *American Archives,* 4th ser., VI, 725.

94 The *Journal* is so cut and dried that it is impossible to determine whether there was any opposition to the substance. *Jour. Prov. Cong.,* I, 475, 481.

Unlike their colleagues at home, the New York delegation in the Continental Congress could not avoid the question of independence. Virginia presented its motion for
independence June 7 and the debate flowed on through
June 10. None of the New Yorkers seems to have sanctioned independence, at least not at that juncture, but
they divided as to whether they had the power to cast any
vote or only a negative vote on the motion.[95] Undaunted
by his voteless status, Robert R. Livingston joined James
Wilson of Pennsylvania, John Dickinson of Pennsylvania,
and Edward Rutledge of South Carolina in the opposition
to independence. Averring their approbation of the measure and admitting the impossibility of a return to the *status
quo ante,* they insisted, nevertheless, that the most propitious moment had not arisen. Let "the voice of the people
drive" Congress to it, they said. As for New York, Livingston maintained that the people of that province were
not yet "ripe" for the break but that they were "fast ripen-
ing."[96] Words, however, were not enough for the New York

---

[95] Edward Rutledge implied to Jay that Clinton, Floyd, Lewis, Wisner,
and Alsop of New York opposed independence. The tone of the letter leads
to the inference that Jay held similar views, an inference which Jay's reply
buttresses: "Your ideas of men and things . . . run, for the most part,
parallel with my own. . . ." Rutledge to Jay, June 29, 1776, Jay to Rutledge, July 6, 1776, Johnston, *Correspondence of John Jay,* I, 67, 68; Edmund C. Burnett, ed., *Letters of Members of the Continental Congress*
(8 vols.; Washington, D.C., 1921-1936), I, 517.

When the Continental Congress resumed the discussion July 1, the New
Yorkers assured their colleagues that they approved the declaration and
"were assured their constituents were for it." McKean of Delaware, long
after the event, positively stated that Wisner voted for independence July 2.
Since New York cast no vote, he may have meant that Wisner approved
independence. Edmund C. Burnett, *The Continental Congress* (New York,
1941), p. 184; Julian P. Boyd, *et al.,* eds., *The Papers of Thomas Jefferson*
(16 vols.; Princeton, 1950-——), I, 314; Burnett, *Letters,* I, No. 753, n. 3.

The June 8 letter of the New Yorkers contained this interpretation of their
authority: "Some of us consider ourselves as bound by our instructions not
to vote on that question. . . ." Since none of them seems to have been
thinking of voting "yes," the implication is that some thought they had
the power to vote "no." *Jour. Prov. Cong.,* I, 488. For a different view, see
Becker, *The History of Political Parties,* p. 271.

[96] Jefferson's Notes of Proceedings in the Continental Congress, Boyd,
The Papers of Thomas Jefferson, I, 309; Rutledge to Jay, June 8, 1776,
Johnston, *Correspondence of John Jay,* I, 66, n. 1.

delegates; they felt keenly their inability to participate in the balloting on the Virginia resolve. Since the source of their authority was the Provincial Congress, on June 8 the Yorkers drafted a letter in urgent terms to that body in which they requested instructions on how to cast the colony's vote on the motion for independence.[97]

The plea from Philadelphia for directions produced a stir in New York. When the continental delegates' letter reached the city on the morning of June 10, the Third Provincial Congress promptly resolved itself into secret session to deliberate on the matter, but it deliberated inconclusively.[98] Late that afternoon the deputies wrestled again with the problem, wrangling over the interpretation of the New York Provincial Congress's powers, the continental delegates' powers, and the election resolutions of May 31. The last item provided Jay with a stratagem to postpone any decision until the Fourth Provincial Congress would meet in July. On the next day he introduced two resolutions which the congressmen amended and passed unanimously. The first of these declared "that the good people of this Colony have not, in the opinion of this Congress, authorized this Congress or the Delegates of this Colony . . . to declare this Colony to be and continue independent of the Crown of Great Britain."[99] The second resolve proposed that the people at the June election invest their representatives with sweeping discretionary power "to delib-

---

[97] Becker, *The History of Political Parties*, p. 271. In view of the supreme importance of the independence question, one would suppose that the representatives would have explained to their colleagues in New York that the debate had begun. That would have been the fact of the matter, since they dated their letter June 8, the second day of disputation, and one of them had participated in the exchanges. Nevertheless, they gave no intimation of this state of affairs: "Your delegates here expect that the question of Independence will very shortly be agitated in Congress . . . and all wish to have your sentiments thereon. The matter will admit of no delay." *Jour. Prov. Cong.*, I, 488.

[98] *Ibid.* The resort to secrecy was a cardinal indication of the majority's attitude toward independence.

[99] *Ibid.*, I, 489, 490. See Becker, *The History of Political Parties*, pp. 271-72 and n. 103.

erate and determine on every question whatsoever that may concern or affect the interest of this Colony, and to conclude upon, ordain, and execute every act and measure which to them shall appear conducive to the happiness, security and welfare of this Colony. . . ."[100] The final clause recommended the electors to "inform" their deputies of their "sentiments" on independence.

Having chosen a means to prevent any positive action until the newly elected legislature met, the Provincial Congress reversed itself and nullified its unanimous agreement. It voted to postpone publication of the resolutions until after the elections. Since the resolutions could not take effect without the elections, it would have to revise the resolutions at a later date to provide for a special referendum on the matter of independence. If this were not true, the motion to postpone publication rendered the resolves meaningless.[101] The parliamentary meaning of the postponement was that the Provincial Congress had moved to reconsider the previously adopted motions. However, such immediate reconsideration was a violation of the house's rules of procedure: "That after the determination of any matter or thing, the same shall not be resumed but with the consent of such majority as aforesaid, *upon notice of a motion for that purpose, previously given at least one day before the same is made.*"[102] Nevertheless, after empowering Jay and Remsen to "draft an answer" for the direction of the Philadelphia deputies, the house dropped the whole subject.[103]

The Jay-Remsen draft denied the colony's delegates any authority to vote on independence. If the Provincial Congress formally approved the letter, it did not record its action

---

100 *Jour. Prov. Cong.,* I, 490.
101 Becker, *The History of Political Parties,* p. 272, n. 103. The letter to Philadelphia specifically stated that a later election would be held on the question of independence. Force, *American Archives,* 4th ser., VI, 814.
102 Italics mine. The rules adopted by the Third Provincial Congress are in the *Journal,* I, 450.
103 *Ibid.,* I, 490.

in the *Journal.* The reply reiterated the sense of the first resolution on the lack of power to act. It professed to see that the question of independence would be divisive within the province and would exercise "an unhappy influence" on the cognate question of a new government should both problems be submitted simultaneously to the electorate. Hence it would be "imprudent" to obtrude the first matter upon the people.[104] The Provincial Congress assured its representatives that "the earliest opportunity will, however, be embraced of ascertaining the sentiments of the inhabitants of this Colony on that important question. . . ."[105]

Since Livingston and his associates in Philadelphia knew that the Continental Congress would resume the subject of independence July 1, this information from New York must have made it clear that they would be without power to vote on the question. The delegates knew that the scheduled elections would occupy the third, if not also the fourth, week of June. Therefore, they could not receive their authorization to vote before July 1. Proof of the delegates' knowledge of the situation in New York derives from the following. Jay specifically promised Livingston that he should have the "earliest advice" of the May 31 resolutions on forming a government. Two of the Continental Congress delegation, Alsop and Lewis, who had visited home, did not set out for Philadelphia until June 1, so they possessed all the necessary information. Moreover, Gouverneur Morris arrived in Philadelphia June 10, so there was no dearth of news from the Provincial Congress.[106] Nonetheless, when the delegates acknowledged receipt of this

104 Force, *American Archives,* 4th ser., VI, 814; Becker, *The History of Political Parties,* p. 271. Becker incorrectly uses "inexpedient" for "imprudent."

105 Force, *American Archives,* 4th ser., VI, 814.

106 Jay to Livingston, May 29, 1776, Johnston, *Correspondence of John Jay,* I, 64, 65. On Morris's presence in Philadelphia, see Hancock to Provincial Congress, June 11, 1776, Burnett, *Letters,* I, 484. Lewis, *et al.* to President of Provincial Congress, June 17, 1776, *Jour. Prov. Cong.,* II, 197.

letter of instructions, they did not inform the Provincial Congress of their lack of time nor did they exhort that body to move swiftly to hold the referendum.

The New York delegation's comportment contrasted unfavorably with that of the Maryland delegation. Writing to their council of safety, the Marylanders observed that Congress had delayed a vote on independence for three weeks in order to give some delegations an opportunity to consult their "constituents." They urged the council to call the provincial convention into session that that body might express the sense of the people on the subject. As late as June 27 the New Yorkers had occasion to correspond with their congress but made absolutely no mention of the impending deadline.[107]

If the Provincial Congress could have demonstrated its ignorance of the events in Philadelphia, it might have technically justified its actions, but the contrary was the case. Edward Rutledge, writing Jay on June 8 from Philadelphia, described the course of the arguments and told of his fear of being unable to block a victory for independence. It is even possible that Rutledge dispatched his letter in care of the same express rider who carried the New York delegation's letter of the same date. In that event Jay would have received it June 10. Even if this were not true, there is other evidence to consider. When the Continental Congress suspended discussion of the question, it appointed a committee to draft a declaration and set July for resumption of the argument. Since Gouverneur Morris was present in Philadelphia from the final day of debate, June 10, until June 13, it is inconceivable that Livingston, a close friend, did not tell him of the whole business. Indeed, Morris may very well have attended Congress, since he bore a special letter from New York to the President of Congress. In view of the fact

---

107 Maryland delegates to Maryland Council of Safety, June 11, 1776, Burnett, *Letters*, I, 484; *Jour. Prov. Cong.*, II, 238.

that in May Morris had urged the necessity of independence, it is remarkable that upon his return to New York on June 15 he made no effort to reintroduce the matter in Provincial Congress. Thus at least two leading members of the New York Provincial Congress were cognizant of the crucial nature of affairs in Philadelphia but did nothing to enable their delegation to participate in the voting.[108]

Although the June elections came and went, no one in the Provincial Congress moved to reconsider the resolutions of June 11. Indeed June faded into July without a word on the subject. Whatever the intentions of the congressmen may have been, their conduct displayed a dubious standard of responsibility toward their constituents. It will be recalled that they had implied to the people that they would instruct the colony's delegates when the question arose on the floor of the Continental Congress.[109] But they did not fulfill their promise.[110] When the British invasion fleet hove in sight, they voted to meet in White Plains July 2 and hastily adjourned. Jay, who was in Elizabeth Town, reacted angrily to this news: "to my great mortification am informed that our convention influenced by one of G. Morris vagrant Plans have adjourned to the White Plains to meet there Tomorrow. This precipitate ill advised Retreat I fear will be not a little injurious to the publick. . . . This Stroke of Morrisania Politics quite confounds me."[111] Not being able to assemble a quorum on July 2, the Third Provincial Congress expired without committing the colony to independence.

These Fabian tactics probably owed part of their success

---

[108] Johnston, *Correspondence of John Jay*, I, 66, n. 1; *Jour. Prov. Cong.*, I, 496.

[109] See above, p. 164.

[110] Becker, *The History of Political Parties*, p. 273; *Jour. Prov. Cong.*, I, 512.

[111] Jay to Livingston, July 1, 1776, from *John Jay* by Frank Monaghan, copyright 1935 by the Bobbs-Merrill Company, Inc., R. 1962 by Frank Monaghan, reprinted by permission of the publishers, p. 83; Livingston, *Revolutionary Letters of Importance*, No. 27.

to the disorganized state of the city and countryside. Washington had converted the port into an armed camp, and most of the able-bodied males were in the army. By June most of the noncombatant population had left the city for safer regions. In this abnormal state, the radicals could not have brought decisive pressure to bear on the Provincial Congress. Furthermore, the revelations of the Tory plot against Washington monopolized so much attention and energy that there was little opportunity to call public meetings on the question of independence.[112] Perhaps the lack of strong leadership by the Provincial Congress on this issue retarded any independent steps by the people elsewhere in the province. Be it noted, however, that in some districts in Albany County the people seized the initiative and voted for independence on June 24.[113] Elbridge Gerry of Massachusetts thought that the people of the colony had outstripped their political leaders: "I do not affirm that either of these [i.e., New York and Maryland] are of the neuter gender; but on the other hand am persuaded the people are in favour of a total and final separation, and will support the measure, even if the Conventions and Delegates of those Colonies vote against it."[114]

If popular opinion approved independence, why did the Provincial Congress shy away at the mention of the word?[115]

---

112 Nettels, *George Washington,* pp. 291-94.
113 At King's District "a full meeting of the inhabitants" voted unanimously for independence. A similar meeting occurred in Spencer Town. *N.Y.P.,* July 4, 1776; Force, *American Archives,* 4th ser., VI, 1056.
114 Gerry to James Warren, June 25, 1776, *ibid.,* 4th ser., VI, 1067.
115 Becker, *The History of Political Parties,* pp. 272-73, sums up the situation in this manner: "The cause was simple: affairs in that province were directed by cautious and conservative politicians, who, in the face of an armed foe and surrounded by domestic enemies, were determined to preserve the essential features of their ancient political system from what they conceived to be monarchical encroachments on the one hand, as well as from rash democratic experiments on the other. And this achievement, if it could be effected, they were determined should be formally declared by the colony and not by the United Colonies.
"How much weight the latter consideration had, it is impossible to say."
By June of 1776 the threat of "monarchical encroachments" no longer had any bearing on whether to hasten or delay independence. As Becker

Many of the influential personages may have felt as did Livingston: "though at present I wish to join hands with a nation which I have been accustomed to respect, yet I am persuaded that the continuance of the war will break my shackles. . . ."[116] Accompanying this reluctance to break with tradition was a realization of the cost of the war in lives and property. Furthermore, since their leaders asked the people to make these sacrifices for the sake of freedom, might not internal disturbances arise over questions of local reform? Some symptoms of discontent had appeared already.[117] In the critical days of late June "Spartanus" had

---

himself admitted (p. 266) the Continental Congress's resolutions of May 15 "could have but one sequel, the declaration of independence. . . ." Thus when New York approved these resolutions May 31, the conservatives accepted the same destiny. Furthermore, as the above pages have shown, the New York leaders privately had seen the logic of events, but other factors deterred them. The latter part of Becker's argument is difficult to follow. The only way in which New York could preserve for itself the right to declare independence would be to do so before the Continental Congress, as did Rhode Island in May. If the Yorkers thought that their opposition would prevent the Congress from acting, they ran the risk of isolating their colony. With the Continental Army occupying New York, such a policy would indeed have been rash, and rashness was not characteristic of these men.

116 Livingston to Duane, February 16, 1776, Bancroft Transcripts: Livingston Papers, NYPL.

117 Some of the Dutchess County tenantry were demanding improved leases. Henry B. to R. R. Livingston, May, 1775, Livingston, *Revolutionary Letters of Importance*, No. 30.

The method of choosing the continental deputies became a controversial matter. In 1775 some of the counties chose their own representatives for Continental Congress, but the provincial convention overruled these choices and selected a representation for the whole province. The issue rose again in 1776 when the Mechanics demanded that right for the people. So bitter was the controversy in Ulster County that the Provincial Congress had to choose between the two sets of credentials: one that reserved the right to the people to elect continental deputies, another that authorized the provincial deputies to do so. None of these challenges succeeded. Becker, *The History of Political Parties*, p. 256; *N.Y.J.*, August 24, 1775, April 4, 1776; Jay to McDougall, April 11, 1776, McDougall Papers, NYHS; *Jour. Prov. Cong.*, I, 460, II, 199-200. See below, p. 205.

Some of the local committees ignored the property qualifications for voting. Sullivan, *Minutes of the Albany Committee*, II, 1030. On the same subject, Robert G. Livingston to Gilbert Livingston, January 1, 1782, Gilbert Livingston Papers, NYPL.

The practice of voting by secret ballot took root in some counties. New York General Committee to the People, *N.Y.J.*, April 11, 1776; Robert Boyd, Jr. to Clinton, July 3, 1776, George Clinton, *Public Papers of George Clinton, First Governor of New York* (10 vols.; Albany, 1899-1914), I, 244.

warned newspaper readers to beware of those who have
dragged their heels but now "speak fair." Let them gain
power, he wrote, and they will subject the people "to a
tyranny and oppression . . . not much better" than the
British.[118] Early in 1775 William Smith cautioned Schuyler
about the hazards of a Pandora's box: "Why raise a military
spirit that may furnish unmanageable adventurers on this side
of the water unfriendly to a province in which you and I
have something else to lose?"[119] James Duane expressed
concern about "licenciousness" and the "means of assuring
the Reins of Government when these Commotions shall
subside."[120] McDougall worried over the dual dangers of
the "licentiousness of the people" and of the army. "The
former feel their own liberty in the extreme," he wrote to
Jay; a sentiment with which the latter concurred.[121]

Probably one of the chief reasons for the excessive caution of the New Yorkers in the Provincial Congress was
their fear that the consequences of an unsuccessful rebellion would be confiscation of property and execution. John
Adams, Richard H. Lee, and George Wythe accused New
York of hanging back "that their particular prospect might
be better even in the worst event."[122] In a private conver-

---

[118] Quoted in Becker, *The History of Political Parties*, p. 267; "Spartanus,"
N.Y.J., June 20, 1776; Force, *American Archives*, 4th ser., VI, 996.

[119] Smith to Schuyler, May 16, 1775, Schuyler Papers, NYPL; Benson J.
Lossing, *The Life and Times of Philip Schuyler* (2 vols.; New York, 1873),
I, 321-22.

Two months later Schuyler incorporated a draft by Smith in orders
issued to the troops in New York City. Among the ideas voiced was this:
"Let us evince to the world that in contending for liberty we abhor licentiousness. . . ." Smith, Memoirs, IV, July 3, 1775; Lossing, *The Life and
Times of Philip Schuyler*, I, 346.

[120] Duane to Robert Livingston, Jr., June 7, 1775, quoted in Beverly
McAnear, "Mr. Robert R. Livingston's Reasons against a Land Tax,"
Journal of Political Economy, XLVIII (February, 1940), 76.

[121] McDougall to Jay, March 20, 1776, Jay to McDougall, March 23, 1776,
John Jay Papers, CUL; Johnston, *Correspondence of John Jay*, I, 49-50.
Smith says McDougall told him in February that he opposed independence.
Smith, Memoirs, V, February 12, 1776.

Livingston once commented that the leaders must "yield to the torrent
if they hoped to direct its course." Livingston to Duer, June 12, 1777,
R. R. Livingston Collection, NYHS.

sation with McDougall, William Smith remarked in passing
on the risks to which the Whig leaders exposed themselves,
noting "the wrath manifested in the King's speech ag[ains]t
them as the misleaders of his American subjects."[123] Although the British no longer exercised authority in the
province by the summer of 1775, Admiral Graves wrote
home that "there are many in [the violent party] who wish
to keep the peace in New York on account of their property."[124] That fall a Tory merchant declared that the Whigs
of "prosperity are afraid of their estates, and are coming
about fast."[125]

Some patriots prudently left the danger zones at critical
moments. When Howe appeared before New York, a number of Whigs departed hurriedly. Among others, Philip
Livingston parted from the Third Provincial Congress
rather abruptly. Jay said that Livingston gave no other
reason than that he was going to Philadelphia. "The ways
of some men like Solomons Serpent on a Rock, are past
finding out," Jay concluded disgustedly.[126] After the loss of
New York in September, 1776, the conduct of Gouverneur
and General Lewis Morris caused bitter complaint. Robert
R. Livingston wrote to Edward Rutledge of South Carolina:
"Gouverneur thro' what cause God alone knows has deserted in this hour of danger retired to some obscure corner
of the Jerseys where he enjoys his jest and his ease while
his friends are strugling with every difficulty and danger
& blushing while they make those apologies for him which
they do not themselves believe."[127] Lewis Morris's behavior
provoked comment in Westchester and in the state Con-

---

122 Jefferson's Notes of Proceedings in the Continental Congress, Boyd,
The Papers of Thomas Jefferson, I, 312.
123 William Smith, Memoirs, V, January 8, 1776.
124 Graves to Stephens, July 16, 1775, *Cal. H. O. Papers*, p. 394.
125 V. P. Ashfield to Isaac Wilkins, November 4, 1775, *ibid.*, p. 482.
126 Jay to R. R. Livingston, July 1, 1776, Livingston, *Revolutionary Letters of Importance*, No. 27.
127 Livingston to Edward Rutledge, October 10, 1776, Bancroft Transcripts: Livingston Papers, NYPL.

vention. The Convention had granted him a few days leave
to see to his family in Philadelphia upon his express promise
to return promptly to his militia regiment. The general not
only violated his word, but implied to the continental delegates that he had come to Philadelphia on Convention
business. Since he evaded the requests of the Convention
to return to the state, that body peremptorily ordered him
home. Rutledge gave this account of Morris's presence in
Philadelphia:

> he left us near three weeks since from some hints which his
> friends here took the liberty of giving him, and declared he
> would never return until he had conquered it [i.e., fear]. Should
> he be worse than his word & pay us another Visit, I'll answer
> for him that he will not stay here above two Days to rest him-
> self. Indeed I much doubt whether he will be able to call
> those, Days of rest, for I will immediately make a Party to
> plague his very heart out. Philadelphia shall not be a place of
> Safety for him I assure you.[128]

Having committed themselves to independence, the
Whigs prepared themselves for misfortune. Robert R. Livingston explained, "I am amazed at the composure I feel
tho' I have everything at stake, & the enemy are already
in actual possession of one third of my income."[129] The
grim prospect of capture by the British induced fearsome
thoughts among many. Gouverneur Morris in 1777, describing the impact on the first legislature of the American
defeats in the mid-Hudson, which included the loss of Forts
Constitution, Montgomery, and Clinton, confessed: *"We*

---

128 Rutledge to Livingston, October 19, 1776, *ibid.; Jour. Prov. Cong.,* I,
666; Morris to Convention, September 24, 1776, Force, *American Archives,*
5th ser., III, 211.

129 Livingston to Rutledge, September 27, 1776, Livingston, *Revolutionary
Letters of Importance,* No. 95. In a later letter to Rutledge he depicted
graphically the dangers of a revolutionary career: "Every day discovers new
plotts a regular plan was formed to carry me off, headed by a relation and
only defeated by a discovery that very night in which it was to have been
executed. Bullets have been shot at night into the very beds of some of our
active people & others been fired at & wound'd on the ambush." Same to
same, October 10, 1776, Bancroft Transcripts: Livingston Papers, NYPL.

are hellishly frightened but don't say a word of that for we shall get our spirits again. . . ."[130] One contemporary attributed the caution of the great landed families to property considerations: "Such extensive property is perhaps too great a stake to be risked in a struggle with a bold invader. . . ."[131] The fears deriving from the foregoing considerations exercised a marked influence on the members of the Provincial Congress and manifested themselves in the advocacy of a go-slow policy.

Since the militancy of public opinion in the colony outran that of the Whig leaders, the delaying tactics of the leadership did not bring New York any closer to pacification. However much John Adams might rail against the timidity of the Yorkers, every important step they took, however halting, was a step farther down the road to independence. The Whigs understood that New York was "a nut in the jaws of a nutcracker."[132] British military strategy centered upon the capture of the province by an attack from Canada as well as from the sea. With these military threats hanging over the province, it is understandable why New York was not in the van of the revolutionary movement.

---

130 Morris to R. R. Livingston, October 8, 1777, R. R. Livingston Collection, NYHS.
131 "The Real Farmer," *N.Y.J.*, February 1, 1779.
132 Nettels, *George Washington*, p. 282.

SIX

Government Prior to the Constitution of 1777

THE Provincial Congress was the nerve center of the revolutionary movement. Its formation greatly strengthened the Whigs in that it united under central direction the county and local committees who lacked overall authority. Since many of the leading patriots served in the Provincial Congress, the people looked to that body for direction. This support in turn enabled the provisional legislature to mobilize the citizenry and their resources. Furthermore, the Whigs now had the means to apply uniform policies throughout the counties. Equally important, the Provincial Congress could and did speak in the name of the whole colony, constituting the only significant group with whom the British could negotiate. Lastly, the Provincial Congress replaced the royal administration as the governing authority.

Although the Tories labored mightily to block the calling of a congress, they had toiled in vain even before the news of Lexington reached New York. When the colonial assembly had refused to name representatives to the Second Continental Congress, the moderates and radicals in the city Committee of Sixty had cooperated to push through a call for the election in April of a provincial convention that would meet solely to choose the continental delegates. The Provincial Convention met in New York City April

20, 1775, completed its business, and dissolved April 22. When the news from New England arrived in town the next day, the conditions requisite for summoning a provincial congress had matured.[1] On April 28 the city committee appealed to the counties to elect deputies to represent them in a provincial congress to assemble in May. The committee's circular letter justified the call by painting a grim picture: "The distressed and alarming situation of our country, . . . threatening to involve this Continent in all the horrors of a civil War, obliges us to call for the united aid and council of the Colony. . . ."[2]

When the colony completed the balloting, either by direct choice or by the local committees, it had deputed 113 men to attend the First Provincial Congress. Not all of these counted themselves Whigs and eventually nineteen joined the loyalists. Although the election circular had set May 22 for the opening of the First Provincial Congress, a majority of the county delegations did not appear until the next day. Some of the absentees came in later in the session, but Gloucester County did not send a deputation at any time. Individual attendance left much to be desired and the numerous absences impeded the legislature's effective operation. From May through July attendance ranged from a low of forty-two to a high of eighty-two.[3]

According to the rules of procedure drawn up by the Provincial Congress, a majority of the counties constituted a quorum. Moreover, each county had to have a quorum of its delegation present in order to be able to vote. Definition of the quorum varied from county to county, some requiring a delegation majority, others from one to four men. Since the counties cast unit votes, each deputation had

[1] Carl L. Becker, *The History of Political Parties in the Province of New York, 1760-1776* (Madison, 1909), pp. 193, 201.
[2] *Cal. Hist. Mss.*, I, 4.
[3] Becker, *The History of Political Parties*, p. 208.

to decide the county's position first before voting. Debate
and dickering among the counties preceded the apportion-
ment of voting strength. The resultant compromise gave
New York four votes, Albany three, and the other counties
two each.[4]

Having established a framework within which to labor,
the Provincial Congress began to tackle the multitudinous
problems that led it to exercise the power forfeited by the
royal government. Although the members wrestled with
many pressing questions, they devoted most time to those
which related to military preparations, the Tories, and
finances. Plagued by decreasing attendance, the Provincial
Congress adopted a suggestion of the Continental Congress
to transfer its provincial authority to a committee of safety
for a stated period. Each county had one vote on this committee except New York which had two. All of the committee's acts were subject to ultimate approval by the
Provincial Congress. This device permitted it to adjourn
for the months of July and September but to leave in its
place a functioning executive.[5]

By October the First Provincial Congress prepared to
end its life and passed resolutions for that purpose. It
named November 7, 1775, election day for the choice of
representatives to the Second Provincial Congress. It proposed to dissolve November 14, the day its successor convened. Having defeated a suggestion to use the written
ballot, the majority relented and extended the suffrage to
nonfreeholders who held lands assessed at £80. Notwithstanding its November 14 deadline, the Provincial Congress
broke up in confusion November 4.[6]

However, it did not assemble on November 14. In

4 *Ibid.*, pp. 207-8; *Jour. Prov. Cong.*, I, 8.
5 Alexander C. Flick, ed., *A History of the State of New York* (10 vols.;
New York, 1933-1937), III, 263; *Jour. Prov. Cong.*, I, 222.
6 See above, pp. 109-11; Becker, *The History of Political Parties*, p. 227.

fact, it did not have a quorum until December 6. Despite this inauspicious beginning, the Whigs congratulated themselves on the new membership of the legislature. The local committees had dropped thirty-nine former delegates in favor of more ardent patriots, or so they thought. During most of its life the Second Provincial Congress remained adjourned, having created a committee of safety to carry on. Thus it fell to the lot of the Committee of Safety to accede in the middle of April, 1776, to Washington's demand for the isolation of the British warships in the harbor. Although some of the radical Whigs grumbled over the slow progress of military preparations, by spring they had less cause to complain as the presence of the Continental Army in New York pressured the Committee of Safety into more vigorous exertions. Before its March adjournment the Provincial Congress provided for the election of the Third Provincial Congress in April and its own dissolution May 14.[7]

A further weeding-out process occurred in the April, 1776, balloting; no less than thirty-two members of the Second Provincial Congress yielded their seats to new men. The number of Tories, however, remained almost constant at eight. All the counties chose deputies and revised downward the number necessary to form a delegation quorum. Consequently, the Third Provincial Congress did not have to wrestle with the quorum issue. A change in the distri-

---

[7] *Ibid.,* pp. 232-35, 252.

These decisions about sessions reflected the difficulties of congressional government. The revolutionary situation required protracted periods of meeting but most colonials had no prior experience with this kind of procedure. The provincial assembly usually met for three months and then adjourned. The executive organs enforced the laws. There was no revolutionary executive and the Provincial Congress could not adjourn unless some agency could take the reins to prevent the Tories from reasserting control. The Whigs solved the problem by setting the life of a provincial congress at six months and by clothing the Committee of Safety with executive authority only. Therefore, the Second Provincial Congress in December, 1775, agreed upon April, 1776, as election date for the Third. *Jour. Prov. Cong.,* I, 223.

bution of the unit votes increased New York's share from one-seventh to one-sixth of the total. The new arrangement gave New York eight votes, Albany six, Dutchess five, Suffolk four, Ulster four, Westchester four, Queens four, Orange and Tryon three each, Kings, Richmond, Charlotte, and Cumberland two each, and Gloucester one.

Although the Third Provincial Congress had a brief existence, it considered three key problems: suppression of the Tories, instructions to its delegates at the Continental Congress on the question of independence, and the formation of a new governmental structure for the colony. A majority deemed it best to refer the last issue to the people, calling for the election in June of a new Provincial Congress with power to draw up a constitution. When General Sir William Howe appeared off New York at the end of June, the Third Provincial Congress adjourned June 30, 1776, to reconvene July 2 at White Plains. Since it could not muster a quorum at White Plains, the Third Congress gave way to its successor.[8]

Many of the changes in the personnel of the Fourth Provincial Congress were a result of a decrease in the size of the delegations. Whereas the Third had a nominal membership of 136, the Fourth had only 106. Fully thirteen of the thirty who did not serve again had represented the three counties (Kings, Queens, and Richmond) which the Tories largely controlled. Only eight of the congressmen were new members.[9] Since the Continental Congress had declared independence, the Fourth Provincial Congress joined the other former colonies in independence on the first day of its meeting, July 9. In accordance with its new status, the Fourth Provincial Congress transformed itself

---

[8] Becker, *The History of Political Parties*, pp. 259-61, 273.

[9] *Jour. Prov. Cong.*, I, 516-931; Edgar A. Werner, *Civil List and Constitutional History of the Colony and State of New York* (Albany, 1888), pp. 408-9. Becker mistakenly states that about one-third of the Fourth Provincial Congress were new men. *The History of Political Parties*, p. 274.

into the Convention of Representatives of the State of New York on July 10.

Thus opened the most difficult period in the history of the state's provisional governments. The Convention had to govern the state, conduct the war, write a constitution, and stay out of the hands of the British invaders, all of this in the midst of a series of major American defeats and retreats from southern New York in 1776-1777. In this confusion the Convention appointed a committee of safety to assume its functions and the committee sat for most of the ten months of the Convention's life, July, 1776–May, 1777.[10]

The two years from May, 1775, to May, 1777, witnessed the steady elaboration of congressional government. The Provincial Congress, of course, worked out specific policies and often depended upon the county and local committees to execute them. At the commencement of the first session the Provincial Congress assumed the subordination of the local bodies to its authority when it directed the formation of committees where nonexistent to enforce the resolutions of the Continental and Provincial Congresses.[11] On numerous occasions the deputies created special committees to carry through their plans, but sometimes, when key men served on more than one committee, this practice precipitated a personnel crisis. For example, the Provincial Congress appointed Jay, R. R. Livingston, and Robert Yates to a secret committee to obstruct the Hudson to the British but in August also put them on the constitutional committee. Since the trio neglected the latter for the former, the constitutional committee accomplished nothing for some time.[12] Using various methods, the Provincial Congress extended its authority over major areas of government. It

---

10 *Jour. Prov. Cong.*, I, 579-824.
11 Becker, *The History of Political Parties*, p. 212; *Jour. Prov. Cong.*, I, 18.
12 See below p. 219.

exercised jurisdiction, for example, over raising, equipping, and supplying the army, finance, suppression of the loyalists and seizure of their property, confederal relations, and Indian affairs.

Military preparations naturally absorbed much of the time and energy of the delegates. Raising an army involved the organization of three types of units. The Continental Congress directed the formation of the regular units, the line regiments, but the colonies nominated their officers and actually recruited them. New York authorized the first recruiting campaign June 28, 1775. The five regiments that resulted participated in the ill-fated Canadian expedition 1775-1776. Since the men's enlistments expired December 31, 1775, their units underwent reorganization after the campaign. When the Provincial Congress prepared to raise four more regiments in January, 1776, the deputies differed over the selection of the officers. They resolved their differences by circularizing the counties, requesting the county committees to nominate two persons for each position. In their first efforts in February to raise the regular regiments the Provincial Congress worked out quotas for each county, but in December they revised their procedure. They appointed the officers, then assigned them recruiting districts in each county.[13]

The militia comprised the second component of the armed services. Although the Continental Congress advised New York in May, 1775, to commence planning its militia organization, the First Provincial Congress did no more than to appoint a committee to consider the situation. Not until August 9 did the much-revised committee hand in a report which was approved. Five days later the legislature published its detailed resolutions, which governed the organization, training, discipline, and pay of the troops. They

---

[13] Alexander C. Flick, *The American Revolution in New York* (Albany, 1926), pp. 133-34; *Jour. Prov. Cong.*, I, 268-69, 306-7, 712-13.

set the strength of the basic unit, the company, at about eighty-three officers and men. Five to ten companies joined to compose a regiment, and each county had one or more regiments. The regiments combined to form the colony's six brigades, each of which was under the command of a major general. In addition, there were previously in existence certain independent formations (hussars, artillery, and grenadiers) which retained their original structures. The men chose their own officers below the rank of major, leaving to the Provincial Congress the appointment of the field ranks. When the companies had organized, one-fourth of the company's number volunteered as minutemen. These volunteers constituted minute companies which might be called into action immediately.[14]

The Provincial Congress drew up a code of regulations for the militia. The rules required each man to provide himself with "a good musket or firelock and bayonet, sword or tomahawk, a steel ramrod, worm, priming wire and brush, . . . a cartouch box, to contain twenty-three rounds of cartridges, twelve flints and a knapsack. . . ." The militiaman had to supply his own ammunition, a pound of powder, and three pounds of bullets. Having accoutered himself, the part-time soldier had to train one day a month for four hours. Since the larger units needed experience also, the regiments would mobilize "at least two days in every year." Penalties for disobedience and refusal to serve ranged from fines to imprisonment. Those who would not enlist would suffer advertisements as enemies to their country.[15]

The New York Provincial Congress dispatched circular letters of militia instructions in August to the county committees and the latter commenced the task of actual militia organization. Since the parent organ did not vigorously

---

14 Flick, *American Revolution in New York*, pp. 138-39; *Jour. Prov. Cong.*, I, 16, 21, 69, 103, 104, 114-16.
15 Flick, *American Revolution in New York*, p. 139; *Jour. Prov. Cong.*, I, 114, 115.

press the matter, these activities proceeded at a very uneven rate. Suffice it to say that by the close of 1775 most of the counties had completed some part if not all of their assignment. Many problems arose which compelled the Provincial Congress to amend the militia law in December, 1775. Some of the regulations in respect to the election of officers, training, brigading, and minutemen underwent modification. This remained the basic statute until June, 1776, when the Provincial Congress again revised it, abolishing the minutemen.[16]

The third component of the armed forces, denominated levies, did not have a separate organization. When the military situation demanded it, the government ordered a portion of the militia into the field for a specific period of time. These constituted the levies. If volunteers did not fill the quotas, the counties drafted the necessary numbers.[17]

New York did not neglect the other branch of service, the navy. The colony had no ships of the line, but it did encourage privateering. A clear picture of the privateers' operations cannot be found, but about a dozen of them took to the seas in the period under consideration. One of them, the *Montgomery*, captured eight prizes by 1777 with a total value of £11,000.[18]

When the Provincial Congress plunged into the intricate task of supplying and equipping the army, it encountered bewildering problems of every description. Not only did the state lack manufactured goods essential to the prosecution of the war but also it experienced great difficulties in procuring and transporting its abundant agricultural commodities to the camps or supply bases. Furthermore, despite the

---

16 Flick, *American Revolution in New York*, pp. 140-41; *Jour. Prov. Cong.*, I, 135, 139, 152; *Cal. Hist. Mss.*, I, 38, 61, 83, 84, 85, 119, 120, 121, 122, 123, 127, 132, 133, 134, 135, 138, 144, 145, 147, 148, 149, 158, 164, 169, 177, 193, 198, 261.
17 Flick, *American Revolution in New York*, pp. 141-43.
18 *Ibid.*, pp. 145-47; *Jour. Prov. Cong.*, I, 859, 915.

heroic labors of devoted officials, a certain amount of pecula-
tion and speculation impeded the functioning of the supply
services. Noting these circumstances, Schuyler remarked
to Jay that military spending in the Northern Department
alone ran at five times the annual rate of the most expensive
year in the previous colonial war.[19]

Since the Provincial Congress failed completely to grasp
either the magnitude or the nature of the supply problem,
the delegates reacted spasmodically, moved to action by
especially urgent situations. It took the first step to create a
commissariat at the direction of the Continental Congress.
The latter body resolved to have New York furnish provisions and stores for the newly captured forts at Crown
Point and Ticonderoga. On June 2, 1775, the Provincial
Congress offered the position of commissary to Peter T.
Curtenius, New York merchant. The scope of the resolutions implied that Curtenius would be employed to purchase
other supplies as the New York Provincial Congress desired.[20] For his services the commissary received a 1.5 percent commission if he spent his own funds, or a 1 percent
commission if he expended congressional funds. If he spent
his own money, the Provincial Congress would allow him
lawful interest for its use. Finally, Curtenius would obtain
reimbursement for all expenses.[21] Having selected a purch-
asing agent, the Provincial Congress the next day presented
him with a large order which they directed him to forward
to Lake George. Among the items Curtenius set out to procure, 1,000 pounds of oakum represented the largest quantity, but he also had to hire artificers and seamen for the
same destination.[22]

---

[19] Schuyler to Jay, February 1, 1777, John Jay Papers, Iselin Collection, CUL.
[20] *Jour. Prov. Cong.*, I, 27.
[21] Flick, *American Revolution in New York*, p. 181; *Jour. Prov. Cong.*, I, 27.
[22] *Ibid.*, I, 28. Flick, *American Revolution in New York*, p. 182, refers to a later order as the earliest.

When occasion demanded, the Provincial Congress by-passed the commissary and appointed a committee of its members to fulfill certain tasks. An incident of this nature arose during the first few weeks of Curtenius's tenure. The Continental Congress instructed the New Yorkers with admonitions of secrecy to provide 5,000 barrels of flour for the army near Boston. The Provincial Congress promptly chose Isaac Sears, Abraham Walton, and Joseph Hallett to carry out the project.[23]

Even though his staff grew commensurately, Curtenius's responsibilities multiplied so rapidly they exceeded his ability to discharge them effectively. He had under his direction one agent, three deputies, seventeen subcommissaries, eight commissaries of purchases, and numerous storekeepers and clerks. Although the supply service had become complicated, the Provincial Congress did nothing to simplify its organization until events forced the legislators to do so. When General Charles Lee arrived in February, 1776, to fortify the city, apparently he or his staff "suggested" that the Committee of Safety appoint a special issuing military commissary to have charge of all army stores in New York County. The committee complied and instructed Curtenius to transfer such stores to Richard Norwood, whom they appointed to the new post.[24]

When New York and continental troops began to pour into the city in February, 1776, the supply problem became very complex. The Provincial Congress requested Curtenius to supply the necessary rations, but the commissary declined. Accepting Curtenius's explanation of the pressure of his duties, the New York legislature turned to Abraham Livingston to fill the gap. Livingston operated under a contract with the legislature, but his duties did not carry through until the end of the provisional government. Since

---

23 *Jour. Prov. Cong.*, I, 39-40.
24 *Ibid.*, I, 290.

the colony's militia was under the command of the continental commander in New York City and since this was true later in the Northern Department, most of the victualling contracts came under the jurisdiction of the Continental Army. When the militia remained under the state's authority, one of numerous commissaries contracted for the rations.[25]

The difficulty of supplying the troops with adequate clothing provoked the Committee of Safety to take steps ultimately to reform that aspect of the service. Prior to this time Curtenius and others bought semifinished and finished goods. Late in 1776 the committee initiated tentative steps to establish a state clothing store, but its organization did not reach fruition until the appointment of John Henry as State Clothier in February, 1777, at a salary of 10s. per diem.[26]

The Convention of Representatives further modified the system in May, 1777, when it charged John Lasher with complete authority over all military stores. To the rank of colonel the deputies attached a salary of £200 per annum and expenses and empowered him to impress teams and carriages if necessary. At the same time they chose David Currie to furnish the troops with items not supplied by the commissariat. In this category fell wine, beer, sugar, chocolate, coffee, tobacco, and staples. The Convention allowed Currie three dollars a day and expenses.[27]

The acute shortage of guns, cannon, and ammunition compelled the Provincial Congress frequently to resort to various expedients to procure desired quantities. The state had few skilled gunsmiths upon whom to rely but did contract with these few to manufacture specific quantities. The Provincial Congress sought to import arms and powder, ap-

---

25 *Ibid.,* I, 303, 315, 360, 362, 365, 367, 388, 405, 436, 761.
26 Flick, *American Revolution in New York,* p. 187; *Jour. Prov. Cong.,* I, 695, 698, 807.
27 Flick, *History of New York,* IV, 133; *Jour. Prov. Cong.,* I, 920.

propriating £4,000 for the purpose in September, 1775. Driven to seek other alternatives by the continuing shortage, in March, 1776, it resolved to loan £200 without interest to anyone who would produce the greatest number of gunlocks and to give a premium of 4s. on each piece to the producers. Similarly, the delegates sought to stimulate the manufacture of gun barrels and bayonets. Exertions to secure light and heavy cannon encountered similar obstacles. On one occasion, despite the pressing need, the Provincial Congress rejected a contract for brass cannon because the price of 4s. a pound was too high. On the other hand, lack of skilled labor and uncertainty as to the needed quantity caused the Committee of Safety to forgo the employment of a foundry owned by Robert Livingston, Jr., for casting heavy cannon. Exorbitant prices did not always deter the Provincial Congress from accepting a contract. A critical lack of grapeshot caused the legislature to pay double the market price.[28]

Insufficient quantities of two other products closely associated with munitions, lead and powder, plagued the revolutionaries. The Provincial Congress directed Curtenius to collect the lead window weights of private dwellings, promising later compensation. In this manner Curtenius received more than 100 tons. The state promoted the search for, and working of lead mines, but none of these attempts proved fruitful. Bounties and loans produced a more favorable situation in regard to powder. Venturous individuals erected a number of powder mills, but at first the mills could not manufacture rapidly because of the scarcity of sulphur and saltpeter. Again the state intervened to promote the location of sulphur deposits and the production of the latter. Both efforts succeeded. Sulphur mined in

---

28 Flick, *History of New York*, IV, 135-36; *Jour. Prov. Cong.*, I, 148, 268, 307, 358, 363-64; Peter Force, ed., *American Archives* (9 vols.; Washington, D.C., 1837-1853), 4th ser., V, 278-79.

Tryon County became the mainstay and saltpeter from small shops and households tended to relieve the shortage in that article.[29]

The state looked to its own resources for adequate supplies of hemp, flax, and wool. Under the advice of the Continental Congress, New York in April, 1776, pleaded with its farmers to increase the acreage of hemp and flax and to increase and improve the breed of their sheep. Even prior to this action, the New York Provincial Congress had voted £1,333 to hire the poor of the city to spin flax. In October, 1776, the Convention selected a committee to provide work in weaving and spinning for the New York City refugees. Such improvisations produced a considerable quantity of cloth. The state imported hempseed in large quantity and distributed it to the farmers without charge.[30]

Given the scope of the task and the inexperience of officials, it is no surprise that confusion and waste loomed large. A large portion of the provisional government's expenditures for 1775-1777 went to pay for the huge quantities of these supplies discussed above. In these two years the Provincial Congress spent at least £500,000 for all purposes.[31] It is to the credit of the government that it managed to achieve what it did.

From the outset the revolutionary government contended with two deficiencies, guns and funds. When the need for funds arose, the congressmen pledged their personal wealth as security. Obviously, the delegates would not bankrupt themselves to finance revolutionary operations, so they had to find an alternative. The financial question thrust itself to the fore on the second day of the First Provincial Con-

---

29 Flick, *History of New York*, IV, 138-41. Measures to import powder encountered price difficulties and occasional congressional reluctance to pay extravagant prices. See the case of Nicholas Low, *Jour. Prov. Cong.*, I, 235, 241, 254, 340, 502.

30 Flick, *American Revolution in New York*, pp. 184-85; *Jour. Prov. Cong.*, I, 414-15.

31 New York State, Treasurer's Accounts, 1775-1778, NYHS.

gress, May 23, 1775, when the delegates read a letter from
the Continental Congress urging the removal of arms and
stores from Fort Ticonderoga. After debating the matter,
the delegates referred it to a committee for study. In its
report the committee the next day suggested the appointment of a committee "to consider of ways and means for
providing moneys" to accomplish the Ticonderoga task.
The Provincial Congress approved this report but did not
choose a committee of ways and means. The inaction was
not equivalent to a death sentence, however. It would seem
probable that private discussion continued because on May
26, without a recorded motion or discussion, the house
selected a committee to prepare a report on a continental
paper currency.[32] Simultaneously, the members drafted a
letter to their representatives at Philadelphia in which they
stated that they had the financial question under study.

The letter and the later committee report are important,
since they throw some light on attitudes toward taxation.
The letter made two basic points. Considering the drift
toward war, the authors declared "an uncommon levy" of
money would soon be a necessity for the Continental Congress and, therefore, the latter body would probably discuss
the feasibility of paper currency. As to taxation, they wrote,
"it is clearly impossible" to raise the requisite funds by
this means. The committee reiterated this view in its report
on May 30, insisting that the Continental Congress would
have to issue some form of paper and that each colony would
have to sink its own share. Significantly, the house approved
the committee's recommendations unanimously.[33]

There the matter rested for two months, when rapidly
rising expenditures induced another plea to the men at
Philadelphia. New York, the Provincial Congress asserted,
had spent a large sum for continental purposes and an equal

---

32 *Jour. Prov. Cong.,* I, 9, 10, 14.
33 *Ibid.,* I, 14, 19, 20.

amount for the province. Taxation, therefore, had become a necessity, but "prudence or policy" dictated the adoption of that mode which would be least liable to arouse "popular disgust or perhaps, opposition." The letter proposed an alternative which would have achieved two objectives. They asked that the Continental Congress repeal the ban on tea consumption, set a maximum price on it, and tax the vendor 1s. a pound. Since New York tea merchants had "a considerable quantity" of smuggled Dutch tea on hand, the ban's repeal would release their capital for investment in the importation of direly needed Dutch goods. Moreover, the brunt of this tax would fall on those who violated the association, the "obstinate consumers" of the brew.[34] This overture came to naught because the Yorkers failed to rally any other colony to their view.

Without waiting for a reply to their tea tax application of July 28, the delegates on August 5 voted another committee on ways and means to study financial measures. The Albany delegation informed its county committee that many congressmen favored an immediate tax, but it added that it could not say whether a levy would carry. Although the house listened to the committee's statement on August 11, it postponed a decision until August 15. It seems possible that the committee recommended a levy up to £30,000, but when recorded in the *Journal* weeks later, the report specified a minimum of £15,000.[35] Since the Provincial Congress did not discuss the matter again, despite its intention, until August 30, perhaps growing opposition to the

---

34 Becker, *The History of Political Parties*, p. 217; Arthur M. Schlesinger, Sr., *The Colonial Merchants and the American Revolution, 1763-1776* (New York, 1939), p. 583; *Jour. Prov. Cong.*, I, 92.

35 Becker, *The History of Political Parties*, p. 218; *Jour. Prov. Cong.*, I, 101, 105. The Albany delegates, writing home immediately after the action of August 11, declared that the tax would raise a sum "not exceeding £30,000." J. Sullivan, ed., *Minutes of the Albany Committee of Correspondence, 1775-1778 and Minutes of the Schenectady Committee, 1775-1779* (2 vols.; Albany, 1923, 1925), I, 185, 196.

levy caused its proponents to compromise on the lower figure.

Led by Gilbert Livingston, the opponents successfully amended the report. They substituted an emission of £45,000 in paper for the tax, committing the Provincial Congress to fund by taxation one-third of the total each year over the next three years. Upon reconsideration the house voted to reduce the funding period to two years. The resolution directed the creation of the necessary tax officials, providing for supervisors, assessors, and collectors. It granted the collectors authority to collect from defaulters by "distress upon the goods and chattels" thereof. Since the measure distributed the tax among the counties on a quota basis, the members sought to bargain for the lowest quota. The endless maneuvering brought on a deadlock which the First Provincial Congress never resolved.[36]

It is difficult to interpret the significance of the paper money triumph solely on the basis of the voting record. The counties cast unit votes and it is impossible to determine from the *Journal* how the members voted within the delegation to decide their county's ballot. Even though Albany, Ulster, and Richmond voted against the bills of credit, it is risky to conclude therefrom that these delegations represented creditor groups.[37] If one accepts the sincerity of the deputies' avowed intention to fund the debt, then the problem resolves itself into one of timing. It should be noted also that by decreasing the funding span to two years, the house increased the tax funds for each year to £22,500, whereas the original committee recommendation had advocated a £15,000 levy.

Having wet their feet, as it were, in the paper ocean, the

---

36 Thomas C. Cochran, *New York in the Confederation* (Philadelphia, 1932), p. 28; *Jour. Prov. Cong.*, I, 128, 133-34.
37 Cochran, *New York in the Confederation*, p. 44 and n. 5. New York County divided evenly.

congressmen were not loath to return for another dip. The
Provincial Congress voted two more emissions in January
and August, 1776, which amounted to £255,000. These
proved to be final, so that New York had mortgaged itself
for £300,000 in all. Both of the last issues indicated the
deterioration of the strength of the proponents of taxation.
Although the January resolution laid down a three-year
funding plan, it made no reference to the tax quotas essential to carry it out. By August even the funding operation
disappeared from the resolution and the Provincial Congress drew up a substitute: "That the public faith of this
State be pledged for the redemption of the said bills of
credit, and that this Convention, or some future Legislature of this State, will make effectual provision for that
purpose."[38]

Fortunately for the prosecution of the war, New York
could borrow from the Continental Congress. When the
latter organ struck off continental paper, it dispatched some
£150,000 to the Provincial Congress, 1775-1777. In addition to this source, the New York legislature borrowed from
individuals to an undetermined amount.[39]

Whatever the reasons for the provisional Congress's hesitation to lay a tax, the creditor-debtor relationship and the
fear of political opposition are not sufficient explanations.[40]
John Jay long criticized the paper policy, prodding Mc-
Dougall occasionally to seek a change. On March 27, 1776,
Jay adverted to the political effects of taxation in these
words: "There is much money in the Province, the Produce
of the Country retains its Price & a moderate Tax would be
borne without a Murmur."[41] McDougall revealed something

---

38 *Ibid.*, p. 38; *Jour. Prov. Cong.*, I, 223, 316, 326, 330, 336, 338, 339, 540,
560, 571.
39 New York State, Treasurer's Accounts, 1775-1778, NYHS; *Jour. Prov.
Cong.*, I, 116; Flick, *American Revolution in New York*, p. 114.
40 See Becker, *The History of Political Parties*, p. 217; Cochran, *New York
in the Confederation*, p. 44.

of the situation's complexity in his reply of April 16 to Jay:

> I have long been of your opinion on the subject of taxing, but I
> confess there are weighty difficulties in the way. The great stag-
> nation of commerce, and the removal of the inhabitants out of
> this city were important reasons which induced my assent to
> delay that measure. If we had taxed, where should the rich men
> of this capital who have taken their flight be taxed? And how is
> the poor freeholder of it, to pay his, when he can receive no
> [rent]? I was determined & delayed the tax for these difficulties
> as the country members seem bent on saddling us with one third
> of the colony expence.[42]

It is worthy of note that these reasons gave Jay pause and
he confessed they had not occurred to him.[43]

The colonial treasurer's position was an ambivalent one.
When the Provincial Congress needed funds in May, 1775,
it called upon the treasurer of the colony, Abraham Lott, to
lend the required money on the personal guarantee of the
deputies. Although he was a royal official, Lott complied
and this procedure obtained for a considerable length of
time. Meanwhile, the First Provincial Congress appointed
Peter Van Brugh Livingston as its treasurer in July, 1775.
The office proved too burdensome for Livingston, an elderly
man, and he chose a deputy, Gerard Bancker, whom the
house approved. Henceforth, Bancker bore the major
burden of the office and in recognition the Convention
changed his title in January, 1777, to Vice-Treasurer.[44]

When Lott presented a memorial to the revolutionary

41 Jay to McDougall, December 23, 1775, March 27, 1776, McDougall
Papers, NYHAS; Henry P. Johnston, ed., *The Correspondence and Public
Papers of John Jay* (4 vols.; New York, 1890-1893), I, 40.
42 John Jay Papers, Iselin Collection, CUL.
43 Jay to McDougall, April 27, 1776, *ibid.* and McDougall Papers, NYHS;
Johnston, *Correspondence of John Jay*, I, 57.
44 Flick, *American Revolution in New York*, p. 108; *Jour. Prov. Cong.*, I,
216, 774. In November, 1776, Bancker wanted to give up his subordinate
position, but neither Livingston nor the Convention would listen to him.
When Bancker repeated his intention on January 14, the Committee of
Safety replied by making him Vice-Treasurer. *Ibid.*, II, 316-17; *Cal. Hist.
Mss.*, I, 593.

legislature in March, 1776, he stimulated that body to action. The substance of his letter concerned the funding of the 1771 bills of credit of which one-tenth fell due in April. A committee recommended that the payment of the principal be suspended and that any sums paid in be loaned out again. Furthermore, the committee declared that the Provincial Congress must "attend to the proper application of the public moneys now in the hands of the said Abraham Lott, Esquire." Lott evaded the directive but the Provincial Congress did nothing. It is surprising that Governor Tryon did not instruct him to bring his papers out to the British warships in the harbor. In September, 1776, the Convention demanded an accounting and forbade Lott to act as treasurer. Whatever expectations the Convention may have entertained as to the funds in his possession, the final outcome dashed those hopes. Although the records demonstrated the existence of £25,000, Lott possessed only £3,000 and the Convention labored in vain to obtain that sum. Lott had invested the large balance in the Danish Islands.[45]

The deepening rift between Whigs and Tories in the summer of 1775 posed one of the thorniest problems that ever confronted the New York Provincial Congress: the disposition of the Tories. It did not formulate a general policy for several months, leaving most action in the hands of the local committees. When a serious incident occurred, such as the enlistment of recruits for the British army, the deputies heard the evidence, then voted on the verdict. Those adjudged guilty might be imprisoned locally or shipped off to Connecticut.[46]

The activities of the Tories in Brookhaven early in

---

[45] *Jour. Prov. Cong.*, I, 347, 350; Flick, *American Revolution in New York*, pp. 108-10. Flick confuses these events with a committee accounting with Livingston and Bancker in February.

[46] Becker, *The History of Political Parties*, p. 216; Flick, *American Revolution in New York*, p. 210; *Jour. Prov. Cong.*, I, 89, 93, 100, 127, 129, 135.

August caused the Provincial Congress to prepare its first overall measures against them. After much debate extending over three days, the deputies agreed upon several resolutions. The resolves defined sundry forms of opposition and actions as punishable by imprisonment but placed their enforcement in the hands of the local committees. If the committees or militia apprehended any individuals who were in arms or enlisted in the British forces, they would hold the prisoners for disposition by the Provincial Congress.[47]

Since these first steps did nothing to quell the Tories in regions which they dominated, such as Queens, the Provincial Congress voted additional measures. The local Whigs lacked the numbers and force to take effective action and pleaded with the Provincial Congress to intervene. By December, 1775, the open defiance of the revolutionaries by Queens and Richmond Tories constrained the Second Provincial Congress to strike at them. Fearing retaliatory bombardment by the British warships, the Provincial Congress instructed its delegates in Philadelphia to ask the Continental Congress for aid. The latter obliged, ordering Jersey troops to Queens to disarm the Tories and apprehend the ringleaders. Approximately 600 residents surrendered their weapons and 19 their persons. Early in February the New Jersey Provincial Congress complied with a request from New York to perform a similar sweep on Staten Island.[48]

The Second Provincial Congress in the form of its Committee of Safety, prompted by a resolve of the Continental Congress, took an additional step against the Tories. It instructed the counties to disarm the "disaffected," employing, if necessary, the militia.[49]

---

[47] *Ibid.*, I, 105, 127, 129, 131-32; Becker, *The History of Political Parties,* pp. 223-24.
[48] *Ibid.*, pp. 238, 244-45.
[49] *Ibid.*, p. 262; see above, pp. 143-45.

The Third Provincial Congress had scarcely organized in May, 1776, when Washington exerted pressure on it to take vigorous action against the Tories. The Commander-in-Chief, taking the congressmen into his confidence, revealed to them intelligence of a Tory plan to unite the disaffected on Long Island and adjacent Connecticut and to join the British. The Provincial Congress spent most of May 19 as well as the day and evening of May 20 discussing the evidence and remedies. It seems to have concluded its deliberations by referring the whole business to a committee headed by John Alsop.[50]

When the committee reported May 21, the house ordered the secretaries to transcribe a fair copy. After three days of intermittent but prolonged debates, the deputies approved the lengthy report which recommended that the Provincial Congress cooperate with Washington to round up the most dangerous of the opposition and that the county committees apprehend not only all civil and military crown officials but also all those suspected of hostility to the American cause.[51]

The following day, May 25, the congressmen charged a committee of Scott, Jay, Morris, Haring, and Remsen to draw up enabling resolutions, but the Provincial Congress did not approve the draft until June 5. The committee submitted its report on May 28 and the delegates immediately commenced consideration of it. Other affairs intervened and prevented final disposition until a week later. The heart of the "laws" approved were those sections creating a committee to seize, try, and punish Tories. The committee consisted of seven men: Gouverneur Morris, John Ten Broeck, Henry Remsen, John Haring, Thomas Tredwell, Lewis Graham, and Joseph Hallett. Among the other resolutions, the Provincial Congress conferred similar

---

[50] Curtis P. Nettels, *George Washington and American Independence* (Boston, 1951), p. 290; *Jour. Prov. Cong.*, I, 450, 453.
[51] *Ibid.*, I, 456-57, 459-60, 461.

powers on the county committees and authorized the local committees to arrest and hold any suspects until the county committees met to dispose of the cases. The resolutions directed the congressional committee to arrest about a hundred of the leading Tories in the city, Richmond, Kings, Queens, and Westchester.[52]

After some delay the "secret committee" set about its labors on June 15 with a slightly altered cast; the most important changes were the addition of Jay and Philip Livingston. Over the next two weeks the "inquisitors" examined numerous suspects, heard witnesses, and disposed of cases. In arriving at decisions, the committee voted in accordance with the voting rules of the Provincial Congress, that is by county unit. Most of those summoned, if convicted as no "Friend to the American cause," secured their release on parole or posted bond.[53]

Scarcely had the secret committee begun hearings when Washington imparted fresh intelligence to the Provincial Congress which halved the committee's membership. On June 17 the legislators chose Jay, G. Morris, and Philip Livingston a "secret committee" to confer with the Commander-in-Chief relative to this information and "take such examinations . . . as they shall think proper." Thus began the unraveling of the celebrated Tory plot, a plot intended to unleash operations against Washington's army on the arrival of the British army. Governor Tryon planned to have Tories strike at ammunition stores, sabotage cannon, and destroy Dykeman's Bridge across Kingsbridge Creek which linked Manhattan with Westchester and New England. Three days thereafter the Provincial Congress granted this second committee power to apprehend and secure certain persons in "such manner as they may think most prudent." The trio worked closely with Washington in

---

52 *Ibid.,* I, 461, 464, 476-78.
53 Flick, *American Revolution in New York,* p. 213.

rounding up the ring, but whether they tried the prisoners or entrusted that task to the first secret committee (of which they were members) cannot be determined.[54]

The British arrival disrupted the work of the committee and prevented consideration by the delegates of the committee's report. On June 28 Jay requested and obtained leave for the committee to continue sitting, since it had not finished its task. He presented a report of his board's activities with the supporting evidence, but the delegates deferred even receiving it "as the House is very much engaged in other necessary business." The house did not return to the business because Sir William Howe's appearance disrupted the proceedings. Before the Provincial Congress closed its session, it gave Washington power to "take such measures for apprehending and securing" dangerous persons "as he shall think necessary."[55]

When the Fourth Provincial Congress or Convention assembled on July 9, it merged the two "secret" committees. The Convention specifically repealed the broad powers to seize suspects Washington had received from its predecessor, resolving that "it would be unreasonable longer to burthen the General with matters for which this Congress ought to provide. . . ." Having taken this precaution to safeguard civil authority, the deputies instructed their committee to proceed in a manner "most agreeable to the dictates of justice and humanity," and "most advancive of the public good, the oath which they have taken notwithstanding." Just how this committee functioned is not clear, since the Convention itself heard numerous cases and prescribed punishments. Late in August the Convention directed the county committees to exercise their discretion in releasing minor loyalists whom the Convention had arrested but not to liberate any person confined for "treasonable practices."[56]

---

54 Nettels, *George Washington*, pp. 290-91; *Jour. Prov. Cong.*, I, 497, 500.
55 *Cal. Hist. Mss.*, I, 341, 348; *Jour. Prov. Cong.*, I, 509, 512.

The deteriorating military situation and increased activity of the loyalists caused the Convention on September 19, 1776, to take a new look at its loyalist policy. During the subsequent debates the members hammered out more drastic resolutions, establishing a standing committee of seven with broad powers for "inquiring into, detecting and defeating all conspiracies." Jay, William Duer, Pierre Van Cortlandt, Leonard Gansevoort, Charles DeWitt, Zephaniah Platt, and Nathaniel Sackett composed the committee. The committee had troops at its command, either militia or special ranger companies, its own intelligence network, and express riders. During the four months of its existence this committee presided over perhaps 500 cases. Many prisoners incurred sentences of banishment to New Hampshire jails.[57]

When Carleton in October, 1776, advanced down Lake Champlain toward Ticonderoga, the Committee of Safety established a new committee in response to Schuyler's appeal for reinforcements. They detailed a special committee to repair to Albany to cooperate with Schuyler. The new committee possessed practically a blank check which included authority to call out the militia of the northern counties. However, this special committee devoted an important portion of its time and energy to the apprehension of loyalists. It is highly unlikely that the labor of this special committee of "arrangement" duplicated that of the committee of seven to defeat conspiracies. The Committee of Safety's correspondence indicates that the committee on conspiracies did not lack for business elsewhere. Where circumstances warranted it, the house resorted to special

---

[56] Flick, *American Revolution in New York*, p. 218; *Jour. Prov. Cong.*, I, 633, 634, 637-39.

[57] Flick, *American Revolution in New York*, pp. 218-19; *Minutes of the Committee and of the First Commission for Detecting and Defeating Conspiracies in the State of New York, 1776-1778*, New-York Historical Society *Collections*, LVII (1924), I, 3-5; *Jour. Prov. Cong.*, I, 693.

committees to supplement the work of the existing committee on conspiracies.[58]

Driven by the pressure of innumerable problems, the Convention devised every conceivable stratagem to maintain adequate attendance by releasing members from committee assignments. On February 11, 1777, the Convention dissolved the committee on conspiracies and replaced it with a commission of three nonlegislators who drew 12s. per diem for their service. The deputies picked three men from Dutchess to fill the new posts: Egbert Benson, chairman of the county committee, Colonel Jacobus Swartwout of the militia, and local committeeman Melancton Smith. The commission seems to have inherited the rights of its predecessor, although the *Journal* does not specifically state that it did. When the Convention resolved on March 7, 1777, to offer political prisoners an act of grace and thereby clear the jails, it inundated the commission. The terms of the resolution extended to all offenders except those who had taken up arms against the United States, those who had recruited for the British or had supplied them with provisions, and those who had conveyed intelligence to them. This meant that the commission interrogated not only those imprisoned in New York but also those incarcerated in other states. The prisoners' discharge depended upon their taking a special oath of allegiance. Failure to comply entailed banishment within the British lines or imprisonment as "open enemies." Although the Convention dissolved May 13, 1777, the succeeding Council of Safety continued the commission. Similarly, when the Council of Safety expired September 10, 1777, a convention of members of the new senate and assembly authorized the commission to proceed as before.[59]

---

[58] *Ibid.*, I, 684, 693, 694-95, 700, 910-11; *Cal. Hist. Mss.*, I, 525.
[59] Flick, *American Revolution in New York*, pp. 218-19; *Jour. Prov. Cong.*, I, 803, 807, 827, 1061.

Having instituted measures against the persons of Tories, the Provincial Congress soon felt obliged to appropriate their property. The house embarked on a confiscation policy on September 1, 1775, when it voted seizure of the personal property of those who joined the British army or took up arms against America. The local committees assumed trusteeship of such personalty, but the people tended to interpret the resolution as authorizing confiscation. The Declaration of Independence spurred some of the committees to wholesale confiscations of personalty and in some localities the committeemen sold the property. Later the Convention instructed the committee on conspiracies to sequestrate the effects of loyalists who broke their parole.[60]

The military situation in Westchester helped to precipitate further confiscations. A Convention committee cooperating with the army in Westchester pleaded with the parent body to dispatch 600 to 700 militia reinforcements to hold the lower part of the county. William Duer, chairman, pointed out that if New York called in Connecticut troops, these would probably seize the property of loyalists who had fled or joined the enemy army. Two days afterward, February 22, 1777, the Committee of Safety ordered the public sale of Westchester loyalist personalty. The next month the Convention applied the Westchester action to the whole state. The resolutions created three commissioners in each county to dispose of the personalty of absentee loyalists by public sale, alloting to their families their apparel, furniture, and three months' supply of food. Income from the sales went to the state treasury "to be hereafter paid to the respective owners thereof, or otherwise disposed of at the discretion of the legislature. . . ." Although the Convention marketed personalty, it did not deal with realty in the same fashion. All houses and estates seized with personalty re-

---

60 Flick, *American Revolution in New York,* p. 220.

mained in trust until further disposition by the legislature in 1779.[61]

Since the distribution of powers between the Continental Congress and the states was not defined until the adoption of the Articles of Confederation, the Provincial Congress's interpretation of these relationships is difficult to ascertain. New York seems to have accepted without question the Continental Congress's primacy in the direction of the war, but from time to time it challenged Congress or its agents on specific issues.

Although the New York Provincial Congress depended in its relations with the Continental Congress upon delegates chosen from among its members, opposition to this method of determining representation cropped up in the spring of 1776. Sentiment for having the people elect the continental deputies arose in New York City, and Orange and Ulster counties. In the city the mechanics sought to rouse popular support for direct election but with indifferent success. The inhabitants of Goshen district, Orange County, deprived their provincial representatives of the power to choose continental delegates. A serious dispute occurred in Ulster on this question, but the county committee adhered to the current practice. Jay defended the New York Provincial Congress's position in the matter, arguing that all the colonies chose their delegates to the Continental Congress in this fashion. Furthermore, since the people gave their deputies that specific power in the elections for the Third Provincial Congress in April, 1776, Jay did not comprehend how the exercise of this power would injure the people's "right of election." After this incident, no further challenge developed.[62]

---

61 *Ibid.*, p. 221; *Jour. Prov. Cong.*, I, 808, 811.

62 Becker, *The History of Political Parties*, pp. 256-57, 259; *Jour. Prov. Cong.*, I, 460, 467, 499, II, 199-200; Jay to McDougall, April 11, 1776, McDougall Papers, NYHS; *N.Y.J.*, April 4, 1776.

The question of continental-provincial relations arose early in the First Provincial Congress. In May, 1775, Isaac Low, seconded by Gouverneur Morris, presented a resolution: "Resolved, As the opinion of this Congress, that implicit obedience ought to be paid to every recommendation of the Continental Congress, for the general regulation of the associated colonies; but that this Congress is competent to and ought freely to deliberate and determine on, all matters relative to the internal policies of this colony." After much debate, the opposition, led by Scott, carried a motion to table. Only Richmond County voted against tabling. Whatever the delegates may have said about the propriety or substance of Low's proposal, they did not entertain any idea of subordinating the colony to the authority of the Continental Congress. May 24, the day after this discussion, the house approved a letter to the Connecticut government in which it promised "that in this and all other matters, we will pay the highest attention to every recommendation of the Grand Continental Congress. . . ." This language hardly qualifies as unconditional acceptance of continental supremacy.[63]

Having blocked the attempted definition of spheres of interest, Scott counterattacked on May 25 with a resolution "to fully approve of the proceedings of the [First Continental] Congress." This motion did not win approbation either, since the house tabled it without a formal division. However, a day later the members approved the General Association, signed it, and circularized the county committees to have every inhabitant sign it. One clause in the association pledged the deputies to "adopt and endeavour to carry into execution whatever measures may be recommended by the Continental Congress or resolved upon by this Provincial Congress for the purpose of preserving our

---

[63] Becker, *The History of Political Parties,* p. 212; *Jour. Prov. Cong.,* I, 8, 11.

Constitution, and opposing the execution of the several arbitrary and oppressive acts of the British Parliament. . . ."[64]

Friction arose in January, 1776, when Washington ordered General Charles Lee to New York to fortify the port against a possible British attack. Fear that Lee might precipitate hostilities with the British men-of-war in the harbor drove the Yorkers to protest the expedition. Hearing of the New York reaction, the Continental Congress, under the prodding of the New York delegates, dispatched a committee to the city to investigate the expediency of the operation and to exert supervisory authority over it. The Committee of Safety assigned Scott and McDougall to wait upon the continental committee and to bring back a report. The committee informed the two Yorkers that the General came to take measures and to consult with the continental members for the defense of the city and not to begin a battle. The continental committee also requested supplies and barracks for the first contingent of the troops, which would arrive that evening. In the course of the debate in the Committee of Safety which the request provoked, Comfort Sands moved that the troops be halted until the committee conferred with the continental emissaries. Sands's motion lost by a vote of 4 to 3 with Scott voting in the negative and McDougall in the affirmative. Scott then advocated that the troops be admitted upon condition that the Committee of Safety control them until the Yorkers met with the continental committee and General Lee and until "further order to be taken thereon, with the consent of this Committee . . . or further direction of the Continental Congress." This motion carried by 5 to 2 with McDougall shifting to support Scott.[65]

---

[64] Becker, *The History of Political Parties*, p. 212; *Jour. Prov. Cong.*, I, 13, 15; *Cal. Hist. Mss.*, I, 86.

[65] Becker, *The History of Political Parties*, pp. 246-47; *Jour. Prov. Cong.*, I, 275-77. Becker attributes the situation to the conflict between nationalism and sectionalism.

The Committee of Safety achieved nothing by this last maneuver. The continental committee rejected these conditions on two grounds: first, that its instructions from the Continental Congress precluded their acceptance and second, that the assurances first given by it to Scott and McDougall rendered the conditions superfluous. Furthermore, Colonel David Waterbury, commander of the Connecticut units which were enroute to the city, practically defied the Committee of Safety. He refused to submit the troops to the committee's command and insisted he would "march them into the barracks." In the face of this resistance the Yorkers asked the Philadelphia committee for an immediate conference. Taking refuge in a technicality, the Committee of Safety argued that since General Lee would not accompany the first contingent and since the troops entered the city without any particular order of the Continental Congress, the Committee of Safety ought to have command of them. The committee from Philadelphia silenced the Yorkers by producing their instructions from Congress which gave them authority over Lee's forces. The Committee of Safety yielded because it had no alternative. The issue lay not in the question of continental versus local command, since Stirling's succession to Lee's authority in March brought no protest from the Provincial Congress. Rather the Committee of Safety apprehended that Lee's rashness might induce him to attack the British ships.[66]

Before quitting the scene, Lee stirred the wrath of the New Yorkers by ordering the imposition of test oaths on the Long Island Tories. He first hinted at the desirability of an oath on March 4, but the Provincial Congress did not reply. On March 5 Lee ordered his acting adjutant general, Isaac Sears, to offer a test oath to a list of Tories and to arrest those who refused to take it. On the seventh the General asked the New York Provincial Congress for a reply

---

[66] *Ibid.*, I, 278-79.

to his proposal on the Tories, but the provincial body ignored the request. Sears carried out his orders, but the Provincial Congress made no official protest, perhaps because Lee handed over his command to Lord Stirling on March 8. On March 12, Daniel W. Kissam of the Great Neck Committee, Queens, presented himself before the house to complain of Sears's conduct. These proceedings, Kissam asserted, "tend to convert whigs to be tories." After hearing Kissam's account of these events, the Provincial Congress entertained a motion to summon Sears before it to explain his authority for his undertaking. The *Journal* noted that the house expended a "considerable time" in debating the motion but came to no decision. Although the deputies postponed the business to the next day, they did not revive the matter.[67]

This seeming oversight in connection with the test oath may have derived from action in the Continental Congress. The New York delegates in Congress heard of the affair and on March 8 won approval of a resolution which condemned the imposition of test oaths by military officers. Their letter to New York on the subject implied a rebuke to the province for not having protested to the Continental Congress, since the military had encroached upon the civil authority.[68]

A long-standing contest among New York, New Hampshire, and Massachusetts over adjoining lands disturbed continental-state relations in 1777. Some of the inhabitants of these counties (variously denominated the Grants, New Connecticut, or Vermont) memorialized the Continental Congress to admit their representatives as delegates from an independent state.[69] The New York Convention, having intelligence of this maneuver, prepared in April, 1777,

---

67 *Ibid.*, I, 336, 343, 354, 355, II, 148.
68 *Ibid.*, I, 379.
69 See Chilton Williamson, *Vermont in Quandary: 1763-1825* (Montpelier, 1949), chaps. v-vi.

a forceful letter of instructions to their delegates in Philadelphia. If Congress should vote to seat the Vermonters over
the opposition of the Yorkers, ran the letter, the Yorkers
should protest in the state's name and "forthwith return
to this state." The Convention added: "You are from time
to time to oppose, . . . all such resolutions of Congress, as
may impliedly or expressly infringe the rights or jurisdiction of this State." Lastly, the Convention threatened to
withhold approval of any plan for confederation unless the
Continental Congress upheld it on the Vermont question.
Perhaps the threat of withdrawal from Philadelphia had
its effect, for in June Congress vindicated New York, refusing to recognize Vermont as a state.[70]

The royal Indian Superintendent, Sir Guy Johnson, had
aroused hostility toward the Whigs among the Indians and,
as a result, the First Provincial Congress was forced to give
its attention to Indian affairs early in its proceedings. After
hearing disquieting reports from the Albany County Committee on Johnson's maneuvers, the congressmen in June,
1775, discussed the feasibility of suggesting that the Continental Congress establish an Indian superintendency. They
outlined their idea to the Yorkers in Philadelphia, giving
them discretionary power to introduce the matter in Congress. Ultimately, the Continental Congress appointed a
number of Commissioners of Indian Affairs, three of whom
came from New York. The Provincial Congress relied on
its committee system to meet such Indian problems as came
before it, although it frequently had recourse to the services
of the Albany County Committee to hold conferences with
the Six Nations.[71]

In 1777 the Committee of Safety moved tentatively to
revise Indian policy. A complaint from some of the Six
Nations in Tryon County, alleging a land swindle by George

[70] *Jour. Prov. Cong.*, I, 778-79, 820-21, 854-55, 869, 998-99, II, 418.
[71] *Ibid.*, I, 24, 30, 32-33, 39, 82, 95, II, 47-48, 56-59, 419.

Croghan of Pennsylvania, impelled the Committee of Safety in February to touch briefly on the general subject of Indian relations. Besides enjoining James Duane and Gouverneur Morris to investigate the complaint, the committee ordered them to draw up a proposal for regulating Indian affairs. Duane and Morris did not report back to the committee, nor did they make any presentation to the Convention when it reconvened in March. When the Convention dissolved itself in May, 1777, it "resolved and ordered" that the two men report to the succeeding Council of Safety. The committee did work out recommendations, but the Council of Safety never formally received them. The suggestions would have deposited authority to regulate Indian affairs in the hands of special commissioners who would "superintend, manage and direct all Publick Business" of this kind.[72]

Although the Provincial Congress combined legislative and executive functions, it did not assume responsibility for the normal administration of justice. After the Declaration of Independence the Convention ordered all Whig judges to proceed as before, provided that "all processes and other their proceedings, be under the authority and in the name of the State of New York." The Convention, however, did intervene on two occasions to appoint judges. In July, 1776, the Convention instituted a court of admiralty and offered the seat to Richard Morris, a prominent judge. When he declined, the legislature commissioned Lewis Graham to fill the post. The second essay into judicial affairs originated in military necessity. Recruiting for the Continental Army regiments in Westchester centered around Peekskill, a supply base. William Duer complained that the lack of a justice of the peace in the vicinity to administer an oath hampered enlistments. The Convention responded by appointing William Paulding "with the like powers, privi-

---

[72] *Ibid.,* I, 801, 802-3, 930; *Cal. Hist. Mss.,* II, 645.

leges and authority now or heretofore enjoyed and exercised by a justice of the peace in this State."[73]

The committee system was the mainstay of governmental procedure. The house did not grant its committees autonomy but maintained a close check on their operations. No doubt duplication of effort did occur. Possibly a more serious handicap for the government lay in the shortage of manpower, since most members divided their time and energies among a number of committees. Notwithstanding its inefficiencies and mistakes, government by committee did see the state through a most critical period and did prevent a breakdown of the war effort. Equally important, the Convention wrote the first state constitution in the midst of great difficulties.

---

[73] *Jour. Prov. Cong.,* I, 527, 550, 554, 556, 566, 765.

SEVEN

Making Haste Slowly: Framing the Constitution

WHEN the Fourth Provincial Congress opened its proceedings on July 9, the primary business of the day was not a constitution but the Declaration of Independence. The Provincial Congress promptly adopted resolutions that heartily endorsed the Declaration and that made New York the thirteenth colony to vote approval. The next day the delegates converted themselves from an illegal, revolutionary body into the Convention of Representatives of the State of New York; the Fourth Provincial Congress had but a fleeting life.

If the people expected the Convention to plunge into the task of constructing new political foundations, they were disappointed. When the matter was first discussed on July 10, the house agreed to defer consideration until July 16.[1] On the appointed day an influential group blocked debate by pleading that "the present dangerous situation . . . demands the unremitted attention of every member. . . ." This sentiment prevailed and the members consented to set aside debate until August 1.[2] It is quite likely that the difference over this point concealed more profound disagreement, indicating the marshaling of the hostile elements for the grand contest over the constitution. A Connecticut observer explained the circumstances this way: "the Toryfied in the House prevailed to have it postponed, the Whigs say they were willing to have it so, as they [expec]t that by & by they shall have better grounds to build their new Constitution upon."[3]

On August 1, Gouverneur Morris opened the business with a motion to select a committee to draft a constitution. William Duer seconded it and the proposition passed unanimously. But here the unanimity quickly dissolved as Matthew Adgate of Albany proposed that the house direct the committee to draw up first a bill of rights "as the foundation of such form of government." Morris sought to kill the measure by moving the previous question, but the house voted him down. An amendment by Duer to direct the committee to report simultaneously both drafts carried by a "great majority" and, thus amended, Adgate's proposal received unanimous approval.[4]

Turning to the selection of the committee's personnel, the Convention embroiled itself in controversy over General John Morin Scott's right to hold a seat in the house. The dispute had sprung up the previous day after some remarks by Scott on a matter of Westchester patronage.[5] The patronage involved command of the drafted militia who had mobilized for the defense of New York City. The Convention, on

---

1 Jay described the fluidity of the situation: "We have a government, you know, to form; and God only knows what it will resemble. Our politicians, like some guests at a feast, are perplexed and undetermined which dish to prefer." Jay to Rutledge, July 6, 1776, quoted in William Jay, *The Life of John Jay with Selections from His Correspondence and Miscellaneous Papers* (2 vols.; New York, 1833), I, 62; Peter Force, ed., *American Archives* (9 vols.; Washington, D.C., 1837-1853), 5th ser., I, 40.

2 *Jour. Prov. Cong.*, I, 519, 527.

3 Jedediah Huntington to Jabez Huntington, July 20, 1776, Connecticut Historical Society *Collections*, XX (Hartford, 1889), 312.

4 *Jour. Prov. Cong.*, I, 552.

5 The rush for political plums in the power of the Provincial Congress had begun early in the conflict. An onlooker distastefully commented: "In the disposal of offices, particularly in the military department the most shameful partiality prevails, all or most of the inferior commissioned officers being selected from the creatures and absolute dependents of the governing party. Indeed the conduct of our gentry & principal people has rendered this vile arrangement almost inevitable." Dr. John Jones to Duane, July 13, 1775, James Duane, "The Duane Letters," Southern History Association *Publications*, VII (Washington, D.C., 1903), 249.

Morris's advice, bypassed the senior colonel of the Westchester militia, Joseph Drake, who normally would have
received the post, in favor of a junior colonel, Thomas
Thomas. Thomas's family, locally prominent, had allied
itself with the Morrises. Drake's protest and resignation
might have gone unheeded, but the officers and men of his
regiment refused to serve under Thomas. The obduracy of
the militia necessitated the Convention's intervention. Scott,
as commander of this detachment of 3,000 militia, opposed
Thomas's selection "lest it might injure the service by placing officers in service out of their proper tour of duty or
rank." His comment gave umbrage to Morris who resented
this interference in his own bailiwick.[6]

Counterattacking from an unexpected quarter, Morris
questioned Scott's right to his seat in the Convention. Morris
demanded that Scott not be "permitted to speak or interfere
in the debates of this Convention." He buttressed his challenge with a congressional resolution of June 15 which stated
that no officer in the pay of the Continental Congress or of
the colony ought to have a seat in the Provincial Congress.
In rebuttal Scott "claimed his seat on behalf of his constituents." Leaving aside these broad grounds of defense, Scott
might have countered with some pertinent observations on
generals in the Convention. When the Convention officially
accepted the New York County delegation's credentials on
July 10, Morris offered no objection to General Scott. The
latter did not take his seat until July 31, but Morris did not
object to Scott until after the latter had participated in the
Westchester imbroglio. Furthermore, two other generals had
won election to the house without undergoing any scrutiny
of their rights. In fact, the convention had chosen General
Nathaniel Woodhull, commander of the Suffolk militia, as

---

[6] Henry B. Dawson, *Westchester County, New York, During the American
Revolution* (Morrisania, 1886), p. 30; *Jour. Prov. Cong.*, I, 551; Force, *American Archives*, 5th ser., I, 790, 1428, 1431-32, 1461, 1475.

its president. Also, Westchester had returned to the house General Lewis Morris, commander of that county's militia and Gouverneur's kinsman. It is possible that when he challenged Scott on July 31, Gouverneur Morris was thinking of the next day's debate on a constitution.[7]

The Convention never resolved the issue raised by Morris. After a lengthy exchange of views the members voted to examine the merits of the challenge August 6. Not until the seventh did the Convention revert to the subject, but then it postponed it again to August 14. However, the Convention did not discuss the matter again. Perhaps informal discussion convinced Morris that he could not muster a majority for his contention. In the interim the city committee sent the Convention an irate letter which condemned this attempt to deprive the people of their right "to say who shall represent them" in convention. Pleading the "forlorn and deserted" condition of the city as the reason for not having collected signatures to protest petitions, it asked that Morris's motion be erased and "buried in eternal oblivion."[8]

The Convention did select its constitutional committee on August 1 and did place Scott on it. Although Scott did not attend that day, Morris must have expected that his own constitutional views would differ basically from those of Scott. Consequently, he opposed Scott's nomination to the constitutional committee on the ground that the Convention had not yet determined his status. When the polling on Scott's nomination ended, the General narrowly prevailed through the support of the New York, Albany, Ulster, and Tryon delegations.[9] In addition to Scott the committee comprised Jay, G. Morris, R. R. Livingston, Duer, John Sloss

---

[7] *Jour. Prov. Cong.,* I, 551.

[8] *Ibid.,* I, 551, 557.

[9] The vote was 21 to 20. Westchester, Dutchess, Cumberland, Suffolk, Gloucester, and Queens supported Morris. Presumably Kings, Orange, and Charlotte lacked quorums and could not vote. *Ibid.,* I, 552. Peter R. Livingston to Colonel Robert Livingston, August 2, 1776, Livingston Redmond Papers, FDRL.

Hobart, Abraham Yates, Jr., Robert Yates, Henry Wisner, William Smith (of Suffolk), John Broome, Samuel Townsend, and Charles DeWitt.[10] The Convention ordered the committee to bring in a report August 26.

Since three of the committee (Jay, Livingston, and R. Yates) were serving on a secret committee to obstruct the Hudson to the British, the Convention sent them a letter which informed the three men of their additional duties and directed them "to meet upon this important business as early as possible."[11] Although Livingston hurried to the Convention in response to this news, so far as is known, no committee meetings occurred.

Livingston's presence had some connection with the desire of certain members to have the Convention immediately elect a governor. Neither the precise details nor the persons involved are ascertainable, but Livingston's agency in the business is definite.[12] He tendered the nomination, if not the office, to Philip Livingston then in Philadelphia. Declaring his "unfitness" for the office, Livingston advised the Convention not to select him. Nevertheless, he added, if the Convention should pick him, he would not refuse the post. If this statement seems like the stock reply of the modern politician, it is an unhappy coincidence. His explanation has an honest ring to it. He feared a refusal might "be construed by some as [a] desert[ion] of the righteous causes . . . at a most dangerous crisis. . . . At so critical a moment it

---

10 Of these thirteen men, two, Hobart and Townsend, never attended the committee; four, Smith, Scott, Morris, and Broome, were often absent. Jay, Livingston, and Duer were conservatives and Abraham and Robert Yates, Wisner, and DeWitt were moderates. For the definition of the terms "conservative" and "moderat," see below, p. 231.

11 The Convention had chosen Jay, Livingston, R. Yates, Christopher Tappen, Gilbert Livingston, and William Paulding to be a committee for that purpose in July. *Ibid.*, I, 526-27, 555.

John McKesson urged George Clinton to be present August 26 at all costs. George Clinton, *Public Papers of George Clinton, First Governor of New York* (10 vols.; Albany, 1899-1914), I, 297.

12 Since the matter was important, it was unlikely that R. R. Livingston acted without the foreknowledge of Morris and Jay.

might have a bad effect to have it even supposed that any
one who has had an early part to act in this contest shd.
not remain ready to step forward when called upon by the
Public."[13]

It would appear that word of either these negotiations or
intentions reached the ears of Tory William Smith. Furthermore, Smith harbored the suspicion that a visitor, Peter R.
Livingston, had come to offer him the candidacy: "I suspect
that Mr. L came to sound me on the Design of tendring the
Governor's Place to me & that he was silent upon discovering
by my conversation, that I was opposed to the Disunion of
the Empire."[14] For whatever reasons, the plan, being still-
born, never reached the Convention floor.

The constitutional committee did not meet during the
month of August, probably owing to the absence of Jay, R. R.
Livingston, and Yates who were exerting themselves on the
secret committee. Livingston, however, did spend a week
early in August in attendance at the Convention and expended some energy in persuading his colleagues that the
work of the secret committee was more important than that
of the constitutional committee. In fact this was the ground
advanced to justify their absence and the Convention acquiesced in it.[15]

---

13 Philip Livingston to R. R. Livingston, August 15, 1776, Miscellaneous
Mss: Philip Livingston, NYSL.

14 Smith, Memoirs, V, August 11, 17, 1776. It was perhaps with this interview fresh in his mind that Smith that same day scrawled an abrupt, incomplete note to Schuyler: "I have ten Thousand Things to say to you, but must
suppress at present, except that as a great Landholder, I think your Interest,
at this tremendous moment of forming a new Government, calls you rather
to the Cabinet than the Field. . . ." August 17, 1776, Schuyler Papers, NYPL.

15 With Livingston present, the Convention drafted this letter to Jay and
Yates: "As you are both of the committee for the framing a new government,
the Convention think it highly proper that you should attend upon that
business immediately, *unless your presence is absolutely necessary in the
secret committee* [italics mine]. . . ." The following day the Convention
formally resolved that it would be "improper" to recall Jay and Yates and
gave Livingston leave to join them. However, private correspondence indicated that other motives were responsible. Livingston informed Clinton: "I
wrote likewise to you on our political state & the necessity we are under of
having your assistance, of which you would be fully convinced if you could

The Convention stressed the secret committee's priority over the constitutional committee and the necessity of attendance by Jay, Livingston, and Yates to insure a quorum on the secret committee, but the explanation lacks conviction. Three months later when Washington was retreating in New Jersey, the secret committee received an important letter and survey from General George Clinton relative to blocking the Hudson. This was the committee's reaction: "Mr. Wisner put the survey in his pockett, Mr. Gil[bert] Livingston took the letter with him immediately on a visit to his wife & is not returned. There the obstruction slept till this afternoon [i.e., November 26, three days after]."[16] Although the secret committee flatly stated that without a quorum "nothing further can be done," its letters belie it. On three occasions in July, August, and September it did not have quorums, but that did not impede its labors.[17] The conclusion seems inescapable that a powerful group, which included the Livingstons, Morris, Jay, and Duer, were striving to delay the drafting of a constitution.

The constitutional committee successfully evaded several deadlines. When the day for the committee's report, August 27, arrived, the Convention voted it a reprieve until September 4. Distracted by American military losses at the end of August, the Convention adjourned and journeyed up the

---

attend to the manovers of some persons for one week. Let me hear from you on these subjects as soon as possible." *Jour. Prov. Cong.*, I, 568; Livingston to Clinton, August 18, 1776, Clinton, *Public Papers*, I, 312-13.

16 Clinton to Convention, November 23 [?], McKesson to Clinton, November 26, 1776, *ibid.*, I, 430-31, 432-33. In view of the urgency explicitly expressed by Clinton, Gilbert Livingston's action was odd. Yet this is the same Livingston who complained to the Convention in an oft-quoted letter: "notwithstanding the sense of the House appeared to be at the time we left it, first to endeavor to secure a State to govern, before we established a form to govern it by; yet that a day is fixed to take this important business when a part of its body is absent by the command of the House." *Jour. Prov. Cong.*, II, 280.

17 Secret Committee to Convention, August 13, 1776, Tappen and G. Livingston to Convention, August 26, 1776, G. Livingston to Convention, September 14, 1776, *ibid.*, I, 575-76, II, 219, 293; R. Yates to Paulding, July 22, 1776, *Cal. Hist. Mss.*, I, 426.

Hudson to Fishkill. For the second time the deadline lapsed and not until September 14 did the subject arise in the house. Then a complaisant Convention ordered its committee to report "with all convenient speed."[18]

The representatives' failure to produce even a draft two months after the Declaration of Independence gave rise to uneasiness in certain circles. In a debate in the Albany County Committee Jeremiah Van Rensselaer led the way in criticizing the delay. "The public are impatient in the highest degree," he said, and contrary to earlier promises, some months have elapsed without visible progress. His conclusion depicted an alarming situation: "Suspicions are daily increasing, the usual harmony is in a great measure rent in pieces, their [i.e., the people's] faith in the Representatives tottering."[19] Van Rensselaer moved that the county committee inform their deputies in the Convention that any further procrastination "will be attended with alarming Circumstances." Since Convention delegates Leonard Gansevoort and John Tayler attended this meeting of the county committee, there can be little doubt that these rumblings of impatience reached the ears of the Convention.

The delay in drafting the constitution continued into October. Perhaps coincidentally, the day Gansevoort returned to his Convention duties, September 28, that body directed its committee to report a draft "on or before" October 12 and ordered it to "sit every afternoon till they shall be ready to report."[20] Although the obstructionists had

---

[18] *Jour. Prov. Cong.,* I, 594, 625. The Convention stood adjourned for much of this period, since its power was in the hands of a committee of safety.

[19] September 20, 1776, J. Sullivan, ed., *Minutes of the Albany Committee of Correspondence, 1775-1778 and Minutes of the Schenectady Committee, 1775-1779* (2 vols.; Albany, 1923, 1925), I, 557-58. Van Rensselaer's motion to appoint a committee to draft formal resolutions carried, the committee consisting of himself, Joseph Young, George Palmer, Leonard Gansevoort, and John Tayler. The minutes, however, do not indicate that the committee ever reported.

[20] *Jour. Prov. Cong.,* I, 649, 651. The *Journal* records no formal division. The Convention added Duane to the committee and reduced the quorum to five, which made it easier to have meetings.

suffered a setback, they did not abandon the field,[21] and Wisner complained a week after: "the formation of government goes on very slow indeed; we have done Little or nothing about it."[22] A short time after Wisner grumbled over the situation the committee did commence its business, although, insofar as the *Journal* records, the Convention did not adhere to its resolution of September 28. So rapidly did the committee's labors proceed that by October 18 Secretary John McKesson proudly declared: "The plan of government and justice (a child of Heaven) is so far come to maturity that I had the honor yesterday to make a copy of it for some other members of the committee on government, and has not yet been further exposed to view."[23]

Since McKesson seems to have transcribed a preliminary draft which contained incomplete or unsatisfactory sections, the drafting committee returned to its labors in November. Fragments of the committee's meetings, dated November 5 and 6, indicate that the members were debating problems relating to the election of senators and the governor. A proviso for the indirect election of the senators prevailed by a 4 to 2 vote, but there was unanimous agreement to have the governor elected by the freeholders and the secret ballot.[24] The committee's rate of progress encouraged the Committee of Safety to adopt a resolution November 12 which notified the county committees that the Convention was at work on the constitution and bade them to insure their county's prompt attendance.[25]

It is instructive to note that the members deemed two weeks sufficient time for the committee to hammer out a draft.

[21] R. R. Livingston indicated the defeat to Schuyler: "The Convention have determined to take up the matter of government peremptorily on the *12th inst.* You promised to write to me on that subject, let me hear from you as soon as possible." Livingston to Schuyler, October 2, 1776, Schuyler Papers, NYPL.

[22] Wisner to Clinton, October 4, 1776, Clinton, *Public Papers*, I, 368.

[23] McKesson to Clinton, *ibid.*, I, 384. Other deputies informally discussed the committee's efforts. William Smith, Memoirs, V, October 18, 1776.

[24] Voting for the measure were Livingston, Scott, Duane, and Smith; opposed were R. Yates and Wisner. *Cal. Hist. Mss.*, I, 552, 553.

At this juncture constitutional principles became entangled in political maneuvering. The next day, November 13, a move to postpone execution of the resolution provoked lengthy exchanges, but this proposal did not owe its inception to the desires of the obstructionists. On the contrary, it was the adherents of Scott and Clinton who argued for a stay of the proceedings. Since both men were with their army commands, they could not participate in this vital business. Their opponents, led by R. R. Livingston and Duane, countered by insisting that those officers had volunteered to take active command and that they must have expected that the Convention would write the constitution without their participation. If necessary, the opposition argued, the Convention might request General Israel Putnam to give them leave when the draft was in the final stage. The Livingston-Duane motives paralleled those of the Scott-Clinton adherents. The former disclosed that the Dutchess County members (among them Livingston) would stand for reelection in December and, not having finished the constitution, might not win, especially since the county's freeholders were in the army "fighting the battles of the Convention" and could not vote. The exclusion of the Dutchess men, after they had been "steady" and "done great service to the public," would be an injustice. "Justice to the freeholders" and those "heroes of the county" in arms demanded that the Convention brook no delay in forming a government. The Livingston-Duane leadership triumphed and copies of the resolution went out to the counties.[26]

---

25 *Jour. Prov. Cong.*, I, 710. Duane indicated that most of the work had been completed but that one of the remaining major problems was the constitution of a court of appeals in error. Smith, Memoirs, V, November 6, 1776. See also Ebenezer Hazard to Pierre Van Cortlandt, November 6, 1776, Force, *American Archives*, 5th ser., III, 548.

The Committee of Safety governed until December 4 but under a stipulation by the Convention could not debate the constitution. *Jour. Prov. Cong.*, I, 677.

26 The *Journal* does not record any of this dispute. McKesson to Clinton, November 15, 1776, Clinton, *Public Papers*, I, 424-26. The Convention did

In the ensuing weeks the constitutional committee alternated between industrious labor and inaction. At times of inactivity the Committee of Safety had to prod the committee's members once again.[27] Schuyler expressed his apprehension of the evil that would result from further procrastination by the committee. It will be more difficult "to bring the unprincipled and licentious to a proper sense of their duty," he warned.[28] While the General was writing this warning, the committee resumed its meetings. Shortly thereafter, Chairman Abraham Yates, Jr., gave notice that the committee would submit the long-awaited draft to the Convention on December 20.[29] There followed two postponements in rapid succession on December 20 and 21, and two days later the chairman obtained permission to leave the Convention.[30] Although both Yates and Duane unequivocally stated that the committee had completed the draft, it did not report the draft to the Convention.[31]

---

not meet until December 5 and then only for the day. The Committee of Safety governed with some exceptions until March 6.

The matter of the Dutchess elections is obscure. No evidence of a December election can be found. It is possible that the county committee extended the life of the delegation.

McKesson said that at least one member opposed delay because "people had not Time to think or Criticize; they would greedily accept such form of Governm't as might be proposed. That in winter & more Leisure many more difficulties & of course delays might arise." *Ibid.*

27 R. R. Livingston to E. Rutledge, November 13, 1776, Bancroft Transcripts: Livingston Papers, NYPL; Gansevoort to Schuyler, November 17, 1776, Schuyler Papers, NYPL; *Jour. Prov. Cong.,* I, 722.

28 Schuyler to R. Yates, December 6, 1776, Force, *American Archives,* 5th ser., III, 1101.

29 He wanted McKesson to transcribe the draft. *Jour. Prov. Cong.,* I, 737, 741, 749; Smith, Memoirs, V, December 16, 1776.

30 Charles Z. Lincoln, *The Constitutional History of New York* (5 vols.; Rochester, 1906), I, 494. The Convention *Journal* for December 14-31 is missing.

31 Robert Yates to Duane, December 25, 1776, Force, *American Archives,* 5th ser., III, 1421; Smith, Memoirs, V, December 27, 1776. The curious silence suggests further disagreement within the committee. Indirect support for this idea comes from the further revisions that were made in the draft after December. It would seem that the introductory section on the state's boundaries was one element in this situation. The sharp language in this paragraph was aimed probably at New Hampshire with whom New York had been entangled in a protracted contest for control of the Vermont lands.

For a brief time February gave promise of being the decisive month but it too joined the ranks of the months of unrealized expectations. The Committee of Safety in early February detailed Duane and Robert Yates to collect "sundry maps and materials" to enable the drafting committee to "describe the boundaries" of the state.[32] On February 11 in a one-day session the Convention stated its intention of opening its consideration of the constitution on February 19 and voted to inform the county committees of its plan. Explaining this decision, Duane said that unless the government acted, some of the delegates whose terms expired in May would have to face their constituents empty-handed.[33] Notwithstanding its intent, the Convention did not assemble February 19 and the matter lapsed.

The end of the committee's work, however, was in sight. The members seem to have completed even the determination of the state's boundaries late in February. Copies of the draft constitution began to circulate outside the confines of the committee; some Convention delegates displayed it to friends.[34] As a matter of fact, the obstructionists could not deny much longer the pressure for action. When the Convention resumed sitting March 6, the house accepted without a division Gansevoort's motion ordering the constitutional committee to bring in its report on March 12. Thus on March 12 the long-awaited draft made its debut.[35]

It will be useful to pause here to ascertain the stages through which the draft progressed. The committee's labors extended in uneven fashion over the months from October

---

The territorial description was worked out in February. Lincoln, *Constitutional History of New York*, I, 501.

[32] *Jour. Prov. Cong.*, I, 795.

[33] *Ibid.*, I, 782, 802, 803; Smith, Memoirs, V, February 15, 1777. The notification to the counties was intended to procure a Convention quorum since the Committee of Safety could not debate the constitution.

[34] John H. Livingston to R. R. Livingston, February 28, 1777, R. R. Livingston Collection, NYHS.

[35] *Jour. Prov. Cong.*, I, 821, 823, 826, 833.

to March, but the members concentrated most of this effort in the first three months.[36] The committee produced a first draft in two weeks but then took two months to revise and expand it. It should have presented this revised copy to the Convention in December. Although the constitution would go through four more revisions before reaching the house floor, none of these would drastically alter the December draft.[37] Only two members of the committee, Hobart and Townsend, did not participate in its work during these three months. The Yateses, Smith, Duane, Livingston, Wisner, Jay, Duer, and DeWitt were present most frequently, while Scott, Morris, and Broome attended least.[38]

Historians hitherto have given Jay principal credit for inditing the constitution, believing that the Convention produced only one copy.[39] Charles Z. Lincoln, however, discovered in the State Library two drafts and addenda which he reprinted, thereby rendering students an invaluable

---

[36] The committee does not seem to have functioned at all in January but spent most of February and two weeks in March on revisions.

[37] See below, pp. 237-40.

[38] Since the constitutional committee sat as part of the Committee of Safety or of the Convention, the attendance recorded in the *Journal* provides a clue to the committee's operation. However, the secretary did not always record latecomers as present and some committee members did not always check in with the Committee of Safety before joining their committee. The *Journal* consequently is not an accurate guide, but it does yield the minimum attendance of the committee members. The statement on attendance, therefore, is a minimum estimate based on the *Journal*. *Ibid.*, I, 661-750.

[39] The source for Jay's role has been the biography by his son, William Jay, *The Life of John Jay*, I, 68, which was written while the father still lived. George Pellew, *John Jay* (Boston, 1899), p. 68; Frank Monaghan, *John Jay* (New York, 1935), p. 94; Jared Sparks, *The Life of Gouverneur Morris with Selections from His Correspondence and Miscellaneous Papers* (3 vols.; Boston, 1832), I, 120; Howard Swiggett, *The Extraordinary Mr. Morris* (New York, 1952), p. 32; E. Wilder Spaulding, *New York in the Critical Period, 1783-1789* (New York, 1932), p. 87; Alexander C. Flick, ed., *A History of the State of New York* (10 vols.; New York, 1933-1937), IV, 156; Alexander C. Flick, *The American Revolution in New York* (Albany, 1926), pp. 83, 85; DeAlva Stanwood Alexander, *A Political History of the State of New York* (3 vols.; New York, 1906), I, 14; Lincoln, *Constitutional History of New York*, I, 496; Thomas C. Cochran, *New York in the Confederation* (Philadelphia, 1932), p. 14; Thomas J. Wertenbaker, *Father Knickerbocker Rebels: New York City During the Revolution* (New York, 1948), p. 123; Allan Nevins, *The American States During and After the Revolution* (New York, 1924), p. 159.

service.[40] Accepting the verdict on Jay, he concluded that these documents were working copies of the Convention's deliberations since one of them, draft B, seemed to be in McKesson's hand and to be a revised copy of draft A.[41] Fortunately, a third fragment of eighteen pages has survived among the Yates Papers, making possible a more precise identification of each.[42] A careful collation of the three drafts and the debates in the *Journal* reveals that Lincoln's copies were not working copies but were in fact committee drafts.[43]

---

[40] The capitol fire of 1911 destroyed the papers. Lincoln, *Constitutional History of New York*, I, 501ff.

[41] *Ibid.*, I, 498-99.

[42] Evarts B. Greene and Richard B. Morris, *A Guide to the Principal Sources for Early American History in the City of New York* (1st ed.; New York, 1929), p. 110; Flick, *History of New York*, I, 157; Minutes of the Convention which formed the Constitution of the State of New York, n.d., Abraham Yates, Jr., Papers, NYPL (hereinafter cited as Min. of Conv.). The first ten pages of the ms. are missing as are those numbered beyond 29.

[43] Since the debates proceeded clause by clause, it is possible to check the changes proposed and adopted against the drafts. For example, the house adopted the first paragraph without change. The final text, however, does not agree with the drafts. The latter had a section on the territorial limits of the state, which does not appear in the former. The draft under consideration could not have contained this section, otherwise the *Journal* would have noted its deletion. The same thing is essentially true for paragraph two. The word differences between Lincoln's drafts and the final text can be explained only by the conclusion that Lincoln's were not under debate. An important illustration can be found in the fifth paragraph. The changes proposed by Morris cannot be fitted into Lincoln's copies. The subject of this fifth paragraph was voting by ballot and in the drafts consisted of a long section of almost five pages. Morris's alterations would have eliminated voting by ballot in favor of the existing voice vote. As given in the *Journal* he moved to strike out "by ballot" and substitute "according to," and to strike "shall continue to have their full effect." A comparison with the pertinent portion in Lincoln, *Constitutional History of New York*, I, 507-8, will make it apparent that Morris's substitutions do not pertain to the Lincoln drafts. "And this Convention doth further ordain that all Elections for representatives in General Assembly shall be made *by ballot* in every county out of the Freeholders personally residing in each respective county. That the laws in force in the colony of New York for regulating elections *shall continue to have their full effect* where they shall not be repugnant to the Constitution hereby established and until they shall be altered or repealed by a future legislature." Morris wanted to delete the italicized words. Furthermore, these changes would not have eliminated ballot voting since the following sections set out in detail the method to be adopted in balloting. Therefore, in order to complete the change, Morris would have had to move to strike out everything after the last line quoted above, but he did not. *Jour. Prov. Cong.*, I, 834, 836. For other differences compare *ibid.*, I, 836, 843, 867, 869, 873, 886 (paragraphs 6, 8, 13, 15, 22) with Lincoln, *Constitutional History of New York*, I, 514, 515, 523, 524, 531.

There is a sequential order to these versions of the constitution. An important clue for establishing the precedence of the various drafts is the preliminary section delimiting the territory of the state. Since the committee did not elaborate this proviso until February, the territorial section must have been one of the addenda to draft A in Duane's handwriting which grew out of the revision in early February of the December copy.[44] Therefore, draft A was probably the committee's December version.[45] Draft B is not the corrected version of A but rather the revision of the fragment in the Yates Papers. The last work, which we may for convenience denote draft C, incorporated the changes in A and the addenda plus other minor variations. In effect then, C was the third revision and the committee finished it in February. Still not satisfied with their handiwork, the committee revised C, in some instances returning to the terminology of A. This was B and it reached completion by the end of February.[46]

Although the committee had finished revision B, it chose to refine it further. Up to this point it seems clear that the constitution was the product of the joint labors of the committee, but it is also clear that the committee did not report the B copy to the House for debate. The committee submitted to the Convention a fifth copy which was very likely Jay's handiwork. Substantiation for the tradition comes from Chancellor Livingston and a pseudonymous writer who consulted the Convention manuscripts then in the possession of John McKesson's nephew. This unknown author, "Schuyler," stated that the draft of the constitution among these papers was in Jay's hand.[47] It is possible that the committee

---

44 *Jour. Prov. Cong.,* I, 795.

45 Lincoln, *Constitutional History of New York,* I, 501, does not specify to which draft this quoted section pertains. Lincoln followed an earlier observer in attributing the addenda to Duane. *Ibid.,* I, 498-99.

46 John H. Livingston obtained his copy from Albany delegate Abraham Ten Broeck on February 27 or 28. John H. to R. R. Livingston, February 28, 1777, R. R. Livingston Collection, NYHS.

assigned to Jay the task of polishing the draft, a task which
he accomplished in the first twelve days of March.[48] Jay
seems principally to have contributed clarity and economy of
language, for McKesson declared the day after the report
that it "omitted the method which proposed for electing by
Ballot & sundry other matters by which the report is much
shorter than when it was last copied."[49] A reconstruction of
Jay's draft from the *Journal* furnishes only a general skeleton
of his labor, but it does reveal that he adhered closely to
draft B, retaining the same topical order. He eliminated
completely two sections, that describing the territorial boundaries and that prescribing oaths of office. Undoubtedly the
most important alteration was the curtailment of the section
on balloting for assemblymen in which was set forth in detail
the requisite procedure. Jay retained that portion which
enunciated the general principle of voting by ballots, deleting
the several pages of minutiae.[50] Other than these, there are

---

[47] Lincoln, *Constitutional History of New York*, I, 498-99. This article by
"Schuyler" appeared in the *New York Columbian*, June 16, 19, 1821 and is
reprinted in part in Nathaniel H. Carter and William L. Stone, reporters,
*Reports of the Proceedings and Debates of the Convention of 1821, Assembled
for the Purpose of Amending the Constitution of the State of New York*
(Albany, 1821), p. 692.
 The Chancellor in uncomplimentary fashion attributed a version to Jay
amidst the scurrilous gubernatorial campaign of 1792. In an anonymous
piece addressed "to ——— M——, Esq., Representative of ——— County"
Livingston referred to "the constitution as first reported by Mr. Jay" as being
in McKesson's possession. A later piece signed "Aristides" challenged Jay
to name that proviso of his draft which would uphold his claim to eminence
as a statesman. Internal evidence suggests "Aristides" is the Chancellor. "To
——— M——, Esq.," *N.Y.J. Extraordinary*, March 31, 1792; draft dated March
7, 1792 in R. R. Livingston Collection, NYHS. "To Timothy Tickler, Esq.,
C—— J—— of the U—— S——" by "Aristides," *N.Y.J.*, April 4, 1792.
 [48] Morris moved in Committee of Safety on March 1 to direct the drafting
committee to meet the following day, but the Committee of Safety rejected
the motion. On March 4, however, the committee did order the constitutional
committee to sit. It is likely that on this occasion the latter group discussed
Jay's draft. On March 6 the newly assembled Convention set March 12 for
the constitutional report. *Jour. Prov. Cong.*, I, 821, 823, 826.
 [49] McKesson to Clinton, March 13, 1777, Clinton, *Public Papers*, I, 657-58.
 [50] If one takes into consideration the changes proposed on the Convention
floor and the phraseology of draft B, this balloting paragraph may have
resembled the following reconstruction: "That all elections for representatives
in General Assembly shall be made out of the freeholders personally residing

no substantial differences in content between the two drafts.[51]

Although the Convention on August 1, 1776, had resolved unanimously to direct its committee to prepare simultaneously a constitution and a bill of rights, there is no evidence to indicate that the committee prepared the latter document.[52] Furthermore, no one formally challenged the committee for contravening its explicit instructions. The house could not construe anything in the draft as a bill of rights, although separate paragraphs guaranteed voting rights, religious freedom, and trial by jury where currently practiced.[53] The debates afforded full opportunity for amendments and changes, but no one introduced anything that resembled a rights bill. Gilbert Livingston moved and the Convention adopted a limited guarantee that preserved to the individual all rights and privileges granted by the constitution, unless removed by the "law of the land and the judgment of his peers."[54] The failure of the more radical delegates to criticize the omission of these vital principles remains unexplained, even though they did strive to democratize other sections of the draft.

---

in each respective county by ballot; the laws in force in the colony of New York for regulating elections shall continue to have their full effect where they shall not be repugnant to the Constitution hereby established and until they shall be altered or repealed by a future legislature." Lincoln, *Constitutional History of New York*, I, 507-8; *Jour. Prov. Cong.*, I, 836.

51 It is possible that Jay's proposed amendments on the floor were the consequence of their rejection in committee. See Alexander, *A Political History of New York*, I, 14, for a different explanation.

52 Robert Yates, writing in 1788 under the pseudonym "Sydney," threw some light on the fate of the bill of rights. Those who favored the bill based themselves on English precedents: the Petition of Right, 1628, and the Bill of Rights, 1689. Those opposed denied the analogy, comparing New York to a "state of nature" without any constitution; therefore, any new constitution would operate as a bill of rights. Moved by these considerations and the provisions for frequent elections and impeachment, the Convention dropped the idea. *N.Y.J.*, June 13, 1788; Paul L. Ford, *Essays on the Constitution of the United States, Published During Its Discussion by the People 1787-1788* (Brooklyn, 1892), pp. 297-314.

53 Lincoln, *Constitutional History of New York*, I, 522, 541, 547. Although the old charter of 1683 had granted the right to indictment by grand jury, the revolutionaries did not adopt it. *Ibid.*, IV, 69.

54 *Ibid.*, I, 522.

Historians frequently have ascribed the eight months' delay in producing a constitution to three factors: the proximity of the British army, the critical military situation which absorbed the energy of the delegates, and the long absences of more radical members who were fighting the war rather than attending the Convention.[55] No doubt on specific occasions any one or combination of these elements caused a postponement, but more than a century ago Sparks put forward a different explanation:[56] "There was a party, who thought this movement for a constitution premature, that it would be safer to wait for a period of more tranquillity, and a fairer prospect of calm reflection and deliberation among the members, and when the people likewise would be in a better condition to understand and receive the results of their labors." Documentation does exist to support Sparks's interpretation. As he pointed out, Jay was a proponent of this attitude: "The difficulty of getting any government at all you know has long been an apprehension of little influence on my mind; and always appeared to be founded less in fact, than in a design of quickening the pace of the House . . . the birth of the constitution was in my judgment premature. . . ."[57] The sharp political conflict in

---

55 *Ibid.*, I, 491-92; Flick, *The American Revolution in New York*, p. 81; Spaulding, *New York in the Critical Period, 1783-1789*, pp. 94, 95; Flick, *History of New York*, IV, 165; Monaghan, *John Jay*, p. 97; Pellew, *John Jay*, pp. 74-75; Jay, *The Life of John Jay*, I, 68; Nevins, *The American States During and After the Revolution*, p. 160; Carl L. Becker, *The History of Political Parties in the Province of New York, 1760-1776* (Madison, 1909), p. 275; Elisha P. Douglass, *Rebels and Democrats: The Struggle for Equal Political Rights and Majority Rule During the American Revolution* (Chapel Hill, 1955), p. 62.

56 Sparks, *The Life of Gouverneur Morris*, I, 120. Spaulding in Flick, *History of New York*, IV, 156, thought it likely that political differences delayed the drafting.

57 Jay to Morris and Livingston, April 29, 1777, Sparks, *The Life of Gouverneur Morris*, I, 126-27; Henry P. Johnston, ed., *The Correspondence and Public Papers of John Jay* (4 vols.; New York, 1890-1893), I, 135. Abraham Yates, Jr., writing under the pseudonym "Rough Hewer" in 1788, said of the drafting committee: "A diversity of opinion soon took place in this Committee not whether the government should be of the republican form partaking of monarchy, aristocracy and democracy; but what proportion of ingredients out of each should make up the compound." Yates Papers,

Pennsylvania where the radicals had been instrumental in establishing a constitution in 1776 stimulated edifying comments among New Yorkers. Responding to Duer's description of the conservative defeat in Pennsylvania, Livingston observed: "You know that nothing but well timed delays, indefatigable industry, and a minute attention to every favorable circumstance could have prevented our being exactly in their situation."[58] The New York conservatives, fearing radical triumph in an immediate debate on a constitution, drew deeply and successfully on their political experience to avert a reversal.

Any division of the Convention delegates vis-à-vis the constitution into conservatives, moderates, and radicals entails the risk of creating a separation which had no reality. Nevertheless, an analysis of the sundry informal proposals of the members, the committee drafts, and the final document warrants the categorization of the membership into these three broad groups. For example, the conservatives divided the electorate, permitting broad participation in the choice of a lower house but imposing high property qualifications for voting for an upper house and chief magistrate. The radicals extended the ballot to all white, male taxpayers, making no differentiation as between various houses of the legislature and offices. The moderates adopted the tax-paying qualification for the election of a lower house but insisted on a £40 freehold condition for the choice of an upper house and governor. The fact was, however, that the moderates had no commitment to any program and in the floor debates sometimes switched positions in order to vote for conservative propositions.[59]

NYPL. See also Duer to Schuyler, June 19, 1777 and Duane to Schuyler, June 19, 1777, Schuyler Papers, NYPL; Egbert Benson to Livingston, December 3, 1777, R. R. Livingston Collection, NYHS.

[58] Duer to Livingston, May 28, 1777, Livingston to Duer, June 12, 1777, R. R. Livingston Collection, NYHS. See also Philip Livingston, Duane, and Duer to President of New York Convention, April 29, 1777, *Jour. Prov. Cong.*, II, 428.

Writers have cast little light upon the constitutional ideas prevalent either among the populace or among the Convention members. Fortunately, the committee drafts were not the sole evidence of contemporary thought on the subject. While the press furnished suggestive material indicating the various political currents, hints have survived elsewhere as to the attitudes of the delegates.

The newspapers at least partially mirrored the public discussion of the projected charter of government. Some of the contributors to the newspapers stressed the need to break with tradition, to build "a new form of government . . . without destroying private property."[60] "Spartanus" would have dispensed with the colonial legislature in favor of a unicameral assembly, holding up the Roman Republic as the proof of bicameralism's fatal weakness.[61] The legislature would exercise executive power also and during its recess would transfer this authority to a legislative committee. The house would choose provincial officials, but the people would elect local officials. In the former category were the provincial secretary, treasurer, attorney-general, and judges of the supreme court; in the latter were the county judges, justices of the peace, sheriffs and other officials, and all town officials. The people would vote annually for assemblymen and magistrates. The county election districts were to give way to small, equal election districts.[62] Although "Spartanus" did not discuss the suffrage qualifications, "Essex" would have broadened the voting base by granting the right to landholders owning realty valued at £40, to £40 leaseholders and renters, to those having personalty of £40, and to widows paying taxes on property in one of the foregoing

---

59 For further discussion of moderate shifts on the Convention floor, see below, pp. 241-42.

60 "The Interest of America," Letter II by "Spartanus," *N.Y.J.*, June 13, 1776.

61 The conflict between patricians and plebeians destroyed the Roman Republic, "Spartanus" asserted. *Ibid.*

62 Letter III, *ibid.*, June 20, 1776.

classifications. Those unenfranchised by these regulations would not pay taxes for the support of the legislature.[63]

Other commentators adhered to the customary forms of governor, council, and lower house. One writer suggested Connecticut's government as a model for the distribution of powers and for election requirements.[64] Another, "Independent Whig," would have had the council chosen by the house for three-year terms. He expressed uncertainty as to who was to elect the governor, first placing that power in the hands of the legislature but then offering it to the people at large. Both governor and house were to be selected annually by ballot. His prescription for the suffrage was vague, "sufficient property to connect him [i.e., the voter] with the community," but the ballot was to be a written one. Keeping the British system in mind, he ruled out dual officeholding ("places of profit should be few, and profits of places should be small"). Furthermore, the governor and council would not have the authority to suspend laws.[65]

Writers on the religious question proposed freedom of conscience except for atheists. Every sect would have to finance itself by voluntary contributions. Although "Independent Whig" conceded that the majority might enforce the sabbath as a sacred day, prohibiting business and pleasure, he discountenanced compulsory public worship. The use of force to win converts, he wrote, was not tolerable. The only method to which to resort was the employment of "good sense, rational and scriptural arguments." In this fashion America would not give people cause to look to the British for religious protection and would attract Catholics to the defense of American liberty.[66]

---

63 *Ibid.*, March 7, April 14, 1776. He proposed also that the people elect the delegates to the Continental Congress.

64 Anon., "To the Freeborn Sons of America," *N.Y.P.*, March 21, 1776. He proposed popular election of local officials in order to "shut the door against the mean, wicked arts of bribery and corruption."

65 "Independent Whig," *N.Y.J.*, February 29, 1776.

In a number of respects, where comparison with the committee drafts is possible, the preceding ideas are more radical than the committee's. Whereas the committee conceived of a governor chosen by the £40 freeholders for a four-year term, the essayists proposed a governor chosen annually by all voters.[67] The committee first favored an upper house which the £40 freeholders elected for four years to operate as a check on the lower house, but some of the newspaper partisans simply dispensed with an upper house.[68] In the committee drafts the governor and legislature absorbed the appointive powers of the crown, but the polemicists urged the popular election of all county and town officials.[69] Lastly, the committee adopted the existing practice of legislative appointment of delegates to the Continental Congress, whereas the press argued for the right of the people to choose them.[70] However, both committee and press held at least three concepts in common: religious freedom, ballot voting, and equal representation in the assembly.[71] On one very important issue, the franchise, the committee assumed a more radical position than the press, permitting those paying state or county taxes to vote for assemblymen.[72]

Since the preparation of a constitution was a fundamental task of the Convention, the deputies engaged in extensive private discussion of the content to adopt. Evidence of this attention appears in the circulation among the members of no less than three plans unrelated to the committee's draft. Peter R. Livingston sent one of them to loyalist William Smith for his comments. Happily, Smith copied it into his

---

[66] "Independent Whig," No. 3, *ibid.*, March 14, 1776; anon., *N.Y.P.*, August 15, 1776.

[67] In the last two drafts, B and Jay's, the committee raised the qualification to £100. Lincoln, *Constitutional History of New York*, I, 524-25.

[68] The last drafts raised the estate to £100. *Ibid.*, I, 516.

[69] *Ibid.*, I, 531-32, 535, 536.

[70] *Ibid.*, I, 536-37.

[71] *Ibid.*, I, 506, 507-12, 541.

[72] *Ibid.*, I, 514.

Memoirs.[73] Consisting of sixteen brief paragraphs, this constitution represented a radical point of view. A council and house of deputies would share legislative authority and would be elected annually without regard to property by ballot by all taxpayers. The councilors would have executive functions also, which they exercised with a president. The president, chosen by ballot out of the legislature in joint meeting, would serve three years. The executive branch would enjoy no veto on laws. It would not possess, furthermore, much appointive power, unlike the colonial executive. The assembly would name all state officials to hold office during good behavior. The citizenry would elect triennially all county and local officials. Even where this plan did award appointive authority to the executive, it did so in very restricted fashion. The assembly would recommend to the president and council the appointment of military officers. The president would combine the duties of commander-in-chief, chancellor, and ordinary. By prohibiting assemblymen from holding salaried offices, this plan preserved the assembly's independence. Finally, the people would elect the representatives to the Continental Congress.[74] No wonder Smith "reprobated" the whole document, complaining to Livingston: "The new Government will be intirely in the Hands of the Peasantry and the commercial Interests of the Capital derive no Safety from the petty Privilege of two members in the Council."[75]

---

[73] Dorothy R. Dillon, *The New York Triumvirate: A Study of the Legal and Political Careers of William Livingston, John Morin Scott, William Smith, Jr.* (New York, 1949), p. 145; Smith, Memoirs, V, October 14, 1776.

[74] *Ibid.*

[75] He sent P. R. Livingston his detailed objections to the draft, objections that could not fail to arouse misgivings among the great landholders. For example, on the question of the franchise, he wrote: "It is dangerous to Society to admit Persons with very small Property to participate in your Councils. The richest Member of the Community under a Government elective, annually elective and that too by Ballot is put upon the same Term with one who has scarce a Farthing to lose. What Security from such a Legislature against an agrarian law and all sorts of Rapine and Plunder! If every individual Legislator is not opulent, yet certainly they ought in

The conservatives, too, entered the contest for the deputies' votes and briefly sketched the main outline of a constitution. The author of this draft simply modified the colonial establishment to fit an independent state. Governor, council, and assembly would have the same powers each possessed under British rule. Contrary to past practice the people would elect assemblymen annually by ballot, but only freeholders might vote. Members of the assembly could not serve in any other office. The assembly would select out of itself or from another source a council of twenty to hold office during good behavior. Council eligibility depended upon the ownership of lands worth £10,000. The plan required the assembly to meet at least once a year, but the governor could not adjourn, prorogue, or dissolve it without the council's advice. Carrying the principle of indirect election further, the draft prescribed the choice of the governor from the councilors for a three-year term by joint legislative ballot.[76]

Publication of this conservative plan of government provoked a direct rejoinder to it. This alternative would enfranchise all taxpayers and permit them to be candidates for any office. The government would consist of an assembly of one hundred, a council of twenty, a president, and council of

---

general to be above the Temptations of Indigence. The Poor being the Majority ought not to refuse a Security to others against the Spoil of their Property. They lose Nothing by being obliged to elect Men of Substance attached to the Territory." *Ibid.*

76 This draft and the following one seem to be the products of the Suffolk County delegation, who divided sharply in their views. The conservative plan specified "Barons of Exchequer" among the judges to be created, but the other draft rejected any "Barons." Although neither outline bears a date, it is likely that they were written in 1776, probably between July and October. The production of a committee first draft in the latter month renders any later date unlikely. *Cal. Hist. Mss.*, II, 117-18.

Robert Yates, twelve years after the event, declared that some delegates circulated this draft "to try . . . the temper" of the members. It provoked a sharp off-the-floor debate, particularly over the suffrage qualifications. Yates affirmed that general agreement existed on the desirability of enfranchising the "middling" class, since rights and liberties were endangered by the two extremes, rich and poor. "Sydney," *N.Y.J.*, June 13, 1788; Ford, *Essays on the Constitution*, pp. 297-314.

safety. The first two bodies would constitute the legislature
and the latter two the executive, which lacked any legislative
authority. All voters would choose the legislature by ballot.
Although the president and council of safety might convene
the legislative houses on special occasions, the former could
never dissolve the legislature. Otherwise, the legislators
themselves would control their meetings. The people would
elect the executive council yearly in the same fashion as the
legislature, but the two houses would select the president
annually by joint ballot out of the council of safety.[77]

Although there is a broad gulf between the conservative
and radical concepts of fundamental law, there are a few
places where they coincide. These—ballot voting, annual
assembly elections, elimination of placemen from the assembly—derive from their colonial experience. It is clear from
the preceding information that the radicals among the
Convention deputies not only had concrete proposals but
also had evolved a coherent, general draft. However, the
major strife, in which the radicals played a peripheral role,
was not between radicals and conservatives but between
moderates and conservatives.

Although few of the radical ideas won acceptance in committee, an examination of the generally analogous concepts
in the drafts will clarify the extent of the radical influence.
The chronological order of the four drafts is A, C, B and
Jay's. Draft A, and probably C, stipulated semiannual
meetings of the legislature, but B and Jay's lengthened the
interval to one year.[78] All versions adopted annual assembly
elections, and A went so far as to authorize carving the
counties into assembly districts. Since someone challenged
this unorthodox step, the committee struck it out, adhering

[77] *Cal. Hist. Mss.,* II, 117-18.
[78] Lincoln, *Constitutional History of New York,* I, 501; *Jour. Prov. Cong.,*
I, 834. Since the first four articles are missing from draft C, their substance
is guesswork. However, the content of the succeeding articles in most cases
does not differ radically from draft A. Min. of Conv.

to the traditional county-at-large method.[79] Although the committee elaborated a detailed procedure for the employment of written ballots which it retained through the first three revisions, Jay cut off everything after the opening paragraph, retaining only the principle.[80] On the crucial issue of the electorate's nature, A and C set forth the payment of both state and county taxes as the prerequisite for assembly voting rights. The committee broadened the electoral base further in the last two revisions, extending the ballot to those who paid either state or county taxes. All four drafts confined candidacy to freeholders.[81]

Unlike the radicals, the committee envisaged the senate as a check for the great landowners on the popular assembly. As first conceived in A and C, Article IX conferred the senatorial ballot on the £40 freeholders, but the conservatives narrowed this right in B and Jay's draft to the £100 freeholders. They opened the candidacy, however, to all freeholders.[82] Unanimity prevailed in the drafts on the four-year

---

[79] Lincoln, *Constitutional History of New York*, I, 505-6; *Jour. Prov. Cong.*, I, 834, 842, 884. Since A and B were practically identical, it is unlikely that C differed essentially.

[80] Lincoln, *Constitutional History of New York*, I, 507-12; *Min. of Conv.*, pp. 11-17; see above, p. 226, n. 43, and p. 228, n. 50. Robert Yates advanced an interesting hypothesis for the popularity of the secret ballot. Its origins arose out of the political battles prior to 1775 when both De Lanceyites and Livingstons expected that eventually the British would convert the governor's council into an hereditary house of lords. Therefore, election victory became mandatory, if the anti-De Lancey faction were to share in the spoils. They despaired of winning because the practice of voice voting enabled the De Lanceyites to pressure their tenants to cast their votes for them. The secret ballot was thus envisaged as the key to success and the "outs" worked assiduously just prior to 1775 to win adherents to the idea of ballot reform. It was this opinion which forced the inclusion of the written ballot in the draft constitution. As to the reasons for its deletion on the floor of the Convention, Yates is disingenuous. He suggested that either the proviso was too lengthy or the elimination of the Tories as a political faction made it unnecessary. Of course, had there been no political differences among the Whigs, it might have been deemed superfluous, but as Yates, a member of the drafting committee, well knew, the differences were many. "Sydney," *N.Y.J.*, June 13, 1788; Ford, *Essays on the Constitution*, pp. 297-314; Milton M. Klein, "Democracy and Politics in Colonial New York," *New York History*, XL (July, 1959), 231-232.

[81] Lincoln, *Constitutional History of New York*, I, 505, 507, 514; *Min. of Conv.*, p. 17; *Jour. Prov. Cong.*, I, 836, 843, 867.

term of office, but on the matter of the number of seats there were disagreements that had their origins in dissimilar means of election. In its initial version, the committee grouped the counties into four roughly equal districts, each district having four senators. Dissatisfied with this solution, the members discarded it in favor of an indirect choice. Increasing the number of seats to twenty-four, the new provision directed the selection by county of electors who would chose the senators. Still not content with this device, the committee retraced its steps in the last two revisions to the principle of direct voting as in A but did not adopt the distribution of seats in the latter. Carrying over the additional eight members from C, the committee redistributed the twenty-four senators unequally among four districts.[83]

The striking fact about the office of governor was its weakness, a conspicuous contrast with the colonial governors. All the drafts specifically confined legislative power to the senate and assembly, excluding the governor from any voice in legislation. The suffrage restrictions for senator in A and C, both as to voting and candidacy, became valid for the governorship. When the committee revised upward the property requirements for senator in the B and Jay drafts, it applied the new yardstick also to the chief magistrate.[84] The nominal parallel between governor and senator extended in all copies to the term of office, four years. Although A and C did not confer prorogation powers on the governor, the later revisions invested him with authority to prorogue the legislature not more than sixty days in one year.[85] As a further limitation on his executive power A and C estab-

---

[82] Lincoln, *Constitutional History of New York,* I, 516; Min. of Conv., p. 18; *Jour. Prov. Cong.,* I, 843.

[83] Lincoln, *Constitutional History of New York,* I, 517-21; Min. of Conv., pp. 18, 22-25; *Jour. Prov. Cong.,* I, 843.

[84] Lincoln, *Constitutional History of New York,* I, 501, 525; Min. of Conv., p. 19; *Jour. Prov. Cong.,* I, 834, 870, 871.

[85] Lincoln, *Constitutional History of New York,* I, 525; Min. of Conv., p. 19; *Jour. Prov. Cong.,* I, 870, 871.

lished a council of state to assist the governor in the administration of the state. The council of state was to consist of five freeholders chosen for five-year terms by joint ballot of the legislature. When the committee revised C, they accepted the new organ but then struck it out.[86] The earlier versions distributed the appointive power between the legislature and the governor and council. Although the governor could only nominate civil officers to the legislature, he could appoint military officers with the advice and consent of the council of state. With the deletion of the council of state from the B and Jay drafts, the governor held the sole exercise of military appointment.[87] A major exception to the governor's appointive authority was the state treasurer. Under the provisions of drafts A and C the assembly chose the treasurer by ballot. He remained in office "during their will and pleasure." In the succeeding revision the committee modified this method so that the assembly nominated the treasurer and appointment was by act of the legislature.[88]

In most of the draft revisions cited above the committee tended to place limitations on popular participation in the electoral process. A major exception was the ultimate defeat of the clause for the indirect election of state senators. Since the committee had boosted the voting qualification for senator from the £40 to the £100 freeholder, it did not see the need for further restrictions.

Although the committee in later drafts had revised key sections to check popular influence in the government, the Convention further modified some clauses. The deputies basically altered the provisions which related to the qualifications of the assembly electors and voting procedures. Under

---

[86] Lincoln, *Constitutional History of New York*, I, 525, 528; Min. of Conv., pp. 21-22.

[87] Lincoln, *Constitutional History of New York*, I, 531-32, 535-36; Min. of Conv., pp. 25-26; *Jour. Prov. Cong.*, I, 873, 874, 877, 882.

[88] Lincoln, *Constitutional History of New York*, I, 531; Min. of Conv., pp. 20, 25; *Jour. Prov. Cong.*, I, 871.

the new requirements three classes of voters emerged. First, the voter must have possessed a freehold valued at £20 above and beyond all debts thereon. Or, second, he must have rented land whose annual value was at least 40s. Or, third, he must have been a freeman of Albany or have obtained freemanship in New York City on or before October 14, 1775. Having reduced the number of electors, the Convention went on to circumscribe the exercise of the suffrage. The first amendment on voting that the Convention approved dropped the secret ballot in favor of the colonial voice vote. But, reversing themselves, the deputies provided for a trial of the written ballot after the war. The experiment would govern legislative elections but the legislature, if it saw fit, might drop the secret ballot later by a two-thirds vote.[89]

When the Convention amended the paragraph which prescribed a broad suffrage for assembly elections, it did not act primarily to disenfranchise the poor farmer but to bar the New York City mechanics from the polls. Robert R. Livingston opened the piecemeal attack on the offensive prescription, moving the insertion of a land-renting qualification for nonfreeholders who could vote. Since most rural taxpayers were either freeholders or tenants at will, this change in requirements did not affect them. Since most mechanics were neither freeholders nor tenants at will, they could not qualify under the land-rental provision. The delegates saw that this was the underlying meaning of the amendment and only the New York City members and Leonard Gansevoort of Albany voted against it.[90] Thus amended the paragraph stood for three weeks when Gouver-

---

[89] However, the Convention provided for use of the secret ballot in the election of the governor. Lincoln, *Constitutional History of New York*, I, 512-15.

[90] Even the Ulster moderates (Christopher Tappen, Matthew Rea, and Charles DeWitt) voted for the amendment. Other moderates (Matthew Adgate of Albany, Isaac Paris and Benjamin Newkirk of Tryon, Henry Schenk of Dutchess, and Henry Wisner, Sr., of Orange) also voted for the provision.

neur Morris renewed the attack. Morris moved to amend the unqualified freehold proviso to require that the freehold be of £20 value. Although this restriction sacrificed the very small freeholder, the sole rural delegation to vote nay was that of Ulster. The New York City members voted against the Morris amendment; in this instance at least, conservatives John Jay, James Duane, and Philip Livingston were opposed to a restriction of the suffrage. The moderates in the other counties joined with conservatives to adopt the proposal.[91] There were occasions such as this one when it was difficult to distinguish a moderate from a conservative.

The Convention did not deem it necessary to restrict further either senatorial or gubernatorial suffrage, but it did modify some of the provisions which set forth the governor's powers. It shortened the governor's term from four years to three. On the other hand, the more conservative members pushed through amendments that strengthened the governor's powers. Whereas the Jay draft had practically excluded the governor from the appointment power, the Convention relented and created a council of appointment which consisted of the governor and four senators, but in which the governor could only cast a tie-breaking vote. The governor might fill positions "with the advice and consent" of the council. In a second major respect, the Convention reversed its committee and granted the governor a voice in legislation. It did not clothe him with an absolute veto but established a council of revision which consisted of the governor, the chancellor, and judges of the supreme court. The governor had a full vote in this body, which decided on a veto by majority vote. The legislature might override the council's veto by a two-thirds vote of those present.[92] These changes

---

[91] Tappen, DeWitt, and Rea of Ulster voted against the restriction. Adgate, Gansevoort, and R. Yates of Albany, Henry Wisner, William Allison of Orange, Joseph Drake and Ebenezer Lockwood of Westchester, moderates, voted for the limitation. *Jour. Prov. Cong.*, I, 836, 867.

obviously represented a compromise between the group who
desired a strong legislature and a weak governor and those
who desired a strong executive.[93]

The Constitution of 1777 was a compromise but was
weighted on the conservative side even though the defenders
of the *status quo* did not attain some goals. Since some conservatives opposed direct election of the governor, acceptance
of that official's popular election represented a concession by
them. Also, there were conservatives who argued for life

---

[92] Lincoln, *Constitutional History of New York*, I, 526, 529, 532-34; *Jour.
Prov. Cong.*, I, 894-96.
The Convention had amended the governor's powers in March and had
given him an absolute veto. Smith of Orange introduced the matter in the
form of a declarative statement that there should be three branches of the
legislature instead of two and that the governor shall have a "negative upon
all laws." After debating the amendment, the Convention heard Duane
move the previous question, i.e., whether the house should now vote on the
motion. Since the house decided not to vote on the question, this in effect
killed the motion. Gouverneur Morris took the floor to reintroduce Smith's
amendment in altered form. The form of Morris's proposition suggests
what had been the source of disagreement in the preceding debate. He added
a proviso "that the governor shall have no power to originate or amend any
law, but simply to give his assent or dissent thereto." Even with this modification, some of the conservatives were uneasy and secured a postponement until
the next day. March 14 the Convention accepted Morris's amendment by a
vote which demonstrated an almost absolute conservative-moderate division.
Those in favor of the motion were Gilbert, James and Robert R. Livingston,
and Zephaniah Platt of Dutchess; Abraham Ten Broeck, Gansevoort, and
John Tayler of Albany; Duane, Peter Pra Van Zandt, Philip Livingston,
Anthony Rutgers, W. Denning, D. Dunscomb, and A. P. Lott of New York.
Gansevoort and Lott usually voted with the moderates. Those opposed to
the motion were Henry Schenk of Dutchess; Adgate of Albany; Tappen, Rea,
DeWitt, and Arthur Parks of Ulster; Isaac Paris, Volkert Veeder, and Ben-
jamin Newkirk of Tryon. Two counties were evenly split: Westchester and
Orange. In Westchester the conservatives were Morris, Pierre Van Cortlandt,
and Lewis Graham; the moderates were Joseph Drake, Zebediah Mills, and
Zephaniah Lockwood. In Orange the conservatives were Smith and Isaac
Sherwood: the moderates were Wisner and William Allison. Since these
counties divided, they could not cast a vote on the motion.
It is apparent that some among the conservatives were not content to
permit the governor to have an absolute veto because Jay, Morris, and R. R.
Livingston, after having discussed the subject in April, moved to reconsider
this paragraph. Their substitute was the council of revision. *Ibid.*, I, 834,
836, 843, 857, 860, 862; George Dangerfield, *Chancellor Robert R. Livingston
of New York, 1746-1813* (New York, 1960), p. 90.
[93] John Adams thought his letter to Wythe on Virginia's constitution influenced the Yorkers. Adams to Jefferson, September 17, 1823, quoted in Flick,
History of New York, IV, 156: Charles F. Adams, ed., *Works of John Adams*
(10 vols.; Boston, 1850-1856), X, 410.

terms in the upper house and a £10,000 qualification for candidacy. Furthermore, the conservative Suffolk plan carried over the royal governor's absolute veto power. The moderates, on the other hand, gave up substantial ground when they dropped the almost universal male suffrage proviso for the assembly and agreed to raise the £40 freehold requirement for senatorial and gubernatorial balloting. Although they excluded the governor from participation in legislation at first, they relented and allowed the chief magistrate to share the veto with the chancellor and judges of the supreme court. Similarly, the moderates proposed that the governor exercise his executive power jointly with a council of state, but they permitted amendments which abolished the council. In the reported draft the governor and council of state held the appointive power with the legislature but the moderates accepted as a substitute a council of appointment which consisted of four senators and the governor. Finally, the moderates surrendered the secret ballot until the war's end.

If the conservatives were a minority, why were they so successful? One writer stresses the persuasive powers of the aristocracy and the magical aura of their past leadership.[94] The Convention votes on the suffrage question suggest rather political fluidity and an absence of sharp antagonism between conservatives and moderates. Moreover, the roster of Convention members tends to belie the thesis of a radical majority but instead lends itself to the supposition of a narrow moderate plurality.[95] Since voting was by county unit, totals of conservatives and moderates have little mean-

---

[94] Dangerfield, *Chancellor Robert R. Livingston*, pp. 92-93.

[95] See the list in Lincoln, *Constitutional History of New York*, I, 484-86. Estimates of political views are necessarily moot, since precise data are unavailable. In this case the generalization derives from what is known of the political careers of individuals, 1774-1778, and supposition. The journals of the several committees and congresses are helpful for the host of lesser figures, although there are some twenty-five of the 107 men about whom there is no information.

ing.[96] What did matter was a majority within the county delegation to control its unit vote. A major obstacle to comprehension of this facet of the problem is the way in which the Convention recorded its ballots. If the members desired, the secretary noted their dissents to their counties' votes. Otherwise, the entire county vote appeared in one column and it is difficult to identify positively majority and minority.

Examination of the recorded votes which the deputies cast on important political issues provides data for drawing tentative conclusions relative to the strength of each group.[97] A crude tally of moderate and conservative votes suggests

96 The Third Provincial Congress formulated the distribution of county votes which the Convention retained for itself. Voting strength was Albany 6, Charlotte 2, Cumberland 2, Dutchess 5, Gloucester 1, Kings 2, New York 8, Orange 3, Queens 4, Richmond 2, Suffolk 4, Tryon 3, Ulster 4, Westchester 4 which totaled 50. However, Richmond did not elect deputies, and during the debates in 1777 Queens, Kings, Cumberland, Gloucester, Suffolk had no quorums most of the time and could not vote. Suffolk managed to maintain a quorum for the last week of the debate. The effective maximum vote in the Convention, therefore, was 35. *Jour. Prov. Cong.*, I, 834-98.

97 There were eight occasions which lent themselves to usage as political criteria. Three of these instances occurred on March 14 and included a motion to give the governor an absolute veto, a motion to delete the provisions for voting by written ballot, a motion to narrow the suffrage base by requiring non-freeholders to be renters of land. A vote for these motions rated as conservative; a vote against them ranked as moderate. The fourth indicator which took place April 2 was a motion to strike out the governor's veto and substitute the Council of Revision. Categorization of the votes on this matter was complicated because some moderates probably voted for the Council as a lesser evil than the absolute veto. Yet some moderates rejected the Council because they desired a return to the original draft in which there was no veto whatsoever. Nevertheless, the tabulation rated a vote for the Council as conservative. Although he was a conservative, Jay moved April 5 to reinsert ballot-voting. The computation placed aye votes in the moderate column and nay votes in the conservative camp. Voting qualifications supplied the sixth and seventh criteria on April 6 when Gouverneur Morris proposed to restrict freehold suffrage to £20 holders and Philip Livingston advocated reduction of residence requirements to six months. An aye voted for a £20 qualification put it on the conservative side whereas a nay vote went to the moderate group. A vote for the Livingston motion was characterized as moderate and its opposite was conservative. The last event was the Abraham Yates motion of April 20 to make the written ballot permanent which the Convention technically did not decide because it voted on the previous question rather than the motion. A deputy's vote for the previous question was a vote to kill the Yates proposal and therefore it belonged in the conservative tally; a vote against the previous question was a score for the moderate position. *Ibid.*, I, 835-92.

that the New York, Tryon and Ulster delegations cast more moderate than conservative ballots, that Albany, Dutchess, Westchester and Orange voted conservative more frequently than moderate.[98] In terms of unit votes the moderates could have mustered only 14 to 18 of the opposition. Of course, this is hypothetical but it supports an hypothesis either of minority status for the moderates and radicals or a propensity of the moderates to accept conservative proposals.

Two other affairs which took place on the same day, August 1, 1776, appear to corroborate this formulation. One was the dispute over the nomination of John Morin Scott to the constitutional drafting committee and the other was the selection of the additional members of the committee. Gouverneur Morris opposed Scott's nomination because he had previously challenged the General's possession of a seat in the Convention.[99] Scott's supporters called for a division which sustained his right to serve on the constitutional committee. It was the votes of the New York, Tryon, Ulster and Albany delegations which gave Scott his victory.[100] With the exception of Albany these were the counties which voted moderate most often.[101]

The second matter, the personnel of the committee, presents a more complex problem. The thirteen men whom the Convention selected represented a cross-section of political opinion. There were six conservatives, five moderates,

---

98 The tabulations are
New York, 44 Moderate votes, 31 Conservative votes
Tryon, 15 Moderate votes, 3 Conservative votes
Ulster, 24 Moderate votes, 6 Conservative votes
Albany, 14 Moderate votes, 22 Conservative votes
Dutchess, 17 Moderate votes, 22 Conservative votes
Westchester, 10 Moderate votes, 34 Conservative votes
Orange, 9 Moderate votes, 25 Conservative votes
Ibid.
99 See above, pp. 214-16.
100 *Ibid.*, I, 552.
101 Albany's switch can be accounted for by the county's attendance on August 1. Two of the three men present, Matthew Adgate and Robert Yates, were moderates and so determined the casting of the county's ballot. *Ibid.*, I, 552, 834-98.

one radical, and one of indeterminate views.[102] Since the striking aspect of this distribution is its near-balance of conservatives and moderates, it is tempting to attribute these proportions to a similar allocation in the Convention. Unfortunately, the *Journal* did not record any formal divisions over the nominations; indeed, all those nominated were put on the committee.[103] Since there was no ascertainable vote, it is possible that each county chose its nominees in accordance with a pre-determined quota. The successful candidates were fairly consistent reflections of the political coloration of their delegations.[104] Moderate influence in the committee was the prime element in the writing of a draft constitution which was less conservative than the amended version of April, 1777.

Since the foregoing discussion implies the importance of the delegates' constant attendance in the Convention, and since attendance during March and April, 1777 averaged only 35 percent of the entire membership, an inquiry in this area has special relevance.[105] A tenable contention might hold that if all or most of the deputies had participated in the voting, the moderates might have prevailed and have

---

[102] The conservatives were Robert R. Livingston, Gouverneur Morris, William Duer, John Sloss Hobart, John Jay and Samuel Townsend. However, the last named fell into this group on the basis of his opposition to the nomination of Scott. Townsend was not in the Convention after August, 1776. The moderates were John M. Scott, Abraham Yates, Jr., Robert Yates, Henry Wisner, Sr., and Charles DeWitt. The radical, an associate of Isaac Sears, was John Broome. Broome was not present in Convention in March and April, 1777. Although William Smith of Suffolk was in constant attendance, his county had quorums only on August 1 and April 20. On the former occasion Suffolk voted against Scott and on the latter supported Yates' moderate proposition for permanent use of the written ballot. *Ibid.*

[103] The deputies represented the major counties with the exception of Tryon. The exclusion of Tryon and the inclusion of Charlotte, a newer county, were possibly the consequence of an unrecorded, general agreement on the size and character of the committee. *Ibid.*, I, 552.

[104] The exception was New York which chose a conservative, moderate and a radical. Perhaps this was the intent, since the deputies present reflected the three broad-gauge views. Dunscomb and Rutgers were conservatives; Beekman and Lott were moderates; Brasher and Harpur had radical proclivities. *Ibid.*, I, 552, 834-98.

[105] *Ibid.*, I, 834-98.

given the people a more democratic constitution. However, analysis of the county representation points toward an opposite conclusion. If all the men on the Albany, Dutchess, Orange, Westchester, Cumberland, Gloucester and Charlotte delegations had fulfilled their obligations as legislators, these counties would probably have had conservative majorities with a total of 23 unit votes. Two counties, Ulster and Tryon, would have fallen into moderate hands with 6 unit votes. New York with 8 votes might have gone in either direction. Suffolk might have divided evenly and so lost its 4 votes.[106] It is not stretching the imagination to put Queens and its 4 votes among the conservatives even though these representatives' views are not clear. This tabulation ignored Kings and Richmond because neither county sent any members to the Convention.[107] The preceding estimate roughly corroborates the calculation of moderate and conservative votes within county blocs.[108]

Although these considerations place the conservative character of the constitution in better perspective, they do not suffice to account for the course of the floor debates. Nevertheless, the evidence makes more meaningful the Jay and Robert R. Livingston comments relative to the uncertainties of the situation and to the employment of Fabian tactics prior to the committee's report in March, 1777.[109] When the voting behavior of the moderates comes under scrutiny, the failure of these men to adhere rigorously to basic positions suggests the emergence of a moderate-conservative consensus. There are other factors as well. Nowhere is there any hint of effective organization among the moderates and

---

106 An evenly divided delegation could not cast its county's votes.

107 It is assumed that in some delegations a majority might have resulted from an alliance of moderates and radicals.

108 Although the interpretation in the preceding paragraphs makes no claim to precision, it derives from a distillation of the deputies' votes in the several committees and congresses and of their political activities from 1773-1777.

109 See above, nn. 1 and 58.

radicals which might have enabled them to defeat the conservatives. Moreover, a comparison of leadership redounds to the advantage of the conservatives. The moderates and radicals did not have, with the exception of John Morin Scott, men of prestige and ability to compare with Jay, Robert R. Livingston and Gouverneur Morris.[110] Possessed of these solid benefits, the conservatives, seasoned wielders of power that they were, triumphed over a less able opposition.

---

[110] The fact that this trio differed among themselves over primary clauses, such as balloting and the governor's veto, might have offered an exploitable weakness to an aggressive, keen opposition. The *Journal* does not reveal any moderate efforts to profit from conservative differences.

EIGHT

Reconsiderations

EVEN though one cannot analyze statistically the Whig and Tory strength, the direction of events from 1774 to 1776 provides us with a crude index to the division of the people. After Lexington and Concord the New York Tories were unable to turn back or contain the upsurge of Whig opposition. The Tory failure was significant in two respects, as a commentary on the government's weakness and as an indication of inadequate popular support for the Tories in the rural districts. Theoretically, the government possessed two advantages, power and prestige, but it was not able to maximize either one because in reality it had little of either. Tory paralysis in the countryside can be attributed neither to a deficiency of leaders, since there were numbers of Tory gentry, nor to an absence of will. Indeed the one county in which the Tories were at first successful became eventually the symbol of their defeat. The Johnsons organized their tenantry to defend the crown but they could not rally the rest of Tryon County behind them. Throughout the province the unwillingness of the people to rebuff the Whigs manifested itself in the last elections for the General Assembly in January, 1776, when the electorate returned a Whig majority. The political trends of 1775-1776 suggest the desirability of a reexamination of the Tory question. Perhaps some of the research techniques in quantification could be fruitfully applied here.

Unquestionably, the timid leadership of the Whigs needlessly handicapped the entire revolutionary movement. The vacillation of the leaders induced confusion, if not disgust, among the people and this in turn dampened the militancy of the population. A converse effect of the wavering policy was the temporary encouragement of the Tories in their covert and open resistance to Whig measures. Another difficulty which timidity compounded was the appearance of competition for leadership and position within the Whig group. The experience of Cumberland, Charlotte, and Dutchess suggests that this factor may have existed in other counties.[1] The Whigs' lack of vigor was in no way a consequence of their being in a minority position; in fact, they were a majority. If they were a conspiratorial minority, they could not have constructed a durable revolutionary organization. It was precisely because the Whigs mustered a majority that they were able to carry the colony down the road to independence and statehood.

There was one sphere, polemical writing, in which the reluctant leadership was unable to quell the ardor of the militants. The newspapers played a vanguard role in presenting to their readers a stream of pleas for independence.[2] The significant factor was the writers' abandonment in late April, 1776 of opposition to separation from Britain. Since none of the moderates found it desirable or expedient to rebut the arguments for breaking the ties, they may have wished to avoid exacerbating public sentiment because that opinion was far in advance of the moderate leadership.

An implicit but nonetheless real theme of the revolution-

---

[1] George Dangerfield, *Chancellor Robert R. Livingston, of New York, 1746-1813* (New York, 1960), p. 462, n. 13; Staughton Lynd, *Anti-Federalism in Dutchess County New York: A Study of Democracy and Class Conflict in the Revolutionary Era* (Chicago, 1962), pp. 57-58.

[2] For the continental situation, see Arthur M. Schlesinger, Sr., *Prelude to Independence: The Newspaper War on Britain, 1774-1776* (New York, 1958), chap. xii.

ary years was class strife. This conflict was spasmodic and disorganized and did not produce a program or sense of class solidarity, nor did it clearly draw lines between classes. Furthermore, it occurred on multiple planes, embracing tenants at will and landlords on one level and mechanics and merchants on another.[3] These were examples of a simple antagonism but there were others that involved complicated class coalitions. Thus, in May, 1776, the Committee of Mechanics warned the Provincial Congress against adopting a new form of government without submitting it to the people for ratification. The house, drawn from the large and middle landholders and commercial middle classes, buried the Mechanics' memorial.[4] The constitution-drafting process in 1776-1777 reflected still another facet of class conflict. It is apparent that the reform group of middle-class farmers sought to broaden the base of popular participation in government but were defeated by a combination of the elite and middle freeholders.[5] Since the lesser-propertied classes neither controlled the revolutionary movement nor were able fundamentally to alter social relations, many historians have denied that class struggle was a factor in the Revolution.[6]

The Revolution in New York was not primarily a question of which class would control the state. For the Whig leadership of landed magnates, merchants, lawyers, and middle-class freeholders, it was a war of liberation. Although the necessity of maintaining a united front against

---

3 The correspondence of Robert R. Livingston is replete with examples of tenant antagonism. Henry B. Livingston to R. R. Livingston, May, 1775, Robert R. Livingston, American Art Association Catalogue, *Revolutionary Letters of Importance: The Unpublished Correspondence of Robert R. Livingston* (New York, 1918), No. 30; Lynd, *Anti-Federalism in Dutchess County*, chap. iv; Richard B. Morris, "Class Struggle and the American Revolution," *William and Mary Quarterly*, 3rd ser., XIX (January, 1962), 13.
    The attempts of mechanics to influence nominations to committees was one manifestation of this spirit. See above, pp. 149-50.
4 See above, pp. 155-59.
5 See above, chap. vii.
6 See Morris, *William and Mary Quarterly*, 3rd ser., XIX, 3-29.

Britain was a powerful centripetal force among the leaders, the coalition evinced signs of strain when it confronted such major questions as independence and the constitution. By and large the prewar elite were preponderant in the revolutionary organs, but the very nature of the conflict with the parent nation opened the door to power to the middle-class farmers, who were learning political self-reliance and independence.

APPENDIX

THE FOLLOWING examples of inaccurate or uncritical use of materials by Flick in his *Loyalism in New York During the American Revolution* suggest that a new look at the New York loyalist problem might produce interesting material.

One of Flick's sources, loyalist historian Thomas Jones, wrote that the British formed a New York City militia organization in 1779 of 6,000 men. All of these males, he said, were inhabitants of the city prior to the British occupation. A little arithmetic will demonstrate the unreliability of the latter statement. If 6,000 men between the ages of sixteen and fifty lived in the city, the city's population would be *ca.* 30,000 but this is a much larger number than any contemporary estimate. Moreover, this calculation excludes the Whigs, who, if added to the 30,000, would have made a total population greater than any city in America. Since thousands, a majority, did not return after the American defeat in 1776, the 6,000 militia could not be original inhabitants. Sir Henry Clinton explained that many of the militia were "persons attached to the different army and navy departments consisting of sailors, watermen and others."[1]

According to Flick, "a large part of the 6,000 seamen in the metropolis were loyalists." The figure derives from one of Tryon's letters, but the Governor noted that they were not all Yorkers. He stated that 6,000 men, partly from New York, composed of landsmen and seamen, partly drawn to the colony from the several provinces, had filled the crews of the royal ships.[2]

In July, 1776, Tryon allegedly began to enlist 1,300 men on Long Island and Staten Island. The source of this fact is the unsupported statement of an inhabitant who did not reveal how he acquired this information. Moreover, the informant in no way indicated how many actually enlisted. Howe remarked to Germain that the Governor participated in the Battle of Long

Island in August with two companies of New York loyalists. The maximum strength of the company was 57.[3]

When Governor Tryon raided Danbury, Connecticut, in 1777, his force supposedly comprised 2,000 Long Islanders. Jones, Flick's source, simply stated that the raiders numbered 2,000 without identifying them. As it happened, all units were regular British army corps; no loyalists participated.[4]

Although Flick quotes in part a Tryon County Committee letter to show that half the county was Tory, the implication is not accurate. The Tryon committee declared that half the people would not bear arms to defend the county against a British invasion because the state had neglected to send troops to aid them. Believing themselves abandoned by the state to the enemy, half the people were unwilling to sacrifice themselves, their families, and their property in vain and so would surrender. This can hardly be termed Toryism. In fact, when St. Leger did invade the county in 1777, between 700 and 1,000 men sprang to arms and their determined resistance at Oriskany and Fort Schuyler blocked a union with Burgoyne.[5]

In 1779 William Axtell obtained a commission to recruit 500 loyalists, but this did not prove he did so. Jones, Flick's source, notes that Axtell raised only 30 men, but drew pay and provisions for the 500.[6]

---

1 Thomas Jones, *History of New York During the Revolutionary War, and of the Leading Events in the Other Colonies at that Period,* ed. Edward F. de Lancey (2 vols.; New York, 1879), I, 322-23; General Sir Henry Clinton, *The American Rebellion,* ed. William B. Willcox (New Haven, 1954), p. 455; Alexander C. Flick, *Loyalism in New York During the American Revolution* (New York, 1901), p. 112.

2 Flick, *Loyalism,* p. 107; Tryon to Vice-Admiral Arbuthnot, June 29, 1779, Edmund B. O'Callaghan, ed., *Documents Relative to the Colonial History of the State of New York* (15 vols.; Albany, 1856), VIII, 772.

3 Flick, *Loyalism,* p. 105; Peter Force, ed., *American Archives* (9 vols.; Washington, D. C., 1837-1853), 5th ser., I, 120; Sir William Howe, *A Schedule of Sir William Howe's Correspondence as Produced to the House of Commons* (extracted from the *Parliamentary Register,* XI, 1779) (London, 1779), p. 342.

4 Flick, *Loyalism,* p. 105; Jones, *History of New York During the Revolutionary War,* I, 177-78; Howe, *Schedule of Correspondence,* p. 391; Serle to Dartmouth, May 1, 1777, Benjamin F. Stevens, ed., *Facsimiles of Manuscripts in European Archives Relating to America, 1773-1783* (25 vols.; London, 1889-1898), XXIV, No. 2059.

5 Flick, *Loyalism,* p. 110; Tryon Committee letter in Jones, *History of New York During the Revolutionary War,* I, 700-701.

Since Long Island, excluding Suffolk, was a Tory stronghold, there are numerous references in Flick to the enlistment of loyalists from the area. When added up, the result is curious. Omitting all numbers which do not give a specific county of origin, the total for Kings and Queens is 3,600. The 1771 census credited the two counties with 11,205, or *ca.* 7 percent of the colony's total. If we allow for a 1776 population of 208,000, the two counties with 7 percent would have 14,560. The age group between sixteen and sixty would number perhaps 3,640 men. We are led to believe, therefore, that the British recruited almost every male in this age bracket into their active units, leaving no militia. Difficult as this may be to accept, it becomes impossible when we consider that Flick also states that one-fifth of the Queens militia was Whig. And what about the Kings militia? Small as it was, there was more Whig sentiment in the latter county than in Queens. General Sir Henry Clinton doubted the loyalty of "a great part" of the Kings inhabitants.[7]

Another example of New York's loyalism was the De Lancey brigade, which was to have 1,500 men from Kings and Queens. Jones was careful to say only that De Lancey held a commission to raise 1,500. The difference was important, since Howe cited the brigade's strength at 693 in November, 1777, and 707 in May, 1778. The unit records show that *ca.* 1,095 officers and men served in the brigade, but not all of them were New Yorkers.[8]

In a vein similar to his comment on Tryon County, Flick tagged Lewis Morris's militia regiment as overwhelmingly loyalist, as having only a "colonel's command" of Whigs in it. This is a misconstruction of what Morris wrote to the New York Convention. After the American defeat in Manhattan, Morris

6 Flick, *Loyalism*, p. 112; Jones, *History of New York During the Revolutionary War*, I, 304-5.

7 Flick, *Loyalism*, pp. 95-112; Clinton, *The American Rebellion*, p. 69.

8 Flick, *Loyalism*, p. 106; Jones, *History of New York During the Revolutionary War*, I, 264-65; Sir William Howe, *Narrative of Lieutenant-General Sir William Howe in a Committee of the House of Commons on 29 April, 1779 Relative to His Conduct During His Late Command of the King's Troops in North America: To Which Are Added, Some Observations Upon a Pamphlet Entitled, Letters to a Nobleman* (London, 1780), p. 52; W. O. Raymond, "Loyalists in Arms," New Brunswick Historical Society *Collections*, II (St. John, 1904), 220; Arthur W. Eaton, "New York Loyalists in Novia Scotia," *The Grafton Magazine*, February, 1910, p. 174.

stated that "not more than a Colonel's command was left" in his Westchester regiment. But this letter was part of a sorry affair which has to be seen in its entirety in order to evaluate Morris's judgment of his regiment. The Convention had called upon Morris to explain his desertion of his command and flight to Philadelphia. As justification he alleged the unit's decimation and the disaffection of many of the survivors. The Convention rejected his defense; indeed Morris had refuted himself in his correspondence. When the Convention ordered his regiment on active service in August, Morris informed Abraham Yates, Jr. that the men reported with "cheerfulness," a most un-Torylike characteristic in this connection. In other areas Tories refused to serve when called up for duty. In a private exchange R. R. Livingston and Edward Rutledge bluntly attributed Morris's action to fear, not to loyalists. Morris's assessment of political loyalties then is highly suspect, since it directly involved his own reputation.[9]

Referring to one of Governor Tryon's letters, Flick comments that Tyron believed the whole province would take up arms for the crown if the British drove out the rebel army. The letter itself does not bear out this interpretation. The Governor described a sortie with 1,000 men into Suffolk in the course of which the people dutifully dissolved their committees and repudiated the resolves of the congresses. He then went on to declare that he thought the whole province would do likewise when the British would destroy the rebel army. Be it noted that both Howe and rebel John Sloss Hobart attributed the submission to compulsion. We may leave this aside, however. For a defenseless people to dissolve revolutionary committees under the menace of 20,000 to 30,000 guns of an army of occupation is not to be equated with voluntarily shouldering arms to defend the King and Parliament.[10]

---

9 Flick, *Loyalism*, pp. 108-9; Force, *American Archives*, 5th ser., III, 211; *Jour. Prov. Cong.*, I, 666, II, 281; Livingston to Rutledge, October 10, 1776, Rutledge to Livingston, October 19, 1776, Bancroft Transcripts: Livingston Papers, NYPL.

10 Flick, *Loyalism,* p. 100; Tryon to Germain, November 28, 1776, O'Callaghan, *Documents, Colonial, New York*, VIII, 692; Hobart to Convention, October 7, 1776, *Jour. Prov. Cong.*, I, 671; Howe, *Narrative*, p. 44.

A Note on Sources

STUDIES of revolutionary politics would be impossible without the great manuscript collections in the depositories of New York City and of course the indispensable lode-star to these is Evarts B. Green and Richard B. Morris, eds., *A Guide to the Principal Sources for Early American History (1600-1800) in the City of New York* (New York, 2nd ed., 1953). Among the riches of the New-York Historical Society the Robert R. Livingston Collection has much to offer those investigating political and economic history. There is also important correspondence in the Alexander McDougall Papers and James Duane Papers. Less useful for this study were the Livingston Family Papers, the John Lamb Papers and the William Duer Papers, although the Duer manuscripts contain significant economic data. Scattered items came from the John McKesson Papers and New York State Treasurer's Accounts, 1775-1778.

Columbia University Library's Special Collections have two pertinent, major groups, the Gouverneur Morris Papers and the John Jay Papers. For these years, the sources of many of the quotations which, sometimes in altered form, appear in Jared Sparks, *The Life of Gouverneur Morris with Selections from His Correspondence and Miscellaneous Papers* (3 vols.; Boston, 1832) may be found in the Morris Papers. Although many of Jay's letters are in Henry P. Johnston, ed., *The Correspondence and Public Papers of John Jay* (4 vols.; New York, 1890-1893), the manuscript collection supplements the printed works and has many illuminating letters to Jay.

The third major depository, the New York Public Library, has several groups of vital papers for this area of study. The Samuel Adams Papers and the Adams correspondence in the Bancroft Transcripts have exchanges between New Yorkers and Adams in addition to descriptions of New York affairs. The

Philip Schuyler Papers are a labyrinth, but the rewards are well-worth the necessary investment of time. Among the William Smith Papers the most important manuscripts are Smith's Historical Memoirs which are conveniently printed in William H. W. Sabine, ed., *Historical Memoirs from 16 March 1763 to 25 July 1778 of William Smith* (2 vols.; New York, 1956, 1958). There are very informative letters to and from Robert R. Livingston in the Bancroft Transcripts, a number of which are excerpted in the American Art Association Catalogue, *Revolutionary Letters of Importance: The Unpublished Correspondence of Robert R. Livingston* (New York, 1918). Three other Livingston groups, the Gilbert Livingston Papers, Livingston Family Papers and Philip Livingston Letters, have useful items. Although the correspondence in the Abraham Yates, Jr. Papers is disappointing, these papers contain a very rare draft of the Constitution of 1777. The huge loyalist collection, Transcript of the Manuscript Books and Papers of the Commission of Enquiry into the Losses and Services of the American Loyalists Held Under Acts of Parliament of 23, 25, 26, 28, 29 of George III Preserved amongst the Audit Office Records in the Public Record Office of England, 1783-1790, is one of the sources for details about various Tories.

Two other libraries, the New York State Library and the Franklin D. Roosevelt Library, hold collections which provide relevant data. The Andrew Elliot Papers in Albany have a valuable account of the turbulent early months of 1775. The Legislative Papers and Dutchess County petitions in the Miscellaneous Manuscripts furnished isolated details. The Livingston Redmond Papers at Hyde Park were most valuable for events in the summer of 1776.

One of the fortunate consequences of conflict among the political factions was the production of broadsides which often clarify otherwise obscure events. Both the New-York Historical Society and the New York Public Library have extensive holdings of these flyers.

Colonial newspapers are major repositories of political opinion, contributing clues to trends of thought. All of the New York newspapers have essential data but recourse must be had

to some of the Connecticut and Philadelphia papers. Especially
valuable for Sears' raid on Rivington's shop are the (Hartford)
Connecticut Courant, (New Haven) *Connecticut Journal* and
(New London) *Connecticut Gazette.* Some important material
is in the *Pennsylvania Gazette, Pennsylvania Journal* and *Pennsylvania Packet,* all of Philadelphia. The researcher would be
lost without Clarence S. Brigham's *History and Bibliography of
American Newspapers, 1690-1820* (2 vols.; Worcester, 1947)
which identifies and locates all of the newspapers.

Official records are fundamental to research about the Revolution in New York. The most rewarding of these are the *Journals of the Provincial Congress, Provincial Convention, Committee of Safety and Council of Safety of the State of New
York, 1775-1777* (2 vols.; Albany, 1842); Charles Z. Lincoln, ed.,
State of New York, Messages from the Governors, 1683-1906 (11
vols.; Albany, 1909); Berthold Fernow, ed., "Calendar of Council Minutes, 1668-1783," New York State Library *Bulletin 58*
(Albany, 1902). The *Calendar of Historical Manuscripts Relating
to the War of the Revolution, in the Office of the Secretary of
State* (2 vols.; Albany, 1868) has some Convention committee
minutes. Charles Z. Lincoln, *The Constitutional History of
New York* (5 vols.; Rochester, 1906) prints copies of the destroyed drafts of the Constitution of 1777. An important collection of Vermont land warrants is in the *Calendar of New
York Colonial Manuscripts Indorsed Land Papers in the Office
of the Secretary of State of New York* (Albany, 1864). Compilations of military service are in James A. Roberts, comp., *New
York in the Revolution as Colony and State* (Albany, 2nd ed.,
1898) and *Supplement* (Albany, 1901). Tory sentiment may be
traced in the *Calendar of Home Office Papers of the Reign of
George III, 1773-1775* (London, 1899). Insights into the local
problems of revolutionary conflict are found in Samuel L. Frey,
ed., *The Minute Book of the Committee of Safety of Tryon
County* (New York, 1905) and J. Sullivan, ed., *Minutes of the
Albany Committee of Correspondence, 1775-1778 and Minutes
of the Schenectady Committee, 1775-1779* (2 vols.; Albany, 1923,
1925). Standing in a class by itself for more than a century is
that wonderful *mélange* of official and unofficial documents,

American Archives ed. by Peter Force (9 vols.; Washington, D.C., 1837-1853). Other useful compilations are Nathaniel H. Carter and William L. Stone, reporters, *Reports of the Proceedings and Debates of the Convention of 1821, Assembled for the Purpose of Amending the Constitution of the State of New York* (Albany, 1821); Washington C. Ford and Gaillard Hunt, eds., *Journals of the Continental Congress* (34 vols.; Washington, D.C., 1904-1937); J. Shannon, comp., *Manual of the Corporation of the City of New York, 1868* (New York, 1868); U.S. Bureau of the Census, *Historical Statistics of the United States, Colonial Times to 1957* (Washington, D.C., 1957).

Much correspondence is accessible in printed form in several types of collections. Two groups of general correspondence are Edmund B. O'Callaghan, ed., *Documentary History of the State of New York* (4 vols.; Albany, 1850-1857) and Edmund B. O'Callaghan, ed., *Documents Relative to the Colonial History of the State of New York* (15 vols.; Albany, 1856). Two of the British Historical Manuscripts Commission's reports, *Fourteenth Report, Appendix Part X* (Manuscripts of the Earl of Dartmouth) and the *Report on the Manuscripts of Mrs. Stopford-Sackville of Drayton House, Northamptonshire* (3 vols.; London, 1895, 1904, 1910), help to fill some gaps in American publications. There is a substantial amount of pertinent material in *The Letterbooks and Letters and Papers of Cadwallader Colden* (11 vols.; New-York Historical Society *Collections*, 1876-1877, 1917-1923, 1934, 1936) and *Lee Papers* (New-York Historical Society *Collections*, 1871). Although they are poorly edited, the *Public Papers of George Clinton, First Governor of New York* (10 vols.; Albany, 1899-1914) have important letters on politics and Tories. Additional valuable papers are in Clarence E. Carter, ed., *The Correspondence of General Thomas Gage with the Secretaries of State, and with the War Office and the Treasury, 1763-1775* (2 vols.; New Haven, 1931, 1933); *Huntington Papers* (Connecticut Historical Society *Collections*, XX, Hartford, 1889); "The Duane Letters," Southern History Association *Publications*, VII (1903), 170-85, 247-56, 362-68; Johnston, *Correspondence of John Jay; New York City During the American Revolution. Being a Collection of Original Papers*

(Now First Published) from the Manuscripts in the Possession of the Mercantile Library Association of New York City (New York, 1861); Benjamin F. Stevens, ed., *Facsimiles of Manuscripts in European Archives Relating to America, 1773-1783* (25 vols.; London, 1889-1898); Isaac N. P. Stokes, ed., *The Iconography of Manhattan Island* (6 vols.; New York, 1915-1928); John C. Hamilton, *Life of Alexander Hamilton: a History of the Republic of the United States of America, as Traced in His Writings and in Those of His Contemporaries* (10 vols.; Boston, 1879). The most useful of the writings of major personalities are Edmund C. Burnett, ed., *Letters of the Members of the Continental Congress* (8 vols.; Washington, D.C., 1921-1936); Charles F. Adams, ed., *Works of John Adams* (10 vols.; Boston, 1850-1856); Julian P. Boyd *et al.,* eds., *The Papers of Thomas Jefferson* (17 vols.; Princeton, 1950-   ); John C. Fitzpatrick, ed., *The Writings of George Washington from the Original Manuscript Sources, 1745-1799* (39 vols.; Washington, D.C., 1931-1944); Gaillard Hunt, ed., *The Writings of James Madison* (9 vols.; New York, 1900-1910); Harold C. Syrett and Jacob E. Cooke, eds., *The Papers of Alexander Hamilton* (9 vols.; New York, 1960-   ); Jared Sparks, ed., *Correspondence of the American Revolution* (4 vols.; Boston, 1853).

In addition to the sources already cited there is abundant data on several aspects of the Tory problem in *Minutes of the Committee and of the First Commission for Detecting and Defeating Conspiracies in the State of New York, 1776-1778* (3 vols.; New-York Historical Society *Collections,* 1924-1926); John Burgoyne, *A State of the Expedition from Canada as Laid Before the House of Commons* (London, 1780); M. K. Couzens, *Index of Grantees of Lands Sold by the Commissioners of Forfeitures of the Southern District of the State of New York Situate in The Manor of Philipsburg, Westchester County, New York* (Yonkers, 1880); Albert G. Greene, *Recollections of the Jersey Prison-Ship* (Morrisania, 1865); Sir William Howe, *Narrative of Lieutenant-General Sir William Howe in a Committee of the House of Commons on 29 April, 1779 Relative to His Conduct During His Late Command of the King's Troops in North America: To Which Are Added, Some Observations Upon a*

Pamphlet Entitled, Letters to a Nobleman (London, 1780); *A Schedule of Sir William Howe's Correspondence as Produced to the House of Commons* (London, 1779); Samuel Seabury, *An Alarm to the Legislature of the Province of New York* (New York, 1775) and *What Think Ye of Congress Now* (New York, 1775); David L. Sterling, ed., "American Prisoners of War in New York: A Report by Elias Boudinot," *William and Mary Quarterly*, 3rd series, XIII (1957), 376-93; John A. Stevens, Jr., ed., *Colonial Records of the New York Chamber of Commerce, 1768-1784* (New York, 1867); Margaret W. Willard, ed., *Letters on the American Revolution, 1774-1776* (Boston, 1925); Thomas Jones, *History of New York During the Revolutionary War, and of the Leading Events in the Other Colonies at that Period*, ed. by Edward F. de Lancey (2 vols.; New York, 1879).

The investigator of revolutionary New York owes much to his predecessors who have made his task lighter by their labors. The one work which holds a unique place in this field because it is a brilliant piece of research is Carl L. Becker, *The History of Political Parties in the Province of New York, 1760-1776* (Madison, 1909). Studies which supplement Becker are Oscar T. Barck, Jr., *New York City During the War for Independence* (New York, 1931); Alexander C. Flick, *The American Revolution in New York* (Albany, 1926); Staughton Lynd, *Anti-Federalism in Dutchess County New York: A Study of Democracy and Class Conflict in the Revolutionary Era* (Chicago, 1962); Richard B. Morris, ed., *The Era of the American Revolution* (New York, 1939); Arthur M. Schlesinger, Sr., *The Colonial Merchants and the American Revolution, 1763-1776* (New York, 1939); Arthur M. Schlesinger, Sr., *Prelude to Independence: The Newspaper War on Britain, 1764-1776* (New York, 1958); Thomas J. Wertenbaker, *Father Knickerbocker Rebels: New York City During the Revolution* (New York, 1948); Chilton Williamson, *American Suffrage from Property to Democracy, 1760-1860* (Princeton, 1960); Carl Bridenbaugh, *Cities in Revolt: Urban Life in America, 1743-1776* (New York, 1955). Basic examinations of the Tory problem are Alexander C. Flick, *Loyalism in New York During the American Revolution* (New York, 1901); Claude H. Van Tyne, *The Loyalists in the American*

Revolution (New York, 1902); William H. Nelson, *The American Tory* (Oxford, 1961); Paul H. Smith, *Loyalists and Redcoats: A Study in British Revolutionary Policy* (Chapel Hill, 1964). Helpful biographies are Edward P. Alexander, *A Revolutionary Conservative: James Duane of New York* (New York, 1938); George Dangerfield, *Chancellor Robert R. Livingston of New York, 1746-1813* (New York, 1960); Don R. Gerlach, *Philip Schuyler and the American Revolution in New York, 1733-1777* (Lincoln, 1964); Dorothy R. Dillon, *The New York Triumvirate: A Study of the Legal and Political Careers of William Livingston, John Morin Scott, William Smith, Jr.* (New York, 1949); Frank Monaghan, *John Jay* (New York, 1935).

Renewed interest in the structure of colonial politics has resulted in an expanding periodical literature. Among the recent articles are Milton M. Klein, "Democracy and Politics in Colonial New York," *New York History,* XL (July, 1959), 221-46; Richard B. Morris, "Class Struggle and the American Revolution," *William and Mary Quarterly,* 3rd ser., XIX (January, 1962), 3-29; Nicholas Varga, "Election Procedure and Practices in Colonial New York," *New York History,* XLI (July, 1960), 249-77; Staughton Lynd, "The Mechanics in New York City Politics, 1774-1788," *Labor History* (Fall, 1964), 225-46 and "The Tenant Rising at Livingston Manor, May, 1777," *New-York Historical Society Quarterly,* XLVIII (April, 1964), 163-77; three essays by Roger J. Champagne, "New York and the Intolerable Acts, 1774," *New-York Historical Society Quarterly,* XLV (April, 1961), 195-207, "New York Politics and Independence, 1776," *New-York Historical Society Quarterly,* XLVI (July, 1962), 281-303, and "New York's Radicals and the Coming of Independence," *Journal of American History,* LI (June, 1964), 21-40.

INDEX

Abeel, Garret, 74n25
Activists. *See* Radicals
Adams, John, 104, 177; accuses New York of lagging, 174
Adams, Samuel, 31, 51, 104, 112
Adgate, Matthew, 243n92, 246n101; moves to instruct constitutional committee on bill of rights, 214
Albany, N.Y., 98
Albany County: formation of committee of inspection, 42; districts vote for independence, 172; voting power in Provincial Congress, 180, 182; delegates vote against paper currency, 194; Convention delegation voting behavior on constitution, 246 and n
Albany County Committee of Correspondence, 89; delays seizure of Tory arms, 145; uneasiness over delay in drafting constitution, 220
Allison, William, 243n92
Alner, James, 148n51, 149 and n
Alsop, John, 26n64, 31, 39n99, 131n78, 148, 166n95, 169, 199; suggests new pacificatory measures be sent to Continental Congress, 120-21
Alva, Duke of, 138
Anthony, John, 38n97, 39n99
Anthony, Theophilus, 39n98, 72n21
Apthorpe, Charles, 8n11
Apthorpe family, 48
Ashfield, Vincent P., 112
Asia: cannonade by, 103
Aspinwall, John, 27n67
Auchmuty, Rev. Samuel, 68
Austin, Thomas, 64n6
Avery, Alpheus, 64n6
Axtell, William, 8n11, 78n37, 255
Ayscough, Captain: divulges Tryon's shift on tea ship, 18

Bache, Theophylact, 39n99
Bancker, Evert, 72n21, 148n51, 149n
Bancker, Gerard, 196
Bassett, Francis, 38n97, 39n99
Bates, John, 64n6

Bayard, William, 39n99
Bayley, Jacob, 116
Bedlow, William, 74n25
Beekman, David, 72n21
Beekman, George, 39n99
Beekman, James, 127, 148n51, 149n
Bennet, Isaac, 64n6
Bennett, John, 64n6
Benson, Egbert, 203
Benson, Robert, 72n21
Berrien, John, 39n99
Beyea, James, 64n6
Bicker, Victor, 39n98, 72n21
Billop, Christopher, 131n78
Blackwell, Jacob, 131n78
Blagge, Benjamin, 48
Blagge, John, 48
Bleecker, John J., 122 and n
Bogart, Nicholas, 74n25
Booth, Benjamin, 39n99; resigns as tea agent, 12
Boston, Mass., 9, 10, 13 and n, 15, 24, 30, 31; opposition to landing tea in, 12; news of Tea Party in, 17
Bowne, George, 39n99
Boycott. *See* Continental Association; Nonimportation
Brantigan, Frederick, 64n6
Brasher, Abraham, 39n98, 72n21, 124, 148n51, 149n
Brinckerhoff, Abraham, 72n21
Brinckerhoff, Dirck, 131n78
Brookhaven, N.Y., 198
Broome, John, 12n, 15n30, 72n21, 148n51, 149 and n, 150, 153, 217, 225, 247n102
Broome, Samuel, 12n, 59
Brown, John, 64n6
Brown, William, 64n6
Buchanan, Walter, 65-66
Bull, Joseph, 39n99
Bulyea, Abraham, 64n6
Bulyea, Henry, 64n6
Bulyea, John, 64n6
Burgoyne, Gen. John: recruitment of loyalists, 97-98
Burling, Lancaster, 39n99

Butler family: encourages loyalist declaration in Tryon County, 85

Byvanck, Peter, 72n21

Canadian expedition, 184

"Candidus": assails British colonial system, 161

Carleton, Sir Guy, 202

Case, John, 56

Chambers, Capt. James: destruction of tea cargo of, 19-22

Champlain, Lake, 202

Chandler, Rev. Thomas B.: recipient of royal annuity, 53

Charleston, S.C.: action on tea, 17

Charlotte County, 115; election for Second Congress, 116; voting power in Third Congress, 182

Charlotte precinct (Dutchess County): vote for provincial convention in, 86, 87

Church party: description of, 6-7. *See also* De Lancey faction

Clarkson, David, 72n21

Class antagonism, 23n53, 29n71, 150; tenant vs. landlord, 103, 173n117; Mechanics' petition as manifestation of, 163-64; as factor in demand for political reform, 173n117; "licentiousness" of people as form of, 174; as implicit theme of revolution, 251-52

Clinton, George, 131n78, 217n, 218n 15; describes militia response, 98-99; said to oppose independence, 166n95; sends information to committee to obstruct Hudson, 219; postponement of constitutional report advocated by adherents of, 222

Clinton, Sir Henry: loyalist troop returns of, 94; panic induced by arrival of, 101; comment on militia in New York city, 254

Clopper, Cornelius, 72n21

Clopper, Peter, 74n25, n26

Clossy, Samuel, 64n6

Coercive Acts: effects of, 24-29; measures to counter, 31-35

Colden, Cadwallader, 8 and n11, 77, 90, 124-25; acting governor during Tea Party, 20 and n45; approves land patents in Vermont, 48; uses land as reward for political loyalty, 49-50; accused of being royal pensioner, 52; declines to recall assembly, 62-63; convenes council to con-

Colden, Cadwallader *(continued)*: sider *James* affair, 66; accused of asking ministry for troops, 74; describes collapse of government's authority, 76; boldness of, 80-81; meeting with council on Dartmouth's instructions, 81; asks for substantial numbers of troops, 83

Colden family: directs disarming of Queens Whigs, 108

Colonial system: assailed by "Candidus," 161

Commissary: functions and authority of, 187; responsibilities exceed abilities, 188; appointment of additional, 188-89

Conciliation: proposals for in Provincial Congress, 118-29

Connecticut, 146, 206; source of loyalist recruits, 95; place of imprisonment for Tories, 197

Conscience, freedom of: newspaper discussion of, 233

Conservatives: definition of, viii-ix, 71 and n20, 231; social base of, 2; representation on Committee of One Hundred, 72-73; growing divergence of views from moderates, 140-41; oppose idea of constitution, 148; ticket in election for Third Congress, 148-50; factors in reluctance to accept independence, 172-77; conception of constitution, 235; concessions in constitution to moderates, 243-44; voting behavior on issue of governor's powers, 243n92; explanation of success in shaping constitution, 244-48 and nn, 249; emergence of moderate-conservative consensus, 248. *See also* Moderates; Radicals

Constitution: New Yorkers debate idea of, 146-48· idea of taken up by Provincial Congress, 150-55; Mechanics raise question of ratification procedure for, 155-59; bill of rights, 214, 229; factors in delay in drafting, 219, 223n31, 230-31; uneasiness at delay in drafting, 220, 223; preliminary draft of, 221; committee debates on election of governor and senators, 221; identification of drafts of, 224-29; attendance at constitutional committee meetings, 225; public conceptions of, 232-33; comparison of newspaper conceptions with com-

life itself

NOVELS OF PACO IGNACIO TAIBO II
IN ENGLISH TRANSLATION

AN EASY THING
THE SHADOW OF THE SHADOW
SOME CLOUDS
NO HAPPY ENDING
FOUR HANDS

PACO IGNACIO TAIBO II

TRANSLATED BY BETH HENSON

THE MYSTERIOUS PRESS

Published by Warner Books

A Time Warner Company

Mysterious Press books are published by Warner Books, Inc
1271 Avenue of the Americas, New York, NY 10020.

 A Time Warner Company

The Mysterious Press name and logo are registered trademarks of
Warner Books, Inc.

Printed in the United States of America
First printing: October 1994
10 9 8 7 6 5 4 3 2 1

Library of Congress Cataloging-in-Publication Data

Taibo, Paco Ignacio, 1949–
    [Vida misma. English]
    Life itself / Paco Ignacio Taibo II ; [translated by Beth Henson].
        p.   cm.
    ISBN 0-89296-518-5
    I. Henson, Beth.   II. Title.
PQ7298.3.A58V5313   1994
863 20   93-46514
                                                                CIP

This book is for: Marc Cooper, Los Angeles journalist; Carlos Monsiváis, writer in the Portales; Esther, owner of a bookstore in Zacatecas; Héctor Mercado, attorney; Juan Carlos Canales and Fritz Glockner, from Puebla . . . and for all the minor characters of this story.

Note: The mining town of Santa Ana in the north-central part of Mexico does not exist, and neither was there a red city government nor a chief of police who wrote detective novels. That story proudly belongs to the terrain of fiction. The majority of its characters exist only in the pages of this book, and even those whose names or distinguishing marks I have taken from life say things that can be attributed only to my imagination. I make this declaration so that nobody thinks, on the other hand, that the country we speak of is not real. It is all too real, and I live with it every day.

Note II: For the non-Mexican reader, the PRI is the official government party that, since the close of the 1920s, has ruled Mexico in a civil dictatorship rife with violence and electoral fraud; members of the PRI are called "priístas." "Cacique" is a term for the political boss of an agrarian zone; originally the word meant "Indian chief." Since the 1920s, Mexican labor unions have operated under heavy government control; in their opposition to these organizations, "red" independents refer to them as "yellow unions."

life itself

And, in the rain, with luck you will see
that in that which gave you life, you fear death.
    Francisco de Quevedo

So, the heroes belong to the books.
    André Malraux

1. Raining in Mexico City

"If it didn't rain in this city, I would have abandoned it a long time ago," thought José Daniel Fierro, immediately registering and filing the thought. There were ideas that were work, reusable thoughts that made up sentences that were later taken up by the keyboard. The rain-reflection was his, but could be made to serve as that of the old Villista who worked in a hardware store in the middle of the third chapter of the novel he was writing. "If it didn't rain . . ." he wrote at the head of the page, watching the drops of water drum on the double panes near his white table and imagining without hearing the splash, the small plop. He had to get into the sentence a bit of the sound of the wind that pushed the rain against the window and that made a literary image, shaking the solitary laurel of the ridge, making it dance. "If there were no laurel," he could go as well; him, not the old man in chapter three. Every day he wrote about leaving and yet he stayed. He lit a Mapleton from the butt of another. Ana, seated at his back in a white armchair, looked up from the book she was reading and stretched out her hand to steal his cigarette.

"You know what it costs us to smoke?"

José Daniel stroked his big black moustache, watching the rain.

"Forty-two thousand pesos a month, what do you think of that? Emphysema is the most expensive disease to acquire in the world," said Ana, without waiting for a response.

"Once I heard of a syphilis that cost a guy two hundred thousand pesos."

"That's nothing. A minor matter," said Ana. "Would you like some coffee?"

"A double cognac."

"Come to think of it, alcoholism is even more expensive," she said, walking to the kitchen. The ringing doorbell made her change direction.

José Daniel Fierro touched his elbow. The rain brought him a touch of arthritis.

The beginning of a chapter must be convincing. Only a mediocrity would begin "If it didn't rain in this city . . ." He tried to keep the conversation in the doorway from breaking his line of thought. He almost had it. He typed, destroying the foul whiteness of the paper: "A good detective only lives in cities where it rains like this."

"Daniel, you have visitors," said Ana, almost breathing the words down his neck.

José Daniel turned and contemplated the three arrivals: a disheveled young man wearing boots and a jacket and very thick glasses; a bearded forty year old with a fierce look; a man of thirty-five, dark, with green eyes, whom he had seen many times in photographs.

"Come in, sit down," he said to the three, who were trying not to get mud on the white carpet. They approached, offering their hands. The writer turned his chair to face them, offering them the two armchairs; Ana stayed by the door, vigilant in her role as hostess-proprietor.

"We are from the commission," said the youth with glasses.

"It's raining buckets," said José Daniel, just to say something.

"They called you, didn't they?" asked the man with green eyes.

"You are Benjamín Correa," said the writer, and the youth nodded.

"Macario, leader of Section Twenty-three, and Fritz, director of our radio station," he answered, indicating his two companions.

"No, nobody called me, but there's no problem," said the writer. "What can I do for you? The Festival of Culture in Santa Ana? I already said yes, I would go, and signed the manifesto. It came out today, didn't it?"

"We would like you to sign another little piece of paper," said the leader of the miners.

"A check?"

The three characters laughed.

"No, Compañero Fierro, worse than that," said Fritz Glockner.

José Daniel smiled.

"We want you to be the chief of police of Santa Ana," said the mayor of the radical town. The three laughed again.

José Daniel emitted a doubtful chuckle.

"You want me to write a detective novel about Santa Ana?"

"No. We want you to be chief of police of Santa Ana."

"What in the world!" exclaimed Ana.

"Are you serious?" asked the writer.

"Of course," said Benjamín Correa, lighting up a Delicado without filter. Macario, the miner, assented with a sly smile.

José Daniel Fierro observed them fixedly, trying not to meet his wife's eyes.

"Wait a minute, let me get this straight. You want me to go to Santa Ana and take over the police department? The municipal police?"

The three nodded.

"I think what you're doing is extremely important. Your experience is fundamental in the midst of so much bullshit. As far as it goes. Let's be clear. I sign manifestos, march in demonstrations, write about you where I can if I have something to say, give money, go to Santa Ana to take part in the Festival of Culture; these are things I know how to do, that I can do. Until now, once again . . . To be chief of police is madness. I'm fifty years old . . ."

"Fifty-two," said Ana.

"Fifty-one and my birthday's next month . . ." he answered quickly. "I've never shot a pistol in my life."

"Really?" asked Macario, who found it hard to believe there was anyone in Mexico who had never shot a gun.

"But in *Death in the Afternoon* it tells everything about the .45, the impact, the backfire, the precision, the cleaning . . ." said Fritz Glockner, smiling.

"I got that out of an Italian manual on firearms," the writer apologized. "And moreover, what does it matter? I have no real experience with the police. Only fiction, only literature."

"In *The Head of Pancho Villa* you tell the story of a bank fraud, that's how we knew what was happening in Santa Ana."

"Okay, that's how it happens. Son of a bitch! Do I have to tell you the difference between life and fiction?"

"There is no difference," said the red mayor. "It is only a question of miles. Who does know about the police in Mexico? No one. Only you, the writer. Who has eleven novels published? To be sure, I missed one, the one about the migrant workers . . ."

"*The Line*," said JD. "I have copies around here somewhere . . ."

"Probably what's happening is that we're not explaining it very well," said Fritz. "Look here: in one and a half years they have assassinated two municipal chiefs of police in Santa Ana. The state judicial cops have us by the balls, we need someone good, someone they can't kill without the whole country going up in arms, even the whole world. For example, a writer who just won the Grand Prize for Detective Literature at Grenoble, who gives interviews to the *New York Times*. A left-winger who comes out on Rocha's TV program when he publishes a book. Someone they can't kill, and who has a brain, ideas, an investigative mind, someone who serves the people and freaks out the PRI and the state government. Someone who can make his mark on Santa Ana."

"I understand all that, but you must take something into account. I am a coward. I'm afraid. Every day this country scares me more. If I go on writing and talking it's because I'm even more afraid to keep silent."

"Bravery is no problem, we can handle that part," said the mayor. "We have ten guys who would go into the lion's den, handcuffed, and kick the beasts in the crotch . . . We want someone like you. Just imagine: José Daniel Fierro, chief of police of Santa Ana."

"I can imagine."

"I'll divorce you, do you hear me?" said Ana.

"Whose idea was it?" asked the writer.

"We were looking around, asking people, and Carlos Monsiváis was the one who suggested you."

"Son of a bitch, what an idiot joke."

"Think it over, maestro. You're not only doing us a service in Santa Ana, think of the number of detective novels that you'll get out of it. Our crimes are really far out," said Fritz.

"They've got us by the balls," said the mayor again, and José Daniel realized how he had gotten the job. He put such intensity into his words, he grabbed you by the throat and didn't let go. "They surround us, cut our budget, the bosses hassle us, they cut off the municipal funds, provoke us, surround us with the blackest publicity campaign in the history of Mexico. The elections come up in eight months: if we win, they'll bring in the army, if we lose, they'll tear apart the whole Popular Organization we've created. We need all the help we can get. We need a chief of police . . . What do you say?"

"Does it rain a lot in Santa Ana?"

"Every day," said Macario.

"Never," said Fritz Glockner.

"Say the word," answered the mayor.

"I'll divorce you," said Ana. "I swear I'll divorce you."

2. Notes for the History of the Radical City Government of Santa Ana
José Daniel Fierro

I have discovered at least six ways of beginning the history of the radical city government of Santa Ana, after only one day in a car on the Pan American Highway heading north with three singular companions. One of them would be to tell the story of the struggle of Section 23 of the miners' union to become independent of the yellow union in the middle of the 1970s; another would be to follow the threads of what is called *La Voz del Pueblo*, the weekly paper begun by Correa seven years ago, which gave birth to the Popular Organization where the miners united with the students who had come back home after studying in Guadalajara, Monterrey, or Mexico City;

another would be the personal story of Benjamín Correa, the antlike persistence that led him to know Santa Ana as no one before him (and when I say *know* I would have to even include the biblical sense, for the jokes in the car ran to at least seven "little houses" with wives included, while he remains officially a bachelor); another would have to do with the work that two old communists did here, one a miner named Don Andrés, now retired, and a shopkeeper, who in the end was one of the ones who pushed the experience onto the electoral path. There is a fifth way of approaching the story of the government, which has to do with the people's law office organized by Mercado, which for three years gave legal support to farmers kicked off their land, market vendors, and schoolteachers fired for unjust cause. The sixth way is to follow the trajectory of the genesis of the popular government from the abuses of the PRI bosses to the popular revolt. Just for starters.

My traveling companions in the beat-up Renault suggest the story of the dead as a seventh option: pug-nosed Madera, shot from a hoist when the miners began to organize. The death by a stray bullet of Doña Jerónima, who sold chickens in the marketplace and who fell in the demonstration of the 20th of April. The death of Quintín Ramírez, forty-five-year-old peasant, strung up in the doorway of his hut by the landowners' thugs. The death of seven children in an epidemic at the end of the 1980s. The death of Daniel Contreras, run over by the drunken son of Simpson, manager of the Santa Ana Mining Company. The death of Lisandro Vera, a law student born in Santa Ana and the first chief of police of the popular government, shot as he left the jail. The death of Manuel, a Coca-Cola worker, knifed on the picket line by a scab paid by the company. The death of the schoolteacher Elpidio, the second chief of police of the radical government of Santa Ana, as he pursued a truck loaded with marijuana ten miles outside of town.

That would be another way of telling the story of this city, which until now I only knew by way of photos and which I always imagined as a big ranch full of red flags. Which I am now beginning to see up close: a mixture of cobblestone and asphalt streets, a municipal plaza, and an intricate complex of passions and powers, a bookstore(!), 11 movie theaters, 11 houses of prostitution (known and stable), 3 taxi stands, 117 crimes of passion weekly, 1,654 weddings a year, 231,000 inhabitants, 21 churches, 42 primary schools, 4 middle schools, 1 high school, 3 supermarkets, a movie director, 16 hotels, 28 percent of the country's production of tin, a circus every two months, a radical government that won the elections by 86,000 to 12,000 votes, and a mountain of dust and loose dirt that muddies the mountain air.

3. *Dear Ana/April 13*

Dear Ana/April 13

Well, so here I am, looking out over the town from my window in the Hotel Florida (I pushed a bureau over to the window and set up my office; the typewriter is up very high, I hope I don't hurt my back since the chair is very low). I hope you are not in a rush to accuse me of abandonment, but if I were to sit down and talk it over with you, I would never leave home. Send me a package by Frontier Bus Lines, a bunch of black ribbons for the Olivetti portable, the cotton ones they sell at the shop on the corner, as well as the original, which is in a red briefcase with a lock, and a pile of novels by J. P. Machette that I left on my side of the bed, there's maybe seven of them, you'll find them immediately. And if it's not too much trouble, send me the bottle of gringo aspirins, the ones with the sealed cap, and the blue turtleneck sweater.

Don't ask me what I'm doing in Santa Ana, I still don't know, and if I tried to explain it to you now it would be pure rhetoric. Forgive me, one more time in so many years.

Kisses. JD

4. Hotel Florida

It was dawn and the light from the east filtered slowly down the main street of Santa Ana, illuminating the white houses at three hundred yards and licking the nearest walls.

From his room on the fourth floor of the Hotel Florida José Daniel Fierro thought that he would never be able to reveal the quality of that light; that he could be chief of police of Santa Ana, because life is sufficiently strange and creates roads, waterfalls, and bends in the roads, but that he would never be able to tell anyone just how that soft light came advancing toward him, entering into his room.

Because chiefs of police improvise, but the narrators of dawn are the product of years of words.

His eyes were irritated by sleeplessness, but the window

drew him like brown and sticky flypaper, the kind that no longer exists, which he remembered from childhood vacations in Veracruz.

From the window of his hotel room he could see ten or twelve streets, even the main avenue, which curved away toward the north and hid itself behind a four-story building with a movie theater on the first floor. A solitary street, with its lights still on, useless in the precipitant approach of dawn.

José Daniel searched in his travel bag for a flask and wet his lips with warm cognac. The whole town was covered with graffiti: sidewalks, fences, light poles, columns, even some low rooftops, house fronts, walls, trees. All painted over many times and by many hands, in many styles; differing hands piling up slogans and signs, advice and insult, calls to conscience, logos of the Popular Organization, calls to the future, memories of the past, cryptic half-written warnings whose final rushing letters fell to the ground.

The walls told the story of the last two years in Santa Ana, inviting one to think of the heat of a bonfire, of malevolence, of verbal warfare. Who said that revolutions advance on a highway of words?

José Daniel Fierro winked an eye at the principal street of Santa Ana and promised himself to buy a notebook and write down what the walls were saying, even to take a few photos.

"Chief of Police, sir, I want you to meet the assistant chief of police," said the voice of Benjamín Correa at his back.

José Daniel turned around.

"Barrientos, alias—more than alias, official name—Blind Man."

A short man of square shoulders and body, with eyeglasses of fifteen diopters on each side, moustache and eyebrows that met in the middle, smiled at him, almost thrusting his teeth out of his mouth.

"Pleased to meet you."

"The pleasure is mine, sir," said the short man, fluttering his eyes behind the heavy lenses. "I have already read six of your novels. The one I liked best is the one about Pancho Villa."

"Thanks a lot, man," said José Daniel, ceremoniously offering his hand.

"They call him Blind Man because he can shoot the balls off a fly with a .45 at forty yards. Not because he's nearsighted," declared the mayor.

"That's good to know."

"The official inauguration will be tomorrow morning, but Blind Man tells me that while we were gone there was an assassination, so I thought . . ."

José Daniel looked at the dawn from the corner of his eye, as if to memorize it, gave another pull on his flask of cognac and smiled timidly.

"Let's go."

She was a campesina of thirty, with her hands firmly clasped, her eyes irritated by tears that were no longer there, wearing a blue blouse printed with flower garlands.

"They tell me you killed your husband, señora, why did you do that?"

The woman looked at her hands, which were dried up by years of work.

"With a machete? You gave him six blows with a machete while he was sleeping? How did this happen, señora?"

She was seated on a cot in the cell, barely lit by the sixty-watt bulb that hung from a wire.

"Her name is Margarita," said Blind Man.

"Let's see, Doña Margarita, why did you kill him? or are you going to say that you didn't kill him? Because we found you with the machete in your hand, next to the dead man, just you and him in the room, and him in bed . . . Tell me why."

The woman lifted her head, looked at José Daniel for a moment, and then looked at the little window where the light was beginning to come in.

"Who is this gentleman?" she asked Blind Man without looking at him.

"He is the chief of police, señora."

"Did we appoint him ourselves?"

"He was appointed by Benjamín. He's very knowledgeable."

"Do they feed us in here?"

"Three times a day, señora, not like before."

"And why does he want to know?"

"To be sure it was you, so we don't make a mistake, and so justice is done," said José Daniel.

"Justice has been done," said the woman and looked at him from the corner of her eye.

"What justice? To kill a man is justice?"

The woman did not answer.

Blind Man took José Daniel by the arm and led him to the door of the cell. They walked out toward the street.

"You don't lock the cell?"

"They lock the door to the passage that leads to the cells, Mateo will lock it now. We have no prisoners today, they left for the weekend."

"Take me to the crime site, Barrientos."

"Sir, call me Blind Man. If you don't I'll feel weird."

"We are all blind, that's what the lady would say."

"That's what she said, but the blows were well placed."

"Why?"

"Only she and God know," said Blind Man.

"According to my enormous knowledge of criminal themes, this is known by herself, God, and the neighbors . . . page one hundred sixty-three of *Dead without Memory*."

"I didn't read that one," said Blind Man.

"You didn't miss much," said José Daniel, lighting a Mapleton and offering one to his companion, who tore off the filter before lighting it. "Do we have a patrol car?"

"Two motorcycles, two bicycles, and a Volkswagen with a grille between the seats, but it's out patrolling the town. You'll see . . . We'll walk, it's toward the La Gracia neighborhood."

José Daniel let himself be guided by the rapid pace of Blind Man, closing his eyes even more against the sunlight. They walked down alleyways and left the asphalt to start on dirt roads and cobblestones; they soon began to run into milkmen, miners in khaki overalls, women carrying fruit and vegetables to market. It was cold.

"You're going to like it here," said Blind Man. "Something happens all the time."

José Daniel agreed.

5. Notes for the History of the Radical City Government of Santa Ana
José Daniel Fierro

◣▬▬◢◣▬▬◢◣▬▬◢◣▬▬◢◣▬▬◢◣▬▬◢◣▬▬◢◣▬▬◢◣▬▬◢

Benjamín Correa is thirty-two years old, a medical doctor,
graduate of the National University of Mexico (UNAM),
born in Santa Ana. This is a recording that I made of him
while we came here. To be overly precise, it was on the long
straightaway between San Luis and Matehuala, where you talk
for a long time, pouring your heart out, because the highway
without trees or lights makes you cough up everything you've
got inside. The punctuation is mine.

Correa: . . . forgive me, writer. You could be moved by
other things: by prestige, a cold conscience, responsibility,
hatred, whatever; me, by guilt. Santa Ana and I are married

by fucking guilt. Better yet, by guilts: better to speak of many guilts. In 1976 I went to Mexico City to begin my courses, and they said to me, "Stay for the demonstration, it's going to be good," and I took to the road and left. I already knew enough medicine to cure the wounded, and on the next day there were thirty people wounded by gunfire, by sticks, by dog bites, by machete, and the asshole was in his classroom studying X rays of the chests of old Swiss gentlemen, because this is what the professor had to show, to see if they had tuberculosis in 1950 and how. And here they died alone. My cousin Evelia with two bullets in her belly . . . There's no mystery. Just guilt. And that's just one, there are many more. I have a list, this long!, of all the times I was quiet, of all the times I ran, of all the times I gave in . . . Now I sleep well, and if they kill me, I'll sleep even better. If everyone did what they had to, we'd be better off. That's the key to the game of the Popular Organization. Ask the people to each do what they have to do, not what would be better, not what would be more convenient, nor more beneficial, nor more revolutionary. Just simply what they have to do.

JDF: It sounds good. It's the best political theory I've heard in the last few years.

Benjamín Correa: It sounds like shit. If we lose, they'll send the town back to the nineteenth century.

JDF: The nineteenth century was a son of a bitch, Juarista liberalism and all that.

Benjamín Correa: To the nineteenth century of Santa Anna.

Fritz: You're very apocalyptic, one would have to . . .

Macario: They're going to cut off our balls.

Benjamín Correa: I hope they leave me something, because we're all going to be just delighted with our dicks made into mincemeat.

Macario: Don't scare the chief of police, assholes . . .
Do you like frijoles charros? Here in Santa Ana they're
bitching.

JDF: A while ago . . .

Benjamín Correa: Pure guilt, do you understand?

6. The Baseball Cap

"That shirt fits you perfectly, chief," said Blind Man.

The city provided the police uniform: brown shirt and trousers, a sheep-lined jacket for cold, Stetson hat or baseball cap. José Daniel chose the baseball cap with the inscription SANTA ANA WILL WIN above the visor. A little brunette rummaged a long time to find pants in his size in the cooperative store; "long and with a bit of belly" according to Blind Man.

They left the store, full of people at eight in the morning. José Daniel smiled, he felt "uniformed" and moreover had found two of his novels with yesteryear's prices in the shop.

"Do I get a sheriff's badge?" he asked his second-in-command.

"The truth is, I never asked. They do give ID."

"Without a badge, I feel half out of uniform," said José Daniel, stopping at a toy stand. He picked through the buttons: there were Snoopys, ALL YOU NEED IS LOVE, Che Guevara, the Sandinista Front, Rafael and Rocío Durcal. He chose one that showed Spiderman in a posture of challenge.

"Do you want one?"

"I don't think so," said Blind Man.

José Daniel pinned it on his new shirt.

"Okay now. One madness more or less . . . Hell, I feel thirty years old."

"Me too."

"How old are you?"

"Shit, I'm twenty-eight."

They walked around the downtown area. Low buildings that opened to shared central patios, grocery shops. Everything painted. Everything, not one inch of free space. Beer advertisements everywhere. Blind Man led him to an enormous public building. José Daniel began to get his bearings: City Hall here, the hotel, the jail . . .

He climbed a high stairway with a half-finished mural that showed the devil, Reagan, and two men in sombreros playing cards.

"Who are they?"

"The old boss and his brother, the Barrios. The PRI bosses in Santa Ana. You had to remind me of their faces. Those two screw us over more than Reagan and the devil put together."

The stairs led to a balustrade around a central patio with a colonial fountain. The offices, with their doors of white wood in doorways carved of quarrystone, bore enormous letters: COORDINATOR OF CULTURE, MEDICAL DISPENSARY, RADIO SANTA ANA, CHIEF OF POLICE.

"This whole side of the building is ours. This and the jail

are ours. The mayor and the sombrero cooperative occupy the left wing."

In the doorway of Radio Santa Ana, Fritz was arguing with a delegation of middle school students who were demanding that he let them broadcast a soap opera about *Chucho the Broken*, directed by the professor of dramatic arts. Fritz waved and pointed to José Daniel's new cap.

Blind Man opened the door of the police office, removing an enormous iron padlock.

"Half of the personnel are here, you'll see them soon. The others are in the offices down the side. This office is just for you."

It was a room worthy of Philip Marlowe. A wooden desk made in the 1950s, venetian blinds that let in slits of light, a coat rack for hanging nonexistent trench coats and hats, two gray metal file cabinets with signs of having been forced with a crowbar, a chair on wheels, and a reclining chair with slats on the back. A new coffee maker, strangely out of place.

Blind Man met José Daniel's eyes.

"The coffee maker belongs to Elpidio. Okay, belongs to his widow. That was the only thing he brought. Nothing else."

José Daniel walked slowly to his chair, let himself fall, and put his feet on the desk. He pushed back the visor of his cap and half closed his eyes to dream other dreams.

"Elpidio's pistol is in the drawer. Since you don't know shit about it, anything will do, although I recommend a shotgun, because it shoots wholesale and hits anything at ten yards."

"How serious are things around here?" asked José Daniel, stretching to turn on the coffee maker, "because I feel like I'm in the movies, and in the movies . . . No, wait, in a novel, and as Malraux said, heroes are from literature."

"What do you mean, serious?" asked Blind Man, letting

himself fall on a three-legged stool in front of the desk. "Serious as in do people kill? Yes, they kill, and to tell you the truth, I don't like it. I don't like it when they kill in cold blood. I don't like it when they kill and then celebrate. I don't like it when they let fear loose in the streets. This was the land of the bosses, sir, a company town; here they beat you up for breathing, and even more for smiling. There's a lot of bastards still running around loose . . . A lot of fucking bastards running around loose. And they don't like what we're doing."

"And what are we doing?" said José Daniel, staring at the assistant chief of his yet-unseen police force of his still half-guessed-at city.

"Popular power, my good man. What kind of a fucking question is that, excuse me? Do you think you could be chief of police of a PRI town?"

"Of no town, more likely . . . What did you do before, Blind Man? Before you were a cop?"

"Secretary of the Interior of the taxi drivers' union."

"Why did you change jobs?"

"There are things that have to be done. Hasn't that ever happened to you?"

"I don't really know what happened to me. Do you know what it's like to be fifty years old?"

"Not yet, but I'm getting there . . . Although I'm not rushing."

"It's like knowing that everything's over, bullshit like that . . . I have gray in my moustache, you know that?"

"Blind Man, run, Blind Man, get a move on!" cried a voice that materialized into a hairy and charmless personage who ran into the office red-faced.

"Say hello to the chief, Greñas."

"Chief," said Greñas, saluting. "I report an emergency.

They say that the girls are calling for help from the bathroom of El Refugio. A kidnapping, that is. I have the car."

"Did you see them?"

"I was told."

"Let's go, said another blind man," said José Daniel, getting up and feeling the cramp in his knee.

The patrol car was a dented Volkswagen, scarred with rust, painted red and black in two horizontal stripes. Greñas took the wheel, Blind Man gave José Daniel the back seat to shrink into.

"My legs don't fit."

"We should have taken the bike."

"Should I turn on the siren?" asked Greñas.

"No way."

Raising dust, the car ran a dozen blocks and stopped by some department stores on the main street. The trio entered the store, as if pushed by a childish hand to some promising place. They crossed the women's clothing department and were advancing through fabrics when they were stopped.

"Where are you going, Blind Man?" asked a man in a suit, standing in their way and blocking the back part of the counters.

"Are you speaking to the assistant police chief of Santa Ana?" asked José Daniel in full drag, changing from Bogart into Clint Eastwood and pointing a finger at the suited man's belly. "You are obstructing a police inquiry."

"My ass," said the man, slapping off the writer's accusatory finger.

"We know you have some girls shut up in the bathrooms," said Blind Man with his .45 in hand.

"In the women's john. They shut themselves in."

Fifty shoppers were closing in.

Greñas advanced toward the passage behind the counters. They passed the perfume section and the electrical appliances. Far off they saw people running. José Daniel followed the hurried steps of his aides.

Two men were standing by the women's john. The door was surrounded by empty boxes, cardboard tubes that had served as towel holders, and great pieces of granulated polyethylene used to pack stoves and refrigerators; they gave the end of the passage the air of the backstage of a theater.

"Look here, the big honcho of the CTM*, neither more nor less," said Blind Man, pointing to a fat man in a blue shirt standing in front of the door.

"Are you in line for the women's bathroom, sir?" asked José Daniel, doing a Lew Archer with a light touch of Woody Allen.

Blind Man, more expeditious, motioned for them to move away with the barrel of his revolver.

"Are they here?" cried Greñas.

"Let us out . . . We're not going to sign," came a chorus from behind the door.

Greñas tried the knob. Locked.

"Get back," he yelled, and knocked down the flimsy door with a roundhouse kick.

The onlookers, including the owner of the department store, were milling about in the aisles. José Daniel lit his last Mapleton and threw the empty package on the floor.

Four women came through the door, tripping over themselves and pushing the bystanders.

"They locked us up to make us sign with the CTM," said one to Blind Man. "They hit me."

*Federation of Mexican Workers, a yellow union.

"They said we would stay here without food until we signed," said a young cross-eyed woman, smiling. The bystanders returned her smile.

"Who locked you up, ladies?" asked José Daniel.

"Domínguez, the owner."

"Him, Domínguez, and the yellow leader of the CTM, Martín Guerra, that revolting fathead."

"None of that, now," threatened the fathead.

"To jail with the two of them, Blind Man," said José Daniel. "Accused of kidnapping. We'll indict them right now."

The bystanders raised a timid applause.

Blind Man moved the barrel of his gun alternately between the owner and the union honcho. In a low voice he asked the new police chief, "Are you sure?"

"Lock them up and we'll see," replied José Daniel Fierro, who then, very nicely, in full Robert Mitchum, offered his arm to the young cross-eyed woman.

7. *Dear Ana/April 14*

Dear Ana/April 14

For now, more vaudeville than tragedy, although there's
something in the air that tugs at the corners of the eyes and
sometimes you walk with a wrinkled brow. A little while ago
I took official possession of the role of chief of police of Santa
Ana. Attended by friends from the Popular Organization,
bystanders, and journalists from Mexico City, Monterrey,
and Torreón. Who runs the public relations department of the
radical town? They do a wonderful job. The idea that Benjamín
and the town leaders drill into me, that the town must call on
all possible help, they keep very firmly in mind.

Do I take myself as a joke or do I take myself seriously?
I'm laughing at myself a little bit, but Benjamín's speech at

my inauguration made my hands sweat. For a few minutes I felt part of a project that fights for survival in a country defeated by so much cynicism, shamelessness, official lies, and barbarity running around loose. That country we know in Mexico City that appears to have no end in sight, that tells us day after day that we're among the defeated, that every dream is impossible except for the nightmare that is installed here among us.

So I opt for the middle road. I regard myself as a joke, but I take very seriously the experiment of the radical city government of Santa Ana.

And by the way, it's true, there's material here for a dozen novels, although I will never be able to write them.

The local radio station is in the office next to me. You would love it. They are the most extraterrestrial people I have met in Santa Ana. Fritz, the coordinator of production, is mounting speakers on the telephone poles. He produces agricultural programs, epic radio novels, radical commercials, at the same time avoiding a system of interference put out from a neighboring peak by the state government to prevent diffusion of the signal. Juan Carlos Canales, incredibly tall and thin, who acts as announcer, master of ceremonies, and funder of the project, told me two things he's working on this week. One, a live program on the prostitutes of Santa Ana (in which they denounce the owners of the brothels and organize), and a radio novel based on the Bible with a Priísta as Lucifer.

My joints ache. I suppose because the town is so dry. Now it's beginning to get cold, send me the aspirins.

I love you from afar. JDF

8. Rum during Office Hours

"Sit down, Chief of Police."

"I sit, Mayor."

"Would you like a rum?"

"I don't drink during working hours."

"I beg your pardon?"

"No, man, I'm putting you on. It's just that all of a sudden I'm getting to say things I've never had the chance to say before. This town is sending my head to a piece of Hollywood that I had tucked away in a corner of my brain."

"It sounded like bullshit to me, because except for the time when I'm sleeping, when I can't drink, every other hour in Santa Ana is a working hour; and without any liquor at all we'd be worse off than we are now."

"I'm seeing a rum on table two, Mayor."

Benjamín Correa took the rum from God knows where under his desk, in a paper cup but with ice and all, and put it in front of José Daniel Fierro. Behind his back was the red and black flag with the logo of the Popular Organization, but missing were the photos of radicals—there was just one displayed. José Daniel made an effort. That photo in particular he had never seen before, but remembered others of the same man from a chain of prisoners: Librado Rivera.

"You have an anarchist on your wall?"

"I keep him because when I despair I read his biography. No one understood better than he did that the revolution in Mexico will be a case of stubbornness."

José Daniel Fierro sipped his rum, letting it heat up his throat. If he continued his Hollywood repertoire, he could choose between Bogart and Peter Lorre: cynical or apparently stupid. He chose Fred Astaire. He stood up and danced a few steps of tap, then smiled.

"In the 1950s I attended an academy of dance. We danced to a piece by Tommy Dorsey till we were exhausted, it must have been the only record they had. What were you doing then?"

"I was a child in the 1950s, Chief Fierro . . . Wasn't Chief Fierro one of the mice in the Mickey Mouse comic books?"

"Damned if I know . . . and so? How'm I doing?"

"Fifty percent."

"I'm all ears."

"Here everything is politics, and arresting the owner of one of the big department stores and the head honcho of the CTM is political. And you have to be very careful with this, because if we push them too hard, they will bring in the army and the experiment will be over. That is the fifty percent bad; before getting into things like that, you have to talk it over with us. This is what I've learned in the last two years."

"And the fifty percent good?"

"That with pressure, we'll force them to let the girls remain in the democratic union instead of making them go with the yellows."

"Will there be a trial?"

"How can there not be, if all the judges are with them?"

"I take note, Brother Mayor," said José Daniel Fierro, slapping his baseball cap against his thighs and standing up.

"Where did you get the Spiderman button?"

"I bought it here. Why?"

"Get me one, would you?"

9. Dispatches Cast on the Wind

He guided his reading with one finger. The breeze that crossed between the two windows moved the pages and he had to hold them with his left hand. Blind Man walked from one side of the room to the other, stopping to watch him every three steps, to be sure he wasn't losing pages, that no paragraphs jumped out, and no letters were eaten.

"Two big ones, three small ones," said José Daniel with his finger on the final comma of the final sentence of the last dispatch.

"Two big ones, three little ones," repeated Blind Man and re-counted with his fingers, so that not a detail was lost between hand and memory.

"That is what we have pending."

"Plus what happens every day," remembered Blind Man.

José Daniel agreed. Not only the breeze entered the windows, but also a number of songs of the Spanish Civil War. He had heard nearly all of them in the home of his sister who was married to the son of exiles. He himself was a foreigner. In only two days he was an absolute and total stranger. It was not bad. Not bad at all. Not at all bad.

"So, when do I get my pistol?"

"I already thought about it, and it seems to me we should give you Lacho Vázquez's shotgun; with that you could shoot a plow at five yards. Breech loading, six shots, cheap ammunition. The city can afford it and you won't kill anyone by accident."

"Blind Man, you don't have much confidence in me."

"You're a champ at reading dispatches, Señor Chief of Police. You read them three times faster than me."

"Which should we start with?"

"Up to you . . . Are we speaking in tú or usted?"

"As the wind blows."

"Then why don't we start with one of the small ones. The shooting at the tavern on Calle Cuatro a week ago."

"I need a chalkboard," said José Daniel.

"What are you going to give classes in?"

"In the detective novel, my esteemed assistant, and I want that agent who signs himself Luix Lómax."

"Popochas."

"Yes, indeed."

"I'll be right back," said Blind Man, and left to do his assignments. José Daniel lit another cigarette and took his flask from his back pocket. He had gone from Mapletons to Delicados with filter, and from Spanish brandy to cane alcohol. Wasn't this an obvious sign of proletarianization? That morning he had slipped out of bed at the Hotel Florida with the firm intention of comparing Santa Ana with other cities. He had proposed to demonstrate that Santa Ana was better than Reims and Houston, than Seville and Maracaibo. He had only to find the right arguments. Write them, put them down on paper and it would be true. However, the blank paper had won the battle. Son of a whore, cane alcohol was worse than the combustible oxygen gas the taxis used in Madrid. The blank paper won the battle. Right now he had to make history instead of writing it. What history? This, two guys wounded in a tavern? Santa Ana was better than Rome because here the couples walked hand in hand through the square full of shame and made love an act of innocence. On a piece of paper he wrote a name, "Barrio." Underneath he wrote, "Seville, birds, bread." He poured out another shot of alcohol. He could lay aside the toothbrush forgotten in Mexico City. The local cane alcohol did the job very well.

"Ready, chief," said Blind Man, entering the office with a borrowed chalkboard.

"And Popochas?"

"On his way; I had him called over the radio. Since the whole town is full of loudspeakers, we'll have him here in no time."

"Let's see, Blind Man, let's reconstruct," said José Daniel professorially. "We have a tavern with seven people, right? Let's sit them down."

"Where?" asked Blind Man.

"On the chalkboard. Then we're going to ask ourselves who they are. Then we're going to find out why five of them don't want to say who shot at the two who were wounded, then we're going to ask ourselves why the two wounded don't want to say who shot them, then we're going to ask ourselves whose gun was on the floor, what was the trajectory of the bullets . . . We're going to ask ourselves what they were eating, who they were, what the fuck they wanted from life, and how they were dressed."

"All that on a chalkboard?"

"That's what it's good for, to erase when it's full and to start over again. What, you never do paraffin tests here?"

"Why should we when they would all come out positive?"

"Improve your sense of humor, Assistant Barrientos."

"You'll see . . . As Canales—a poet as well as an announcer—says, everything is contagious, even love."

10. *Notes for the History of the Radical City Government of Santa Ana*
José Daniel Fierro

There are two dates that are regularly cited in conversations with the Popular Organization, the popular forces of Santa Ana: the demonstration of April 20 and the meeting of December 24. Curiously, I do not recall the date of the electoral victory (I believe it fell in August) among the material gleaned from conversations turning around in my head. It would appear, and here one is once again interpreting instead of narrating, as if the victory was the result of the Demonstration—with a capital D, although I must have been told of three others that have their own particular names and glory. The demonstration when Lacho climbed up City Hall by the portals like an African ape or the demonstration with gunfire in 1973 or the demonstration that lasted two days. But the Demonstration was that of April 20, and, in the parlance of radical Santa Ana, December 24 has nothing to do with Santa Claus or the birth of Christ Jesus but instead has to do with the Meeting.

I tell you because collective memory is perhaps the best political evaluator, the best revealer of realities, the best index of importance. I tell you what they tell me. I don't even know which came first, the meeting of December 24 or the demonstration of April 20. I would guess that logically the meeting preceded the demonstration by a few months and that by then the Popular Organization already existed.

The characters are alike and different. The Meeting, in the talk of the PO and the popular militants, made equal stars of Benjamín, the lawyer Mercado, old Güicho, and the dead ex-chief of police and teachers' leader, Elpidio. It also has its celebrated phrase, "If they don't stop talking bullshit, I'll shoot myself to show an example," uttered by Don Güicho. And its amulets: Don Güicho's pistol, the bloody shirt of Quintín Ramírez, on which all or nothing is sworn, and the Panama hat my assistant Barrientos wore that day that everyone remembers (I must remember to ask him what the hell happened to that hat).

The Demonstration is more properly common property. Everyone has his six or seven personal favorites: Benjamín Correa, of course, Elpidio, who was at his side, the narrator himself, a cousin of his who was passing through, Lacho, and Doña Caro and Doña Jerónima, now dead. It has its slogan: "Let them kill us all, dead we are real motherfuckers," coined by Benjamín to stop people from running away when the shooting started. And it has its own place, engraved forever in memory by blood and stone: the corner of the square, entering from Benito Juárez, where the flower cart and the taco stand stood.

Now a few years have passed, a very few years, and there is a communal middle school, full of teenagers in green uniforms, whom I see every day at dawn walking down the highway into town, and the school is named April 20. The kids, happy kids, smile like an interminable toothpaste ad and know why the school is named that way. Some of them marched in the demonstration, some of them picked up the wounded. They have their own version of what happened. They have their own hierarchy of memories. The smallest speak of the machine gun at the palace, with two feet, no three, supported on the balustrade. The big ones speak of the blood that flowed down Benjamín's white shirtfront, and how everyone believed he was dead, and that no, it turned out the blood was not his, it belonged to other people.

Yesterday I asked Benjamín whose blood it was. And he instantly replied, "Everyone's."

When I write these notes, I have to keep that bloody shirt in mind, so I'm not fooled by the peaceful cobblestone streets, the occasional car that passes in front of the Hotel Florida, and the treacherous light, the marvelous dawn in Santa Ana.

11. Dear Ana/April 15

Dear Ana/April 15
Domestic tales:

I have gone to Delicados with filter. First, I smoked Mapletons because you stole them from me, and I liked the way the house smelled. It turns out I don't like them so much now that no one is smoking at my side. Second, they are hard to come by in Santa Ana. Third, everyone I offer them to looks at me strangely. Populism has its eccentricities.

I have a voracious appetite. I eat whatever they give me in emormous quantities.

I have a baseball cap (I'm enclosing a photo you can send to my nephew Marcial). You see me not only with the cap on but in full small-town sheriff drag. Without comment. The local correspondent of *unomásuno* took it, so I suppose it will come out in the paper. Did anyone call you with the news? Tell the editors not to worry, the novel will be ready by the middle of May, as we had agreed.

I'm cold and sleepy. I don't want to read this note, I'll find out I'm illiterate and infantile. I'm happy.

Yes I love you: JD

12. There's Nothing like a Lawyer

"Whoever is free from madness, let him cast the first stone," said José Daniel Fierro to himself while he thought how ridiculous it was to sleep switching his pajama tops and bottoms on alternate days. Later he advanced to further reflections and made a list of his own idiosyncracies while he rubbed his eyes furiously, trying to open them to the light:

a) Making orange juice by hand, even when he had an electric juicer in the house. Idiocy that he defended against wind and tide, to the extent of cutting the cord of the electric juicer when Ana suggested repairing it, since he concealed his madness by saying it was broken.

b) Opening his sandwiches to eat the two halves separately, for which all sandwich makers have hated him for the past forty-five years of his life, seeing him as a destroyer of the art of the sandwich, a violator of tradition, and a dirty son of a bitch who should roast in hell.

c) Urinating sitting down. A feminine habit, dangerous in case of discovery, which originated a thousand years ago with the pleasure of reading shut up in the bathroom, isolated, sequestered behind a locked door and secure from disturbances from the outside.

d) Picking the wax from his ears with a match and then setting it on fire, although it almost never caught, but limited itself to an acrid and foolish smell.

He stopped his list, which could go on indefinitely, and dressed only in a pajama top walked to the window of his room, ready as ever to let Santa Ana enter his eyes before he accepted it in his mind. The city was there.

The knock on the door did not surprise him. He was waiting. Santa Ana was like that. First it entered the eyes, tamely, then it knocked at the door. He tried to put on his pajama bottoms while preparing to say, "Come in," and almost made it. His "Come in" was uttered while he caught his right foot and fell, trying to hold himself up on the gilded metal post at the foot of the bed. He did not succeed. The attorney Héctor Mercado found the sheriff of Santa Ana rubbing his knee with his balls in the air.

"Are you hurt?"

"Shit in a box," he said, employing a curse he had learned twenty years ago in Salamanca, when he had lived there on scholarship studying the literature of Spain's Golden Age.

Mercado turned his head away to laugh.

"Laugh all you like, there's nothing sillier than someone who falls to fucking pieces at seven in the morning."

Mercado walked to the bed and sat on it, after leaving his briefcase, which was always with him, by the washstand. He was younger than JD, some ten years younger; he would be approaching or just past forty years old, with juvenile whiskers and dusty hair, a bit stiff, a characteristic common to Santa Ana, upon which JD had speculated and noted on a piece of paper, "the water? loose dirt all over the city?" José Daniel could not avoid raising his hand to his own hair as he pulled the string on his pajamas to pull them up. His hair was rough. He would spend half his salary on lemon shampoo, or apple. The Señor Clairol he carried inside attacked him again.

"And what brings you here, Mercado?"

"The mayor sent me to have a brief word with you about the elephant traps of legality to cover your ass a bit."

"Are there many?"

"No, for me it's easy. I will explain to you the jurisdiction in which you should remain. If you want to go further, consult us and we will all decide together if we all go, if you go alone, or if you stay quiet. It is more or less simple. We're all here to serve the people, that's rule number one. How to serve the people, that's open to interpretation. The ones who're out to fuck the people over interpret it the opposite way. The law is written on paper. You follow it to serve the people, you abandon it to go on serving. The only real law is moral . . . Things like that."

"It sounds like a complicated business to me."

"Complicated it is. Get dressed and we'll have a breakfast for big people and I'll tell you about it."

JD looked in the mirror. What he saw did not bother him too much. He could live inside the guy he saw in the mirror. He had gray hairs in his moustache. They were his.

Half an hour later, with plates of eggs before them, Mercado said: "The municipal police are preventative, their work is limited to making arrests in flagrante or by denunciation. In other words, it is the first recourse of law. Simpler cases go to the justice of the peace, who can in turn pass judgment on minor or administrative infractions. All the bigger cases go to the state, where the Public Ministry orders investigations, and remands them to the state judiciary and not the local municipal police. They take charge of common crimes, robbery, murder, rape. Their prisoners go to the state penitentiary. In cases of drug trafficking, treason to the country, and contraband, the Federal Public Ministry takes charge and the feds intervene, under charge of the attorney general of the republic. The municipal police can testify in serious cases and help in investigations, that is to say, they can lend a hand."

"And where does all this leave us?"

Mercado took his time in chewing an enormous mouthful of eggs and tortilla.

"It leaves us in the middle . . . We have no federal agents here, and when we do they're up to no good. We have a judicial detachment, led by Durán Rocha, a very well connected gangster. You'll see for yourself. We have an agent of the state Public Ministry, who in turn has a pair of agents under him whom you'll meet soon. What that means for now is that all major investigations will be impeded and that when you detain a murderer in flagrante, the state will let him go after a rigged trial in the capital, and so on."

"And so what do I do?"

"The best you can, my friend. I remind you of the cardinal rule: when it's a big deal, consult us and we'll see how to make it smaller."

JD gazed at the lawyer with dirty hair. Nothing was clear.

13. Notes for the History of the Radical City
Government of Santa Ana
José Daniel Fierro

~~~~~~

Santa Ana has a hit parade of sons of bitches. They have certain similarities to the national hit parade. If you study them, you find small oscillations, minor variations like raising the son-in-law to number seven instead of leaving him at the fifteen that he averages. Nevertheless, in the judgment of Benjamín Correa, the hit parade is not exact. I always thought the advantage and disadvantage of the class struggle (as in wrestling) is knowing the enemy, the conversion of symbols into names, the personification of constant capital and the agricultural bourgeoisie as Jack and Jill. Correa maintains that no, Santa Ana has its own lights and shadows, its own endowment of classist zebras, full of white or black lines as you wish to see them. That is his theory and he got it somewhere, and I don't doubt his virtue as an observer. However, in view of the fact that his information stays at the enigmatic level of maintaining doubts, I keep in mind the results of the survey I've made in the last few days:

Indisputable number one in the hit parade: Melchor Barrio, boss of the PRI, brother of the phantasmal agrarian cacique, toothless and with bad breath; in delincuential material (maybe it's not said like that but the word enchants me), violator of minors of age.

Number two and hard on the heels of the one before and not only figuratively, Sabás, just like that, Don Sabás if you're being polite. Homeowner, brother-in-law of the former, and yet they don't get along and have bad blood between them. They say that Melchor killed a son of Sabás's years ago in a fight over land. Sabás's crimes are not clear, he appears to be mixed up in everything and nothing. He is whispered to be involved in marijuana traffic with the ranches north of Santa Ana. Very friendly with the chief of the judicial police, one Durán Rocha, number four on the list despite only six months in town.

Number three, all agree, and numbers one and two on certain anonymous lists, Manuel Reyna, Blackie. A hired gun who runs the shock troops of the PRI in Santa Ana. Responds directly to the will of the state capital, doesn't treat with the local powers. Everyone says it was he who fired on the April 20 demonstration with a machine gun from the church tower. Someone told me that before being a gunman he sold agricultural equipment. They call him Blackie because he's an albino. Good to know that. Better to notice him from afar. Someone told me that he doesn't sleep in Santa Ana, that he keeps his cot in González Ortega, a small town that is the head of the neighboring municipality, about nineteen miles northeast of Santa Ana.

A tie for number five between the bosses of the CTM and the CROC,* half a dozen of one and half a dozen of the other. They even look alike. The difference might be that Martín Guerra, as well as being a union honcho (now all he's got is a pair of unions maintained by force by the bosses), is the owner of three butcher shops that the PO has been boycotting in response to a call put out by Radio Santa Ana, which has made him purple with rage.

Place number seven is collective, divided between the foremen of the mine and the gringo director, who is not out and about town these days because he is having his balls operated on in Houston, as I've been told by my agent Lómax, who is involved with his maid.

In eighth place, a lawyer, mentioned little but always by those who are well informed, Querejeta, from Mexico City, who wears dark glasses and sleeps in the hotel across the street from mine, as much a stranger here as me, a bird of misfortune who carries disgrace in his luggage.

The list goes on to contain some two hundred and seven more sons of bitches.

---

*Revolutionary Confederation of Workers and Peasants, another yellow union.

14. *Nothing like a Few Shots Before Dinner*

He remembered a quote from Ross Macdonald that appropriately explained what happened in the middle of dinner. The one that went: "He was less a man of action than a man of interrogation, a conscience from which the significance of other lives emerged."

But not even the quote could get rid of the bad taste in his mouth.

It happened like this: After a dusty tour of the commercial district of Santa Ana with Merenciano and Luix Lómax, "just to take a look-see" and on Blind Man's recommendation, he had stopped by the office for a bit and from there, along with the popular Canales, broadcaster of Radio Santa Ana, and his assistant, he had gone to eat at a tavern.

"I read all your novels, chief," Canales had told him.

"I hear that every day," José Daniel had answered.

"No one cares, you're hostage to the public."

"Breaded steak with lots of potatoes," said Barrientos.

"And how does it work, that new radio system you're putting up? Sometimes you hear it all over town and sometimes it's turned off."

"It's a stab at the limits of democracy," said the thin, eternally optimistic Canales. "You think if someone wants to hear, they turn it on and that's that. We don't have to force you to hear, but sometimes it's important to communicate with the whole town, so then the radio goes public, obligatory, in the streets; that's why we connected that system of loudspeakers. Now we're just testing, that's why you wake up to *boleros* by José Feliciano and when you're just at the point of solving a crime, you have to do it with the farm news at full volume . . . But it won't be so bad . . . I have millions of ideas. Start off Sundays with Tchaikovsky's *1812* Overture at full blast, cannons included. Public serenades to beatified mothers, once in a while news of a famous Priísta arrested for adulterating milk or raping his niece . . . Can you imagine? One hundred sixteen speakers telling that story. Son of a bitch . . ."

Canales got dreamy with the Hollywood perspective drifting through his head.

"It also serves to call for help in case of fire, or to pass on organizational slogans, or for . . ." Barrientos had said, in a more practical vein.

"No need to abuse it," José Daniel had recommended, thinking of Orwell's Big Brother.

"Abuse is when you turn on the TV and there's only bullshit," Canales had replied.

"Exactly," replied JD.

The tavern only had four tables, and the food was so home-made you could see it cooking on the hearth from the middle of the counter. There were no tricks; you simply decided and if you wanted the steak with onions, you pointed and they put it on the charcoal grill.

Canales got up and went to the fridge for beer.

JD smoked, watching the street. He witnessed the arrival of the two guys with shotguns, jumped up from the table and went running to the only safe place in the tavern, the bathroom. He would never remember if he screamed or if the cry remained locked up inside him. He heard the blast, and felt the scattered shot that searched him out, blowing apart a hardware store calendar featuring a big-assed blonde whose head was twisted oddly to look at the camera.

Of the three, maybe Canales, returning with the three beers in one hand, had the best view. He saw JD jump up and flee to the bathroom, caught a brief glimpse of the guy with the shotgun, and managed to see Blind Man under the overturned table shooting toward the entrance. He saw how the bullets hit one of the gunmen in the face, blowing his hat back. He saw how the second fled, firing into the air to make room, to comfort himself, to give himself courage.

When JD stuck his head out, Blind Man Barrientos was kicking the dead man's shotgun away, so the faceless corpse could not twitch and press the trigger in death.

For a moment, silence settled on the little tavern, broken only by the meat hissing on the fire, and the noise of the street.

The other patrons, a pair of campesinos, had not had time to figure out what was going on, and now contemplated the stars of the drama with admiration.

"What happened, chief?" asked Blind Man without looking at José Daniel.

"What the fuck do you think happened, asshole?"

"I don't know, suddenly you were there and just as suddenly

you weren't, like the magician Chen-kai. You disappear very prettily."

JD vacillated between answering, hiding his head under his wing, instantly resigning his post as chief of police of Santa Ana, or going back to the bathroom. It wasn't clear which was more dangerous, the guys with the shotgun or Blind Man's sarcasm.

"What speed!" said Blind Man, loading the clip of the .45 with bullets from his pocket.

"Okay, okay, I warned you. And what was I going to respond with, my fork?" he had asked, holding up his knife and fork.

"Canales, call the Red Cross to come get the stiff."

"Who is he?" asked JD.

"Nobody from around here," replied Blind Man.

15. *Dear Ana/April 16*

~~~~~~

Dear Ana/April 16
   This is . . . like life itself.
   I shall abandon literature to dedicate myself to writing the words to *boleros*. Everything's clear.
   Absolute fucking life itself.
   And I didn't know until now.
   I love you as always and a bit more because distance works miracles on marriage, José Daniel, alias "Chief Fierro."

16. *Daylight Photo and Rotten Meat*

"I heard they shot at you yesterday."

"I ran like hell."

"That's how it's done, chief, we can't let them kill us. And you know what, I didn't think they'd allow it either," said Mayor Benjamín Correa to José Daniel Fierro, while they moved to the wall to form up with the rest of the municipal cops of Santa Ana for the photo.

"Maybe they didn't shoot to kill," replied JD, "but nobody told me."

"And how do you feel?"

"Like shit . . . It's never happened to you?"

"Experience doesn't help. Every time they shoot at you is like the first time."

"Close in," said the photographer.

José Daniel put his arm on Blind Man Barrientos's shoulders; he had taken his hat off so his face would show up well in the photo.

"So, Benjamín, do we get a new patrol car?" asked Popochas, legally registered in Santa Ana as Luix Lómax.

"You've got something better, shitface, the best town in Mexico under your care."

"All right then," said Merenciano, who posed with his .45 in hand and leaning a bit to one side.

The photographer, hidden behind his old tripod camera, scolded:

"Now shut the fuck up, or you'll all come out with your mouths crooked."

"Your ass is crooked," shouted Lómax.

"Can you prove it, motherfucker?" asked the photographer, ready to interrupt his work to beat up the cop.

"Calm down, Señor Photographer, sir, you'll get three days in jail for striking a police officer in uniform," said JD.

"Shut that guy up, chief," replied the photographer, pointing to Lómax with his finger.

"Popochas, control yourself."

"Whatever you say, chief."

It was still early and you could hear the sparrows and footsteps in the street. The six cops and the mayor stayed still and smiled for an instant. The flash never went off, only the click.

"Another," ordered the photographer.

"Go," said Benjamín Correa.

In the office half an hour later, José Daniel Fierro discovered that he could see a tree from his window, just as he could from his window in Mexico City. It was not a laurel but an ocote, but it was a tree.

"Does it have birds?"

"What?" asked Blind Man.

"The tree across the street."

"It must have, that's what it's for, isn't it?"

JD wanted to write down his assistant's words.

Merenciano came in leading an old woman by the hand. She was radiant, very dark, with two braids held with red cords in hair turning gray, dressed in blue percale.

"Chief, my mother says they're selling rotten meat in the butcher shop run by the honcho of the CTM."

JD got up, giving a furtive glance at the tree.

"Who's in charge of such things in the government?"

"We have a veterinary student two doors down."

"Bring him here in a flash, Assistant Barrientos."

"Shit, the way things move around here."

17. Dear Ana/April 17

Dear Ana/April 17

So that there's a record of my people somewhere there in Mexico City, I send a photocopy of the payroll list (in case nobody wants to believe me) and a photo (I'm the one in the middle). With guys like these and Spitfires, Churchill could have won the Battle of England in one and a half months.

• Barrientos, alias "Blind Man," my assistant chief, former taxi driver, wonderful marksman, future bigamist, lover of poetry, participates in a literary workshop with Canales at midnight, Tuesdays and Thursdays, in a bar.

• Luix Lómax, alias "Popochas." Studies law by correspondence school. Changed his name legally. Childhood polio, limps with his right leg, from Guanajuato. Subchampion in the fifty-yard dash in the mini-Olympics for the handicapped. (I'm serious! Look in the *Ovaciones* newspaper of May 1980 if you don't believe me.)

• Marcelo (no last name whatsoever), alias "Greñas," former insurance salesman, born in Santa Ana. Gets red in the face at times of crisis. I have found no medical explanation among the local eminences for this phenomenon.

• Merenciano, alias "With Mouth and Hand." Gossips say he is an ace at masturbation. Silent. Goes around town on a motorcycle. When I ask him a question, he answers with another. Was a bartender. The owner threw him out when he refused to water the drinks.

• Martín Morales, alias "the Russian." Teachers' union activist from the early days. A year ago the judicial police kidnapped him and beat him for two days to make him sign a false confession involving our mayor. He didn't sign a fucking thing.

The biggest scientific advance I've made in a week was to organize, at Marcelo's suggestion, an interpolice tournament of dominos by pairs.

Isn't it wonderful?

I adore you. JD

18. Notes for the History of the Radical City Government of Santa Ana
José Daniel Fierro

Tape recording made with Mario Lapiedra Cruz, shopkeeper.

"I arrived here in 1959, after two weeks in jail at Matías Romero, with the railroad workers. I was assistant to the telegraphist in the days of the movement and affiliated with the Mexican Workers Communist Party . . . sixteen pesos for bread, sweetheart . . . And I was on the run from that but my ideas were still firm, moreover I had a few pennies inherited from the wife's dad, now dead, both of them, my wife and her dad, and so I set up the store. See? Outside you see written "The Winner," the lettering is from back then, because I didn't want to keep tasting the beating they had given us, and so I put "The Winner" in red letters with black trim. No, the black trim very light, so no one would see it was a flag, and to disguise it I painted two bulls, one on each side of the sign, but if you look hard you'll see the horns on the left are bigger . . . Leave it, I'll weigh it, the melon is very good, sir . . . You see the sign outside, it's old now, right? Like me, but I haven't changed it, it's from the old days. So I came and opened the store, with a boy who went north later on, his name was Isaías, religious, one of those guys who pray all night long, son of a bitch, okay. And I stayed quiet in 1959, in 1960, in 1961, in 1962. So quiet that if you had seen me then you'd have said that guy is a complete sissy. A fag. But I was waiting. In 1963, the leftist Presidential candidate passed by on tour and I approached him at the hotel and said: You take down the address of a supporter, Mario Lapiedra, and when you need me, send for me. He never sent word, he must have thought I was just a big mouth, and there you have it, quiet for another twelve years. And sometimes I said to myself: Something has to happen in this town, here or somewhere else. But it made me mad not knowing what to do. So I felt like climbing a ladder and changing the name of the store to "The Pussy" but then I would not only be a failure but left without customers too. So I contained myself, for that and because my wife had been sick since 1971. Until in 1982, when Benjamín arrived and said to me: They tell me you were a Vallejista. And I told him, 'Now is the time.' . . . Grapes at eight hundred pesos, sweetie."

19. At Fifty Yards

At fifty yards José Daniel Fierro appears an ungainly character who miraculously broke through the barrier of silent film to arrive alone and desperate in the commercial cinema of the 1960s: movies about drug running on the border and so on.

At fifty yards, the house where 153 kilos of marijuana were being guarded looked neither like the House of Usher nor the pantheon of that celebrated Mexico City chief of police in the middle of the 1980s. At fifty yards it looked more like a white mansion surrounded by roses, for a bucolic film with Jorge Negrete and a few grande dames of Mexican movies.

Nor was it clear at the same fifty yards if the man seated in the rocking chair with the shotgun in his arms was alert, dead, or asleep. But Blind Man with his glasses of fifteen diopters sees more than the eye of God and he indicates with humility:

"No, chief, he's smoking."

"He wouldn't be farting by any chance?" asked JD, cowering on the ground and trying to see more than was possible through the bushes.

"Farts don't smoke," responded his assistant, carefully hidden near the same bush, but with a stone between him and the shotgun of the man seated in the rocking chair.

"You who see everything, Blind Man, tell me if our forces are now in place."

"Popochas just arrived, limping, he's maybe twenty yards in back of us, and Merenciano is settling in behind the gate."

"Then let's go, I want to smoke a cigarette too," says José Daniel Fierro, who still does not get up because he does not want to be shot.

"We'll drag ourselves out there and take off his shoes?" asks Blind Man, who has made enormous advances in sarcasm these last few days.

"It's just that it strikes me as ridiculous to shout 'You're surrounded,' " says the chief of police of Santa Ana, excusing himself.

"You're the writer, say something far out."

But José Daniel Fierro couldn't think of anything memorable.

At fifty yards you wouldn't know if the man in the rocking chair smiles or suffers from pancreatic colic. And José Daniel Fierro thinks that, fortunately, at fifty yards the man couldn't see how yellow he was either. So he gets on his knees and cries, "Surrounded!"

Which must have been interpreted by the man in the rocking chair as "Impounded," and seeing a man on his knees at fifty yards, does not know what to watch, nor what is being impounded, nor what he's supposed to do, except to get on his feet and aim.

Fortunately, the act of aiming is interpreted by Merenciano as a direct assault on the recently inaugurated chief of police of Santa Ana, and an invitation to shoot the guy in the thigh with a bullet from a .22 rifle, because it's the only one he's got, and the guy in the rocking chair lets go of his shotgun and curses the fucking mother of the marksman who caught him unawares.

A cat comes out the front door of the house, and then a few minutes later a woman with nothing on but a tiny pair of panties, whose breasts sway from east to west, provoking Blind Man to distraction so that he doesn't see the machine gun barrel poke out the second-story window.

So it goes, and when the first burst of fire raises dirt near José Daniel Fierro's bush, Blind Man doesn't know if the one with big tits fired from her two powerful nipples or if someone else is trying to get them out of the game, and while he figures it out, he throws himself behind the rock and opens fire with his .45.

José Daniel Fierro feels like he's pissing and he is in fact pissing. Terror invades and paralyzes him and the dirt flies around him.

Blind Man, in front, his back to him, takes up firing position and lets loose at the window with the whole clip of his .45, one after another, although after the third there's no one in the window, just his shots breaking the silence. With the seventh he gets up, José Daniel follows, feeling his knee joints creak and his kidneys hurt, with a stinging pain that diminishes little by little as his fear gives way.

At fifty yards, Merenciano and Popochas advance on the house with their eyes wide open, measuring every step, but there is only silence.

"Is it over?" José Daniel asks his assistant.

"I guess so," he says, shaking off the dust without turning around, leaving his chief time to recover his presence of mind.

"Good, because if they start shooting again I won't be able to piss anymore," says Chief Fierro, smiling, because he knows that fear does not define a man, but sincerity does.

20. No Way

He let himself fall, bouncing on the mattress, without taking his boots off. He hurt from the hair on his head to the toes of his feet. He would not be able to sleep. He had never been able to sleep when he was tired. He should get up, take a hot shower and two aspirins, drink two cognacs, listen to Schubert. I won't sleep, he said to himself, tracing the lines drawn on the ceiling with his eyes.

He caught a movement from the door to the bathroom and immediately looked for the shotgun he had left in a corner of the room. A woman's voice aborted the planned leap from the bed.

"Steady now, little friend, I didn't come to hurt you, just to make you happy."

She was young, a fair-skinned brunette, with long loose black hair that fell to a strapless red dress, sewn onto her flesh by a skilled seamstress. A whore from the Mexican cinema of the 1950s. Even the way she talked.

The woman slid to the bed. She walked with difficulty because her dress was so tight it made her move her legs like the arms of a compass of short arc.

"Just relax and let go."

"Miss, I need your name."

"María, my dear."

"Okay, María, who sent you?"

"I came by myself, as a favor to the city. I try out all the important visitors who come here."

"What strange traditions remain in the provinces."

María lifted her arms to her back looking for the zipper. José Daniel felt tempted to help her. For reasons that were not strictly erotic, simply because it hurt him to see her sewn up so tight. He controlled himself. In high school, way back in 1947, a Basque professor of his, named Belascoarán, had instilled in him the sage maxim that he should not go putting his dick into women he didn't know. Advice as hard to defend as the rights of an author.

As the whole world knows, sex is a chain of reactions that begins with noises (a zipper running, the whisper of silk, a strangled sigh, a little cry muffled by a pillow between the teeth) that travel to the brain, which sends signals to the penis. All of this would be under control if one were deaf, but JD was not.

The woman stood up and let the dress slide over her body. Obviously she had nothing on underneath. The nipples of her two full breasts stared at José Daniel. A twinge reminded him of his headache and he narrowed his eyes. The woman interpreted his gesture as disgust.

"Don't you like them, papacito?"

She advanced toward the bed, to the post on the headboard, and began to masturbate. Her breasts knocked on the metal, swaying the mattress.

Obviously she wants to fuck, thought José Daniel in a last attempt to maintain his lucidity. Who? Why? The woman moved the mattress to and fro, knocking the slats of the bed with her pubis and staring at him.

José Daniel got up and went for the shotgun. He cocked it.

"Don't play with that, papacito, just take off your clothes instead."

José Daniel aimed at the woman's navel to avoid temptation.

"Who sent you, María? I'm giving you one minute to answer me. If you don't say, I'll shoot your leg and say you tried to kill me with a razor blade. You'll see yourself in hell with that red dress and crotch."

"What a bad boy you are."

"You've got thirty seconds left . . . I'll count them for you . . . twenty-nine . . . twenty-eight . . ."

"Don Sabás sent me, but not for anything bad. He just told me, fuck him. That's all. Nothing's going on. It was in good faith."

José Daniel gestured with the shotgun, indicating the door. "Out."

"Now be good. Just let me get dressed."

"Nope. As you are," said the chief of police of Santa Ana, planting a boot on the red dress.

The woman backed out with her eyes on the shotgun. Then she turned and fled the room.

José Daniel, hypnotized, watched the pair of swaying buttocks that fled their destiny. "What a chump," he said of himself.

He picked up the phone. Dialed five numbers.

"Greñas? . . . Do you know where Don Sabás lives? . . . There's a naked woman in the hallway of my hotel, a whore whom I believe is named María. Arrest her on morals charges, and take her to Don Sabás . . . That's what I said . . . Are you married? . . . Better yet . . . Take her to the front door and tell them that the chief of police ordered she be delivered there, because the lady gave that as her address . . . Exactly."

He hung up, advanced to the door and pushed an armchair against it. Then returned to bed and fell on the mattress. He passed his hand across his face and dried the sweat. Now he would be able to sleep. But he would sleep badly.

Six hours later he was awakened by a knock on the door. The sun was pouring in the window.

"Chief, there's a rumor going around town that you're a fag," announced Blind Man Barrientos, opening the door and sticking his head into the room.

José Daniel walked to the bathroom and carefully washed his face.

"What's to be done?"

"It's a blot on the force. If we don't fix it, no one will have any respect for us, no matter how well armed we are and even though we buy a new squad car."

"I can show the whole world a photo of my grandchild," said José Daniel while he dried his face.

"It won't work, chief."

"Then what?"

"Right this minute we're going to the whores, you and me. With the union Canales organized the other day. They're our very own."

"No way," said José Daniel.

21. Dear Ana/April 18

Dear Ana/April 18
   Today, I'd better not tell you anything.
   But I love you.

                                                         JD

22. Science

▲▲▲▲▲▲▲▲▲▲▲▲▲▲▲▲▲▲▲▲▲▲▲▲▲▲▲▲▲▲

"Lómax, repeat," said JD, leaning on the omniscient chalk-board, which was full of schemes that were at this height incomprehensible.

"Half an hour before, go over the road they're coming in on and check all the rooftops."

"Barrientos?"

"Maintain a volunteer guard . . ."

"Of helpers called the Baker Street Irregulars."

"Of kids, then. Put the kids in front of the offices of the state judiciary and let them whistle if they see any strange movement."

"Define 'strange movement.' "

"More than one person leaving with a long weapon."

"Morales, alias the Russian?"

"Watch the main street with a walkie-talkie and if a car turns off toward the highway too quickly, advise Barrientos."

"Barrientos?"

"If he tells me to, I close the street with the patrol car and announce it on the radio."

"Merenciano?"

"Check out the cathedral and then the portals and then station myself in the window over the stage."

"Greñas?"

"I block Calle Siete with a barrier, and don't let any demonstration pass that comes out of the PRI office."

"And if there's a lot of them and they're armed?"

"I advise Blind Man."

"Chief, one question."

"Spit it out."

"What if everything happens at the same time?"

"Everyone look to his saint."

"And where will you be?"

"Everywhere, like Spiderman."

Lómax controlled himself.

"That's not how we did it before," said Merenciano.

"And how did you do it before?" asked JD, ready to learn from the mistakes of others.

"Before we marched in the front with arms."

"That's not scientific," said JD. "Demonstrations have to be scientifically cared for. We are the armed force of popular power."

"That sounds like hot shit, chief, but let's hope there's no gunfire," said Blind Man.

"Amen," answered José Daniel.

23. Riders in the Sky

"And you, why are you with the left?"

"Because in a former life I was on the right and my conscience shit on me."

"No, seriously."

"Let's see," said José Daniel Fierro, scratching his moustache with the barrel of his new shotgun, a tic that Blind Man deplored as being unprofessional. "With what they throw out in the garbage in Queens, New York, in one night, you could furnish a street in Cuzco ten thousand times better than it is now. With the leftovers from one middle-class restaurant in Caracas, sixty Algerian families could eat for five days. The bachelors who go out at night in Buenos Aires could delight all the single women who dream lonely dreams watching the stars of Bangkok. The books I've bought and not read would solve the problems of a middle school library in Camagüey. With the monthly salary of a trolley car driver in Mexico City, you could live for one day at Caesars Palace in Las Vegas. With the speeches of a PRI governor of Mexico, you could drive six lie detectors crazy. With the fire that's in the poems of Vallejo you could cook all the hot dogs consumed in one day in Monterrey. All the words I've used over the last thirty-five years to explain it, if they were stones, could be used to construct the three pyramids of Cheops in Texcoco . . . Do I make myself clear?"

"Would you repeat that for the tape recorder?" asked Canales seriously.

"It never comes out the same."

Canales moved the button that disconnected the turntable spitting out revolutionary corridos and went on live.

"Here, at XELL, Radio Santa Ana, the solitary red star on your dial, broadcasting for insomniacs and middle school students who are studying for their literature exams . . . And for them, especially for them, a bit of music by Glenn Miller, and let me remind you not to buy meat from La Favorita. It is being boycotted by the Popular Organization."

He hit the switch and connected the second turntable.

"How do you know about the middle school?"

"They are my students, they have an exam tomorrow," said Canales, smiling.

"What kind of batteries do you use, Canales? Mine give out with the heat."

Without answering Canales walked to an icebox, the kind only miserable lunchrooms could afford, and took out two soft drinks that dripped freezing water.

"I never imagined myself broadcasting with a novelist here, live, at midnight."

"Novelists don't sleep in Santa Ana."

"You'd be surprised how many people don't sleep. These fucking people have insomnia since we won the elections. Just dreams and nightmares, neighbors."

José Daniel smiled.

"I'm sleeping badly."

"I haven't slept for two months," said Canales, very seriously.

"Really?"

"Really, ask Fritz . . . Have you ever been a member of a political party?"

"I joined the Communist Party in 1959. Until 1962. I left with Revueltas. Then I went it alone, without a party. In 1969 I was about to go out to the country, with a group that was organizing communal lands in Veracruz. I suppose I could continue being left-wing for that. Because the organized left didn't consume me the way it did so many others . . . I've seen the best minds of my generation getting paid by the treasury."

"And before you were a writer?"

"There was no before. When I was nine years old I knew."

"But your first book came out in 1964. You were twenty-nine then."

"I was late in getting clear on what I wanted to write about. For a third worldist who wants to eat the novel with the novel, who thinks that fame and glory depend on his capacity to enchant the metropolis, that is, to fool it, to put fear into his own pen, to darken the text so it appears absolutely transcendent, it is hard to arrive at the conclusion that what I really always wanted to write is a good adventure story. A kind of realism/social realism/adventure, which is not realism, is half socialist, and is completely an adventure. It was hard. While I got that clear, I worked as the manager of a supermarket, an editor, a professor of English literature, an assistant theatrical director, and a commissioned salesman for a rum manufacturer."

Canales stared at him for a moment, then returned to his console.

"And now, for those who are almost asleep, and dedicated to the managers of supermarkets, who if they pressure their consciences a bit will end up being writers of detective novels, 'Riders in the Sky.' "

"Aren't you driving people crazy?"

"They're used to it," said Canales, smiling as his long skinny crossed legs followed the rhythm of the march that sounded like a Western.

24. Dear Ana/April 19

Dear Ana/April 19

If you're going to divorce me, for God's sake send me the blue turtleneck sweater and the aspirins, Manchette's novels, the three books by Rodolfo Walsh held by a rubber band that were on top of the table, the draft of the novel that is in the green folder, the one that says "New Lies," the gray suede boots, the photo of my nephews pissing that I have in the bookcase on the right, the three green notebooks of notes that are in the drawer at the left of the desk, the yellow fountain pen and its cartridges, a novel by Roger Simon (*The Straight Man*) that's in the bookcase in the hall, the dark glasses I kept in the sewing kit, a pair of black corduroy pants, old, with patches on the knees, two boxes of Maalox (you, you're constipated, you don't ever use it), the correspondence with the Strugatski brothers, in a folder under S in the file cabinet, my old address book, the photo of Argel's grandfather (and don't take it out of the frame, okay?), the medium chess set, a cloak-and-dagger novel by Shellabarger that must be under the bed, volume two of *Les Misérables* by Victor Hugo (you'll find it easily, it has a red spine, bound in leather), the box of French paper that's under the desk, and the book of Benedetti's poems, with dedication.

If you've got any time left, send me the last photo of us together.

All this if you're going to divorce me. If you're not, send it all anyway, I'll be even more grateful.

JD, who still loves you.

25. Flowers in the Plaza

For José Daniel, the morning of April 20 began when he looked out the window of his hotel room and a worker for the soft drink bottler let a handful of dahlias fall on the sidewalk at the corner of Benito Juárez. Moments later, there were three or four market women carrying gladiolas. Then close to two hundred children from the middle school with daisies, which they dropped to the ground, as if carelessly, covering the place where Doña Jerónima had been killed four years ago.

José Daniel washed his face carefully, with cold water, which made his skin throb as if it were burning.

He walked out the door of the Hotel Florida. The loudspeakers connected to Radio Santa Ana repeated a song by Silvio Rodríguez, oddly cadenced in waltz time. A song whose chorus repeated: "I know you."

JD walked on, striking the tips of his mining boots on the paving stones. Turning the corner to the portals, he met the lawyer Mercado with a wreath of roses in his hand.

"Want one?"

"Thank you," said JD with a timid smile.

They walked together in silence to the street corner.

The pavement was covered with flowers, and from every corner of the plaza came men and women, children, elders, the ugly, the tall, the beautiful enough to drive you mad with their total splendor, those confused by morning and faraway memories, by the music that blared from the loudspeakers and raised their moustache hairs, the smiles, the recently combed hair, the drops of morning dew between their teeth.

José Daniel Fierro let his rose fall amid the rest of the flowers. And assumed the ritual silence, the felt end to the act. Now, he was one neighbor more in Santa Ana. Their dead were his dead.

26. *You Really Don't Like It?*

His police were transformed. The silent Martín Morales, alias the Russian, howled the rhythmic "Popular power, popular power" with his face bright red; the nose of Marcelo—Greñas—broke the air inches before its owner's face like an icepick, leading forth a character full of security. With a gesture, JD reminded them to occupy their designated places. They retired in protest.

JD found Carlos Monsiváis in the fourth line of the demonstrators advancing toward City Hall, at the edge of the crowd, a bit alien, looking at everything he could without appearing to stare.

"I know you recommended me to this infamous post. You're a fucking traitor."

"You really don't like it?"

"I love it. Aside from being shot at twice, and one of those times I peed my pants, I love it."

"Then I was right," said the other writer.

JD lifted two fingers to the visor of his baseball cap and moved on. He looked toward the rooftops of the buildings searching for nonexistent sharpshooters. He was here in his role as chief of police, not narrator. He saw other things. He could leave for another day the careful observation of women in red and green aprons, armed with posters and wreaths of flowers, who lifted their fists half high as if they still maintained some hint of shame. It was not an orderly demonstration. Miners and farmers, squads of the Popular Organization, elementary school teachers, women from the neighborhood committees, members of the reborn prostitutes' union (two arm in arm with the tall Canales), taxi drivers and small business owners, middle school students, many farmers, workers from the soda pop and gypsum factories, marching all mixed together, some with their own posters in which the spirit was stronger than the spelling.

Entering the plaza he saw Merenciano with his shotgun in the window of City Hall above the stage. When the first contingents began to turn the corner into the plaza, all the loudspeakers surged with the first chords of Beethoven's Fifth. Canales winked at the police chief.

And thus Beethoven and forty thousand citizens of Santa Ana entered the plaza of their city on the 20th of April.

*27. Notes for the History of the Radical City
Government of Santa Ana
José Daniel Fierro*

The leadership of the Popular Organization does not agree on
an interpretation of what is happening. While Benjamín believes in closing the circle and that the key moment will be
within the next six months, before the towns destroy the PRI
dominance in the whole region (at least in the other six towns
that advance stubbornly following Santa Ana's example), Mercado believes that something strange is happening now, and
the leaders of the miners' unions think that the enemy is in
retreat and now is the hour to advance.

We are almost speaking of a problem raised by a game of
divination. In one matter we are all in agreement, the state

apparatus has remained without support in Santa Ana and will have to bring in outside help or break the PO's unity to give itself room. Blind Man says this is the hour of the traitors, but that they must have made themselves scarce.

Benjamín, meanwhile, has elaborated a theory of siege. Basically, he means to oppose the pressure (economic: they hold back city funds collected in taxes by the state government, anticipated federal funds don't arrive, traditional federal support is diverted to other regions: bank loans, highways, public health clinics under construction, publicity, sanitation) with a pressure from inside consolidating the power of the radical city government and extending it to the neighboring zones, gently and cautiously, and with another, external, pressure: a national publicity campaign involving intellectuals, journalists, artists, and even the few left-wing deputies in parliament.

This is what I'm here for, I have no illusions. I'm lending my name to the revolution: the impossible and for that not any less necessary revolution. The difference between me and other writers and journalists who are jumping into the struggle with both feet at the call of the radical city government is that I don't write a thing, and nevertheless, I play at the statues of salt while I walk through town in my uniform and baseball cap.

Whatever comes out of it, it's certain that Benjamín's tactic is getting results, the name Santa Ana is beginning to take on national and even international fame thanks to the foreign press and translations of the Mexican press in French and American magazines.

No doubt the attraction of Santa Ana is the unanimity it presents, the nonexistence of cracks in its justice on the one hand, and two complementary factors on the other. The first has to do with the pride of victory that everyone takes on by extension, in a country that makes us all minorities despite ourselves, that condemns the timid to silence and the daring to isolation. The second is visual: there are no beggars in Santa Ana. Our miracle was not that we extracted petroleum where there was none to be found, but that we have won back the most important human resource in this country: the hundreds of children who work from the age of five selling gum and newspapers, the women who stretch out their hands, the men who sell Kleenex without looking you in the eye. The child care centers, the shelters, the municipal employment plan, the cooperative stores, and above all the legion of voluntary social workers who have thrown themselves on the streets to reconstruct the human landscape, have achieved a great victory.

These are overwhelming arguments for organizing solidarity around Santa Ana, but do nothing to brake the offensive of its enemies.

28. *Dear Ana/April 20*

Dear Ana/April 20

Before you say fifty-two years old, I say nearly fifty-two, and each year is one more in a line, waking you up in the middle of a dream to say I'm an asshole, I should dedicate myself to arithmetic, I don't know how to write, how could anyone be so imbecilic, so absolutely conceited as to have once believed himself master of words and sentences, speeches and paragraphs, entire chapters, when he is really master of nothing, not even the Olivetti Lettera 25 I beat on, or the paper, or the commas in the wrong place and another job before tears flow from my eyes and another fucking job in which the dance from euphoria to depression is not calisthenic, toboggan-like, the leap from the Latin American Tower to the ground in ten seconds; and I tell you that while you cover your head and say it will pass, as if it were the slogan of the Spanish Civil War, *no pasarán,* but it does not pass and goes on at my side accompanying me, the faithful mark of the job the fear of words that don't exist, sentences that say the opposite, inchoate ideas, uncapturable landscapes, erratic characters, vagabond plots, wounded to death, and fuck the book, which then falls from the hands because no fragrance of ink or sentence makes the nightmare a dream and from the dream the tranquillity that comes from finishing the final touches, although later I must correct them a thousand times and the best novel is that which is never finished, is never written, but always thought of, the one carried inside forever that will die with you because of that absurd marriage between the book that will never come about and the man who will never write it.

And who can I tell this to? Because the mirror already warned me it won't take another fucking monologue for depressed assholes.

For you, of course.

I love you: JD

29. Birds

From the window of his room in the Hotel Florida, José Daniel Fierro watched the swarms of thrushes drawing circles in the sky of Santa Ana, crazy gyrations, absurd turns, writing a message in the air that could not be retained . . . They come nineteen miles from González Ortega to sleep in Santa Ana. They eat in the wheat fields of the cañadas and at dusk fly to Santa Ana to fill the laurels of the plaza, shit on pairs of sweethearts, and after warbling an hour and making the trees appear like live, irritated, and palpitating masses of green, they sleep in the city. How far is nineteen miles to a bird? Far? Maybe a bit less, because it is nineteen miles on the highway, and the birds fly in a straight line. Why do they sleep here? For the same reason I do?

The lights of the town begin to go on. José Daniel dries his sweat with a bandana and watches the patrol car pass down below, driven by the Russian, who accompanies Merenciano.

On the little table by the window, an open bottle of brandy stood alongside the typewriter. The only glass was dirty, muddy with cigarette butts tossed in the night before. The birds were disappearing from the sky and he drank from the bottle.

This is the worst hour in Santa Ana, the moment of solitude before he decides to write a bit or listen to music stretched out in bed, or until someone appears to offer a last nocturnal round through town, filling the mortal hour with old stories that to JD appear eternally new, freshly unveiled.

The telephone rang. JD smiled at the apparatus, which guessed at his solitude.

"We have a bizarre death, chief," said Barrientos's voice in his ear.

"Why?"

"You'll see. Come downstairs and I'll be there on the bike in two minutes."

JD hung up and dried his face again. The sky was clean of birds, the last lights were on. The street was, nevertheless, deserted. "They must all be shitting," as Merenciano says when the streets suddenly empty at certain hours of the afternoon and the city dozes among the sounds of creaking bedsprings.

His baseball cap lay on the bed. JD put it on and adjusted it in the mirror, which showed a grim and sullen look.

30. Candles in Church

JDF made his way through the women in mourning, the butcher with his deliveries on the back of his bicycle, two altar boys. The church was dark, and smelled of damp and of rancid death, but the bloody woman was young, the naked body out of place in front of the altar. José Daniel tried to construct a literary image and words like "obscene" or "profane" did not appear, just flashes from pop art, plastic mannequins, Andy Warhol and European design magazines. The murdered woman was that unreal.

"Who is she?"

"I have no idea, chief. All she's got on is the knife she was killed with. The altar boy found her fifteen minutes ago and advised a cop going by," said Barrientos.

José Daniel approached the corpse and took the undone face between his hands, trying to avoid contact with the knife that stuck out from the center of her chest. She was young, blond, her hair fell over one eye in that hairstyle like Veronica Lake that reminded him of a girlfriend he'd had when he studied in London, who looked at him with an intensity that came of using only one side of her face, the other appearing and disappearing in the soft sway of a short mane of hair. The blue eyes looked right through the chief of police of Santa Ana, looking at a killer who was now long gone. The body was still warm.

"Does anyone know her?" José Daniel asked Barrientos. Blind Man shook his head.

"Tell the Russian to come here. Get everyone together here, and bring me the altar boy who found her . . . Lómax! Find me Dr. Jiménez . . . I want to speak with the priest of this church, the earthly proprietor as he would say . . . Doesn't anyone know her?" he asked the spectators for the second time, raising his voice over the Santa Ana cops who were filing in and making a small protective barrier around their chief, ready to obey orders and make suggestions at the drop of a hat. With one theatrical gesture José Daniel made the bystanders, who were filling the church, move back a few paces. The cadaver was lying on the stairs that led to the altar, between the altar and a confessional of black wood.

"I'm the one who found her, Chief Fierro," said a disheveled altar boy who did not reach José Daniel's waist.

"I need more light, light all the candles."

"The señor priest doesn't like it."

"But I do, and this matter is for the Santa Ana police and not God, my child."

The church began to light up as the altar boy ran from one side to the other, touching fire to wick. The butcher and a lay sister began to help him. The body of the blond woman acquired a greater presence as the shadows retreated. It was becoming the center of a new rite that would be remembered years later as the-night-when-Chief-Fierro-found-the-dead-gringa.

"Greñas, come here and take a good look at this knife without touching it. Have you seen one before?"

"Everywhere, chief, they're butcher knives, or taco knives. They sell them everywhere, even in the supermarket."

"Here's the Russian," said Barrientos.

"Catch that altar boy and bring him here . . . Russian, station yourself in the doorway and let me know when the judicial police arrive."

"Should I stop them?"

"No, just tell me."

"Here he is, chief," said Barrientos.

"Okay, kid, how did you find her?"

"I came into the church and there was no one here, chief. And there'd been nobody else 'cept that dead blonde. I went running and called the butcher going by on his bike."

"It was ten o'clock," said the butcher, coming forward. "I went outside and the patrol car went by and I shouted at them real loud."

"And the priest?"

"He doesn't come today, it's his day to visit other towns in the district," said Blind Man.

"And what were you doing, little one, dressed as an altar boy?"

"Practicing, chief—him too," he said, pointing at the second altar boy a few feet away, clinging to a column with such strength that he appeared to be holding up the small temple.

"That's right," said the second witness.

"Thursdays at night we practice."

"And the church is open even though the priest doesn't come?"

"Yes, it stays open, for anyone who needs it."

"With or without lights?"

"I lit the bulb in the sacristy where I change clothes, chief."

"Somebody must have seen you come in. Someone undressed her. They brought her dead or they killed her here, but to run around town with a naked blonde would provoke such a scandal that . . . Greñas!"

"He's in the doorway, chief."

"Assistant Barrientos, grab Greñas and interrogate everyone in the neighborhood, everyone who was hanging out in the doorway, taking a breath of fresh air, all the drunks, everyone on this and the next block. What are we looking for? A car that stopped in front of the church. A group of people with a woman along, two guys who carried a rug where a body would fit, someone who heard a cry, a quarrel, anything out of the ordinary . . ."

JD walks around the body as he continues to talk. He was out of character. He had entered a Mack Sennett comedy. Around the body, small pools of blood fall from the chest wound, one of them had been stepped in; you could barely see the print of a boot heel. He touches her again. She is still warm. As he lets the arm fall, he finds a one-inch tattoo in the interior of her forearm: a small rose with six words in English: Loneliness is the heart of life. Suddenly he wonders if the woman is a natural blonde and examines her roots. No signs of dye, she's blond and always has been.

"Dr. Jiménez!" cries Lómax, and enters running, holding the doctor by the arm.

"When did she die? Did a lefty strike the blow? Was she beaten? Was she raped? How old is she? Is that a new tattoo?"

Jiménez, a gray-haired man of some forty years, stares at Chief Fierro and smiles.

"This is the first instantaneous autopsy I've done in my life, chief. Everything I tell you will be a lie."

"Hurry, because we'll have the feds here any minute."

"I'll take a look, but don't worry. When they take the body, they'll take it to the morgue and the guy in charge there is Luis, who was my student in Durango . . . Just ask them to move back, I don't work in public."

JD steps back as an example and, at his gesture, the whispering crowd that fills the church moves back again. Those seated in the first rows go to the third, and so on, respecting the order of arrival.

"Does anyone know her?"

"You can't see from here," replies an old miner.

" 'Loneliness is the heart of life,' " José Daniel murmurs. "Lómax, have you ever taken fingerprints?"

Luix Lómax shakes his head.

"Does anyone have a Polaroid camera?"

"I do, chief," says one of the middle school teachers.

"Can you bring it?"

"I live far away."

"Lómax, take the teacher on the motorcycle and come right back. Do you have flash?"

The woman nods and smiles at the chief and Lómax.

" 'Fuenteovejuna against the Murderer of the Gringa,' they'll call the play," thinks José Daniel, who has tried to conduct the whole affair in the purest *procedural* style of the stories of McBain's 87th Precinct.

"She wasn't a virgin, doesn't appear to have been raped, she was killed half an hour ago or a little more, and I believe she died here because that's what the blood on the floor says, she died instantly. She has scratches on one arm and the neck, she could have been forced. I don't think she's thirty, but you never know. If she were a compatriot of mine from Durango, I could give her exact age, but she looks like a gringa or a rich girl from Polanco there in Mexico City," says Jiménez.

"How did you do it so well and so quickly?"

"I read all your novels, Chief Fierro."

"Son of a bitch," thought José Daniel, "that's how it goes."

"Cover her with a sheet!"

"Will a blanket do?" asked the butcher, who was of a literal bent.

JD nodded.

"Have you ever seen a knife like this one?"

"I have three of them" said the man, advancing toward the dead woman with a blanket passed up from the third row.

"Should I run the onlookers out of the church, chief?" asked Lómax.

"Why? The dead woman is just as much theirs as ours, they're not bothering anyone," answered José Daniel, who believes firmly in democratic police investigation.

The phrase "loneliness is the heart of life" reminds him of something he read once, but not in Spanish, in translation. Thomas Wolfe? Dylan Thomas? Someone like that.

"What time is it?"

"Fifteen to eleven, chief! Ten forty-eight!" respond the anonymous voices in chorus.

"Little one, what time did you find her?"

"I got here around ten-fifteen, chief."

"Russian, what time did the butcher call you?"

"A bit before ten-thirty, chief."

"Shit, they had just killed her, and here we were going over the business inside instead of following the fresh trail in the street. When I got here, twenty-five minutes hadn't gone by since the murder."

"I could be wrong and it was more like forty-five minutes," said Dr. Jiménez.

"No more than that?"

"No more, she was very warm, and the floor was cold."

José Daniel approached the body covered with a blanket and lifted a corner and the murmuring at his back increased. If he could only see the face without the traces of fear, of anguish, of tension from pain and the rigidity that death was beginning to imprint . . .

"Here's the teacher with the camera," says Lómax, dusty from driving the motorbike at sixty miles per hour in the streets of Santa Ana.

"Will you take them or should I?"

"Oh, no, chief, not me," said the teacher, passing him the camera and retreating a few yards.

"Uncover her, doc."

Slowly, JD begins to shoot photos of the body, the face from various angles, the position of the corpse, general shots. To see what comes out, more or less neatly.

"Here come the judicial police, chief," advises the child.

From the door, arms in hand, the chief of the group of state judicials comes in followed by two confederates in suits.

"Who killed her?" he asks, directing himself to Chief Fierro, who finished the roll in the Polaroid without looking up.

"Nobody here. She was found half an hour ago. No one knows anything or saw anything. Nobody knows her."

"The case is ours," says Durán Rocha.

Chief Fierro looks at him, trying to discover something, but sees only the scarred face of the cop.

"Let's go," he says to the doctor and Lómax, the Russian and Merenciano, but his voice is interpreted by the majority of the onlookers as a communal order, and the church begins to empty, to the judicials' surprise. The butcher puts out the candles as he leaves.

"The witnesses stay here!" says Durán Rocha but nobody pays any attention to him.

"You can come by tomorrow to read my report," answers Fierro, turning his back. The church empties, while the witnesses to the crime and the witnesses to the beginning of the investigation follow the police chief out to the street.

31. Office Hours

~~~~~~

"Permission to go home and sleep is suspended until the investigation is over," said José Daniel, throwing the Polaroid shots on the table before a pair of agitated agents. "Take the motorcycle and hunt up Barrientos and Greñas; they're out doing investigations down the block and around the church, tell them the time of the crime was around ten at night, right there, in the church, the murderer and the blonde went in together, tell them she's probably gringa, tell them to look for her clothes, they must have been thrown away somewhere. Merenciano and the Russian should try the hotels with one of these photos. If you find the hotel where she was staying, call me, and then stand in the door to the room and don't let even a fly get in."

"What are you going to do, chief?"

"I'm going to make coffee. If I'm not here, I'll be at the broadcasting station. I saw a light on when we went by."

JD turned his back and went for the coffee pot. He didn't know if he had them fooled, but he certainly had tried. Them and the whole town. If you give orders so rapidly that the guys who get them don't have time to think, it looks like the guy who's giving them knows what he's talking about. At least that's the way it looks and José Daniel in the role of Chief Fierro has convinced even himself. "What's missing?" he asked himself now in the empty office. He reviewed his arsenal of thirty-five years of reading detective literature: fingerprints, why, to identify her if she is a gringa, I suppose; put a tail on the judicials to see what they do, copies of the photos, what for?

José Daniel Fierro tips his baseball cap and serves himself the first of a long series of cups of coffee.

"Chief, an interview!" said long-legged Canales, entering the office and tripping over the coat rack.

"Do you know her, Canales?"

The skinny one looked at a photo of the dead woman's face, and then at the others.

"Son of a bitch, I saw her today."

"Where?"

"In Esther's bookstore, La Piedra Rodante."

"Who is she?"

"Who knows, but a Spanish-speaking gringa. She was chatting with Esther when I arrived to buy some books."

"What did you buy?"

"A new novel by Semionov."

"And where can we find Esther?"

"She lives above the bookstore . . . But first, an interview. Come to the station next door!"

"And who stays in the office?"

"Let's call Tomás, the night watchman. You give the instructions."

JD stopped. "Is there a way of tapping the judicials' phone?"

"We already have, it's just that we only have two shifts out of three, because not all the operators are with us. What do you want to know?"

"Everything. Who they talk to, about what."

"Wait a minute," said the skinny Canales and lifted the office telephone.

"María? Tell Laura to lend an ear she knows where, and if they call Chief Fierro, pass the calls on to the station, please; call Tomás at the entrance and tell him if the agents arrive to tell them the chief is at the station . . . All the above." Canales hung up and said to JD: "You owe me a supper, which is what it costs me for María to pass on three messages without forgetting anything."

JD walked alongside Canales. The night chilled the building's central patio. The radio station was empty, a revolving long-playing record of classical music and the red indicators on the switchboard were the only things stirring.

Canales took the microphone, threw a switch, and went on live.

"And here, from the broadcasting studios of Radio Santa Ana, a live interview with our chief of police, the famous writer José Daniel Fierro, who will review the facts of the strange murder perpetrated tonight in our city."

José Daniel got serious. Radio had the virtue of making him a character in a melodrama.

"At ten o'clock tonight a woman some twenty-five years old, blond, blue eyes, was murdered in the church on Calle Lerdo. The body was discovered minutes later by accident. She was found nude. She had been killed with a kitchen knife."

"Do you know the dead woman's name?"

"We still have no information, although we are investigating."

"Do you have any leads?"

"I reserve comment so as not to interfere with the investigation."

"Is it true that the judicial police arrived half an hour after you had begun the investigation?"

"That's true."

"Will the Santa Ana police be continuing their investigation of the murder?"

"Yes, although the judicial police are in charge, we will continue with our own investigation."

"Don't you have confidence in the state judicial police, Señor Chief of Police?"

"None at all. The crime occurred in our city, we were the first to discover the body, we will ascertain who killed the woman and why."

"Do you want the town's cooperation?"

"Yes, we're going to ask for various kinds of help. We urgently need to find out who the woman was, so we ask the inhabitants of Santa Ana, if they know or saw a woman who corresponds to the description, to report it immediately. We will put a photo of the body on the board at the entrance to City Hall to facilitate identification. We would also like to know if anyone saw anything out of the ordinary around ten at night near the church on Calle Lerdo. And since the woman was found naked, if a woman's clothing appears thrown out somewhere in town we would like to be informed immediately."

"Chief Fierro, are you asking the town to take up the investigation?"

"I certainly am. A woman died today, brutally murdered in our town. We are all responsible for finding the killers."

"Here, at Radio Santa Ana, live, you have just heard an interview with the city's chief of police, an hour after the murder committed in the Church of Carmen on Calle Lerdo . . . And now for you all, music of the Chilean resistance movement . . ."

Canales switched off the mike and brought up the music. "Do you have any ideas, chief?"

"I have a dead woman, and I take it as a personal offense."

"Against you?"

"Against her."

32. Night Rounds

José Daniel lined up the four paper cups with the remains of coffee. It was his way of measuring the night. He began his report.

"If I'm wrong, if I skip things, if you don't understand me or if I don't understand me, cut me off, we'll discuss it and start over, as many times as we have to."

"We should interrupt you?" asked Merenciano.

"Exactly."

Around him, squeezed into school desks, the Russian and Merenciano, Blind Man Barrientos seated on the metal file cabinet, Lómax on the floor in lotus position, Canales standing in the door (in his capacity as connoisseur of the detective novel and not as broadcaster of Radio Santa Ana). The police force of the radical city government lit cigarettes and served themselves fresh cups of aromatic coffee.

"Yesterday afternoon, probably to attend the demonstration, or God knows why, a gringa arrived in town in a Renault with California plates. She registered at Motel Lucas under the name of Jessica Lange, which must be a pseudonym."

"Jessica Lange, from *King Kong?*" asked Canales.

"Exactly, but she isn't. Look at the photo, she's beautiful but not that beautiful."

"We didn't see her at the demonstration, but that means nothing. At the motel she received no phone calls and all they know is that she slept there and left again today in the morning. The car isn't there, we know it's a red Renault but don't know the plate numbers. Later we'll talk about that."

"But the car was at the motel last night, or else she took it out today," said the Russian.

"How did you know to search at a motel?" asked Blind Man.

"I didn't know, it just occurred to me."

"That's called instinct," said Lómax.

"At the motel," continued José Daniel, "the room was messy, there was no suitcase but some clothes were thrown around, and a few other things: a Los Angeles newspaper dated the eighteenth, a box of American chocolates, a novel in English, a box of tampons and a toothbrush in the bathroom, two dirty changes of underwear near the shower, a Zeiss telephoto lens that must have cost a fortune, a folder with professional black and white photos, two-by-three stills, all of a six- or seven-year-old boy. The folder had fallen behind the mirror. The rest of the luggage was missing. We know it was just one suitcase, of canvas, blue, because the kid who waits on people who arrive there at night told us. That's where we stand. All we've got left is the disappeared car, the disappeared suitcase; we know she was in Los Angeles two days ago, we know she registered under a false name, that she left the motel today . . . We know that she was at the bookstore. Tomorrow we'll follow up on that trail . . . At ten o'clock she was dead and naked at the church."

"Why naked?" asked Barrientos.

"That's one of the clues. They took off her clothes because there's something in them that could serve to identify her or the murderers, or because they want to create a scandal with a dead naked gringa in a church in Santa Ana."

"Why the church?" asked Barrientos again.

"One thing or the other. Either by accident, she was there and they trapped her, or on the other hand . . ."

He paused, ritually, while everyone sipped their coffee. Magnanimously he circulated a small flask of brandy that came back to him empty.

"Shit, it was to flavor the coffee, not to drink coffee with brandy to give it a better color . . . Okay. Somewhere near Calle Lerdo, we still haven't found more than two clues. Somebody saw a red car parked in front of the church, and was at the point of telling them that the priest was away, but . . ."

"Doña Lola," completed Greñas.

"Doña Lola had a sick kid and kept going. When she went by the car was empty. When the altar boys found the body, the car was gone. Two miners on the night shift brought us some women's clothes that they found thrown in Avenida Riva Palacio, behind a garbage can. With that we'll know if they undressed her after they killed her . . . Nobody heard anything else in the street."

"We should go out again and start over," said Barrientos. "We didn't talk to all the neighbors."

"Okay, what do we have? A car. Everyone to the streets to

look for a gringo car with California plates. Not only here in town, on the outskirts too. We'll cut the town in four and divide it. Merenciano and Russian in the patrol car, take the east and the north, Greñas on his bicycle, downtown which is easier, Lómax the south with the motorcycle and follow the outlying neighborhoods and the highways to Chihuahua and Monterrey. Report back every fifteen minutes. Let's go."

33. Red Car Badly Parked

"There's a time to ask questions . . . How would Pete Seeger say it, Canales?" said José Daniel, shadows under his eyes, lining up the nine paper cups.

"And a time to answer questions . . . Seeger according to Ecclesiastes," answered Canales from deep in an armchair. He did not know how to hide his excessively long legs.

Barrientos was still mounted on the file cabinet answering the telephone.

"This is not the time to ask questions. To ask a good question you have to know part of the answer. But still: What was she doing in church?"

"They killed her with her clothes on," said Barrientos, playing with the yellow dress they had brought in, its checked front bloody and torn by the knife. "First they killed her, then they undressed her."

"There was the print of a boot heel in the blood," said JD. And he began to draw it. "Just like this."

"Did you take a photo?"

"It didn't occur to me."

"I'll do it, chief."

"We'll do it tomorrow if the judicials haven't erased it . . . And nothing from that angle?"

Canales shook his head. "They called the capital once to report. They cursed you out various times, chief, for having gotten there first, but nothing else."

JD got up from his armchair and walked to the window. The streets were empty.

"What time is dawn here?"

"In half an hour," said Barrientos. And he stretched to answer the phone.

"Yes? Where?" Then, turning toward José Daniel, "They found the red car."

JD stretched, trying to touch the top of the window frame. He picked up his cap and the shotgun that hung behind the door.

"I'm going, the broadcast is about to start," said Canales. "I have a cot in the cabin. Do you want me to say anything more?"

"Give them a report on what happened last night."

Barrientos set out.

"How are we traveling?" asked JD, rubbing himself to shake off the cold.

"On the other motorcycle, the old one."

JD looked at the sky. The stars of Santa Ana had been out all week: thousands of them, burning like pale suns. His beard grew by the warmth of the stars. Blind Man revved the engine.

JD got on the rear seat, hung the shotgun carefully on his back and cried, "Ready, Assistant Chief."

The motorbike took off like a shot in the empty streets. Sixty miles an hour under the stars, with a frozen wind that made him tremble like he did at the end of a week of drinking. José Daniel Fierro shoved his cap down over his brow with his free hand.

"Almost there, chief. In the Esmeraldas neighborhood. The one behind the hill on the main highway."

"Who lives there?"

"Ranchers, the mine owner, businessmen, Mercado's parents, the director of the middle school, the engineers of the Ag Department's experimental fields, the PRI ex-mayor, one of my sisters-in-law . . ."

"You can stop now."

They entered the highway and Barrientos accelerated even more. Then he took an open curve and José Daniel felt like his teeth would fall out when the frozen air hit his face.

The red car was at the end of a street. Alone. Lómax next to it on the bike. Blind Man braked noisily in front of Popocha's motorcycle, lifting the loose gravel. JD got down, rubbing his hands to bring them back to life.

"No more cars?"

"They keep them all in garages."

JD walked around the car while his boys watched. It was locked. Lómax lit up the inside with a flashlight. The keys were not there.

"One or the other, they abandoned it here without leaving a trail, or they didn't think we would find it so quickly and it has to do with someone who lives in those houses."

"That's it, now you've got it, because in that house lives the big cheese himself," said Blind Man, smiling.

"Which one?"

"Melchor Barrio, the PRI boss."

"Shall we pay a visit?"

"At five in the morning without speaking to Benjamín first? I don't think so."

"Lómax, find the patrol car, and tell them to bring Benjamín here, get him out of bed."

"Which bed?" asked Lómax. "Where's he sleeping tonight?"

"Who knows," said Barrientos.

"Shit," muttered José Daniel.

He walked around the red car again. He heard crickets, and an automatic hose watering the garden behind the stone walls of the house. A street of walls, castles shut off by fences from the rest of the city. Only two houses on one side, and one on the other, that of the PRI boss.

"There are armed men inside there," said Blind Man.

"So?"

"Just so you know, so you don't say I didn't tell you."

"Popochas, bring a tow truck and take the car to the jail patio. I believe that's all for today."

34. *Notes for the History of the Radical City Government of Santa Ana*
José Daniel Fierro

▲▲▲▲▲▲▲▲▲▲▲▲▲▲▲▲▲▲▲▲▲▲▲▲▲▲▲▲▲▲▲▲▲▲▲▲

Since Benjamín and his gang came to power, crime in Santa Ana has been transformed. Murders have increased, no doubt a product of the heightening of social conflicts. Common robbery has diminished, a product of who knows what. Official robbery has disappeared. Sex crimes have increased, maybe the heightening of the class struggle makes some people crazy. Divorce has risen at an alarming rate (from 27 a year to 103). The town's fortune-tellers (two) are receiving fewer clients. Theft of cars, motorcycles, and bicycles has practically disappeared. Street assaults are a thing of the past (some of the gangs joined the movement, and the others, according to Blind

Man Barrientos, were given twenty-four hours to clear out of town). Accusations of insult and injury have multiplied by eight. Arrests for public drunkenness have diminished. Arrests for traffic accidents have diminished. Begging has disappeared. Public attention to venereal disease has almost disappeared. Arrests for offenses against public health have increased. One citizen was arrested for farting at the movies. Six bosses were arrested for not paying minimum wage. It is not hard to draw conclusions.

35. *Hotel Florida, Dawn*

He left the shotgun behind the door. He walked to the small bathroom and verified there was no one inside. Then he stood before the window to watch the light stain the white walls of the main street. In his hands he carried the perforated and bloody yellow dress and a folder with the photos of the child. A six-year-old boy, blond like the dead woman: leaving a nameless school, in a city full of cars with California plates, eating an ice cream cone, smiling before the monkey cage, sleeping in a very small bed with white sheets, sucking his thumb.

José Daniel felt extremely old. He thought he could just as well pack his bags and walk to the bus station. It was a night as good as any other to say goodbye to Santa Ana.

He looked in the mirror. A doom-laden new mania for

confirming that he was still on his feet with his baseball cap.
Santa Ana was making him old. Or was simply making him
a super-survivor at the edge of retirement. He vacillated between getting up to sing "Venceremos" or a Gardel tango that
spoke of gray hair, between falling asleep on his feet like a
horse or masturbating while thinking of Greta Garbo. That
was a symptom of old age. The whole world masturbates
thinking of Jane Fonda or Olga Breeskin, according to their
taste, while he still concentrated on ranchero singers wearing
wide skirts down to their ankles and cowboy hats.

Poor José Daniel Fierro, so much owner of his typewriter
and so out of his element. So much owner of other people's
dreams, so solitary in his own nightmares. So afraid of putting
a comma in the wrong place and so newly rich in wounds,
cadavers, human plunder, and terrors.

As always, Santa Ana's dawn got under his skin and revived
old droughts. He put out the electric light, in the tenuous
gloom his image in the mirror came undone and appeared
cadaverous. He shifted his cap a bit to the right and then
straightened it. If he hadn't wanted to, he wouldn't have accepted. Now he had only to leave Santa Ana with a Guggen-
heim grant, heading into exile with a legion of failures (and
he with the last shotgun in hand); that, or go out walking
alongside the last ambulance without daring to look behind so
that his flaming boots would not turn into salt.

Now he had only to discover the murderers of the girl who
wanted to be Jessica Lange and in whose body they buried a
kitchen knife.

He sat on the bed and looked in the mirror again. He got
up again and walked to the door and picked up the shotgun.

He slept with his boots and cap on, lovingly cradling the
breech-loading shotgun.

Smiling.

36. Confessions

He opened one eye and got up on his elbows, frightened. There was someone in the room, the shotgun fell to the floor.

"No problem, chief, I put on the safety. What an ass you are with firearms, you slept with the safety off."

José Daniel Fierro scratched his head.

"And why are you here so early, Blind Man? What time is it?"

"Eight. You just got two and a half hours' sleep, chief," said Blind Man Barrientos, walking to the washbasin and taking off his glasses. He let the water run from the tap and began to carefully clean the mucus out of his eyes, making walrus noises at the cold water.

"What's new?"

"I went out fishing for rumors, chief, instead of sleeping."

"And how do you do that? You'll have to teach me."

"You go here and there, looking for the worst gossips, you give them two words and get ten in return. It's easy. The only problem is that seven in the morning isn't the best hour for hunting down gossips—around here everyone's a bit fucked up at that hour."

"Including the chief of police."

"That's true . . . During the revolution, there was a Villista colonel who used to come here, Colonel Cabrera Palomec, and he only came for gossip, they told him what was happening hundreds of miles away. He said that nowhere did they speak of the revolution so prettily as in Santa Ana. Once he beat up the Federales in Las Tunas, forty-four miles to the north of here, and he came running to Santa Ana so we could tell him about the battle."

José Daniel pushed gently at Blind Man, who was now using the chief's brush to comb his hair at the mirror, so he could wash his face too.

"And what's the gossip?"

"That this isn't the first time the gringa has come to this town . . . There's shit in the air, chief," finished Blind Man enigmatically.

JD stared at him. Blind Man tucked his shirt into his pants, carefully, hoping for a semi-martial air.

"Our hosts?"

"I sent Lómax and Merenciano to sleep. Martín, the Russian, is guarding the gringa's car; Greñas is out patrolling the town on the bike."

"I'll walk to the office. Ask the owner of the bookstore to come by and see me right now."

José Daniel left the Hotel Florida and was surprised at the force of the sun that stung his face and back. To buy dark glasses would be too expensive. Some middle school students, late for class, crossed his path. He felt their eyes at his back, but it was not the sullen look common to Mexicans when faced with the law, they were looks of solidarity. At first opportunity he would get a middle school pin to put next to Spiderman. The April 20 popular middle school was one of his favorite spectacles in Santa Ana. Hundreds of green-sweatered adolescents walking on the edge of the highway in the middle of the afternoon.

The nine cups of coffee were still lined up on his desk. A brilliant light broke the office into stripes through the venetian blinds. He turned on the coffee pot after verifying there was water, and changed the coffee. Then he walked the few steps to the radio station. Fritz was at the controls; at his side, skinny Canales slept on a diminutive cot from which his legs protruded a foot.

"And we continue with our program to begin the day. For you, the *Clair de Lune*. Music to soothe the early morning here at Radio Santa Ana."

Fritz cued up the record, turned to JD, pointed at the sleeping Canales.

"Look at him, he's got me playing music for siestas. If he doesn't wake up soon, I'll play the Russian army chorus and then Beethoven's *Eroica*. And the other bastards go on interfering with our signal from the mountain."

"Did anyone call?"

"About the dead woman? A lady who has a taco stand on Calle Lerdo, Doña Luisa, half a block from the church. She wouldn't tell me shit even though I told her I had a right to the information. She wants you to go by. Two calls threatening death to Benjamín, saying that now he's in deep shit."

"Is that normal?"

"Every other day."

JD saluted, lifting a finger to his cap, and went back to his office.

Barrientos was serving two cups of coffee when he entered.

"Esther says she can't leave the store right now, she's expecting some cartons of books from Mexico City and you should go by there or wait another half hour . . . They reported a robbery in the Conasupo warehouse, I sent Greñas out there."

"Is the bookstore far?"

"Five blocks alongside the main street, on Revolución, toward the south."

"I'll walk to the bookstore and then go by the jail to see the car, and from there I've got to see a lady at a taco stand in front of the church. You take charge of the robbery and when the Russian appears send him to sleep when Lómax and Merenciano report in . . . It's all very heavy. Sleep a bit here. Steal the cot from our neighbors at the radio."

Barrientos agreed.

The bookstore was very narrow, with two long series of shelves down the sides with floor-to-ceiling books and some small tables in the middle that ended with a desk that served as a counter and the owner's office. JD tried to go directly to her but could not. One and a half yards from the entrance he stopped in front of a bookcase of Latin American literature when he saw Soriano's *There Will Be No More Pain or Forgetting*. A book he'd been looking for for years. Beside it, *The Compañeros* by Rolo Díez, just out, a novel they talked about in Mexico City, about the last years of the Argentine madness and the guerilla movement. He went on browsing, squatting before the bookshelves. He had forgotten why he was there.

"It's true it doesn't look like a small-town bookstore, does it?" said Esther.

"Not at all," answered JD, finding a book of Onetti's stories in the Contemporary Times edition that he had owned and been robbed of years ago. Son of a bitch! There were the first two novels of Iverna Codina and *Bolero* by Lisandro Otero in Cuban editions.

"You have to sign your novels, José Daniel, here in the detective section."

JD took his books and followed the woman to the fourth bookcase. There were seven of his novels, some in old editions no longer on the market. Also the new detective story by Orlando Ortiz and some old editions of Caimán and the Seventh Circle.

"Ouf," said Chief Fierro.

"I knew you'd like it. We have books here you can't find anymore in Mexico City. I go out and buy things here and there. Look, I have something like fifteen books of the Maigret series by Simenon at five hundred pesos."

JD looked at the bookstore owner with admiration. It was much better to read than be chief of police. It made the question that followed an act of masochism.

"The gringa who was killed was here yesterday?"

"Anne? They killed Anne? I thought you wanted to talk about books. Nobody told me anything."

"Her name is Anne?" asked José Daniel, holding out some Polaroid photos. Esther stared at them.

"Poor sweetie."

"Have you known her a long time?"

"She came last year, she was the photographer for a magazine in Los Angeles. We're folkloric, a radical town and all that. She came to the demonstrations. She bought some books here, underground novels of the 1960s that I have in the back, the sort of thing the local gringos like. She was nice, spoke Spanish. This time she came to buy some books, she said she couldn't sleep. She bought a pocket edition of *The Naked and the Dead* by Mailer and a biography of Bob Marley. We talked for ten minutes. She looked tense."

"She didn't say who else she wanted to see? She didn't talk about Santa Ana?"

"She said she was going to take photos of the palm weaving cooperative at City Hall, and she wanted to see Benjamín, but she seemed to be thinking of something or somewhere else."

"And the gringos?"

"Which ones?"

"The ones who live in Santa Ana."

"They're a colony of some fifteen families, Vietnam veterans; almost all of them are retired with pensions for the disabled. With what they get, they live very well here. In Kansas City they would starve. They're nice, they keep their problems to themselves, they don't hang out much with natives like me. They all have something to do: a pottery kiln, one woman paints with watercolors, one studies German by correspondence and doesn't speak Spanish. They come here to buy books and place orders I fill through American Book in Monterrey. I never saw them with Anne."

"Nobody knew her yesterday but you tell me she was here last year taking photos."

"Just for a few days. I remembered her because one day we spent hours talking about photography books. She adored Robert Capa and Cartier-Bresson. She liked the same photographers as me."

"And me."

JD left the bookstore with forty-seven books and not a penny in his pocket. He had spent half his salary on books. He carried them in two packages tied with cord with the shotgun dangling from his back. It was a very strange war. He remembered the Capa photo of the dead parachutist and then immediately the posture of the woman in church. Were her cameras in the car? She too was a photographer.

The Russian showed him the open trunk, inside were the two cameras, a six-by-six Nikon and a Minolta with a wide-angle lens. The blue suitcase was there and the automobile registration with her data: Anne Goldin, 116 Riverview, San Jose, California, the books Esther had told him about, and a two-piece bathing suit, damp.

"Does anyone know how to take fingerprints?"

"Who knows, chief. I could ask Lorenzo, a friend in the PO who's a chemist for the University of Mexico."

"The judicials know we have the car here?"

"They haven't come by."

"Do we have police seals?"

"No. What's that?"

"Papers you tack on the doors with gum and a sign saying that the car is evidence and the seals can't be broken."

"I'll do it, that's easy."

"It won't work for shit," said José Daniel, just to be an ass. "Take my books and the suitcase with the cameras to the office, then make the seals, come and stick them on, and go home to sleep."

"Tomás told me they robbed the Conasupo, can I go?"

JD looked at him strangely. Of all his agents, Martín Morales, alias the Russian, was the taciturn, silent one. He was surprised at the vehemence, the determination in his voice.

"My sister is a cashier there."

JD nodded. The Russian began to carry everything on the back of the motorcycle using string to tie the load. JD left the patio of the jail and tried to orient himself. The church was six blocks down Calle Lerdo, and Lerdo was at the next corner.

He set off with a tired step. The sun shone on white walls, making the graffiti jump out. Lately the most common was a replica of the one the chief of police wore on his cap: SANTA ANA WILL WIN! Who conspired against the city by killing a blond North American, mother of a six-year-old child, and left her naked inside a church?

"There were two, chief," said Doña Luisa, but not before Chief Fierro had accepted a Corona Extra for the heat.

The woman pointed with her whole arm to the entrance to the church. JD nodded.

"I only saw them from afar, because I don't go in there. I'm Protestant, chief, and with the Popular Organization. But from far off I saw there were two guys who got into the car, one with a Stetson hat, the other in a suit. And I thought and I thought all night and I couldn't say anymore. I saw the car and half believed that that heretic priest, that bigmouthed ass-licker of the rich, didn't have a car and much less a red one, it wouldn't stick, and I saw the two leave and start the car. Then I went to see my comadre who's sick and so I didn't know about the trouble till my daughter told me, and I spent the night thinking on how the two of them looked, but I barely saw them. One with a Stetson and the other in a navy blue suit."

"Who drove, Doña Luisa?"

"Let me see," the woman frowned as if reconstructing the scene. "The one with the suit got in the driver's side because the one I saw better was the one with the hat."

"Would you recognize them?"

"Only if they're dressed the same, and you put them far away from me, or in other words I don't think so."

"I thank you very much."

"Get them, chief. Nobody should come to Santa Ana to kill nobody, even from the outside . . ."

"That's what I'm doing."

The woman took the empty beer bottle and gave José Daniel a kiss on the cheek. This disconcerted him. She was short and very fat and had to get on the tips of her toes to kiss him.

"It seems to me the priest is also a fag," she said, amplifying her information in farewell.

JD, who was of Jacobin background, nodded.

He entered the old black stone building surrounded by chattering secretaries returning from lunch. On the staircase the mayor, Benjamín Correa, waited for him, tense. He stopped in the middle of the stairs.

"They're going to try to stick me with the murder, chief," said Benjamín. "I was with her yesterday."

37. *Notes for the History of the Radical City Government of Santa Ana*
   José Daniel Fierro

When you try to put Santa Ana's tensions down on paper
to explain the radical government, its origins, the particular
convergence that permitted the union of forces that impelled
it, the weakness of the enemy that functioned like a stage
curtain for the convergence, one has to combine the study of
slow processes with rapid situations. Santa Ana, like anywhere
else in the country, moves with a combination of tensions
that come from the past, with the rapid succession of small
happenings that go on building into agitated waves. Macario,
the leader of the miners' union, tries to explain it when he
says that Santa Ana is a place where nothing happens because

everything happens. Nevertheless the city I'm getting to know doesn't look like the one they tell me about. I feel as if a backwater had been produced, a time of waiting, a stage when small events accumulate to unfold into something. As for Benjamín, if anything characterizes him it is an irrational sensibility of the social, he repeats to me every time he can: "Something is moving toward us and we still don't feel it, but it will be serious. They're very quiet." Not the product of conscious forces, or that's what he thinks, the government's enemies are waiting, or embarked on reorganization, in mythical operations that give no results, in moments of the great campaign of attrition, which is the only continuum one perceives here, or else they're preparing something big we don't know about. But there are other things, things in the air, responses to calls made a few years ago, illusions buried in the city, cold hearths that are warming. In the long run, Santa Ana is a pit in a country of injustices, there are debts two or three centuries' old, personal affronts that are historical and that originated one afternoon in April in the middle of the nineteenth century when the mine owner made the peons of shaft number two eat the flesh of a dog they had killed by accident.

In the short run, Benjamín's bearded ones have gone around to all the ranches to talk about irrigation and painfully organizing the campesinos of the seven municipalities around Santa Ana. In the short run there is a debate in every household with a child in the middle school over the workers' right to the factories where they work. In the short run there are tensions in the two small steelworks that are all that remain of the union booty of the CTM in the area. In the short run they speak of unionizing the maids, and say that two gunmen came from Mexico City to kill Benjamín.

In the long run there is the problem of the demarcation of

the lands between the colonies of Cerro Viejo and Don Sabás, which remains unresolved only by grace of the old man's machine guns. In the short run there is the debate over how to make the old movie theater a cooperative, and in the long run the debate over whether we should preserve the language of the two hundred Chichimeca campesinos of the Cañada. In the short run Don Eligio, the priest of Santa Isabel, reads liberation theology texts and in the long run the widows, daughters of miners' widows, dream of blood.

I know that I must put things down on paper to avoid surprises. Benjamín, who sees me taking notes, does not believe in private paper, and together with Fritz has spent a week designing a weekly wall newspaper.

38. Nothing to Do

The halls of the first floor of City Hall were occupied by the women of the straw hat weaving cooperative. Be it populist folklore or lack of space, Benjamín moves well among the women making the hats who fill up the space, many times up to the door to his office, joking and singing while they work. On the other hand, the representatives of the state and federal government feel like they're in enemy territory, watched over by witnesses who impede rule number one of Mexican political power: action in the shadows, the coverup. Benjamín's witnesses, symbolic representatives of Santa Ana, make City Hall into a kind of festive factory. The women, nearly all of them more than fifty years old (for this the factory was created, to give work to women who would not be given jobs in industry), have a curious attitude about Benjamín: they consider him a mixture of son and godfather, take care of his meals and pinch his butt when he goes by, bring him beer, and pretend not to notice when one of the secretaries spends more than half an hour alone in the office with its mayor.

José Daniel and Benjamín passed among them that morning, spattered with jokes and recently wetted straw. The office was curiously empty.

"I was with her yesterday afternoon," said Benjamín. "Women will be my ruin, José Daniel. They make me stupid. I met the little gringa last year when she was here shooting photos. Yesterday I ran into her in the street, she stopped her car and took me to the waterfalls, where we had a roll in the hay. But that's all, chief."

"What do you know about the child?"

"What child?"

"She had photos of a child. I believe a child of hers in California."

"First time I've heard. The truth is I don't know anything about her except her name was Anne and she was a photographer."

"Do you know if she had any other relations with the town?"

"I don't think so. Maybe with the gringo veterans, but the truth is I never saw her with them. That is, I never saw her. Last year two or three times when she took photos of the land seizure, and once when she took photos of me here in City Hall, and another time I found her in the bookstore and we had dinner together, but nothing more. She was a good person."

"Where were you going when you found her yesterday? What time was it?"

"Around five o'clock. I found her in Calle Revolución. Or rather she stopped her car and found me. I was coming from a meeting with the organizers of the La Libertad neighborhood, eating an ice cream, and she stopped behind me. A red car with California plates."

"What time did you leave her?"

"Don't you want a beer?"

"No."

"I left her . . . No, she left me here at City Hall, at the corner because the street is one-way, around nine o'clock, I had a cabinet meeting."

"Where were you at ten o'clock?"

"The meeting began around nine-fifteen; here are the minutes."

"They killed her at ten."

"Shit."

"So you have an alibi."

"For what it's worth . . . Who killed her?"

José Daniel shrugged his shoulders. Then he stretched out a hand for the offered beer.

"We found the car in front of the home of the PRI boss. Blind Man didn't dare go in to rouse them without consulting you first."

"The murderers took the car to that house or did they abandon it there?"

"I don't know. It all went very fast, it may be they were meaning to make it disappear."

"She took my photo at the waterfalls. There may be something else on that roll. Did you find the camera?"

JD nodded.

"We have a darkroom here in the offices of the PO, Sarita knows how to develop. Were they color or black and white?"

"Both."

"Chief, mount an attack on Melchor Barrio. If there's no proof, just tighten up. You have a free hand."

"And the judicials?"

"Them we have to stop in their tracks, so that they bite and don't fuck with the campesinos. No way, you'll have them on your back the whole way."

"You didn't have anything to do with the death of the gringa?"

"Nothing," said Benjamín looking him in the eye.

39. *Photos and Bribes*

Radio Santa Ana had been alternating the militant songs of Joan Baez with the more militant tunes of Quilapayún. José Daniel intuited problems while he played at dusting his table with one finger. Before him, Blind Man Barrientos ate tacos of fried pork fat in green sauce with absolute parsimony, not letting a single drop drip on his trousers.

"Let him tell you. I have nothing to say."

"Don't hand me that shit, Blind Man. There's no such thing as two loyalties. You should have told me that Benjamín knew the gringa."

"Who knew her? Benjamín? Let him tell you."

"He already did."

"Okay, so that's that. You just got here. Benjamín and I have always been here, what the fuck are you saying?"

"You can't play if you don't know the game."

"He already told you, didn't he?"

JD nodded and drew hearts and sketches of little paper boats.

"When they kill someone, who are we committed to, respected Blind Man?"

Blind Man concentrated on the pork fat.

"To the dead, right?" asked José Daniel.

"Depending on who dies. If it's the chief of the judicials or a gunman sent from the capital, let his fucking mother watch over him, and let his fucking mother look for the killer."

"This was a little gringa of twenty-five with a six-year-old boy, who took photographs."

"Benjamín didn't kill her. Benjamín couldn't kill a woman. You want the guilty ones? Let's go look for them, don't keep fucking with me, chief."

"Okay, then, love and peace," said José Daniel Fierro. "What's happening with the photos?"

"They must be ready, I'll go and get them."

Blind Man left, trying to balance his pork fat tacos. JD got up and reviewed the contents of the suitcase for the third time; he skipped the clothing, opened the passport and leafed through it again; he preferred this photo of Anne to the Polaroid shots of the body. The girl had crossed the border on the 19th, her passport said she was married, but did not give her husband's name. JD noted the address in San Jose on a piece of paper so he could send a letter. Should the murder be reported to the consulate? He put the books aside. No papers, no letters. Nothing to look at. He lit a cigarette and walked to the door. Only the photos could tell him something.

"Reporting in," said Greñas in the doorway, with his hair over his eyes and his cheeks red, almost purple.

"What happened, Marcelo?"

"The Russian is getting first-aid, he'll be right here. And we left the two assailants in jail, also getting first-aid. So they're all in jail, three of them, getting first-aid."

"What happened?"

"We got scientific, chief. It was a little robbery, a little tiny fucking robbery. Two kids with a knife who emptied one cashbox, not even two. I was dealing with that and calming the cashier, who was really frightened because they scratched her throat to scare her, and the fucking Russian arrived all bent out of shape and asked her who they were. And after not saying a word to me, she told him immediately. We set out for the billiards hall on Calle Cinco, and there they were, two assholes shooting pool. The Russian gave them time to get out their knives and then fucked them both up. He left me watching the party. He bit one in the arm and took out a piece of flesh. That motherfucker won't get better, chief. But he stuck him a little bit. Here and here. Superficial, not submarine, just on top." Greñas pointed at his thigh and his hands. "They had the money on them."

"How's the Russian?"

"Good, chief, he'll be right here. He told me you shouldn't worry, he'll be right here, he's just putting a bandage on."

"And how did science enter into the matter?"

"The way the Russian beat up two of them at the same time. A fine thing."

"Greñas, if you had to choose between your hairdo and your job, which would it be?"

"Is this a game or do I have to cut my mop?"

"A game."

"No, then let somebody else decide. It really doesn't bother me when I'm riding the bike because I tie it back, look."

Greñas demonstrated his Apache drag while Blind Man came in with the photos and spread them out on the table.

"One roll was blank, the color roll; the other had only six photos; four of Benjamín, one of the filthy Priísta, and the other of the cripple who lives across the street."

"In the street where we found the car?"

"Exactly. A rich guy who's always in a wheelchair."

Blind Man pointed with his finger. They were professional photos, shot with a wide-angle lens from very close up, and captured the expressions well. Melchor Barrio, the PRI boss, complacent under a wide-brimmed hat, a cold and angular face, prematurely aged. The invalid, a man some thirty-five years old with very black hair and eyes hidden behind dark glasses, smiling from a wheelchair that a butler in a white jacket with wide shoulders and shining face pushed toward the door of his house.

"Which was first?"

"The one of the Priísta and the guy in a wheelchair. Then the ones of Benjamín. Look at the shadows in this one, it's noon," Barrientos pointed out.

"We're going to visit the bad guy of the film," said José Daniel. After hesitating an instant, Blind Man opened a drawer in the file cabinet and took out the square .45, twin of the one he carried on his belt, together with a box of bullets.

"We're not waiting for the Russian?" asked Greñas. "There's a dozen killers in that house."

"We're just paying a call," said JD smiling. "They don't do anything to visitors."

40. *Dear Ana/April 21*

Dear Ana/April 21

Fritz Glockner made some kind of lay scapulars out of wood, the kind you hang around your neck with a leather thong, and put that phrase that Pablo Milanes made so famous: "No one is going to die, least of all now" inside them and we gave them to the Santa Ana police force. I tell you this because if they lose, it will be your responsibility not to recommend it.

I love you. JD

41. A Four That Comes Out Eight

But Greñas lifted the phone, and after listening five seconds stopped them with his hand.

"Benjamín says not to go anywhere."

"And how does he know we're going out?" asked José Daniel. "Give me the phone."

JD took the phone, his head was beginning to hurt. "Chief of Police, sir, stop by here," said Benjamín, a little more opaque than usual.

"Blind Man, I leave you in charge of the office, take a break," he said as he hung up. He deposited the shotgun behind the door and pressed his temples with two fingers.

"Do you have any aspirin?"

"No, but I'll get you some . . . Lulú, aspirin for the chief!"

*   *   *

Benjamín was seated very formally at his mayoral desk. José Daniel had never seen him thus. Always dancing among people and furniture, always fleeing the formality of you sit here and I sit on the side of power. Always with a button missing from his shirt sleeve, always with a sauce stain on the collar of his jacket, always with a beer in hand when it shouldn't be; always watching the wrong side of the office, the window, the city, contemplating other things.

"They are waiting for you. Inside Barrio's gunmen, outside Durán Rocha's judicial police. They're going to fill you with lead and then mount a riot so they can ask the army to intervene."

"And how did they know we were going there?"

"They have ears here."

"How did you know they were waiting for us?"

"They're not the only ones with ears. I have an enormous ear of a hundred seventy thousand little ears; many of them don't appear as such. What does your baseball cap say? 'Santa Ana will win.' Do you think we would put that on every yellow cap we can find if we didn't even have a chance?"

"Here are your aspirin, chief," said the secretary. JD threw them into his mouth without breaking them and swallowed them without water.

"You have to show me how to do that."

"A trained windpipe. Do you think I could write eleven novels without learning any tricks?"

"The worst is that Barrio believes we are pulling a trick on him. That we want to charge him with the death of the gringa, that's why he's acting so fierce."

"You mean you think he had nothing to do with it."

"You should find out. He or the fifteen killers who live in his house, or his secretary who's an asshole, who when he was in government and thought he owned the city raped ten-year-old girls. You'll see. Or do you want us to believe that he's enraged and in the end the murders are his?"

"What do you suggest?"

"That you wait and later go by yourself, or with all the Mexico City journalists we can get together."

"Let me think about it."

"Let me know. Things are heating up here."

"Anything I should know?"

"The rumor is that they're cooking up something big for us. That's why they're so quiet."

"So?"

"We can't stop, because if we stop we'll die a natural death. Listen, do me a favor: we need to distract the judicials, tomorrow there will be a big land seizure out by La Cañada. Two thousand campesinos with their families and everything. They've been preparing for months. Haven't you heard the rumors? They were communal lands and eleven years ago the caciques took them at gunpoint. Now there's a rumor going around: *Tomorrow we'll come back, tomorrow we'll come back.*"

"You mean I have to entertain the judicials and think about how to get at Barrio?"

"That's it."

"You know the city, Benjamín; who killed the gringa?"

"I have no idea, José Daniel, no fucking idea."

In the hallway he found Martín Morales, the Russian, with bandaged hands. JD put his arm across his shoulders, paternally, and they entered the office together, in silence, JD imagining ten thousand campesinos pulling out posts and wire fences.

"So what now, chief?" asked Blind Man.

"They're waiting for us."

"Are we going?"

"Not till they've stopped waiting . . . Russian, go and tell them at the radio to announce that the dead gringa's car was found in the street where that gorilla lives and that the investigation continues."

The Russian left to fulfill his commission. JD fell into a creaking armchair. Greñas and Barrientos watched him, waiting.

"Greñas, to the street, normal patrol. The town has to see that we're still keeping on."

Greñas left without saying a word.

"Let's see, Blind Man, who lives in those three houses where we found the car? Who is that cripple? What are the houses like inside? You who know everything and invent what you don't know, stuff me with information."

"Barrio's house, the first one, is big, with a garden of some thirty yards in front. I've never been inside. He must have a dozen gunmen, with automatic weapons. No family. No one can stand him. He has a daughter but she left years ago, she's a nurse, she lives in Mexico City . . . In the second house the man in the wheelchair. He's a millionaire, his name is López, he had an accident about five years ago and came to hole up in Santa Ana. They say his family was from around here. He had never been in town before, he was a jet-setter, Rolls-Royce, house in the United States . . . He never goes out. Sometimes doctors come from Mexico City. He has the fag in the photo and a maid, that's all. The fairy pushes the wheelchair and cooks. I've never seen him armed or anything . . . In the third house, on this side, in front of where we found the car, lives the widow of the Chinaman Ling, who owned all the big businesses of Santa Ana. The widow has enough money to paper her walls with. She lives with her daughter, who's very hot shit and wants to be a rock singer. Sometimes you see the young Chinese with the gringos from the Estrella colony. She can't sing for shit, but she comes on good, with that she'll triumph, right?"

"With less than that in Televisa they'll make a six-chapter series with ranchero ambience."

"With a Chinese?"

"With half, Barrientos. I can see you haven't been out much."

"Less than I wanted to, chief . . . Do you really think it's in that street? Just because of the car?"

"It's that you can see everything two ways. Either they had the car parked there because they didn't think we'd find it so quickly . . . but then they would have taken the suitcase and the cameras . . . Or someone put it there to tell us something or to tell them something. It's like those messages that come and go. Even though they don't want to say anything, if you know who they're for, you learn something."

"And why don't we look somewhere else? For the guy with the Stetson hat and the one in the navy blue suit. Them and the car between nine and ten last night."

"And how do you know that?" asked José Daniel, very surprised.

"I spoke with the lady too, chief. Did she give you a beer?"

JD nodded.

"And two for me. Because I'm a native."

JD smiled. "Leave it at that, I believe you . . ."

The chief of police of Santa Ana stopped, hearing cries in the street. It sounded like waves. He looked out the window.

A crowd of miners had congregated before the building, climbing the grillework of the church, raising their fists.

"Shaft number three is on a work stoppage, because of the uniforms . . . It's going to heat up," said Barrientos without looking outside.

JD was by now used to everyone knowing everything, except for him. "And what do we do now?"

"We have to put a guard at the entrance to the mine so the scabs don't enter and provoke fights."

In the street were some eight hundred miners whose slogans began to merge into one, "Santa Ana will win!"

"Chief, another one," said a red-faced Greñas, entering the office.

"Another what?"

"Another death." He let himself fall into the folding chair.

"Now what?"

"They found Blackie dead."

"The PRI gunman?"

"Exactly," said Blind Man. "Where?"

"In the circus, shot six times."

"Son of a bitch, are we going to see him first or shall we celebrate right now?" asked the assistant chief of police of Santa Ana with a smile that almost rattled his teeth.

42. Notes for the History of the Radical City Government of Santa Ana
José Daniel Fierro

Manuel Reyna, Blackie, has a dossier of some fifteen sheets in the files of the municipal police of Santa Ana. The purpose of the file is to preserve the town's history for the day of justice. Justice arrived and no one knows how. That left a strange taste in the mouth. The data now belongs to a cadaver tossed in the middle of the circus ring.

I have read the history twice: a salesman of agricultural machinery, albino, who got into heroin in the petroleum camps of Campeche, beat a woman to death, was tattooed with a plumed serpent on his left arm, and then appeared in Santa Ana to do the dirty work of the state government.

The brains behind every provocation, spearhead in every confrontation, he had (had had) a singular status, answering neither to Barrio nor to Don Sabás, nor to any of the local strongmen; he played ball with neither the judicials nor with those sent by Mexico City, but answered only to the state government. He did not live in town, he was not a tough guy tied by blood and debts to the needs of the local political bosses. He was a gunman on salary, solitary, who sometimes appeared over Santa Ana like a bird of bad omen, always keeping his back covered, always both far and near, always alone and with a fixed target.

In the file were two photos of the day he fired upon the demonstration from the cathedral with a machine gun. Blurred photos, Stetson hat(!). Then incidental news of his travels while the collective assassination got cold in the pages of the Mexico City papers.

An appearance three months ago heading up a group of gunmen hired by Don Sabás to fire on the campesinos of La Piedad ranch. A typed report that accused him of having killed Lisandro Vera, the student and first chief of police of Santa Ana, with his bare hands after having tortured him.

An Instamatic photo that showed him leaving a hotel on González Ortega with two suitcases.

To this one would now add the photos of his cadaver.

43. Watching the Trapeze

The circus had pitched its tents on the vacant lots alongside the highway access; two big tents and a dozen trucks with some mangy bears and zebras persecuted by flies.

In the sands of the central tent, surrounded by dwarfs and trapeze artists and constituting the after-dinner spectacle, Manuel Reyna, Blackie, was thrown down. Hunchbacked, his body giving the impression of furious activity despite its immobility, due to the .45 caliber bullets that had twisted him into knots, leaving him covered with entrance and exit wounds.

"Six shots, chief, all of them mortal, as they say."

"And his pistol, was it fired?"

"No, chief, they got him shitting. He must have got it out when he felt the first bullet, but didn't even have a chance to play with it," said Barrientos, who bit a toothpick between his teeth to keep from smiling.

"Are you happy, Barrientos?"

"I'm sorry it wasn't me who got him."

"Let's see! Don't move around too much . . . What is this? These are the boots of Greñas, and these are mine, look at the defect in the left heel. And those? Make a drawing of them. Surely they're the same as the bloodstains in the church. We need photos. Greñas, go get the teacher's Polaroid."

The best thing to do when faced with a corpse is to have no respect. So you can treat it like an object, without your heartbeat accelerating and your guts turning over. JD took his pulse. It was warm. Macabre cadaver of the albino. Unreal.

"What time was he found?"

"Here is the gentleman," said Greñas, taking the hand of a dwarf who quietly let himself be led to the writer.

"How did you find him?"

The dwarf put on his best circumstantial face to tell the story. "We waited till the shooting stopped and then picked straws to see who would come. There he was. Three-thirty in the afternoon, just a little while ago."

"Did you see him arrive?"

"It was dinnertime."

JD lifted his gaze to the immobile trapezes, the sky that peeked through the holes in the tent, then lowered it to the dead albino. Seen from afar he seemed to be smiling. As if saying, "Just look where I ended up."

"Barrientos, interrogate everyone, find out if they saw any cars at the entrance. Look at the tents. We are on open ground, the two guys arrived from somewhere, the dead man and the killer or killers. This one came from González Ortega as far as we know, he got here somehow. Look for the shells, here's one, there should be six. Take his boots off. Take his pistol and put it in a bag and bring it to the office. I'll be there."

44. The Scent of Seven Machos

One of the few Mexican contributions to the world of scents and perfumes is the cologne Seven Machos. Used in thousands of third-rate barber shops, it has an indescribable odor of overripe violets and cane alcohol. This is what José Daniel Fierro put on after shaving, and with two stiffs in the closet and only two and half hours' sleep on his bones, he went out walking in Santa Ana unarmed and without his cap. The absence of the gun was a matter of comfort; that of the cap, the vague impression that to wear it too much on sunny days would make him bald.

He left the door of the Hotel Florida and headed off to the right. The sun shone even at five in the afternoon, burning the asphalt and drying the few puddles left by the fruit vendors'

melting ice. He advanced down Calle Revolución looking in
the windows of the Chinese shopkeepers and the shoestores of
Guanajuato industrialists who had come with their new boots
to colonize the north of the country at the beginning of the
1980s. Once in a while he passed a traditional hardware store
owned by a Spaniard with a name like Casa Toledo or Los
Fierros de Oviedo, then two bakeries, a repair shop for agricultural machinery, a seed warehouse, a uniform shop. Arriving at the Cine Río, where they were showing *Nocaut,* he
stopped to wait for the judicial who was following him.

"Do you have a moment, writer?" asked Durán Rocha.

"If the chat takes place in front of witnesses, I have no
problem," said JD, smiling and at the same time feeling his
asshole pucker up a bit. The chief of the judicial police based
in Santa Ana awakened his deepest infantile terrors: with a tic
that distorted his upper lip; a scarred face lost forever to any
form of human encounter, forever calculating although there
was nothing to calculate; with cold eyes that had spent thirty
years burning in hell, Durán Rocha inspired panic in him.
But JD had learned to transform his fears into words typed on
a typewriter, and overcame his first impression.

"Right here, in the park."

They walked on, looking for shade under the laurels and a
bench. They sat at a distance, leaving the center of the bench
free, an uninhabitable space, a no-man's-land between them.

"You have nothing to do with this," Durán Rocha began.
"This little game will be over one of these days and you will
leave as if you'd never been here. Neither coming nor going.
Santa Ana is not your concern. Your concerns are the letters
defending human rights and the demonstrations in support of
Nicaragua in Mexico City, cocktails at the Yugoslav embassy . . ."

"I've never been to the Yugoslav embassy, now that you mention it."

". . . and other such bullshit."

They were silent for a moment.

"The gringa and Blackie don't mean shit to me. There is already so much fucking death in this town that two more don't even give me insomnia at siesta time. I don't give a fuck who did it, it may be I did it and didn't notice. Or one of you, to heat things up. I don't give a shit. What I do want is for you to stop setting the journalists on my ass, because if you do it again, I'll kill you. You and all those fucking crippled assholes of the municipal cops. I'll make mincemeat out of you."

"You know what the big difference is, Durán? It's that they're going to kill you in cold blood. Nameless women will drag your cadaver through the streets, spitting on you. You won't even be buried. But if you kill me, you'll have more journalists here than ever before, and they'll give me a funeral that will keep you awake nights. What do you think?"

"Once we're dead it's all the same. If the buzzards shit on me or if they put flowers on your dick, I don't give a fuck."

José Daniel meditated on this response. The nearby benches were filling up with spectators. That was the curse of Santa Ana: you had to hide your fear and play to the audience. It was worse than in Hollywood; one put one's face on display for everyone.

"Who killed them, Durán?"

"I already told you I don't give a shit. I kill with a telegram in hand and there was no telegram for those two. Get out of this fucking town or you and I will not get old together."

José Daniel got up and looked down at the man sweating in a dark suit. He couldn't tell him that he was already aged by their chat. He turned on his heel and left the chief of the judicial police talking to himself before the rapt looks of the spectators, and left behind him the potent odor of Seven Machos.

45. Are You Writing a Novel?

"We have seven reporters from Mexico City, two from Monterrey, and even one from *El Sol de San Luis Potosí.*"

"Send them to the chief of the judicials, and then to Barrio's, tell them the car appeared in front of his house. And then tell them we'll have the pleasure of speaking with them at seven-thirty."

"Can they take a photo of me with the red car, chief?" asked Lómax.

"Whatever they like, my son," responded José Daniel Fierro, paternally. He was dying from lack of sleep.

"The guys at the radio want you to go by and see them for a minute. And Benjamín is waiting for you in his office when you're free," said the Russian.

"How are your hands?"

"Better."

"Tell them both I'm coming."

He remained alone in the room with Blind Man Barrientos. JD lit his tenth cigarette. He was beginning to like the proletarian Delicados.

"What do you think?"

"You first. You're smarter in these things," replied Blind Man.

"There's something that doesn't fit and then many things that even though they don't fit are from the same puzzle. The guys who fired at me in the lunchroom. Do you know anything about that? Who they were? Who they could be?"

"I think they were Blackie's people. If you want I'll go looking in that direction. Shit, so much has happened in just a few days. Now all I need to do is get married."

"And do you have someone to marry?"

"Two," said Barrientos, smiling. "If I don't get married it's because I can't decide for the life of me . . . They look alike. They even have the same name: María, both of them, one just María and the other María Elena . . . But I wish all this noise would die down before I get married, I don't want to leave a widow."

Barrientos was seated on the file cabinet and smoking too, throwing his ashes behind him. José Daniel would have liked to have a tape recorder and make the whole story into a novel, two novels, three novels.

"I keep wondering why the car should have stayed on that street. It pushes me toward Barrio, toward the lame millionaire and the Chinese widow. It gets to me. It's too easy."

"That's probably why they put it there."

"Do you know something I don't know?"

"I know how to shoot."

"And aside from that?"

Blind Man Barrientos shook his head.

"I'll be right back. I'm going to see Benjamín and then to the radio station."

JD left the office, went through the halls and climbed the stairs with a dancer's tread. He went into Benjamín's office without meeting anyone. Around a small round table, bottles of beer in front of them, were the mayor, the lawyer Mercado, Macario, the leader of the miners, two other miners he didn't know, and a campesino who looked very young.

"Am I interrupting?"

"Not at all, chief, we're talking about you and your murders," said Mercado.

"Anything new?" asked JD, pulling a chair up to the space they made for him at the table.

"In *El Heraldo* of the capital they say that the gringa was Benjamín's lover and that he killed her," said Mercado, laughing.

"I spoke with the governor's secretary and he said very nicely that if we push the people against Barrio and cause a riot they will fill the town with soldiers, but he said it as if they would do it anyway."

"That shit is always political," said Macario. "What if it was a crazy person?"

"What if it *was* a crazy person," repeated José Daniel, taken by the thought. "Or two crazy people, one for each crime. Or one of one and the other of others. Didn't we want to kill the albino?"

"It was vile justice, but if I had done it, or Blind Man, or Macario here, we would have taken him in González Ortega, or in Mexico City when he went for morphine at Barrio's daughter's sanatorium."

"The nurse?"

"What fucking nurse? She's the owner of a sanatorium in Las Lomas and she trafficks in drugs with medical prescriptions . . . Fucking rich bitch. Didn't you see the scars on the dead guy's hand?"

"New ones?"

"Old ones, on the right hand. Barrio has some too. They sat at the table in front of each other. They didn't like each other at all, but they used each other. They put a bottle of tequila in the middle and each one lit a cigarette, and then they took turns burning each other's hands, first Barrio to Blackie, then Blackie to Barrio, and the one who stopped smiling was the loser. Fucking pair of jerkoffs."

"Chief, whatever we tell you, you won't know the half of it. There are more than one hundred women in Santa Ana who have the same scars on their hands, from the days when that son of a whore was mayor. Blackie killed Valentín's brother and cut off his balls, and then went and threw them in front of his family's house," said Mercado, pointing to the young campesino. He got up and walked, stumbling a bit, to a bucket full of bottles of beer.

"We're all getting a little bit crazy from all the shit that's come down," said Macario.

"What should I do?" asked José Daniel, suddenly trapped in the vortex of Santa Ana's underworld, tossed by emotions and memories, watching Valentín's knuckles get white around the bottle of beer.

"This is a case for the police. Not to make any grand claims for the Santa Ana force, but before the inefficiency of the judicials, who dedicate themselves only to persecute campesinos and take care of the marijuana dealers so they can get their cut, we must take charge of the investigation. This is the official story and the real one for once. Here no one asks for anything to be covered up. Only for us to act together, because if we fuck up they will bring in tanks and chariots on parade and the most beautiful flowers of the army."

"To say nothing of their pricks," said one of the miners sagely.

"That goes without saying."

"You could have warned me when you brought me here," said JD.

"If we had known we probably would have stayed with you," said Macario.

"No, about the rain, that it doesn't rain," finished JD and left without hearing their laughter.

Another seven halls, another twelve steps. Canales was waiting for him, smoking in the doorway of Radio Santa Ana.

"That asshole Fritz says nobody can smoke in the control room. He's nuts, that guy."

"Let's give him a Veracruz cigar to see if he can resist," said JD, and entered the cabin with the cigar held out in front.

Fritz saw it in the corner of his eye while he was speaking lovingly into the microphone. JD had noticed this before. This amorous relationship, broadcaster/microphone, almost masturbatory, the way professionals took it and caressed it, spoke to *it*.

"Songs for lovers at dusk in the voice of Angélica María of the 1970s, when to be in love was a challenge to destiny. Songs for lovers who are tired and nostalgic, or for irresponsible youth who don't buy their toothpaste in the Campos pharmacy, sponsor of this program . . ."

Fritz let go of the console switch and started the turntable, giving the lever a shove with his elbow. Professional skill.

"Thanks, man," he said, appropriating the cigar and lighting it without further ado.

"We wanted you to tell us how things are going," said Canales to José Daniel but looking at Fritz with murderous fury.

"There's not much to say. Everything is still very nebulous."

"As they say, the novel is at the stage of investigation. When there are so many false leads you don't know where you're going."

"The truth is that in mine everything is pretty clear. I'm going to give a press conference and when I arrange my thoughts to speak with the journalists I'll come and give you the news."

In the middle of the hallway Barrientos was fending off journalists, an ill-tempered look on his face.

"Good evening, colleagues." A pair of flashbulbs went off.

"What do you think of this affair? Not exactly a novel, is it, José Daniel?" said the correspondent of *La Jornada.*

"Do the two murders have anything in common?" asked the one from *El Sol de San Luis Potosí.*

"The commander of the judicial police says that you are an intellectual from the capital who never saw a dead person before. That it was irresponsible of the government to have named you chief of police, and of you to have accepted," said the one from *El Porvenir* in a northern accent.

"Have they identified the dead gringa? Why was she killed in church? Why did they kill that gunman at the circus?"

"Have there been crimes like this here before?"

"Are you going to write a book about all this?"

"Do you know how many killers there were?"

"When are you going to resign?"

"It is true that you have a shotgun and don't know how to take off the safety?"

"How many cops are on the force?"

"Aren't the crimes out of your jurisdiction?"
"How old are you, José Daniel?"
"Are you writing a novel?"
"Are you writing another novel?"
"Are you writing a novel about all this?"

46. Dear Ana/April 21 (II)

━━━━━━━━━━━━━━━━━━━━━━━━━━━━━━━━━━━

Dear Ana/April 21

Me again, but this time not to ask for anything (you could certainly send me the green stapler, though), but to send you a draft of a novel—keep it, it may be that one day I'll write it.

It is a novel of some very fucked-up crimes, but the important thing is not the crimes, but (as in every Mexican crime novel) the context. Here one rarely asks oneself who done it, because the killer is not the one who wants the death. There is a distance between the executioner and the one who gives the orders. The important thing is usually the why.

And so I think this is the story of various whys. The characters are not, as my neighbors at the radio station would say, very lucid; they are more opaque.

There is a touch of exoticism: an American, but she always appears out of place, accidental, caught in a story that is not hers.

There are other characters who are more sordid, more common. It is not the first time they have been involved in a crime, more likely it is the millionth time. Saint-Exupéry would identify them by their hearts, Lombroso by their looks.

They follow the very Mexican trade of hired killer.

I would like to work with that, but I can't identify with those characters, I don't know if their hands sweat or if their eyes water when they exercise.

In this novel they stink, because they dirty the landscape of a city in which there are neither beggars nor rain.

Two hundred pages of the novel must be dedicated to the absence of beggars and to tell how the cacti flower on the slopes of the mountain range; a good chunk to tell of the days of rain. The rest, only the rest, could be dedicated to these grim characters who spoil the landscape. What do you think?

I love you. JD

47. The Smell of Marijuana

He had asked the switchboard to put in a call to Marc Cooper in Los Angeles, an old friend who was a journalist, with whom he had once written the screenplay to a movie, and was stretching himself in the armchair that creaked as much as his joints when the call came through. He spoke with Marc for five minutes at the city's expense, mixing Spanish and English as the words halted or flowed over the telephone line. He was hesitating between a brandy or a coffee when Merenciano appeared: shining, recently bathed, with his hair plastered to his skull.

"Now go to sleep, chief, I'll leave you the patrol car and pick it up later at the door to your hotel. Leave the keys at the desk."

"You'll let me know if something happens?"

"I should let you know if something happens?"

"Exactly, and tell Blind Man to go and sleep, that we'll see each other tomorrow morning and he can tell me . . . If you have a chance, find out all you can about the Chinaman and his widow, Mrs. Ling. Do that for me."

"Mrs. Ling?"

"Exactly."

At the hotel desk they gave him a message before giving him the key:

"There is a gentleman waiting for you in the bar."

He was bald with a gray moustache, with good healthy color, dressed in a black leather jacket and gloves. He looked almost like a paternal and televisable bank official. Too bad about the troubled look and watery eyes.

"You don't know me, I am Sabás, but surely you have heard of me," he said, offering his hand. "I sent you a gift when you arrived and you returned it. Very bad manners."

The bar was empty, with a bored waiter and a television that nobody was listening to. Don Sabás had a bottle of cognac and two glasses in front of him. José Daniel served himself a double (or a triple, depending on the measure) and sat back stretching his legs and leaving the shotgun leaning on the table between them.

"I came to ask you a favor." Don Sabás spoke very slowly, relishing the vowels, as if his companion was slow to understand. "Because you are not from around here, I do not know what you have heard about me; and as we haven't had the pleasure of meeting, I wanted to come and chat with you in person, without onlookers or intermediaries or messengers. I came to tell you that the affair has nothing to do with me. The two murders have nothing to do with me."

"And how am I supposed to know that?" asked José Daniel.

"Because if they were mine I wouldn't come to tell you anything."

"And what are you going to tell me?"

"Things."

"Okay, then tell me."

"I don't know if I should . . ."

JD got up, tossed down the rest of his cognac, and picked up the shotgun.

"When you want to tell me, give me a call. I'm too tired for this today."

"Sit down, don't be so impatient. Just think, you've been in such a hurry you haven't learned some of the things you should know."

"Like what?" asked José Daniel without sitting down.

"Like that the mine is stealing silver. They don't declare a third of what they extract. They are robbing the country. Silver goes from here to the border as contraband."

"I have two corpses, and you say they're not yours. I've been in Santa Ana for one week and the only thing I know is that I don't know why they would be yours, and so, with you here telling me they are not yours, the first thing I think is that they are. I don't know you even by hearsay, and the only thing they tell me is that the hundred and fifty-three kilos of marijuana that we captured the other day were your property, and not for you to smoke by yourself. Now you tell me some bullshit about the mine, and next you'll read me the program for the circus tomorrow . . . Either tell me who's responsible for two murders or we'll each go home to bed."

"Son of a bitch, but you're impatient."

"To be patient one needs eight hours' sleep."

"The gringa was killed by two guys, okay? One you already know, the other was Durán Rocha, head of the judicials."

JD sat down and served himself another double/triple cognac.

"Why?"

"Why else? Because they were paid to do it."

"By who?"

"That would cost more."

"How much more?"

"To forget about my ranches from now till the end of the year."

"Good night," said José Daniel and this time he did not even look back after saying goodbye.

48. Land

A tense voice on the loudspeakers of Radio Santa Ana woke him up:

"Compañeros, they are invading the estates of La Cañada. The campesinos of San Carlos and Los Horizontes are taking back the land of La Cañada. Everyone to La Cañada to support them and offer solidarity with them . . . Attention, people of Santa Ana, the campesinos of Los Horizontes are taking back the estates of La Cañada . . ."

The town bells were ringing. José Daniel got up and put his face under the tap, letting the cold water run. At the door of the hotel Blind Man was at the wheel of the patrol car.

"I thought you might want to go."

JD threw his shotgun in the back seat and straightened his

baseball cap in the rear-view mirror. His kidneys hurt. An old sign of fear.

"Is this inside or outside the municipality?"

"Outside, in the neighboring municipality, San Sebastián."

"So we're there as observers."

"No, in solidarity," said Blind Man, starting the car.

The secondary highway was full of people walking the shoulders on both sides, some with banners and signs. Many striking miners from shaft number three, all the students of the secondary school in their green sweaters, the market women, even the three trucks from the Coca-Cola plant where the unionized prostitutes traveled with red banners instead of bottles.

The police car advanced through the middle of the crowd, among sporadic applause.

"The takeover was at dawn. Everything quiet until now, is what they tell me," commented Blind Man.

"Yesterday I was thinking I don't know how to fire the fucking shotgun," said José Daniel.

"When we go back we can stop around here and I'll teach you."

"Were the boot prints the same?"

"They were different, but we don't know which prints to match with which boot."

"Blackie with the blood print in the church. That's easy."

Blind Man looked at him with a mixture of suspicion and admiration.

"You want more? The print of the boot in the circus will fit the boots of the chief of the judicials."

"Son of a bitch, you're not going to put me in the shade," responded Blind Man. "The guy who fired on us in the lunch-room, the one who ran out, is in González Ortega, hiding in a hotel and shitting with fear."

"And what does he do there?"

"He's waiting for something. And I was right, he was one of Blackie's men. Only now he's left without a boss."

The crowd went off to one side of the highway where you could see torn-down fencing. Behind them, on a small peak, a red flag.

"Shall we visit?"

They saw small fires. The invaders were eating breakfast. José Daniel thought that he would sell his kingdom for some frijoles charros.

49. Raining in Santa Ana

It was raining in Santa Ana when they returned. The city had changed into a phantom collection of little streets whipped by sheets of water that veered from one side to the other of the avenue tossed by wind as if from buckets. The streets appeared narrower and José Daniel realized that the city was sloped and descended to its center; he saw the little rivers of water that poured down the sides of Calle Revolución toward the plaza.

"Do you like the rain?"

"Very much," replied the chief of police. "Do you?"

"It makes me sad," said Blind Man Barrientos. He drove in silence and stopped the car before City Hall. They got out trying to protect themselves under the eaves of the first-floor balconies.

The first sign of alarm hit when they reached the second landing and saw the crowds of people.

"Something in the office?" asked Blind Man and they both ran. The thickest crowd was in front of the door to Radio Santa Ana. José Daniel and Blind Man made their way through. Desolate, Canales and Fritz were contemplating the broadcaster's chair, which they normally shared. A tape spun, whipping its tail. There was a man in the control chair with his back to the door. Blind Man, faster than the chief of police, spun the chair around. The body of Durán Rocha, chief of the judicial police in Santa Ana, stared at them, a third eye some inches from his nose crusted with dry blood and burned flesh. *The vultures have accompanied him*, thought JD.

"Let's go, kid," said Fritz. Canales came over to the microphones and changed the switch. Fritz stopped the tape and passed him the mike.

"We lament the temporary suspension of our transmissions, but we are here in the studio of Radio Santa Ana with Chief of Police Fierro and Assistant Chief Barrientos, performing the preliminary investigation of a crime." The voice of Canales, which trembled at the start, was gaining confidence. "Live from our studio, where someone put a dead man while those in charge of Radio Santa Ana went out to eat . . ."

"There's no blood, he was killed somewhere else," said Barrientos.

"That's true."

"Chief Fierro and Assistant Chief Barrientos comment that the cadaver is the man in charge of the judicial police here in Santa Ana, the famous and little-loved Durán Rocha, and also comment that the assassination was not committed here, as there are no signs of blood. The dead man is found in the chair that your servants normally occupy, so that we will have

to change the chair in the future. He has a hole in his fore-
head . . ."

"A small caliber bullet, a .22, fired close up."

"He's cold," said JD.

". . . And was killed hours ago, because as you've been able
to hear, the body is cold."

"Is there anyone in our office?"

"Do you need anything, chief?" asked Juan Carlos Canales
solicitously. José Daniel couldn't help smiling.

"Please tell the members of the police force to report here
along with someone with a Polaroid camera. Shit, let's see if
we can take up a collection and buy one. And a doctor."

"You've already heard, esteemed radio listeners of Santa
Ana. Chief Fierro needs his crew, a doctor, and a Polaroid
camera, as a gift if possible . . ."

"Blind Man, take prints of his boots."

Fritz touched his arm.

"Benjamín is calling on the intercom."

JD took the apparatus.

"Three judicials are on their way. Avoid trouble. Negotiate.
We don't want any gunfire or trouble. If you want I'll come
down and lend a hand."

"I'll take care of it," replied JD and then said in Barrientos's
ear: "Blind Man, search him and keep everything in a bag.
The traitors are on their way."

Blind Man cocked his .45 without taking it out of its holster,
and then went looking through the dead cop's pockets, putting
the papers he found into a can for recording tape.

A small commotion at the entrance announced the arrival
of the three judicials. The one leading them was wild-eyed,
pistol in hand, shoving with his elbows.

"And now we have here with us three abusive members of

the dead man's police force who are elbowing the onlookers crowding into the door of our studio."

"What the hell is going on here? Who killed the chief?" said the man.

"We know as much as you do. They put him here at dinnertime, when no one was here."

"We'll take charge of the investigation," said the man pushing JD. Suddenly he bent over. Blind Man had taken advantage of the crowd of people to shove the barrel of a .45 in his kidneys.

"You are listening to . . ."

"Just don't push."

"There's a doctor and a photographer on their way."

"No way, we're taking him. So, the crime didn't take place here?" said a second judicial, struggling to get through.

JD pointed to the chair.

"Look, no signs of blood. He's cold. They put him here. Someone wants to confront us."

"Son of a bitch, you are now confronted. If I see you . . ." said the judicial in a louder voice.

"Show some respect, asshole," said Blind Man, shoving the barrel a bit more.

"We are not responsible before the Radio Commission for the bad language emitted in this transmission live from the studios of Radio Santa Ana . . ." said Canales, now truly relishing the affair.

50. Notes for the History of the Radical City Government of Santa Ana
José Daniel Fierro

~~~~~~

Santa Ana was founded by a man who wanted to die and not leave shit behind him. One Hernán Villalar, who had gotten lost on the silver trails on the way from Zacatecas, who carried a Chichimeca arrow in his back that he couldn't get out and that was poisoning his blood. He stayed here because he found two runaway Negroes named Simón and Sebastián who hunted birds with slingshots and gave him bird soup to eat. The fact that this happened in the middle of the seventeenth century does not prevent the official story from having always been played essentially as the adventures of disillusioned men, with no love of life, who founded great wealth without meaning to.

And so the second character in the history of Santa Ana is one of the Salinas family, Frenchified landowners who robbed land from the communities, the land of Indians released from the mines, taking advantage of 19th century land reforms. A Salinas who answered to the literary name of Edmundo, and who committed suicide twice, the first time in Santa Ana with poisoned port wine and the second time in Barcelona when it occurred to the imbecile to challenge a pimp from Seville to a duel, and with that he entered the Pearly Gates.

Santa Ana has had a pianist of moderate fame, and a pair of bucolic poets who achieved distinction in the days of Porfirio Díaz. The three died of tuberculosis, colluding in the creation of the necrophiliac phantom that feeds on the traditional history of the city.

The phantom is nourished by the doings of an Englishman, general manager of the mines, who suffered from chronic boredom, and who collected sexual perversions, albums of photos and paintings of nudes by folk artists. They cut his throat, fortunately in Torreón, while he was taking a Christian boy whose cousin was expert with a razor.

After 1923, the story of the bad-blooded aristocracy was transformed into that of well-fed caciques, beginning with an Obregonista colonel named Salustio, maternal grandfather of Barrio. With him the dross of the postrevolution made its day, building on the stories of others, those who filled the ravines with wheat and excavated the tin to fill the dozens of thousands of wagons, and partook, why not, of the legendary suicides and tuberculars.

The colonel had a niece who threw herself from the church belfry after abusing cough syrup and believing she could fly. But this is a minor story, and the tradition is disappearing.

Since 1972, the Popular Organization entered the chronicle, the chroniclers changed, the big collective characters showed their teeth, threw flowers, and drank beer.

51. New Science

He waited for Popochas/Lómax to count his money and took his place before the cashier. The Santa Ana police were paid at the end of the first and third week of the month (that is, around the 7th and 22nd of each month) and JD was paid his first complete month (a bonus for the shooting, Benjamín had said). After receiving the envelope he stepped aside to let Barrientos take his place before the cash drawer and he started counting the notes.

"Do they make mistakes sometimes, Popochas?"

"No, but it gives me great pleasure to count them."

Instead of going up to his office JD walked to the gate at the entrance to watch the rain. *What a shitstorm*, he thought, while the wind occasionally tossed water in his face.

"You have a call from the United States in the office, chief!" shouted Popochas from the first floor. JD went up running. Barrientos held the phone with one hand and a pen and piece of paper in the other.

"Marc! What do you know?"

His friend's voice, half in English and half in Spanish, began to unfold a story from nine hundred miles away.

JD noted on his paper: *single mother, without husband.*

He drew a butterfly. *Child with grandparents. Grandfather says child's father is Mexican. Friend's darkroom: strange stories father child. She never spoke. Mexico City seven years ago.* He drew a second butterfly.

"Are they coming for the body? You're coming? The *L.A. Times* will pay you? Next week? Yes, of course . . . Bring aspirin . . . A hug, old man."

He hung up and gazed at the paper.

"The Traitor had a bank account," said Barrientos, putting a checkbook on the table. "It says here he made a deposit of a million pesos yesterday," he said, showing the bank receipt.

"Anything else in his papers?"

"A letter from a whore in Juárez asking for money for her child."

"Everyone has children scattered around up there."

"Where are we going, chief? To González Ortega to look for Blackie's helper? To the street where we found the car, to talk to the three neighbors? To walk around town and be seen?"

"What about the boot print?" asked José Daniel.

"What do you know, it's the same."

"Popochas, get out the chalkboard."

"Are we going to have a science class, chief?"

"We're going to put things in order."

José Daniel looked out the window. The rain was stopping. The town outside the window was still the same Santa Ana, but he was not the same innocent stranger of the first days. Was it the rain? or so many things in so little time? The rain, he decided.

"Let's see. If this were a novel we would not need science— it would be clear as day that the Chinese widow hired the judicial cop and Blackie to kill the gringa, and then the cop killed Blackie and the Chinese killed the cop. Since it is not a novel, let's put what we do know on this side:

"Between nine and ten at night on April 20, they killed Anne Goldin with a kitchen knife in the church of Carmen. Two men: one we know by his boot prints is chief of the judicials, Durán Rocha, and the other, who was wearing a Stetson hat, could be Blackie . . ."

"What should I put on the chalkboard?"

"April 20, Anne/knife/nine to ten/Durán Rocha and Blackie, that last with a question mark at the end . . . Exactly. What questions shall we ask, Assistant Chief Blind Man?"

"How much does a bottle of Bacardi cost if the price of sugarcane in Veracruz has gone up seventeen percent in the last year and the vampire on the label is more cross-eyed than ever?"

"Where do I put that?" asked Popochas.

"Nowhere. All right, Blind Man, leave literature for Canales's garret. Questions?"

"Why? Why in the church and naked? Who paid?"

"Okay, put under Durán Rocha the million pesos that we know he had in the bank . . . How did those two get along?"

"Not very well. Gypsies don't read each other's hands. But it was competition. Durán Rocha had more friends among the town Priístas, he hung out more with them. Blackie was solitary. He came and went. For example, I never saw the two together."

"Neither did I," said Popochas.

"Neither did I, chief," said Greñas, joining the group of scientists.

"Okay, we'll go for the second round: the red car. The killers took it. It appears an hour and forty-five minutes later in a street where there are three houses."

"What do I write?"

"Red car. Street . . . What is the name of that street?"

"La Escondida."

"So. Then three houses: Widow Ling, Barrio, what is the cripple's name?"

"López, Engineer López."

"Okay. Greñas, why did the car appear there?"

"The murderers put it there to get something, to make a point."

"And why didn't they? The suitcase was inside. Why abandon it there?" It was becoming an inquiry, Maigret-style, but with too many questions.

"To confront Barrio," said Blind Man.

"They left the car in front to pressure one of the owners of the three houses. To increase the pressure to get more money. That's why the car was there. They left it there as a calling card," said JD, proudly.

"I like it," said Blind Man.

"Let's see, they paid those two bastards to kill Anne," said JD, nearly spoiling everything by using her name. Anne suddenly reappeared, a twenty-five-year-old California girl with a six-year-old son, not material to make "science" out of.

"Coffee, chief?" said Barrientos, guessing that something was going on. Merenciano entered the office in silence and took a chair, behind him, the Russian. The Santa Ana forces were complete.

JD nodded.

"So, after killing her they take the car and leave it in front of the house of the one who ordered her killed, as a reminder that he owed them something. What do you think?"

"Weren't they taking a risk?"

"We worked very quickly that night, didn't we."

"I guess so," said JD, feeling that after all the clarification nothing was particularly clear. "Third, we know that the judicial killed Blackie at the circus. Six shots from a .45 . . . What pistol did he carry?"

"A .45, like two thousand other inhabitants of Santa Ana, like me," said Blind Man.

"And fourth," continued JD without stopping, "whoever killed him ordered the murders."

"Why in the circus?"

"How the fuck would I know?" replied José Daniel.

"Really," said the Russian. "And why at the radio station?"

"In the church, in a circus, in the radio station . . . It seems to me they want to start an uproar in Santa Ana."

"That points to Barrio," said JD. "The more you know, the less you know, and you know why? Because the more you know, the more questions you can ask."

JD knew he had a story in his head that had formed watching the rain, but it was too literary, too much like a novel to be the truth.

"Who was the last person to see the judicial cop alive? I saw him yesterday in the park at five o'clock in the afternoon. After that . . ."

A hypothesis occurred to him, even more like a novel, without any foundation. A hypothesis that implied there had been a traitor in Santa Ana. That happens in novels, doesn't it? And he had even another hunch, but the story of the Chinese widow belonged to another novel. He had to move, science wouldn't provide the answers he was looking for.

"Greñas and Russian, your turn to investigate the movements of the judicial cop since yesterday. Barrientos, could you get Blackie's helper from the hotel and bring him here?"

"We don't have jurisdiction there. I'd have to go in unarmed."

"Can you?"

"I'll bring him."

"Popochas, get the motorcycle ready, we're going to see the gringos."

Like a small army, the members of the Santa Ana police force began to clean their pistols, smooth their moustaches, comb their hair, shake off fatigue. Better to get moving than to study science.

"And me?" asked Merenciano.

"It's your turn to erase the chalkboard."

52. Tattoos

▲▲▲▲▲▲▲▲▲▲▲▲▲▲▲▲▲▲▲▲▲▲▲▲▲▲▲▲▲▲

A North American outside his country is a vulnerable creature who has to surround himself with bottled soft drinks, toothpaste, and electric can-openers if he doesn't want to die of loneliness.

José Daniel tried to confirm that idea, which he had used in various novels, on entering the neighborhood of San Carlos and seeing the small duplex houses with ten square yards of garden in front and a hose ensuring the brilliant green of the grass although it had rained that morning.

"Lómax, what will you be when you grow up?"

"A cop, chief."

"Don't you think that's a very routine job?"

"But a hell of a lot happens . . . Which house are we going to?"

"The first one you like."

Lómax was slowly braking the motorcycle, coming to rest ten yards from a one-armed gringo who was sweeping the yard with his one hand.

José Daniel got off the bike.

"Pispanish?" he asked directly.

"Yes, I speak a little," replied the gringo, smiling at him.

"José Daniel Fierro, chief of police of Santa Ana," said JD, offering his hand.

"I've read your book," said the North American, pressing firmly. "Johnnie Walker."

"That's a real name?" asked JD, disconcerted, slipping into English.

"No, just a nickname." He turned to the inside of the house. "Betty, the chief of police. The writer!"

Betty stepped out, wearing an enormous apron, giving every indication she had been making an apple pie.

"I've read *Notebook*."

"Did you like it?"

"Very fine plot and the general idea. I also read *All Night Shooting and Dancing*, that's the one Betty likes most. Right?"

"Yes. It's my favorite. JW is also a writer."

"And what do you write?" asked JD, letting himself fall onto the lush lawn. JW followed suit.

"History, mostly."

José Daniel took out the photograph.

"Do you know her?"

"Anne—they killed her in town the other day, right?" said Betty, demonstrating fluent Spanish.

"What do you know about her?"

"The one who could tell you more about her is Jerry Martínez, they're very good friends. Let's go," said JW, getting up.

Lómax and Chief Fierro followed the North American couple, crossed the garden next door, and climbed a porch.

"Do you have books in English, chief?" whispered Lómax.

"Four novels."

"Jerry, the chief of police of Santa Ana," Betty said to a big Chicano who came out to meet them on the porch. He had a moustache as good as that of the chief of police.

"Did you know Anne Goldin?"

"Of course," said the Chicano. "We were very good friends. She was a good person."

"Did you see her Monday?"

"She came by here in the morning to bring me a book that my sister sent me from San Jose . . ."

"What was Anne doing in Santa Ana?"

Jerry stared at the chief of police, then decided to answer. "She came to see the father of Tommy, her son, a guy she located here after looking for many years. A strange story, she never said much about it . . . She came to take our photos, and when we talked we found we had a lot in common, she had studied in San Jose with my sister. And we saw each other a few times last year, and now she brought me that book. Last year she said she'd be back because she had found Tommy's father here in Santa Ana."

"Didn't she tell you who he was?"

"No. Nor did I ask. I don't go out much. I can't move around much because of the lesion." He lifted his shirt and showed an enormous scar above his liver.

"Nothing? Not one clue?"

"That was last year, this year we didn't even talk about it. She said she had brought a photo of Tommy to show me but that she'd left it at the hotel. And last year nothing. Just that. That Tommy's father lived in Santa Ana and that she had found him."

JD shook hands again, declined an invitation to coffee and cake, promised to return when things calmed down to talk about literature and to read JW's manuscript, and went to the motorcycle with Lómax.

"Chief!" cried Jerry after them. "She said something about uniting the tattoos . . . I didn't understand very well, but she had a tattoo on her arm, right?"

53. Declarations

"That guy is absolutely mad. He's having romantic problems so he plays Zitarrosa's song "Stephanie" fifty times. I've gotten twenty protest calls," said Fritz to JD, who had once again become the arbiter of minor conflicts at Radio Santa Ana.

"I have a gift for you in the office," said Barrientos when he saw JD in the hallway.

"Who knows where the judicial was all night yesterday," reported Greñas.

"The mine is threatening to declare a lockout," Mercado informed him when he passed by the door to the bathroom.

"Barrientos, call Dr. Jiménez, ask him if the judicial had

a tattoo—they must have him on the table by now and can look him over," said José Daniel, passing through the door to his office.

"It wasn't me, chief," said Blackie's assistant, tied up in the chair of the chief of police.

"Me either," replied José Daniel to gain time.

54. *Dear Ana/April 22*

~~~~~~

Dear Ana/April 22

The novel continues. It is a novel about tattoos. Its characters are a commander of the judicial police who has a tattoo on his ass that says: *Who arrives here does not leave alive*; also a North American who has a tiny rose on her forearm with the phrase *Loneliness is the heart of life*. Also, so it won't be too easy, an albino gunman who has a plumed serpent tattooed on his left arm.

As you will see, the novel appears to belong to Vázquez Montalbán and not to me.

The protagonist is a Chinese who dedicates himself to commerce and has a double life, because in the back room of one of his businesses he also practices the forbidden art of the exotic

Japanese tattoo (it's a problem that he's Chinese and the tattoos are Japanese, but it can be resolved).

I have various problems: one of them is that the child in the photo has no Asiatic features at all, the other is that I don't feel like going to see the tattoos of the Priísta cacique.

The novel, nevertheless, despite my indecisiveness, goes on filling up with weird stiffs and out-of-place confessions.

What do you think? Tomorrow I'll send you Chapter Three.

An enormous kiss in the solitude of this monkish cell.

JD

55. Resign? No way!

‾‾

"I came to see you because . . ."

"Cut it out, would you?" said JD, leaning back on his metal cot. "All I need now is for someone to arrive at the hotel and say, 'I came to Comala because they told me . . . ' "

Benjamín sat on the carpet at the foot of the bed. "Blind Man told me what the gunman told him. The shots fired at you the other day did not come from on high. I don't know if this is better or worse, but if you want to resign, that seems reasonable to me."

"Resign? No way!" said JD euphorically. Benjamín had interrupted a seriously drunken interlude. And J.D. was only halfway to his intended alcoholic destination.

"Moreover, things are heating up heavy, my chief."

"Did you bring a bottle? I can't give you any of mine. And least of all unless you stop moving, asshole," said JD.

"Son of a whore, you're shitfaced drunk and I didn't even notice. I'll be right back," said the mayor of Santa Ana, and went out, leaving the door open.

JD did not bother to close it. He lowered his trousers and showed his balls to a maid who went running away down the hall.

Benjamín returned in five minutes with his own bottle of brandy, closed the door, sat on the floor and drank a quarter of it in one gulp.

"To catch up with you, bastard."

"You're going to get very fucked up, Señor Mayor, and then the fucking Chinese will get hold of you and cover you with tattoos on all sides, very weird all covered with tattoos, on the sixteenth of September you're going to look like hell ringing the independence bell all covered with tattoos."

"That's what I wanted to talk about. We won't make it to the sixteenth, Señor Chief of Police. They're going to fuck us up first."

"The Chinese?"

"The Chinese will peel our dicks. Lick our balls."

"Our balls," said JD, pointing at his with difficulty. "Our eggs."

"No, I'm talking about the government."

"The government won't lick my balls."

"The governor passed a petition to the state congress dissolving the government of Santa Ana. The state press is accusing me of the murders. They say that you want to trap Barrio and that we're going to use that pretext to kill him. Judicials from all over the state are arriving and closing in on the land invaders. They're bringing the whole works."

"They must want to give us a fucking tattoo on the ass."

"What the fuck is this with the tattoos?"

"No. Let's change the subject. Fuck."

To join the mood, Benjamín dispatched another quarter of the bottle in one gulp that to JD appeared interminable. He took one a bit shorter. Good brandy and bad were meant to be savored.

"What was I saying?" asked Benjamín.

"Now you're drunk, Benjamín."

"I'm never drunk."

"Me either," said JD, and he got up to vomit in the washbasin.

"What a miserable drunk! Police drunk."

"I am a democratic cop," said José Daniel, trying to keep the spittle from running down his lips. Stumbling, he reached the bed and fell down again. The bottle was still there at his right. He took another drink to rinse his mouth.

"You mean shit to me, Benjamín. Santa Ana means shit to me. I was an asshole writing a novel in Mexico City and Santa Ana means shit to me."

"I told you. You mean shit to me, too . . . Who killed them?"

"Who the fuck knows. Do you think I'd be here getting plastered if I knew?" said José Daniel with difficulty.

"They're going to fuck us over."

"No way. I'll find the killers tomorrow, the fag bastards."

"You think so?"

"Of course, the fucking murderers are whores, I'll fuck them tomorrow."

"You mean shit to me, Chief Fierro," said Benjamín before vomiting in the washbasin.

"Son of a bitch, you're fucking wasted," said José Daniel Fierro, smiling at his bottle, which moved less than the mayor.

56. *You're the Only Ones*

It dawned rainy again and the city was covered with damp three-color posters announcing a PRI demonstration at six o'clock. From the door of the Hotel Florida, José Daniel Fierro, tasting metal from his hangover, looked at them wondering if he should cross the street in the middle of the downpour.

The patrol car, with its splendid red and black paint job, stopped before the door to the hotel.

"They fired on the campesinos last night," said Blind Man, opening the door. "Benjamín is giving a press conference right now, do you want to go?"

"Let's go and visit the Calle Escondida."

"Alone?"

"Just us and our shadows."

"Do you want to read the press of the state capital, *El Heraldo* and *El Independiente?*"

"What does it say?"

"They're arguing in the local congress if they should invade us. Now there's a PRI demonstration and also a meeting of the Popular Organization."

"Does the PRI have people in Santa Ana?"

"A few, the rest they bring in from other places."

"Let's go."

Blind Man started up the car and reached the highway in five minutes through the empty streets.

Calle Escondida was full of automobiles. The grim-faced drivers, some of them armed with automatic rifles that they held ready despite the rain, began to move toward the patrol car.

"Say the word," whispered Blind Man.

"What time is the demonstration?"

"At six, they start at six."

"We'll come back then."

The patrol car started up in reverse. A pair of shots rang out, the windshield shattered by a bullet. Blind Man braked and took out his .45.

"Hold it, Blind Man, we'll be back," said JD, grabbing his arm.

Santa Ana was inundated by music. Every two minutes the alternating voices of Fritz and Canales announced the demonstration.

Benjamín was waiting for them in the office.

"The mission of the police force of Santa Ana is to prevent the two demonstrations from meeting. Let's establish a blockade on Calle Revolución, in these three blocks. We can't have any provocations. The national press is in Santa Ana, that can serve as pressure. Can you do it?"

"At Barrio's house there are some fifty gunmen, with automatic arms, against six of us," said Blind Man.

"We'll see what he can do," said José Daniel.

"How do you feel?" asked Benjamín.

"Like an asshole," replied José Daniel Fierro.

"That makes two of us," replied the mayor.

"You're the only ones," said the assistant chief of police of Santa Ana.

57. Dear Ana/April 23

Dear Ana/April 23

The novel continues:

It is a novel of games. People die, and the ones who kill them think they're killing for a motive, but they do it at the suggestion of others, who in turn have another motive, and so on. So that no one really knows exactly why people die in the book.

The characters are an American who comes to Mexico to see her ex-husband to get child support from him, the ex-husband who refuses to give it to her, a pair of hired killers who kill her to pressure her ex-husband, the enemy of the ex-husband who really directs them against him, an associate of the ex-husband who negotiates with the killers, and the town's disoriented sheriff who veers between synthetic glory and madness.

The beauty of the novel is that the sheriff discovers nothing, only that things simply happen. That's what I like about this novel—that it has no ending, no closing, but is, as I've said of my days in Santa Ana, like life itself.

What do you think?

I miss you. JD

58. Notes for the History of the Radical City Government of Santa Ana
José Daniel Fierro

In these last two years, what did the radical city government contribute to the inhabitants of the town?

The question is not easy. It is a government that has not had even a month of normalcy. It has never been able to receive the entire funding it is entitled to. Even so, we can gather some ideas among those that the whole world speaks of, those outside and those inside:

An honest administration of funds, that had many repercussions in minor details: city cleaning, the reconstruction of the market, the birth of six production cooperatives and two big ones of consumers, a big hydraulic irrigation works, a cultural project that I have never been able to see but that everyone talks about behind the municipal House of Culture, the new popular secondary school, a healthier relationship with the authorities, a moralization of the police force, efficient control of business, the reconstruction of the three colonial monuments that are in the city. Things like that.

It is hard to judge based on these things. You would have to have lived in Santa Ana three years ago and I did not.

Maybe most important is that the people were mobilized. Or the inverse, the government was mobilized by the people. And this I have seen. These phenomena of mobilization of the immobilizable, the advance by centuries in a few days, the transformed mentality, are difficult to see in a country in which complaint substitutes for action.

59. Streets

"The patrol car in the middle of the street. On the block that follows the metal barriers. Greñas with the bike at the corner of Revolución and Lerdo. Barrientos in the center. Russian and Merenciano at Revolución and Seis. The street cleared of cars, so that we can see with a simple glance. Blockades down the middle."

At his back the miners go by, formed in columns of four, with axes and picks, with clubs. The noise of the crowd grows in the streets beaten by the drizzle, that fine rain that does not dampen but goes on entering the clothing until it reaches the body. Radio Santa Ana is silent. This morning, the broadcasting plant was sabotaged, the technicians are trying to repair it. They succeed in the middle of the demonstration, and suddenly Benjamín's speech fills the empty streets of Santa Ana and the packed plaza. His voice full of fury: *Let them go, they have nothing to do with our city. No one can negotiate with our liberty. No one can come and tell us how we should live, how we should organize our days, our passions, our needs. No one can come here to deny us the right to work honestly, the right to work together, the right to not let ourselves be exploited. The right to be the free town of Santa Ana. No congress of paid deputies who kowtow to the central power can decree that we do not exist. Here we are! We are the people of Santa Ana! And there will be no voices, nor votes, nor newspapers, nor tanks that can deny this simple but definitive truth: We exist. We do exist. We do exist. Santa Ana will win!* and the rhythm of *Santa Ana will win Santa Ana will win* was repeated like thunder and threatened to tumble the walls and electric cables and to stop the rain.

José Daniel feels the clamor striking him in the back while he tries to guess if the provocation is advancing through the drizzle. If the black city will spit out death. It gets dark. There are only shadows.

"I don't think they're coming," says Barrientos. "They must not have gotten very many people together."

Night falls. The first groups begin to return from the demonstration of the PO. José Daniel orders the patrol retired.

60. *Nocturne*

▲▲▲▲▲▲▲▲▲▲▲▲▲▲▲▲▲▲▲▲▲▲▲▲▲▲▲▲▲▲▲▲▲▲

"My neighbor stands up at night when he thinks that nobody sees him," said the voice on the phone. José Daniel does not need to ask who was its owner. He reacted as a character out of Earl Derr Biggers.

"What else can you tell me, Mrs. Ling?"

"Since yesterday the house of my other neighbor is full of armed gentlemen."

"I thank you very much for the information . . ."

"The American girl saw both of them the afternoon they killed her. She was first in one house and then in the other."

José Daniel scratched his head.

"I thank you, madam."

"I'll be watching them, I'll let you know."

"Very kind of you," said the chief of police of Santa Ana as he hung up.

José Daniel had been bathing when the call came through, but now he could not find the strength to get back under the shower. He was cold. On his table, together with the manuscript he had started about the history of the radical city government of Santa Ana, were Anne's photos. There were two he wanted to see: those of the engineer López, the false cripple, and that of Melchor Barrio, the PRI cacique of Santa Ana. There must be some clue in those photos. *She visited them both.* He already knew that, the photos had already told him. Hours later they killed her. What took place during those visits? Who ordered her killed? Why naked and in the church? What could the gunman and the judicial have told her? What the fuck was happening in this city that was beginning to catch fire? José Daniel had no answers. It was not a logical problem. What did his nephew Javier say when he had no information? *Not computable.* Just so, not computable. He had not even been able to sit down in front of the two men. The false paralytic, the cacique. Was it really useful to know the truth? Would the truth stop the whirlwind from being unleashed on Santa Ana?

José Daniel got dressed again. The rain beat on the window.

At the door of the Hotel Florida, Blind Man waited for him in the Volkswagen patrol car, smoking a cigarette.

"I thought we would have nocturnal visitors, chief."

"You second-guess me too much, Blind Man, I'm going to put you on the list of suspects."

"Of the judicial and Blackie, what the hell, but the gringa no, please."

The automobile took the same route toward the outskirts of Santa Ana but did not enter the neighborhood.

"The paralytic is not paralytic," said JD.

"How do you know?"

"You see, I too have my resources."

"Are we going straight? Do we go sideways? Do we hide? Do we show ourselves? Do we go to the engineer's house? Are we going to Barrio's house? Are we just out for fresh air? You tell me."

"Rule number seventeen of the detective novels I don't like: the murderer is the one we least suspect."

"And rule seventeen of the novels you do like?"

"The murderer is a son of a bitch who almost escapes."

"Which do you prefer?"

"A combination: the paralytic who is not paralytic and Barrio. Together."

"Let's check them out."

The car turned in again at the entrance to the neighborhood. Three times they had been to this street: La Escondida. Barrio's house was dark. There were lights at the house of the engineer, and a dim light on the second floor of the Chinese widow's house.

"Barrio is out of town. He must be in the capital, negotiating the booty, chief."

"Let's go to the engineer."

He knew the man who opened the door, he appeared in the photos pushing the wheelchair. He was bigger in real life than in the photos.

"We would like to speak with Engineer López," said Blind Man.

López appeared, pushing his wheelchair through a swinging door that apparently led to the kitchen. José Daniel took off his cap and hung it coquettishly on the barrel of his gun. Blind Man remained standing near by, measuring the majordomo.

"Who are you?"

"Pal, that's what I should be asking you," said the paralytic who wasn't. "But I've seen declarations of yours in the press with photos, and I even saw you on a television show years ago."

"You are not paralyzed. You are hiding out in Santa Ana. You are Anne's ex-husband and the father of her child. You have a name that is not López. The red car was put in front of your house to pressure you. But you did not kill her."

José Daniel grew still. He waited. Then he walked toward the man and took off his dark glasses.

The man had gray eyes. José Daniel heard a noise at his back and guessed that Blind Man had taken charge of the majordomo. He didn't even turn around.

"Let me see your arm," said JD.

The man remained immobile, looking nowhere, seated in his chair. JD took his left arm and rolled up his sleeve. Nothing. He repeated the operation with his right arm. There was the small tattoo, a rose, with the same words, but in Spanish: *La soledad es el corazón de la vida.*

"I can take your photo without dark glasses and circulate it among the journalists at City Hall. Surely someone there will recognize you. It's only a matter of time."

The man did not try to meet his eyes. Immutable, every hair in place, a gray cravat at his neck. A portrait of other times. JD turned around. Blind Man was tying up the major-domo with a venetian blind cord.

"Blind Man, bring the fucking Polaroid from the car, it's in the glove box."

Barrientos finished his work, checked the knots, and left the house. JD turned back to the man in the wheelchair, who was looking with curiosity at his own tattoo, as if seeing it for the first time. Lew Archer would now begin to speak with the character, carrying him back in time. That was what fascinated Ross Macdonald, men who could not return to the past. José Daniel did not give a damn. He only wanted the truth. Blind

Man came in with the camera. José Daniel Fierro took four or five photos of the man in the wheelchair. He gave them to Blind Man, who left the house in silence.

"We could save ourselves some trouble," said the chief of police. The man did not respond, only gave him a sad smile. José Daniel fell into an armchair with his shotgun between his hands. It was a temporary home, someone had chosen the furniture for the silent man, someone had decided that the brocades went well with a mustard-colored carpet, someone had brought the bar and even filled it with exotic bottles.

"You have a name," said JD to say something.

"There's a suitcase with half a million dollars in the hall closet. Let me buy your shotgun."

"What do you want it for?"

The man shut up again, looking at his tattoo. Then he got up. JD raised his shotgun, but there was no aggression in the movement. The man went to the closet and returned with the suitcase, he put it between them. He pushed away the wheelchair as if he would never need it again, and opened the suitcase on the middle of the rug. It was full of hundred-dollar bills. Five thousand one hundred dollar bills, calculated JD, fifty prettily wrapped packets of one hundred.

"I don't need the shotgun, I have a pistol. I only want two minutes . . ."

"Your neighbor is not here, the lights are out, those two minutes won't help you at all . . . Let's make another exchange. I'll trade you the photos of your son and the photos of Anne's body in the church for another story." JD looked in his shirt pocket. There were the Polaroids of the dead girl in the church. He passed them to him. The man took them as if they would burn him. He looked at them one by one.

"If you don't tell me the story, I'll guess it."

"I don't give a shit," said the man without taking his eyes from one of the photographs.

Shock therapy, JD told himself, and went on pressuring while he stroked the trigger.

"What did Barrio offer you? Security forever? For that he ordered her killed, to go on giving you orders, and in passing, to stir things up a bit here in town. He's a man with a practical mind, a shame I've never met him."

The man let the photos fall in the suitcase.

"I never saw the photos of the child."

"I have them at the office. I'll show you when we get there."

"You don't want the money?"

"I guess not."

"The shotgun was for me. Barrio is at home, dead. He's naked in a bathtub. With a shot through each eye. I turned out the lights when I left."

José Daniel smiled at him.

"You don't want the money?"

"No, I don't need it. Santa Ana pays me seventy-two thousand pesos twice a month and I get something in royalties." He considered explaining that Goldman Verlag was about to publish three of his novels and that they paid in marks, but it wasn't worth his while.

The man arranged the bills and closed the suitcase again. He took the photos carefully and gave them to the chief of police, who returned them to the pocket of his khaki shirt.

"What a bunch of shit, eh?" said the chief of police of Santa Ana, for something to say . . . This ending was no good, he felt trapped in someone else's story.

The patrol car braked before the door of the mansion; the efficient Barrientos would carry out the rest of the drama. But the story did not belong to him. Perhaps a little?

61. Dear Ana/April 23 (II)

▲▲▲▲▲▲▲▲▲▲▲▲▲▲▲▲▲▲▲▲▲▲▲▲▲▲▲▲▲▲▲▲▲▲▲▲

Dear Ana/April 23

End of the novel: The town sheriff understands nothing, although he learns everything without meaning to. The bad guys of the story kill each other off, and he stays behind watching the graveyard.

It was a novel of "uncovered passions," but not of "hidden passions" because nobody writes about them anymore.

Everything turns around a town cacique without a tattoo, who has a lot of dirt on those who do have tattoos. He gives orders to one while he hides him, orders another to kill her, orders others to put the red car in a certain street. It's a bit complicated, the novel. I don't know if I want to write it, I don't think so, it lacks a hook, dramatic architecture, the negative characters (as my Cuban friends would say) are badly drawn. I don't think I'd like to write it.

Rather I'm sure I would not like to write it.

But I love you. JD

62. Here at Radio Santa Ana

━━━━━━━━━━━━━━━━━━━━━━━━━━━

"What's happening, chief?" asked Canales at the door to City Hall.

The plaza was full of campfires, the people were waiting for something. José Daniel entered, accompanied by Blind Man, who brought in the former chief of acquisitions of Pemex, who had disappeared two years ago with eleven million dollars in a suitcase, bound by toy handcuffs that rattled from every link in the chain.

"What's happening here?"

"The state congress dissolved the government of Santa Ana a few hours ago. The cabinet is meeting . . . And what have we here?"

"A pathetic jerk. He just killed Barrio."

"Piss up a rope! Now the shit's hit the fan!"

"One down," said Blind Man, slapping the properly dressed man on the back, who despite everything had not a hair out of place or a wrinkle in his gray cravat.

"Take him to the office, Blind Man. I'm going to see Benjamín. Call the journalists. I'm going to get Barrio's death off the back of the town."

At that moment, loudspeakers began to sound across the town. Surprisingly, not with the "Venceremos" but with "Penélope" by Serrat.

"Fucking Fritz, he's completely flipped out," said Juan Carlos.

The cabinet room was full of smoke. Little blue clouds that ascended from the big table. The lawyer Mercado was by the phone.

"They already gave out the news in Mexico City. Before they finished voting they had already had a press conference, the representative of the local government there. What fucking mugs they are!"

"Okay, we already know what we have to do," said Benjamín. His eyes were irritated. "Macario, tell the boys at Radio Santa Ana that the government is invoking a total and indefinite general strike, close the markets, close the highways. Pass the declarations on to the press. Half the government stays here, the other half, along with the leadership of the PO, already knows where they have to go. Scabs to be dealt with by the neighborhood groups. Serafín, get moving. You have to advise all the communities from here to La Cañada. Every one of them."

The people began to get to their feet. Benjamín came toward José Daniel.

"Shit, we wouldn't have brought you to town for so little time."

"I got my month's pay, and the month isn't over."

"I think I should meet with all the police and speak with them a bit, but I don't feel like it. Blind Man Barrientos knows the emergency plan, and knows about guarding the arms. All in good time . . . I think you should resign and get together with the press. These next few days are going to be a bit brutal, and it wouldn't be a bad idea for Santa Ana to have its own chronicler."

"Let somebody else tell the story," said José Daniel, slapping the mayor on the back.

"Aren't you going to talk to the people outside the building, Benjamín?" asked the young leader of the miners of shaft number three. José Daniel had seen him on other occasions.

"Right now," said Benjamín Correa, stretching.

"I solved the mystery."

Correa looked at him with surprise.

"You solved it?"

"It solved itself. I'll tell you. You know, Barrio was killed."

"By one of us?"

"No, one of them."

"What do you know, that's good news," said Benjamín, going out on the balcony.

José Daniel climbed down the stairs, past the mural of hell. He stared at the image of the Priísta cacique whom he had never met, and imagined him in a bathtub with two shots in his head.

At the entrance to the studios of Radio Santa Ana, Canales stopped him. Fritz was broadcasting: "People of Santa Ana, we have to inform you that a couple of minutes ago two army tanks entered by the main highway."

In that moment, all the loudspeakers began to sound. Fritz had put on a record of the National Anthem.

Wearily, José Daniel covered the steps that led to his office.

63. *Dear Ana/April 27*

Dear Ana/April 27

    I got Canales and Fritz as cellmates, together with my assistant chief, Barrientos. We are designing a four-dimensional chess game. Canales organized a workshop on the poetry of Nezahualcóyotl. I'm writing a novel. Although it causes me remorse to say so, in the midst of so much injustice, of so much aggression hurled at Santa Ana, I am a happy man. Tell the spectators in Mexico City and New York, and in Madrid, that I'm a happy man. I suppose you'll wait to divorce me until they let us out. Meanwhile, you could just as well send me the aspirin and the blue turtleneck sweater that I've asked you for.

I love you, JD

P.S. I've kept my baseball cap.